SOFTWARE DEVELOPMENT WITH UML

Ken Lunn

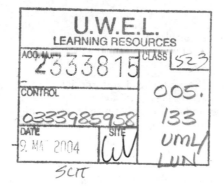

First published 2003 by
PALGRAVE MACMILLAN
Houndmills, Basingstoke, Hampshire RG21 6XS and
175 Fifth Avenue, New York, N. Y. 10010
Companies and representatives throughout the world

PALGRAVE MACMILLAN is the global academic imprint of the Palgrave
Macmillan division of St. Martin's Press, LLC and of Palgrave Macmillan Ltd.
Macmillan® is a registered trademark in the United States, United Kingdom
and other countries. Palgrave is a registered trademark in the European
Union and other countries.

ISBN 0–333–98595–8 paperback

This book is printed on paper suitable for recycling and made from fully managed and
sustained forest sources.

A catalogue record for this book is available from the British Library.

10   9   8   7   6   5   4   3   2   1
12 11 10 09 08 07 06 05 04 03

Printed and bound in Great Britain by
Ashford Colour Press Ltd, Gosport

Software Development with UML

Contents

Preface

The development of computer systems is the great modern adventure. The jungles we have left are now called rain forests and are the haunt of conservationists, not hunters; people in business suits fly over the Arctic with bored regularity and look down upon Greenland with disinterest; great architectural feats pass barely noticed by the scurrying tourist. The natural world seems to have become a much smaller space at the start of the 21st century. The conquering of Everest and the great treks to the poles seem nothing but fragments of history.

Thus, it seems, the artificial world of computers and software has become the one in which people cast their imaginations. As the physical world seems to diminish in our imagination, so the virtual world seems to expand, and it is here where so many now expend their energies and enthusiasm. The time and energy of the modern world seem most intent on information technology.

This is not as poetic and fanciful as it sounds. In the 19th century, great feats of engineering captured the public imagination. History shows then the same mix of triumph and disaster, the heroes and anti-heroes, fame and fortune, ignominy and loss, that we see today among the pioneers of the computing world. That is not to say that we should yawn and discount what is going on as mere repetition of a pattern. Without the railways and roads that came from the endeavours of engineers two centuries ago, the world would be a much poorer place, even if their works seem commonplace and dull today. In time, information technology will surely look as prosaic as civil engineering now seems to the majority. That time, though, is long off, and it is better to be out there among the explorers than to linger with the bystanders and Luddites.

Today there are the enthusiasts who see no limit to the way technology will be used, living in almost a comic-book fantasy world of possibilities. They would have our brains wired into the Internet and our refrigerators doing the shopping. There are the cynics who think that there is nothing but froth in all that is being touted. And there are the pessimists who see nothing but disaster. All this is more to do with psychology than technology. Every new movement has the same mix. No doubt the IT world will one day be monotonous, but today it is vibrant and exciting, and thus has both devotees and opponents.

There is no point boring you with lists of successes of the IT world. All you have to do is look around. Possibly you bought this book over the Internet, and almost certainly the bookshop that sold it used some computer system to log the sale. It is hard to get away from computer systems today. The fact that you bought this book at all indicates that you are among the enthusiasts, unless you are a strange subversive who wishes to cite it as an example of modern decadence and burn it in the street. Equally, there is little point in cataloguing the huge litany of failures. Every computer professional has his or her pet story of disaster, and they are fun to relate. Any computer system development involves risk, and risks result in failures, but the greatest risk of all is in not taking risks.

Which leads us to the point of this book. Developing a computer system that is going to be used for some practical purpose is a great endeavour. There are many paths through this modern jungle. Adventurers may get bitten by snakes or stalked by tigers, and some get eaten alive. Today many IT projects are staffed with people with little more than the equivalent of a compass, machete, and a roughly drawn map given to them by some moonshine salesperson. Over the last 25 years I have been involved in the research and development of a large number of IT systems; I have my share of scars and tales of both woe and success, have swallowed more than my share of moonshine, and I have sold a few bottles of moonshine myself. In that time I have developed some sense of the layout of the jungle, and the meaning of some of the strange noises encountered therein. I am not the most successful adventurer, but I have lived to tell the tales.

I wrote my first computer program in 1973, using Fortran and punched cards. On my mathematics degree I was privileged to be taught some of the best programming practices of the time, and I learnt Algol and stepwise refinement as directed by the then great guru Dijkstra. I thought then that I knew all there was to writing computer program. In 1977 I started my first job as a programmer, using Cobol, and got my first real hint of how little I knew. I taught myself Jackson Structured Programming, from Jackson's textbook, and thought my programming education complete. In 1979 I started a Ph.D. in distributed computing, only to realize I knew even less. Over the following 20 years, I have worked in systems programming and in research and development into artificial intelligence applications; managed large system developments; and used almost every common computer language and operating system. As I develop my knowledge and skills, the sheer scale of what is yet to be learnt grows. I expect the challenges to continue to grow well beyond the day that I finally put my developer's hat on the peg and wander off into the sunset with my fishing rod and watercolour set.

I want to convey to readers, who are likely to be novices in these matters, some sense of the adventure. I would like them to know what medicines to take, and to show them one path through the trees. It is not the only path, nor necessarily the best. Those who stay with me will get a little further into the jungle than they might on their own, and when they venture out by themselves or with some other party they will not be so surprised by the some of the things they see. I cannot promise to save you from being eaten, but I can promise excitement in your future career.

Ken Lunn
June 2002

The Author

Ken Lunn graduated with a degree in pure mathematics from Sheffield University in 1976, and was awarded a Ph.D. in distributed computing by the University of Keele in 1983. He has worked in research and development roles for Air Products Ltd, Systime Computers Ltd, Shell International Petroleum, and Ventura (part of

Next plc). He has also had brief academic roles at Bradford and Liverpool Universities, and he currently is Principal Lecturer in Information Systems at Huddersfield University. He regularly provides training and consultancy in UML and OO design and analysis to blue chip organizations. He co-authored with Simon Bennett and John Skelton *Schaum's Outline of UML*, which is now one of the best selling UML books. He currently leads research and teaching on e-commerce applications.

Intended Readership

This book was primarily written for the undergraduate first and second years for students in a broad range of IT courses. It harmonizes the UML notation with a full software development approach, from project conception through to testing, deployment and enhancement. Few other books approach the topic in this way.

IT managers and developers who have no knowledge of UML and a limited exposure to the management of IT systems and software development will find this useful as an introduction.

The book is filled with extensive examples. This is what I like when I read a book, and it is what most of my students like both at university and in commercial training. There are a number of case studies developed throughout the book, and a complete case study in the appendices.

Web Site and Support Materials

A full set of lecture support material, with slides, further exercises and examples, is available from:

```
http://www.palgrave.com/science/computing/lunn/
```

Acknowledgements

I would first like to thank David Hatter and Chris Glennie who recruited me to this particular project, and provided encouragement and advice along the way. David also recruited me to a previous project with Simon Bennett, and Simon taught me a great deal about writing and publishing, for which I am duly grateful. Thanks are due to Carol Gresswell who reviewed the proposal and the final draft, with many constructive comments, which I hope to have addressed, at least in part, in the final version. Last, but not least, from the editorial team, Rebecca Mashayekh has provided meticulous guidance and management through the final stages.

The list of credits for people who have helped me along the way as an IT professional would run to many pages, so a general thanks is all I can hope to give, for fear of leaving someone out. A special thanks must go to Professor Keith Bennett of Durham University who was willing to take a bumptious Cobol programmer and let him do a Ph.D., and then to put up with supervising him for the next three years. Another mention must go to Dr Allan Robinson at Shell, who gave me great freedom to lead a research group for over six years. And finally, Professor Mike Shave of Liverpool University, for his kindly advice, cooperation and help over a number of years.

The School of Computing and Mathematics at Huddersfield University has proved to be one of the most pleasant environments in which to work, and to continue my research and development career. My colleagues there have given me every encouragement, and the students have provided me with insight into the difficulties of understanding a rapidly changing field of study. In particular, Rob Lloyd-Owen and Steve Wade have provided much useful and constructive comment and discussion on this book; Rob also used some of the text with a class, and the feedback from those students was invaluable. Steve Scott and Dave Brignell provided some valuable proofreading and comments.

And finally, my family and friends, who have provided nothing regarding the content of the book, but who have provided the stimulation, encouragement, diversion, cups of coffee and affection – much needed during its production.

INTRODUCTION AND CASE STUDIES

Reader's Guide

This section introduces the book and the case study material that is used throughout it. Read the first chapter to get an overview of what the book is about. The second chapter gives an introduction to modelling and the Unified Modeling Language; some readers might like to skip that, but if you want to get a quick understanding of modelling notations it will be useful to read it. The case study material is very extensive. You may not want to read the third chapter in detail at the beginning, but you will need to refer to it repeatedly. A quick skim of the chapter is advisable.

Chapter 1: Introduction

This introduces the text, and the main themes of the book.

Chapter 2: Modelling and Notation – The Unified Modeling Language

This introduces the notion of modeling and notation are introduced for those readers unfamiliar with such concepts. The main notation used in this book, the Unified Modeling Language, is briefly introduced.

Chapter 3: Case Studies – ICANDO Oil

Five substantial case studies based on real applications in an oil company are introduced. These will be used extensively throughout the book.

CHAPTER 1

Introduction

1. What the book is about, and the approach it takes to introducing software development
2. What the software development process is
3. The notions of modelling and notation
4. The concept of architecture in software development
5. The role and importance of organization in software development

1.1 Aims and Objectives – the Adventure Begins

You, the reader of this book, are likely to be an undergraduate at the outset of your study, or a software developer at the beginning of your career, or an IT manager or developer who wants to gain an overview of modern software development. In the preface, I introduced IT development as a great modern adventure, akin to the great engineering adventures of the past. This book is very much a 'Cook's Tour', in that we shall visit all aspects of computer system development. However, we shall linger in each of the areas long enough, and give you sufficient pointers, for you to have a real feel of what a computer system development project is about.

The motivation is to provide you with a holistic view of computer development early on in your studies. Many books focus on a limited aspect, or provide over-emphasis on some aspect, or are just a hotch-potch of badly linked material. The aim here is to give you a sense of modern system development using methods, tools and techniques that fit together. It is, to a large extent, a selective view, but a comprehensive view of different methods and approaches would be far too extensive and overwhelming; this is a springboard for deeper and more thorough study later on.

If you are reading this out of general interest, you may follow the Hatter's advice to Alice, and begin at the beginning, go through to the end and then stop. If you are reading this to support a course, you might want to delve into the later chapters, skipping some of the earlier ones. As far as possible, I have tried to make the chapters stand alone, though it gets harder as we move further into subjects such as analysis and design.

This book will introduce four major concepts. Figure 1.1 shows these concepts arranged as the structure of a house. The plot in which the development will take place is the organization that carries out the development. The foundation of a good development is the process by which software is developed. Architecture

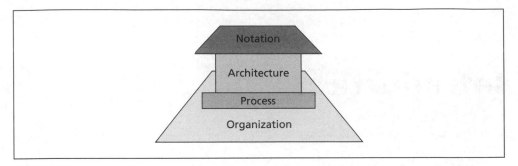

Figure 1.1   The concepts for a successful software development

defines the structure of the product that is being constructed. Notation is the means of recording communication and provides the roof under which the development takes place. The success of any development depends on all of these working in harmony. Though notation is one of the key concepts introduced by this book, notably the Unified Modeling Language (UML), this on its own is not sufficient. It must be used appropriately.

Along the way we will meet some important concepts. One of these is the notion of 'object orientation'. At its simplest, this is very straightforward to understand, and it has had a huge impact on the way software is developed. Like many ideas though, it has gathered a collection of myths and folk tales. This is perhaps the most important base concept to understand, and it will underpin a lot of the understanding of the notation and process. However, object orientation is only one aspect of developing software, and it is possible to develop software without that concept. This book is not truly an 'object-oriented' book, though the basic concepts are founded in the notion of an object. Thus, if you are not expecting to develop in Java or some other object-oriented language, you should still find value in the book, and even in the UML notation, though that is based on object-oriented concepts.

The aim of this book is to make software development accessible and understandable as a complete, holistic endeavour. Along the way, we shall explore some of the best contemporary notations and guidelines. Whatever role you adopt in your career (and it is likely that you will adopt many), it is important to know how this fits into the process of constructing a software system. Understanding the breadth of a software development project makes it more meaningful and more exciting. If this book succeeds for you, you will gain a sense of that excitement and want to go on to your own adventures.

1.2 Organization

The basis for any development is the organization undertaking that development. Organizations vary in size, type and maturity. The larger the organization, the more formal the structure tends to be. Organizations are groupings of people, who mostly specialize in certain aspects of development. Large teams split up into roles, and these roles focus on different parts of the development process. Sometimes people adopt several roles in the development, but it is rare for an individual to undertake all the tasks in software development. People usually have different skills and orientations, and are more suited for some roles than others. I am lucky to have adopted many roles, but certainly not all of them.

Organization is the key to success on major ventures. Edmund Hillary may have been the first to the top of Everest, but there were dozens of people setting up base camps and preparing the path for the final assault, and more people finding funding and supplying goods. Of course, that level of preparation is unnecessary for a fine Sunday afternoon jaunt up Helvellyn in northern England. The bigger the task, the greater the need for good organization. Organizations drive software development processes just as car manufacturers run factories. Mature organizations are able to reflect on their processes and improve them. Immature organizations often invent processes on the fly, and discard them with little reflection.

Development of substantial computer systems is a collective activity that requires a vast number of people with different skills. There are the obvious people, like the analysts and programmers that focus on the design and construction of the system. In addition, there are the senior managers who monitor the overall progress, the project managers who deal with day-to-day progress, the team leaders who organize the craftspeople, planners, testers, trainers, operators, technicians and help desk staff, and the end users themselves. They all have roles in the development of computer systems.

Good organization is something that requires experience and skill. Organizations develop through a range of maturity. Young organizations have to invent processes as they develop. They can be somewhat anarchic, but can be the most stimulating to work for. They are fleet of foot, but often short on memory and frequently reinvent processes. As an organization grows and matures, it begins to reflect on its processes, and change them more methodically. Organizations can also become geriatric, and unable to revise the way they operate.

Organization has a dramatic impact on the effectiveness of individuals. This is something that is difficult for novices to understand. Often there is an intense feeling of frustration in an organization when it seems to be behaving counter to the way an individual thinks is most effective. Again, experience is the great educator. However, some understanding of the typical organization and management of software development is invaluable for a developer. We shall therefore devote Chapter 6 to the way software developments are organized.

1.3 The Software Development Process

The construction of software is a process. It takes time, energy and money. Even the writing of a small program that takes one person a week to complete follows some process. Larger projects with tens or hundreds of people involved for many months or years follow a much more obvious and explicit process, or they would not succeed. One of the great problems of teaching IT is getting the learner to have some sense of the importance of process. Usually we teach only some part of the process, often as if it were the whole or at least the most important part. The greatest problem of education, in terms of giving realistic experiences to students, is that it focuses on individual performance, while great enterprises focus on teams and collective performance.

This book is structured along the lines of a process of construction of software. Sometimes this is known by the grand title of the 'Software Development Life Cycle'. This is an unusual way of introducing some of the elements – most books focus on some part of the process, or start with some later part of the process. We shall explore software development in roughly the order it takes place. The most prominent process for software development is the Unified Process, and we shall discuss that a little along the way. There are, however, many more processes, and every organization that develops software has its own distinct way of carrying things out. There is no single way of constructing software, any more than there is one single way of manufacturing cars.

Unlike the manufacture of goods, such as electronic goods or cars, the process of constructing software is not easy to see or visualize. If you visited a car factory, you could follow the process from beginning to end, and see how each part of the process contributes to the finished product. You would see how metal sheets are pressed into body parts. The wiring harness could be followed through from the point where the strands of wire are pulled off reels to the point where it is bound together and connected to switches and devices in the car. After a while it would be possible for most people to see how the raw materials are transformed into the finished product, and have some idea of how each stage of the process works.

Walk into a software development project, and you see a large number of people peering at computer screens, organizing meetings and engaging in jargon-filled conversations. For the uninitiated, how computer systems are constructed is a complete mystery, just as the first visit to a jungle reveals nothing but greenery, insects and strange, frightening noises. It is a key purpose of this book to unfold this mystery. When you really examine what is going on, it is not that different from any other construction process, except that the tools and artefacts are not that visible.

Figure 1.2 shows a flow of work in the development of any software product. Although this is drawn as a staged process, each of the stages is likely to be running in parallel. For example, a business case may be updated many times during the development of software, as new factors come to light. Systems requirements for part of the system might still be under investigation as a part of the system already constructed is deployed. We shall be considering later how this development process can be organized.

The first stage in any software development is determining what people want and whether it is worth doing. All software development starts with some idea that a new system or a change to an existing system will make someone's life better, or make some money. How those ideas arise depends very much on the organization or individual that desires the development. It might be the bright idea of a senior manager, or a suggestion from an office worker, or some clever sales operation. We will look at some typical examples of how projects arise.

First and foremost in software development is the construction of a business case or some other justification for the development. This can be very formal, and large systems development needs a very rigorous process that determines costs and benefits up front and tracks them carefully throughout the whole of the development process. Smaller systems can be handled much more informally, and the smallest systems are often developed with little formal justification. Whether explicit or not, some decision is made to start the development, and some benefit in the project anticipated.

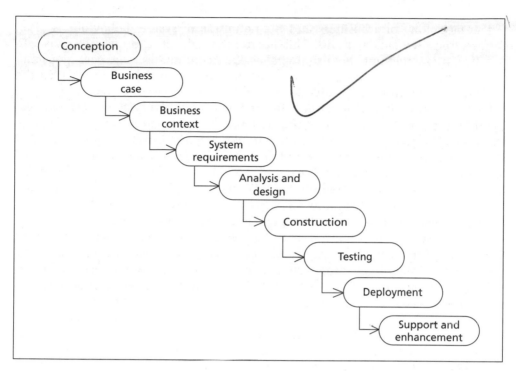

Figure 1.2 The process of developing software

Arguably most of the major tragedies in software development are because this process of justification, monitoring and review is weak. Too many projects overestimate the benefits and underestimate the costs and risks involved. In Chapter 4 we will look at project inception, and how this can be organized to minimize the risks and maximize the chances of success. The continual monitoring of a project throughout its activity is vitally important.

Once the principle of developing some software has been agreed, it is important to understand the context in which the system is to operate. In this book, we will make this an explicit step. We will introduce some UML notation to allow us to describe the services provided by a business, and how those services are provided. Impatient software developers miss this stage at their peril. Software always implies some change in a business operation, or even the creation of a new business operation. The notation we will introduce will permit explicit modelling of the business environment in which the system will fit. These notations will be common to some of those used in the description of the system itself.

With a purpose for the system and a clear understanding of the business environment in which it will fit, the development team is ready to define clearly how the system will meet the goals and fit into the business environment. The core concept we will introduce is known as a 'use case'. A use case is a meaningful unit of work carried out by a computer system. Through the identification and definition of use cases, we determine what the proposed system will do and how it will be used. Use cases have become central to object-oriented development methods, as they represent the core unit of delivery – use cases are discrete pieces of functionality.

The modelling of a business and the definition of system behaviour is often termed 'requirements analysis'. This is often thought of as a discrete phase. In practice, it is something that usually takes place continually, as expectations and understanding grow and change, and the business environment into which the system will be introduced evolves.

Once a clear understanding of the desired behaviour of a system is established, the definition of the operation of the system begins in earnest. Now the detail of the system behaviour needs to be filled in. We begin to introduce notations that are much more computer-specific and that begin to be more precise. This is known as 'systems analysis'. Considerable detail is gathered on the way the system operates and interacts with the environment. We will meet the notion of an object and a number of diagrams that allow us to model the behaviour of the system and its interactions. Here the Unified Modeling Language comes into play in earnest.

Once the behaviour of the system is defined fully, this needs to be transformed into a design that can ultimately be implemented. The design stage is where the physical implementation of the system in terms of computers, networks and interfaces is first considered. Considerable skill goes into the design of good systems. Good design is supported by a good architecture. Just as in the construction of large buildings, there is the need to have a good overall plan and structure to a system, and this is known as the architecture of the system.

From the design, a system is constructed. This is the phase that most people think of when they consider software development. It involves writing computer programs and defining interfaces such as computer screens or Web pages. Although it is a considerable and complex activity that needs substantial skills, it is not the whole process. In fact, in terms of overall cost, the actual programming of a system can be relatively small.

After construction comes testing. Once it is built, does it do what it is supposed to do? Is it reliable and usable? Like hostile invaders, a testing team will push the system until it breaks. Testing needs to be linked back to the requirements capture, and we will look at how to transform the use case definitions and business models into test plans. Testing is something of a Cinderella subject. Yet it is as vital to success as good analysis, design and programming.

Then, when the system is all working sufficiently well to be used, the system needs to be deployed. This involves installing the software, training people in its use, and supporting them in day-to-day use. A huge organization is often required to undertake this. Keeping hundreds of users happy, fixing problems and making sure that they use the system safely and securely is an endless task.

Once the system is operational, issues will arise. There will inevitably be problems with the software. It may stop working, and some urgent action will be needed to correct the problem. It may do something wrong, and part of the system may need to be changed. Someone may want the system to do more or do something differently, and these suggestions need to be collected and considered. The majority of the cost of a system is keeping it live and operational. This is known as software maintenance, or more fashionably today 'software evolution'. Unlike mechanical devices, software does not wear out, but it does present errors caused by faults (known as bugs), and it needs to keep pace with changes in business needs.

As you can see, the journey from a bright idea to something that works and is useful is a long and complicated process. For small systems, the process is shortened, and can be very informal. For big systems, it has to be explicit and formal. Different organizations will provide a different emphasis on each part of the process. However, the nature of the product means that the stages from conception through to support and enhancement must be gone through.

This looks like a staged process. In fact, the phases usually overlap. A large project needs to keep on track and adjust to changes in the environment, so the justification stage is revisited regularly. The analysis and design of part of the system can take place alongside the requirements definition for another part. More often than not, systems are developed incrementally, and are often deployed incrementally (that is, a bit at a time).

The most prominent definition of a software development process is the Unified Software Development Process (Jacobson *et al.*, 1999). This is a comprehensive approach to the development of large-scale software, and advanced students are advised to study this in detail. This book is loosely aligned to this process, and we will refer to it from time to time. There will not, however, be scope to consider it in detail.

Other software development processes exist. A development process that has gained ascendancy in recent years is Extreme Programming (Beck, 1999). This seeks to reduce the amount of intermediate modelling. It folds systems analysis, design and construction together, and has explicit processes for managing requirements and testing. Other methods, such as Rapid Applications Development (RAD) and prototyping approaches, have similar goals. Each of these has different emphases. There is no absolute right or wrong, and approaches will vary in success, depending on the environment and scope of a project and the skill of the practitioners.

However software is developed, it follows some process. Mature organizations have well-developed and finely tuned processes. Novice organizations and those that are immature will have processes that are obscure and are often invented as a system is developed. At the end of the book, you will have assimilated the outline of a process and be better placed to judge or define a process yourself.

1.4 Architecture and Design

Architecture defines the broad structure of the system to be developed. For small systems, this is often informal. The best analogy is building architecture. A garden shed or tree house does not need much architectural planning. A house needs some planning before it is constructed. A tower block needs careful consideration of the architecture, or the craftsmen will get nowhere as they try to construct the building. There are some classical architectural forms that are emerging for software development, and we shall look at these. Architecture is a skill learnt over time. In this book we can only give a flavour of what architecture is about.

Architecture is an increasingly important concept in the development of systems. It is a hard subject to grasp, and a good architect has many years of experience, ideally in different roles. It will be hard to give much more than a fleeting glimpse of architecture in this book. Fortunately for most developers, early in their careers, architectures are already defined for them. However, they must understand and apply the local architectural models as they construct their parts for the whole system and integrate them.

Architecture at the gross level considers the computers and networks that are used to construct the overall system. There is also a definition of the software tools that are used to construct the system, such as compilers, modelling tools, databases and packages. These decisions need to be made early on in a project. Often they are determined by the environment that an organization already has. This is known as the technical architecture.

Within the technical architecture, the software can be broken down into major components that cover items such as the user interface (computer screens and the like), detailed processing, and storage. These need to be distributed over the technical architecture. This is known as the application architecture. Major technologies, such as the Internet, have a distinct impact on the application architecture.

Good architecture is a craft that is learnt slowly. Building architects undertake many years of training, and require long experience before they become masters. The same is true of software architects. The only way to learn is to do. This book cannot hope to do much more than introduce the importance of architecture and indicate how it fits into the overall software development process.

Design involves the gross details of architecture and the fine detail of how individual components of a system are constructed. We will be following an object-oriented approach to design and using the different notations in the Unified Modeling Language to produce detailed designs. As with architecture, good design comes with practice and experience. There are many guiding principles to design, and much to study beyond this book. By the end of the section on architecture and design, you should have a systematic means of approaching design that can reliably lead to implementations that are effective and maintainable.

1.5 Notation and the Unified Modeling Language

Large projects involve a great deal of communication. The more people that are involved, the more complex that communication becomes. Notation is nothing more than a convention for the way we write down ideas, descriptions and designs. It is important, as far as possible, that the members of a project team share a common notation wherever possible. A good notation clarifies communication and helps to structure the thinking in a group.

The notation that we will use in this book is the Unified Modeling Language, usually known as UML. This has become the most widespread standard language in the IT industry for recording analysis and design. This book introduces the language at the point of use, and covers the major features of the language. For those wanting a more detailed and comprehensive description of the language, a book such as Bennett *et al.* (2001) is recommended.

The software development process involves the construction of a series of models, starting with simple descriptions of need and the way the physical environment of the system works, through to the construction of models that can actually carry out work (known as computer programs). Instead of introducing notation in isolation, we will meet the notation at the point in the software development process where it is needed.

Probably the greatest problem in terms of notation is knowing where and when to use it, not how to use it. On the whole, notations are easy to understand, but their application is often puzzling. Notation is about communication, and that communication needs to be concise, accurate and appropriate – knowing all the words in a dictionary will not make you a great novelist. Notations such as the UML are the primary means of recording and communicating in an IT project. Of course, everything could be recorded in a natural language such as English, but most disciplines, such as architecture or engineering, have special languages. Notation allows for more precise exchange of information.

The UML is a diagrammatic notation with some textual additions. This helps in the visualization of the structure of a system. Most modern methods use some visual notation – either the UML or something similar. The UML is based on object-oriented concepts, which are generally accepted as best practice in the development of IT systems. Given the importance of this notation, there is a brief introductory chapter following this one on object orientation and the UML.

1.6 Case Studies

Guides to adventures are best supported by realistic tales. We shall therefore be looking at five case studies of oil industry applications. These are based on my experiences. They have been chosen to represent different sizes and orientations of project. One will look at a large-scale sales order processing system, which, on the face of it, is not very exciting, but in fact is the type of project that can give the most benefit to large organizations. The second is a research and development project that is trying to apply the latest techniques to solving a difficult engineering safety problem. The third looks at an Internet development for retail promotions, which is very much in tune with many contemporary developments. The fourth considers a system for handling retail outlet transactions that involves linking existing systems. The fifth is an oil trading application, akin to many financial trading applications such as commodities or shares.

Each chapter illustrates the concepts with examples drawn from the case studies. There are also exercises for you to undertake. It is largely through doing rather than abstract theorizing that the fundamentals of software development are learnt. There is also a fully worked example in the final chapter that I have used extensively with my students. Experience shows that a variety of case study material best illustrates a complex set of ideas.

1.7 Conclusion

Software Development is a complex and time-consuming activity that involves organization, process, architecture and notation. Software developers need an appreciation of all these aspects in order to contribute to large-scale IT development projects, and to develop expertise in some aspect of IT development.

The aim of this introduction has been to quickly give you a comprehensive overview of the book and the approach to software development that it describes. The rest of the book is opening up the detail and introducing the principles and practice of software development.

At the outset, software development was described as a great adventure. If this introduction has given you some sense of the sweep of that adventure, and a kindergarten picture of some of the creatures and landscape that lie ahead, then it has been successful. Now we shall delve deeper into the forest, and see some of the creatures close up.

REVIEW QUESTIONS

1. **What are the four major concepts that this book is aiming to introduce?**
2. **What does UML stand for?**
3. **What are the stages in the development of software?**

CHAPTER 2

Modelling and Notation – The Unified Modeling Language

IN THIS CHAPTER YOU WILL LEARN:

1. What modelling is and why it is important in the development of large-scale IT systems
2. About the concept of object orientation
3. About the notions of modelling and notation
4. A little about the Unified Modeling Language

Modelling is one of the fundamental tools that are used in software development. Understanding the importance and role of models is necessary. Hence, this brief introduction to modelling has been put at the beginning of the book. If you are unfamiliar with modelling, then reading this chapter carefully will help prepare you for the detail to come. If you have used modelling notations before, then a brief skim through might be sufficient, or you may wish to skip this chapter completely.

A model is some description of a system. It might be a drawing, such as the plans for a house. It might be a description, like the estate agent's details of a house. It might be a prototype of some kind, like a three-dimensional mock-up of a shopping centre. Models are an essential part of the construction of software systems, and all but the most trivial developments will involve some modelling before the construction begins.[1] The output of any stage in any methodology is a set of models that are used as input to later stages. Models are written using a notation, and the notation we shall mostly be using in this book is the Unified Modeling Language.

A model is not the thing it is describing. It is some representation of the thing. But in some very real sense, it looks like the thing. You will find models in almost any discipline. Architects have lots of different models of buildings, such as plans and drawings. Engineers have models of bridges, including drawings and

---

1 Extreme programmers may disagree with this statement. However, the test plans and stories that are used by extreme programming are in fact models; they are not the artefact that is to be built, but some description of the artefact and its behaviour.

mathematical models. Town planners have drawings and prototypes of layouts of streets. Government planners provide complex models of things like hospitals that may be financial models or social models. And of course, computer systems developers construct models of systems before they build them.

We model because it is easier and cheaper to build a model than the real thing, or because the real thing is difficult to carry. An architect draws up plans for a house so that the design can be shown to the customer before building the house – better to spend a hundred pounds on a drawing than a hundred thousand pounds on a building before you find out that the customer does not like the layout.

When you construct a model, you come across problems that are easier to solve at the modelling stage than at the construction stage. It is better to find out that the standard garage door does not fit in the opening *before* you buy it. An engineer can calculate stresses on a model before constructing a bridge and work out the type of materials to use, rather than building the bridge and seeing whether it will take the load. Likewise, when two teams cooperate to build different parts of a software system, they need some plan to make sure that the different parts fit together.

Models are useful for communication. A complex construction will require lots of groups to work together. If they work from models that fit together, then the things they produce should fit together. At another level, models are used to describe things that you want to buy – a travel brochure is a simple model of a holiday resort. In software development, as we shall see, there are many roles and responsibilities, and the communication among members of the project and the various stakeholders outside of the project is paramount to the success of the project.

Models are also useful for planning. When you know how things fit together, and what needs to be done, then you can start planning the construction. You also need models to cope with change. If someone wants to rewire a large building, a drawing of the existing wiring is essential. Models help you to visualize, plan, communicate, estimate and, at the end of the process, provide a better solution than if you started without modelling. We shall see, as we examine the software development process, that the output of a stage is usually a model, and that model is used as input to another stage.

Models are not always essential. If you wanted a fence around your front garden, a model would be rather an expensive precursor. This is true in information systems too. If someone wants a quick program to solve a problem, then often it is easy enough to construct the program quickly in something like Microsoft Access. If something takes a few days, you can afford not to model. If it takes a few weeks, you might want a few models. If it takes years, you'd better get out your modelling kit first. Remember, modelling is not an end in itself. Sometimes people get too obsessed with modelling and model everything. Be sensible – model when it helps.

2.1 Object-Oriented Software Development

As with any human endeavour, there are movements and religions that dominate, are open to interpretation, and cause debate and controversy. Over the last twenty years, the notion of object-oriented software and object-oriented processes to develop software have become dominant. The early concepts of object orientation date back even further, back to the 1960s. It was in the 1990s, however, that it became mainstream accepted practice to adopt object-oriented tools and techniques for software development.

The term 'object-oriented' has become commonplace, and you will come across it over and over again. It is now somewhat overworked. It is used very broadly to describe methods, notations and programming languages that incorporate in some way the notion of an object. In this book I shall not explicitly condone object-oriented approaches, though in general these are considered the best approaches available, and the approach used in this book is object-oriented. The underlying stages of development can be well supported without the notion of an object, and indeed there are developments such as certain Internet technologies that challenge the purist view of object orientation.

Object orientation is based on a very simple concept. A system is made up of a number of cooperating objects. An object has a memory or state, and this is shown as a set of attributes. An object also has behaviour, and this is shown as a set of operations. Figure 2.1 shows an example of the UML notation for an object. Here we have a Bank Account that has a state defined by attributes account number and balance, and operations deposit and withdraw. The attributes are the things that are 'remembered' by the object, and the operations are the things that can be 'done' to or by the object. We shall define these concepts in some considerable detail later.

There are lots of good reasons why the notion of an object has become very important. Some of this is to do with the deficiencies of earlier approaches to development, and some of it is to do with the neatness of the concept and the good correspondence between object interactions in a system and the interaction of entities in the business context where the system is embedded. We shall consider these in detail when we introduce the notion of an object fully, and look at how systems can be constructed as a society of cooperating objects.

Object orientation has become a Good Thing, and vendors like to quote this as a facet of their products. This can be somewhat confusing, and leads to some misrepresentation. Having objects as a part of a tool is neither universally good nor universally bad. The UML has a strong representation for objects, and the methods it evolved from are object-oriented. Yet it contains a number of notations that are not strictly object-oriented, and the UML can be used to support other approaches to software development that leave out the notion of object. There are

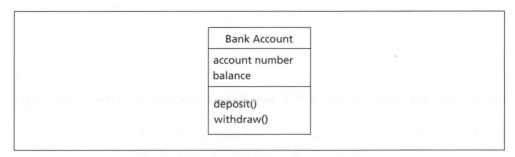

Figure 2.1 The UML notation for a Bank Account object

aspects of good software engineering, such as abstraction and encapsulation, that are well served by objects, and we will discuss some of these.

One misconception that does need challenging is that object-oriented methods require object-oriented languages for construction. This may be an ideal worth striving for, but to discourage the use of a powerful method because the target language is not truly object-oriented is a fallacy. Therefore we will discuss later in the book how we can consider using object-oriented methods and UML for non-object implementation. This is an important consideration, because many software development tools in common use are not object-oriented, or pay only lip service to the idea, but they have strengths of their own.

To keep this book general, I shall adopt a broad church view. Object-oriented concepts are preferred, but if there are good reasons for diverting from the purist view then I will take it, or point out the alternative paths through the jungle for those wishing to explore on their own.

2.2 The Unified Modeling Language

The Unified Modeling Language (UML) is a notation for recording models of computer systems. It is a standard that has been defined for widespread use in the computer industry. It first appeared in 1995, and has evolved since then. It was derived from the best aspects of a large number of different notations that were available before that. It has gained widespread acceptance, and the majority of popular CASE[2] tools support UML. Before UML there were many overlapping and competing notations. Jacobson's OOSE notation, Booch's OO notation and Rumbaugh's OMT notation provide the basis for UML, but elements of other notations have been incorporated.

This book uses the UML notation extensively. Notation is not the same as method or process, just as the way you draw buildings is not the same as the buildings themselves, nor the way you construct buildings. Do not be fooled into thinking that knowing the UML makes you a good designer, any more than knowing English makes you the Poet Laureate. Good notation is important, but there is more to development than just good use of notation.

The UML is not a way of providing models for a project manager. It is really a notation for analysts and developers. There is more to modelling in a project than the UML. There are also limits to the use of the UML for analysis and design, and it is sometimes necessary to use additional notations. The UML does provide some means of extension, through stereotypes and constraints, and we shall see how these can be used.

2.2.1 THE KEY UML MODELS
The UML has a number of models which in turn form part of the models for information systems development, such as the systems requirements. Here we will give a flavour of the models available in UML. Later we will introduce these in detail, as they are needed at each stage of the software development process.

2 CASE – Computer-Assisted Software Engineering

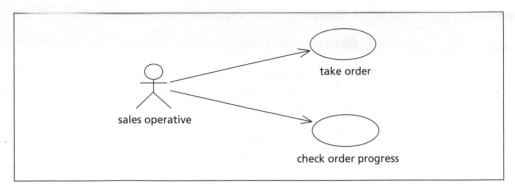

Figure 2.2   A use case diagram to describe aspects of an order-processing system

Use case diagrams

Use cases define exactly the points at which a computer system is used. Use cases define interaction between the users of the system and the system itself. A business process may invoke one or more system use cases, and a use case may be invoked by a number of business processes – we shall see some examples of this later. In Figure 2.2, a sales operative (an actor) may use a computer to take orders (a use case) and check order progress (another use case). These are very high level diagrams, intended to provide a definition of the system boundary. The use cases encapsulate all of the behaviour of the system, and the interactions between actors and use cases define the communication between the system and the outside world. The UML does not provide much by way of detail in the definition of use cases, and we shall introduce some additional notations and conventions to support the description of use cases.

Activity diagrams and statechart diagrams

Activity diagrams, as their name suggests, describe activities and the flow between activities. These diagrams can be used in business modelling to describe workflows in a business, in systems analysis to specify the behaviour of use cases, and in design to specify the detailed operation of complex parts of the system. Figure 2.3 shows a simple activity diagram to describe a business model of payment handling; this involves printing an invoice (activity), sending it to a customer (activity), waiting for payment (state), then processing that payment when it arrives (activity). The dot and bullseye indicate the beginning and end of the process respectively.

Activity diagrams will be used in this book in a variety of roles. They will be used to describe business processes in the business modelling. They will be used to describe the behaviour of use cases. They will also sometimes be used to describe detailed aspects of computer system operation. The notation is much richer than is indicated in the simple diagram in Figure 2.3.

Statechart diagrams are an alternative form of diagram that are used most commonly at the design stage. These allow description of some object (e.g. a customer account) as it moves between states. Figure 2.4 shows the movement of a bank account between states. Once opened it is in credit. It may then move into

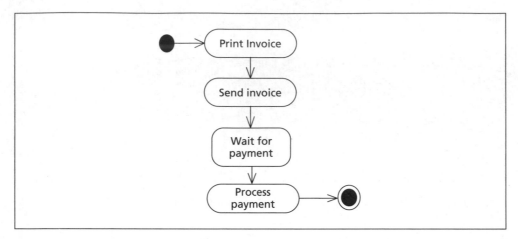

Figure 2.3 A UML activity diagram showing a simple business process to issue an invoice and collect payment

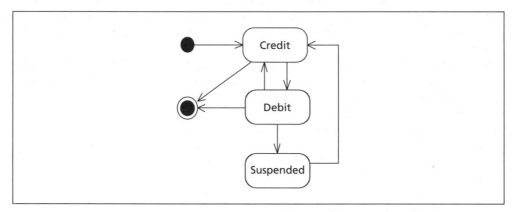

Figure 2.4 A UML statechart diagram to describe the behaviour of a bank account

debit and back to credit. From a debit state, if it is not paid in time it may move into the suspended state, and then can only be reactivated by being taken back to credit. It is only allowed to be closed from a credit or debit state.

   Both activity and statechart diagrams have the potential for nesting behaviour. For example, an activity can be described in detail by another activity diagram. This allows analysts and designers to work at varying levels of detail.

Sequence diagrams and collaboration diagrams
A sequence diagram is a key design drawing that takes a flow of activity and maps it in a two-dimensional way to the internal components of a system. Figure 2.5 shows a sales operative (an actor) using an order entry screen to enter order and delivery details, and the screen in turn will modify the order (an internal object in the computer system that deals with the order) and despatch (another object that processes the despatch of goods).

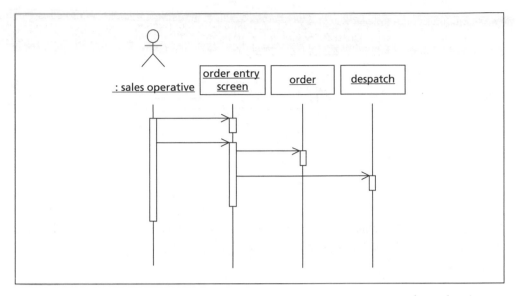

Figure 2.5   A UML sequence diagram to describe the interaction in a simple order processing use case

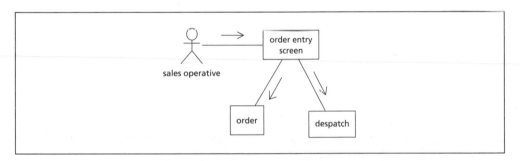

Figure 2.6   A UML collaboration diagram showing a simple interaction in an order processing use case

Again, this diagram is very rich. We shall use this extensively in the design process. It can be used not only to identify interactions, but also as a basis for determining what objects are needed in the system to provide the functionality. This is perhaps the most complicated diagram to grasp and apply successfully, and we shall look at this in great detail.

Collaboration diagrams are similar to sequence diagrams, but they draw out the interactions in a different way. This illustrates that, as with architects drawings for buildings, different drawings may show different aspects, but overlap in detail. Figure 2.6 shows the sales operative interacting with an order screen that in turn interacts with an order and despatch object.

Class diagrams
Class diagrams are really the internal wiring diagrams for a system. They are sometimes called static models, as they define the static and unchanging structure

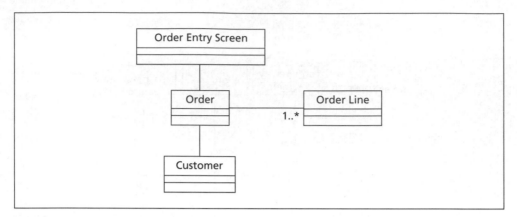

Figure 2.7   A UML class diagram to show the objects and their relationships in a system to support order processing

of the system.[3] In Figure 2.7, an order entry screen will need to use an order, which is made up of a number of order lines, and which is linked to a customer. In this diagram we show the objects that make up the system, and the lines of communication between them. This is the principal diagram for object-oriented analysis and design, and there is a great deal of preparation needed to produce a good set of class diagrams. Lots of information can be included on this diagram, including the data that is to be stored in the system and the processing that takes place.

Component diagrams
Components group together the elements of a computer system into larger units. Systems are then built out of the components. In each component there will be a number of objects, defined elsewhere in class diagrams. The components are then grouped together to cooperate to provide a complete system (Figure 2.8). These components will be deployed among the various computers that are used to implement the system.

2.3 Conclusion

Modelling is a fundamental part of the development of large-scale systems. Each stage of a development provides models that are used by later stages. The level of modelling depends on the size and type of the project, and range from lightweight informal models to large and complicated models. Throughout the book we shall examine the models described above in much more detail, introduce some extra models to supplement the Unified Modeling Language, and relate them to the stages of a software development project.

3 Sequence diagrams and collaboration diagrams are sometimes called dynamic models. Collaboration diagrams and class diagrams tend to have similar structures, but collaboration diagrams show a particular execution of the system, and class diagrams represent the paths for all possible uses of classes.

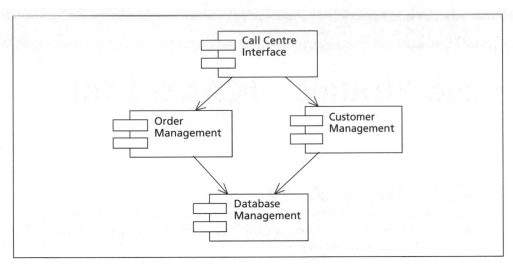

Figure 2.8 A UML component diagram showing the relationship between components that make up a call centre system

REVIEW QUESTIONS

1. Why are models used in software development?
2. What is meant by 'object-oriented'?
3. Are object-oriented programming languages essential for object-oriented methods to be used?
4. Is UML a method?
5. What are the key UML models?

CHAPTER **3**

Case Studies – ICANDO Oil

IN THIS CHAPTER YOU WILL:

1. **Read about three realistic case studies that will be used throughout the rest of the book to illustrate the concepts, and two further ones that will be used for exercises that you can try yourself.**

Information technology is not an end in itself. Its significance lies in the industries it supports. In the developed world, according to the World Bank statistics, many countries spent in excess of 8% of GDP on information technology and communications in 1999. The majority of this expenditure is in support of businesses, including the communications industries such as television and newspapers. Much of the excitement of IT development lies in the transformations that IT can make to the way companies undertake business. For the purpose of providing a realistic background to the examples in this book, we shall look at one major business sector.

The oil industry is a complex and wide-ranging enterprise. Most of us only see the end products, such as oil, fuel and plastics. Many people perhaps do not realize how much of its products they rely on, including road surfaces and the electricity delivered to our homes. To get some idea of the enormity of the industry, OPEC quotes the world demand for oil to be 76.8 million barrels a day (a barrel is 35 imperial gallons), and the three leading world oil companies each had revenues in excess of US$100 billion in 1999. This industry has matured during a century of immense economic development and change. It involves heavy engineering, a variety of technologies, and scientific understanding to find and transform crude oil into countless products. It employs millions of people, directly and indirectly. More than any other industry it has transformed lives, often for the better though in some unfortunate cases for the worse. It is the subject of great controversy, and it has massive impact on society, government, economies and the environment.

The maturity of the industry, and its wealth, mean that it is one of the widest adopters of information technology. Geologists use complicated simulation programs to estimate availability of crude oil. Engineers control complex drilling operations with computer systems. Traders use systems to exchange products and route them to refineries. The refineries themselves have process control systems and optimization programs. A computer system will plan the delivery of fuels and lubricants. A retail outlet has systems to log sales and monitor promotional schemes. Computer programs print out bills for retail outlets, and collect the

22

money from bank transfers. Without computers, the production and delivery of oil products would be a slower, costlier and less efficient process.

During the late 20th century, the expenditure of oil companies on information technology grew tremendously. Vast research programmes included investigations into a variety of uses of IT, from better optimization and simulations, through artificial intelligence, to machine learning. Outside of the leading IT vendors and consultancies, the oil companies are perhaps the largest consumers, researchers and developers of computer systems.

For this reason, and because I worked in this industry for a number of years, the case studies we shall consider will be from the oil industry. The choice has been to consider three types of application. The first is a large-scale order-processing application. This will give an insight into development where there are lots of existing systems. The second is a technical research and development system, where the focus is on technology. The third is an Internet application, of a type that is becoming increasingly common. We shall consider each of these applications all the way through the software development process. In addition, two further applications are described, which will be used as a basis for exercises for you to undertake.

To give you a sense of the complexity of the overall business, we shall describe briefly the various stages in the production of oil products. Broadly the industry splits itself into upstream and downstream businesses. Upstream focuses on finding, recovering and transporting crude materials. Downstream focuses on converting the crude materials into usable products such as gasoline and then delivering these into the marketplace. Figure 3.1 outlines the overall process of finding oil and converting it to usable products.

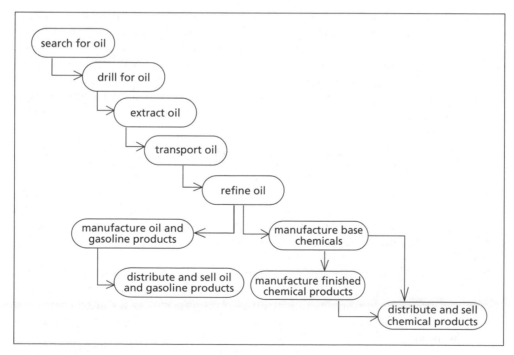

Figure 3.1   Schematic of the oil industry process

The key areas of activity are as follows.

- *Exploration*
  This involves finding oil and gas. Geological structures are studied, and investigations carried out. These include seismic surveys where echoes from explosions give a picture of the underground rock structures. Drilling may also take place, with samples taken from different depths in the Earth's crust. Computer simulations are often used to help geologists picture the way rocks lie, and to identify possible pockets of crude oil and gas.

- *Production*
  Production involves drilling wells, and controlling the crude product as it emerges from the ground. Gas and oil are usually mixed, and the gas needs to be separated. The oil needs to be transported to a refinery, and this is commonly done by ship or pipeline. Production involves lots of uses of IT, from production control, through monitoring of flows, and even the modelling of dispersion of drilling residues.

- *Trading*
  Once oil is out of the ground, it needs to be transported to refineries. All crudes have different characteristics, and a refinery can only handle specific types of crude oil. For example, some crudes have a high sulphur content that needs special treatment. The purpose of trading is to obtain the best deals for moving crude to a refinery. Variances in production rates in different fields and refining rates make it necessary for companies to buy and sell oil; simply moving your own oil to your own refineries is rarely done.

- *Refining*
  Crude oil is a complex cocktail of hydrocarbons. Imagine taking oil, bitumen, gasoline, diesel, methanol and a hundred other oil products and mixing them all together into a black sludge, and you have some idea of what crude oil is. Refining involves separating these out. Basically, this is done by boiling the oil and condensing the vapour at different temperatures. The thicker, heavier products are less valuable, so these are usually processed to break them into lighter products. Thus, out of the goo of crude oil come refined products.

- *Manufacturing*
  The refined oil products, such as gasoline and engine oils, do not come straight out of the refinery. Various chemicals are added to make them perform better. For example, additives to gasoline make it explode properly in an engine and keep some of the engine components clean, and the oil that goes in an engine consists of 10% or more of additives to improve its performance. Some of the outputs involve further processing for the production of base chemicals, such as ethylene, and end products, such as polythene.

- *Distribution*
  Products need to be distributed to the final consumers. For oil and gasoline, this will involve shipping to the retail outlets. For other products this may mean shipping to businesses that use the products, say as input to their own manufacturing processes. Distribution also involves temporary storage in warehouses.

3.1 ICANDO Oil

ICANDO Oil is a (fictional) leading European oil company, that has a diverse business operation involving exploration and production of crude oil, refining and manufacture of chemicals, and delivery into the retail gasoline, commercial gasoline and bulk chemical markets. The overall company is in fact a group of operating companies working in various national settings. There are also small but highly profitable operating companies in pharmaceuticals, agrochemicals and alternative energy sources. It is responding to major changes in the global market place, with rapid development in Eastern Europe and some tentative developments in China. It is ambitious and wishes to compete with the leading players in the oil industry. The company has a highly devolved structure, and has grown by acquisition. Therefore business processes vary widely and the supporting IT systems are very diverse.

3.2 ICANDO Bulk Chemical Ordering

ICANDO Oil has consolidated its European bulk chemicals operations into a single operating company. With the development of the European Union, cross-border trade has become commonplace, and the national chemical companies that form part of the ICANDO group have become artificial and cumbersome, with companies sometimes competing with each other over national boundaries. The restructuring has given opportunities for optimizing production and supply, rationalizing the various business units and improving the quality of products and services. One of the cornerstones for achieving this is a consolidated ordering system.

The business currently has ordering systems implemented and maintained on a country-by-country basis. These support different business procedures and are implemented in a variety of ways on different types of computing system, from mainframes with CICS[1] screens through to LAN[2] systems. Because of the way ICANDO has developed its manufacturing base, the manufacturing systems are more consistent, but there is some variability, particularly in plant where ICANDO has acquired another chemical company.

This problem is common to many companies. As they grow and mature, acquiring new business operations, the diversity of support grows. It makes the support of the business complicated. The prevalence of personal computers and the cheapness of servers mean that small business units often develop their own IT systems independently. A great challenge to any developing business is to rationalize its IT infrastructure.

Probably the key business driver for ICANDO in considering a new IT system for ordering is its relative market performance. In comparison with similar companies worldwide, ICANDO carries far more stock, has far more warehousing capacity, and has higher transport costs. In a price-competitive market this means that ICANDO's profit margins are very small, and a number of product lines are uneconomic. ICANDO has maintained its market through high-quality service and

---

1 CICS is a long-established IBM mainframe operating system.
2 LAN stands for Local Area Network.

reliability, but this is supported by high staff levels. In some countries though, market share has been falling dramatically. The board has been supporting the business through high income in the upstream oil market, but the business needs to return to a healthy profitability quickly.

ICANDO's primary problem in terms of stock management is that there is no consolidated view of ordering and manufacturing. Therefore, to ensure that customer demand can be met, high stocks need to be kept. Stocks cost money to keep and result in wastage, as well as tying up money that could be used for other purposes.

The IT strategy has focused on the ordering system as the first stage of a major revision of the systems to support the business. The reason for choosing this is that potential stock reductions of €147 million have been highlighted by significant changes in business procedures, and annual cost savings of €23 million in annual operating costs have been identified by reducing warehousing costs, transport costs and warehousing to the best levels in the industry. A comprehensive, Europe-wide order-processing system is needed to achieve these benefits.

The technical evaluation has been undertaken. A long look at the package market made package solutions a large contender. However, one of the key business requirements is providing secure access for clients to the ordering process over the Internet, with the capacity to supply added-value services to customers. The package market was marginal by way of cost of delivery, had a lower risk in terms of delivery, but was less flexible and did not give a marketing edge. The decision has therefore been to provide a bespoke ordering system, assimilating some package elements. The time-scale is short, and from project inception to delivery of the first system has to be less than 12 months.

Figure 3.2 illustrates the ideal situation, where a customer can make an automatic order over the Web. This would involve the server automatically scheduling some production at a plant. Once the product is available, it will be scheduled for delivery. The customer would then receive the goods and be invoiced.

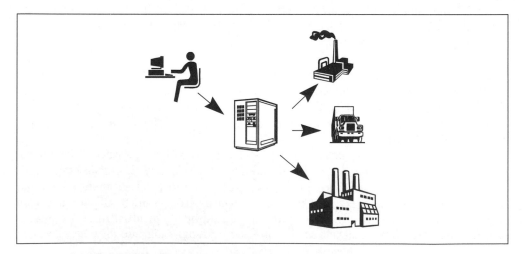

Figure 3.2   Vision of automatic ordering by customers, with automated scheduling of production and delivery

The business requirements have highlighted the following:

1. A consolidated system is needed to allow ordering and delivery to be sourced from any warehouse or plant in Europe.
2. The ordering process will be identical in each country.
3. Order taking will be in the language of the country of the customer.
4. Customers must have the ability to order directly over a secure Internet connection. Product lists will be customized according to the customer's contract.
5. Customers will be given a discount for advanced orders. This will be on a schedule adapted as part of each customer's contract. The reason for this is to optimize production schedules. A minimum of 21 days order before delivery is required to qualify for a discount, with an increasing discount for a further 7 days.
6. There will be an overall operations team that needs overview information of orders, expected orders, stocks and production schedules.
7. An optimization package used by one of the larger countries will be adapted to optimize overall production to meet projected demand. This will be run daily by the operations team. Weekly production plans will be despatched to each plant, with exceptional daily changes issued to individual plant.
8. Delivery will, where possible, take place from production, not from the warehouse. This radically reduces working capital and costs of movement of product.
9. In some cases, delivery is metered at the point of delivery. A form is signed by the customer and the delivery agent to register the amount delivered. Delivery agents must enter their deliveries on a secure Internet link by close of business on the day of delivery. This can be done manually or, for some delivery agencies, via a link with their own systems.
10. Customers are invoiced on the day following delivery. Payment terms are 30 days.
11. Late payment will initially invoke a warning and a restriction on further orders.
12. Non-payment in 60 days will suspend a customer's account.

3.3 ICANDO Site Safety

ICANDO has a number of chemical, petroleum and gas storage sites. A site must conform to rigorous safety standards. These standards specify the quality of storage facilities and limits on the proximity of facilities to each other and to other facilities in the local environment. The reason is to prevent a small hazard from a leak becoming a major hazard causing a chain of unpleasant events.

Site engineers are responsible for maintaining safety and specifying changes to the site. Safety guidelines are substantial documents. ICANDO has its own company standards, and there are often local standards as well. These standards change from time to time. Whenever a site engineer rearranges a site or adds a new facility, the guidelines need to be checked. Failing to meet guidelines is not only dangerous, it can lead to local safety inspectors closing the site.

Central services have a safety audit team that visits sites as regularly as possible. They do find infringements, and often these are because the site engineer has

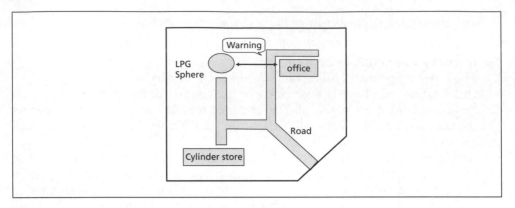

Figure 3.3 Suggested interface to the site safety auditing system

misread guidelines or occasionally overlooked a guideline. They would like some form of computer program to help the site engineers maintain safety standards.

The IT research group is called in, and they propose a drawing tool that allows engineers to quickly draw a site, including all the storage facilities, offices, boundaries and roads. It will take specifications of each of the facilities. Guidelines will be read in, and the site automatically checked against the guidelines, with an audit report. The IT research team sketch out a suggested layout for the interface for the system, as in Figure 3.3.

On close investigation, it is determined by the IT research group that there are two types of rule. The first type of rule states the materials that must be used to construct a facility, specifying qualities such as thickness of container walls. The second type of rule specifies minimum distances between facilities, and the distance depends on the facility and the capacity of the facility. Some of the distance rules are complicated by the fact that firewalls and bunds (mounds of earth) can be introduced to provide a barrier that enables facilities to be located more closely to each other, and distances must be calculated differently.

3.4 ICANDO Retail Petrol Promotions

The UK retail market for gasoline products is very competitive, and the nature of the market with a high number of business drivers means that most retailers use some form of loyalty card system. The ICANDO loyalty card allows users to collect points for every litre of fuel they buy and for every pound's worth of goods bought in the shop. Points can be exchanged for goods or used to obtain discounts on a range of products such as holidays. The UK marketing director wants to improve the image of ICANDO by offering customers a Web site. This will allow them to check their points online and to make orders. The marketing manager has managed to sell advertising space on the site, and has contracts with suppliers to offer additional discounts for offers if they are ordered through the site. The throughput on the call centre at present is 3,000 calls a day. Two thirds of these calls are to cash in points. The rest are for reissue of lost cards, new registration, complaints and general enquiries.

When a customer makes a purchase, she hands over her ICANDO loyalty card. The cashier swipes the card at the till. The details of the purchase are sent to the central server, which allocates points depending on the purchase. The customer has those points available immediately if she wants to use them – the current balance is printed on the till receipt. Each outlet has a small number of standard goods that can be purchased with the points. Every three months a catalogue is sent to the customer, and she can choose from a wider range of goods and also obtain discounts against services such as holidays or theatre tickets.

The Web site will allow the customer to see an online catalogue of goods, and make orders. She may also buy goods and services through the site at a discount in exchange for points, with payment by credit card. The site will allow her to check her points balance, change contact details and order a replacement card. It will also collect her email address, and optionally she can elect to have emails of special offers.

The marketing manager is also keen to explore the possibility of mobile communications, such as WAP.[3] At the very least, he thinks that it should be possible to send SMS[4] messages to a customer's mobile phone with special offers.

3.5 ICANDO Retail Outlet System

The UK retail division of ICANDO oil has signed an agreement with NeverShut, a grocery service that supplies goods to franchised outlets with the brand name NeverShut. The vision is to provide NeverShut goods at petrol stations 24 hours a day, seven days a week. This will substantially extend the range of goods that can be bought at an ICANDO retail outlet. It is expected that this will have a positive effect on the sale of fuels, as well as adding a new revenue stream.

The retail outlet will continue to supply ICANDO products, such as oil and other motor-related products, alongside NeverShut groceries. These will all be paid for at the same till, with goods accepted through a bar code scanner. Each ICANDO retail outlet has an electronic point of sale (EPOS) terminal that is connected to a central system that records all sales. This is done on a 'store and forward' basis, with sales batched up and sent daily. For customers with a loyalty card, the loyalty card number is recorded with each sale.

NeverShut tracks the sales in an outlet, and its own EPOS terminal in its standard shops works in the same way as the ICANDO system. It does not make sense to put a second EPOS system into ICANDO retail outlets.

NeverShut tracks the sales at an outlet, and when stocks are low they trigger an automatic order to restock the retail outlet. Each stock item has a minimum and maximum stock level, and as soon as the minimum is reached an order is despatched to the outlet within 24 hours. When deliveries are made, any stock item that has been reduced by the minimum stock delivery will be topped up to the maximum stock level.

---

3 WAP stands for Wireless Application Protocol, which is used for mobile devices to have a limited Internet-style interface.
4 SMS stands for Short Message Service, a simple text messaging service that is commonly used on mobile telephones.

The ICANDO EPOS system allows for the recording of deliveries. The sales operator reads the product code using the bar code and types in a quantity delivered. This is already provided.

ICANDO need new IT functionality to handle the NeverShut relationship. Firstly, whenever sales are downloaded, the NeverShut sales need to be separated from the ICANDO products. The loyalty card details cannot be passed on to NeverShut. The NeverShut sales for each retail outlet are then passed on electronically to NeverShut's own system, and the restocking is handled entirely by NeverShut.

NeverShut produces a monthly statement to ICANDO for products delivered to ICANDO retail outlets. ICANDO needs to reconcile the NeverShut statement with its own record of deliveries to the retail outlets. Variances are reported, and any substantial variance is investigated by someone in ICANDO's head office liaising with the manager of the retail outlet. A variance will involve adjusting either the amount payable by the retail outlet or the amount to be paid to NeverShut.

The retail outlet receives one consolidated bill from ICANDO for everything delivered to the outlet, whether it is supplied by ICANDO or NeverShut. The manager checks that bill before authorizing payment.

Head Office wants to track the effectiveness of the new deal. There will be a refurbishment cost of €15,000 for each retail outlet taking on the NeverShut brand. This will involve setting up hoardings, extending car parking facilities and increasing shelf space. The initial trial will be with 20 outlets in a selected region over a 6 month period, but if it is successful, it will be rolled out to 300 retail outlets. The expectation is that profitability on the retail goods alone will amount to €12,000 for a typical site. The expectation is that extra petrol sales will amount to an additional profit of €4,000 per site per year. Changes to the information system to accommodate the new deal will cost approximately €500,000.

Reports are needed to split profitability between ICANDO and NeverShut products. There is also the need to track individual purchases, through the loyalty card, to see if the volume of purchases for regular ICANDO customers increases.

The loyalty card will credit points for all sales, not just ICANDO products. There is a plan to offer bonus points for special promotions, including NeverShut products. The system needs to be able to accrue the loyalty points for a customer for each sale, including the special promotion points.

3.6 ICANDO Oil Trading

Oil trading is a major activity for any oil company. Crude oil is mostly transferred by tankers that can exceed a million barrels of oil capacity.[5] With crude oil normally exceeding €20 a barrel, the tankers are carrying huge amounts of stock.

An oil company needs to keep a continuous stream of crude oil into a refinery. Unfortunately, crude oils are very different in characteristics, depending on where they are sourced. Some oils have highly corrosive constituents and need special treatment. Thus a refinery can usually only process a restricted set of oil types. Often the oil that a company recovers is inappropriate for its own refineries.

---

5   A barrel of oil is 42 US gallons, and a gallon is 3.8 litres.

The primary role of the trading arm of an oil company is to keep its refineries functioning with the cheapest available crude. Oil is bought and sold in commodity exchanges, much like shares. Oil can be bought and sold before it is extracted through to when it is in transport. It is not unknown for a tanker full of oil to be traded on route to a refinery and redirected to another refinery.

The trading arm often has a secondary role: to make money by trading. If oil is bought that is surplus to processing needs, then the oil can be sold if the price improves. There might also be bargains that arise because, say, a refinery is offline, and if your company has sufficient storage it may make sense to buy excess crude at low prices. Crude bought at a low price might be sold later at a higher price.

The market is complicated by two features. First, there is the notion of futures. A deal can be struck for oil to be delivered on some date in the future, and for the trade to take place then. Thus the trader is not buying something now, but promising to buy something weeks or months ahead. All this is straightforward until traders start to sell futures. If a future trade is for €20 a barrel and the market price on delivery is €25 a barrel, then the future has a value of €5 a barrel, which means that another trader might buy the future at up to €5. (Equally, the value of the barrel may be lower than the future says, so the future has a negative market value.)

The second complication is the future options market. You buy an option to buy. Thus a trader might pay €2 for the option to buy a barrel of oil at €20 some time in the future. If the oil price is above €20 at the time the option reaches its settlement date, it is worth buying the oil. However, if the oil price is below €20, the trader would let the option go and lose the original €2. Options can be bought and sold. If a barrel of oil looks to be going to sell for €25 and a trader has an option for €20, the value of the option would be €5.

A trader takes risk. The risk is the amount of money the trader could lose if all the deals took place under the worst conditions (all the futures and options contracts were above the market price at the time of delivery, say). The trader tries to minimize risk by balancing promises to buy with promises to sell, and provided the value of the promises to sell are on balance more than the value of the promises to buy, the risk is low.

ICANDO Oil has a substantial trading group. The trading floor has dozens of information feeds. The current commodity market trades are shown, with the prices. The futures market trades and prices are shown. News feeds are shown, and any major event such as a refinery fire or a world event like a terrorist attack or war declaration can have a rapid effect on trade.

ICANDO Oil would like a fully integrated system that allows a trader to sit at a desk and see all the information feeds, see all the portfolio contracts that are held, enter new trades, and show the risk that the portfolio represents. The managers want to be able to see the portfolios of all the traders, and to assess and control the overall risk of the trading floor. If a trader takes on too much risk, the management need to be advised immediately.

Traders also have lists of contacts they use regularly. They deal directly with traders in other companies over the phone, and they need to keep the details of traders available. Also, traders pick up useful bits of information as they talk, and they share that with other traders. An internal bulletin board is needed so that a trader can type in some information that will be seen by other traders.

The supply needs of the refinery need to be managed. Thus, planned and future stocks and production capacity need to be available to the traders. They need to know the types of oil a refinery can process. If a refinery has a production problem that keeps it out of operation for any significant time, it needs to be notified to the trading floor.

INITIATION, ORGANIZATION AND MANAGEMENT OF IT PROJECTS

Reader's Guide

This section introduces the types of organizational environment and the management and initiation of IT projects. Traditionally this is left late in the description of software development, but in practice it is one of the first things that needs to be considered. If your primary interest is in modelling notations and analysis and design, you may choose to skip this section and return to it later. If your interest is more in management and business issues, then you will probably want to study this section in detail.

Chapter 4: Project Conception and Initiation

This chapter gives an outline of how projects are initiated and introduces some useful methods for gathering information, such as stakeholder goals and project risks, to be used later in the software development process.

Chapter 5: Software Development Life Cycle

This chapter gives a thorough introduction to the software development life cycle and how developments can be organized, focusing on iterative development approaches.

Chapter 6: Managing the Process

This chapter introduces different organization types and different ways of managing the software development process.

Chapter 7: The Cost–Benefit Model

This chapter looks in detail at the economic justification of IT projects.

Project Conception and Initiation

1. **The importance and involvement of different stakeholders**
2. **The use of project goals**
3. **The importance and relevance of infrastructure**
4. **The importance of recognizing and tracking risk**
5. **Some useful analysis tools for project inception**

Projects arise in many ways. The simplest developments are the small ones, where only a handful of people are involved – usually these are to solve some relatively minor problem. Large-scale developments have usually gone through a good deal of debate among the senior management teams before anyone starts to think about development. As well as generating the idea for a project, the project inception often considers a lot of information that is important to the development and that is often lost or overlooked.

Major projects usually start with some grand vision. The goals are clear, and unequivocal. As the project matures, that vision is brought closer to reality, and the goals often change. Too often the vision and goals are lost in the process, or become so dislocated from reality that the project ends up shipwrecked with no survivors. Keeping the vision, goals and reality in line is the role of senior management. I recently witnessed a project where this process failed. The vision was valid, but did not readjust to the reality of the project. The project overran and kept missing key deadlines and asking for more money. Ultimately, as a young colleague of mine reflected, reality has a habit of catching up with you, and the result was a cancellation of the project with substantial job losses and damaged reputations.

IT projects are not just about IT. They are undertaken because they have a major impact on business operations. Within an IT organization it is often difficult to get a grip on the importance and impact of IT. The initiation and planning of an IT project is a substantial undertaking for an organization. The actual costs and effort that are spent on IT directly are often dwarfed by the effort and expenditure elsewhere, like the ice jutting out of the sea is but a small representation of an iceberg. For example, the establishment of the software and hardware for a call centre with 200 staff may cost €2 million, but the building to house the call centre will probably cost at least that much, and the annual cost of employment and operation will be between five and ten times that much.

Understanding the initiation and involvement of various people and organizations is valuable to the developer. The analyst needs to know who the stakeholders are and to make sure that views and requirements are collected from all the appropriate sources. Project managers need to know who to keep on board and involved in order to reduce the political risks to the project. Programmers need to know the importance of time-scales and the need for appropriate quality in their work. Steering groups need to be aware of the broader implications of the project to ensure its safe and smooth delivery.

My colleagues teach 'Systems Thinking', which tries to address some of these broader issues. It is often difficult for novices to grasp the importance of these more general ideas. However, as you develop your career, either you are going to grow frustrated by the strange decisions that seem to go on independently of you, or you are going to begin to understand the broader picture. Peter Senge in *The Fifth Discipline* (1990) gives an excellent introduction to the complexity of organizational endeavours. One of his underlying arguments is that consequences are so far removed from decisions that it is difficult for an organization and the people in it to learn. The situation that many software developers find themselves in is producing systems that are flawed in original concept, or that meet a need that has changed dramatically, and frequently they get the blame; that is not to say that developers themselves are universally blameless, just that they are the final stage in a project before the product is delivered, and alas it is true that the messenger is often shot if the message is bad.

In a book of this nature, which focuses mainly on the development process, it is impossible to give a comprehensive overview of this stage. However, it is useful to understand that projects are not delivered by the stork, and that there is a complex and messy process (that is also a great deal of fun) before even the first project plan is put in place.

We will, however, consider some useful tools that can help gather information from the project inception that can be useful in guiding technical decisions later. Figure 4.1 shows the inputs and outputs to a project initiation. A primary output of considering the project inception will be a list of stakeholders that need to be considered throughout the project. The goals of the project need to be gathered and monitored throughout the project. It is useful to know the strengths and weaknesses of situations and proposals, and to look at the drivers and barriers to change; on the diagram this is shown as a situation assessment. Risks need to be identified as soon as they arise throughout the project, and addressed in a timely and effective manner.

4.1 Stakeholders in a Project

A lot of textbooks and methods talk about users and developers as if they were the only people involved in a project. The last project I helped manage called a meeting of all those impacted by the project, and though the analysis and development team were barely a dozen in number, there were well over 50 people in the room, and that did not include all the potential users. In reality, over a hundred

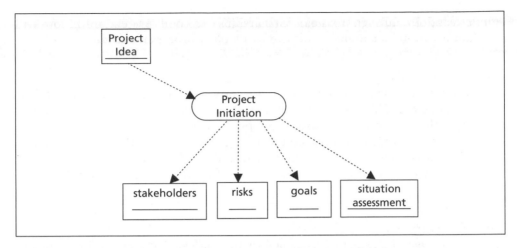

Figure 4.1   The primary inputs and outputs of project initiation

people would have an involvement in the project, even though it was a small pilot exercise. We shall consider here some of the likely stakeholders in any project.

The sponsors

Someone is paying for the project, and usually they want a good deal of say in the project. They are needed to start the project, and they can pull the plug at any time. In a company, the sponsor is usually some budget holder. Depending on the size of the expenditure and importance of the project, the sponsor will apply different controls. The sponsors define the overall goals of the project, and they will generally only continue to pay if they are in sympathy with the goals and they believe that the goals will be met.

The users

For new projects, the users often have little say in the initiation of the project. They usually become involved once funding has been agreed, though the managers of the users are often involved in the decision-making. Sometimes the users of a system do not even exist at project initiation if the project is to develop a system for a new business unit. Users become more important once the project is in development and especially after the first part of the system is deployed and operational. Their response to the system will be critical to its ongoing success. Once a system is operational, many of the enhancements come out of complaints and suggestions from the users. Then they become one of the major sources of new development ideas, as they see how the product can be improved and extended

Suppliers

It may seem odd to consider suppliers as being stakeholders in a system development, but they very much are. Many projects are initiated when a supplier suggests a new solution to a problem. Suppliers are essential for providing packages, equipment and development tools. Their level of involvement varies, from simple vendors through to near-partnerships. A good project initiation will consider a variety of suppliers, and we will look at procurement later.

Employee agencies

One of the large drivers for many projects is improvements in productivity and/or reduction of costs. This usually has an impact on employees who may face radical changes in their work, or even lose their jobs. This needs to be considered early on in the project. In some countries, employee legislation means that advance notice of significant changes in employment need to be notified well in advance. Also, the threat of changes can cause employees to withdraw cooperation or take industrial action.

Internal departments

IT projects typically have a wide impact in an organization, not just in the development team and the commissioning department. Large changes in business operation involve training, reorganization, construction and communications.

Customers

A large proportion of systems development today focuses on customers, either directly through Internet services, or indirectly through customer relationship management. The impact on customers, direct or indirect, is usually one of the key drivers in system development, and the success of the project can stand or fall by how it impacts business performance in the market.

4.2 Goals

It may seem obvious, but projects are there to meet some goal. Understanding the goals of a project are important for guiding decisions on IT choices. For example, a project to try out a new idea will need to be fleet of foot, and make hasty decisions with software that is quick to build but difficult to maintain. A project to consolidate a position in a developed market can afford to take more time, and aim at software that is more robust and long-lived.

Goals, however, can be conflicting. Different stakeholders have different views, and different things they want out of a project. The marketing manager may want a system that is ready in three months and will be operational for five years or more in a growing market, while the IT manager knows that quick software is hard to maintain and more costly in the long term. Understanding the conflicts can help in planning; perhaps the IT department can produce a quick and cheap solution for the short term while developing a robust long-term solution.

Goals often change during the lifetime of a project. The grand ideas often need to be brought back to reality. Also, market changes or changes to an organization may impact a project. Sometimes these enhance the project and make it more important. Perhaps a new opportunity arises, or there is some new insight into how to change the way an organization runs. Setting clear goals at the outset, and maintaining these goals in a way that reflects changes throughout a project, is critical to success.

4.3 Infrastructure

Existing infrastructure dominates the direction of any project. Few IT projects today start with a clean sheet. Usually there is a substantial IT infrastructure in place. It might well be that the best implementation of a project would be using Java on modern servers, but if the IT infrastructure is based on Cobol applications and the organization has a substantial Cobol development team, there may need to be compromises.

Most new developments need to work alongside existing software. This will involve exchange of information. The choice of technology for new projects is usually dominated by existing IT solutions. Long-lived software is more common than you might suspect. I recall one evaluation study I undertook that showed that a number of companies, despite upgrading most of their IT infrastructure, were running invoicing programs that were first written twenty years earlier and had been adapted extensively over time.

4.4 Risks

One of my favourite analogies for risk is the boiled frog. The argument goes like this. If you drop a frog into a pan of hot water, it will leap out immediately. If you sit a frog in a pan of cold water and heat it slowly, it will enjoy the rise in tempera ture until it passes out and boils; at no single point will it realize its life is in danger. I have not personally tried the experiment with a real frog, but I have seen many metaphorical boiled frogs, and I have suffered that fate myself occasionally.

IT projects are risky. This is not inherent to IT; Isambard Kingdom Brunel had more failures than successes in his development of railways, bridges and tunnels – he never did get that tunnel under the English Channel. IT projects are about change, and change itself is risky. A risk is any event or situation that may cause the project to fail, to be delayed, to cost more, or to deliver less than is planned. Risks need to be acknowledged and dealt with early. It is too tempting to sweep risks under the carpet and hope they will go away. A healthy project is one that identifies risks early and takes action to minimize their impact.

Risks arise from many sources. External risks can arise when suppliers fail, or the market changes. Projects are often cancelled not because they failed to deliver, but because the organization can no longer afford them for some other reason. Sometimes a product (say a computer package) does not live up to its claims, or has a serious fault that is not identified in the product evaluation. Internal risks arise from failure of parts of the organization to deliver, perhaps caused by staff turnover or other internal pressures diverting resources. Some-times the planning of a phase got the estimate wildly wrong, and that too is a risk.

Any member of a project team needs to be able to raise a risk. The risk needs to be quickly categorized and someone allocated to investigate. Action needs to be taken if the risk is seen as significant. A mature project can live with a number of risks and deal with them. Sometimes a risk can cause a project to be cancelled, but more usually it causes the project to change direction, perhaps to change its goals or its delivery schedule or funding. A good project plan will include some contin-gency to deal with risk.

Table 4.1 Part of a stakeholder analysis

Stakeholder category	Role in project	Project implications	Actions needed
Sponsor	Provide funding	Will be seeking value for money	Agree budgets
	Chair steering group	Regular reviews of progress, expenditure and risks	Present project plan and costings
Call centre	Operate new IT system	Need for training	Agree training schedule and budget
		Needs to be usable	Use for interface prototype evaluations
	Provide detailed operational knowledge of order processing	Need to capture operational knowledge	Business analysis to focus on call centre staff

4.5 Useful Analysis Tools

4.5.1 STAKEHOLDER OVERVIEW

It is useful to keep a list of stakeholders and their role in the development, with any project implications and actions that need taking. The analysis tool below has been taken from USERfit (Poulsen *et al.*, 1996). Stakeholders are grouped into categories (an individual might fit under a number of different categories). A stakeholder category may have a number of roles in the project. Each role may have a number of implications for the project. Actions need to be devised to address these implications. You may wish to adapt this tool to the needs of an organization. For ICANDO Chemicals the stakeholder overview might include something like Table 4.1. As you can see, this will be useful for various stages in the development process. A table such as this could be quite extensive.

4.5.2 SWOT ANALYSIS

SWOT analysis is a common tool used in strategic planning to work out the Strengths, Weaknesses, Opportunities and Threats of a situation or proposal. Strengths are those aspects internal to a situation that are positive. Weaknesses are those aspects of a situation that are negative. Opportunities are those aspects external to the situation, or that the situation can develop into, that are positive. Threats are those aspects external to the situation that could be negative.

The advantage of a SWOT analysis is that it forces people to think on both sides of an argument. A common fault in many analysis procedures is looking at only one aspect, either only the positive aspects or only the negative aspects. I have also used a variety of thinking tools by De Bono (1994). The opening stages of a project need open thinking rather than closed thinking, to allow people to explore options before coming to firm decisions.

4.5.3 FORCE FIELD ANALYSIS

Force Field Analysis is used to estimate the pressures for and against change in a situation. Pressures for change are listed and drawn on the left of a diagram, as in

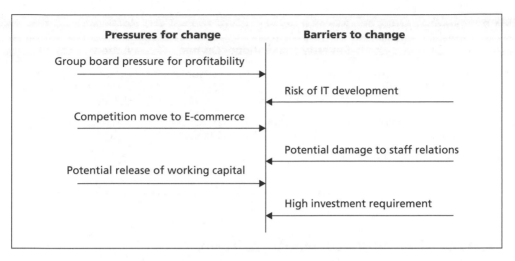

Figure 4.2 Force Field Analysis for ICANDO Chemicals' proposed change to order taking and distribution

Figure 4.2. Barriers to change are listed and drawn to the right of the diagram. Forces have different magnitudes, and often one or two are overriding. For ICANDO Chemicals, the pressure from the main board will almost certainly override the barriers to change.

I have used this to good effect in organizational change when there has been huge resistance to change. Most organizations are conservative, and will not change willingly. Often people only see the downside of change, especially if it impacts them. Getting a fair assessment of the balance of pressures is important for making decision-making explicit. This should not be used as a means of justification, but as a means of careful and objective assessment. People will disagree about the importance of different forces, but grouping all the forces together will help the decision regarding change.

4.5.4 RISK REGISTER

A risk register is used to catalogue and track risks. A risk is anything that may affect a project in a negative way. Managing risks is something that is the responsibility of all project team members. Logging risks and addressing them is an ongoing activity. A risk register should be reviewed regularly. Risks can be categorized in terms of their likelihood and severity, and rated as high, medium or low. High-severity risks are ones that could stop the project succeeding, or delay it severely, or incur substantial costs. Medium-severity risks are ones that can cause significant delays or unplanned costs. Low-severity risks are ones that can cause some delays or unplanned costs. Risks can escalate if they are not managed.

A risk should be notified as soon as it is spotted. The risk needs to be rated, and someone needs to be allocated responsibility for addressing it. A risk register can be kept in a small database or spreadsheet. It needs to be reviewed regularly in project team meetings, and the steering group needs to be advised of high-severity, high-likelihood risks. A risk register for the ICANDO Chemical system might contain items as in Table 4.2.

Table 4.2   Sample entries in a risk register

Risk	Severity	Likelihood	Owner	Action
Industrial action by warehouse staff in response to threat of redundancies	High	Medium	Personnel	Negotiations to be established at project outset
Supplier of communications software in receivership	High	High	IT Project Manager	New supplier being sought
Resignation of technical architect	Low	High	IT Development Manager	Reallocation of duties while replacement sought

4.6 Getting the Project Inception Right

In the early part of your career, you are unlikely to be involved in the inception of projects, except perhaps if there is some aspect of technical feasibility required. However, understanding that projects start in a number of ways, and that there is important information that can be gleaned from the inception, can make the development process much smoother.

As you will see from the worked examples below, the level of effort put into project inception varies considerably. Large projects need careful consideration, though that can often be done very quickly if the pressure is on to produce a solution to meet an urgent need.

The main message I would like to leave in this chapter is that some consideration needs to be made by all individuals in a project about how it arose, and projects should not start on a whim. All projects need an open and broadening thinking phase before decisions are made. No project considers all the aspects at the outset, and there will be surprises and disappointments, but too many ill-considered projects are started without due care. It might only take a few days to consider the broader aspects of a project, but they are days worth spending. The longer it takes to uncover a problem, the harder it is to resolve it. Missed requirements, unconsidered stakeholders, overlooked risk and wrong goals are hugely expensive to rectify.

4.7 ICANDO Bulk Chemical Ordering

4.7.1 STAKEHOLDERS

Sponsors
In the ICANDO Chemicals application, the sponsor is the board of ICANDO Chemicals, led by the chief executive. Their goal is to make the overall performance of the European chemicals business more profitable. As experienced professionals in the business, they know that their operation is inefficient in many ways. Trade reports indicate that they are in the bottom half of the industry in terms of profitability. Parts of their business, however, are very profitable. They have made a strategic decision that the best way to improve the overall business is to

harmonize the order processing and production planning throughout Europe. To do this, they know that they need a single order-processing system, so that orders can be met from the most appropriate plant or warehouse, and that the level of warehousing of product is kept to an absolute minimum.

The ICANDO Chemicals board realize that there is a two-year window in which they can improve profitability of the business before the board of the ICANDO Group decide to intervene. The consequences of failure would be a radical restructuring of the business by the Group board, perhaps selling off many of the least profitable parts of the business.

They are able to raise the capital, partly from retained earnings, and partly from group funds. This will be a substantial sum, and they will want careful control on expenditure and project progress.

Users

The primary users of the ICANDO Chemicals order-processing system will be the staff in the call centres processing the orders, those customers who are granted the right to make direct orders themselves, and a new centralized production planning team. The implication of this is that the design of the system must cater for the needs of these people. Particular care will be needed with respect to customers using the ordering system directly.

Suppliers

Any large IT investment attracts considerable interest from the IT industry, especially when a large established organization is planning a major investment. ICANDO uses a wide variety of software packages, software tools and development organizations. Once the project is announced, sales representatives start to contact senior people in the ICANDO Chemicals team, looking for opportunities.

One of the key category of suppliers that will take an early interest and involvement will be the various software houses that undertake large-scale developments. Often such organizations are involved very early on in the planning of the project, and ICANDO, like many such organizations, will often subcontract large parts or even all of the development of their applications.

Employee agencies

ICANDO Chemicals has two areas of cost improvements. The first is in improved stock management. This will more than halve the warehousing capacity needed, and there will be subsequent job losses in the warehousing that is decommissioned. The programme of decommissioning will take three years, and it is expected that a fair proportion of the job losses can be catered for through natural wastage. A budget is set aside for redundancies, but the company plans to offer alternative jobs where possible. The personnel departments in the various countries notify the government agencies and employee organizations of their plans.

The second improvement will be in order processing. There will need to be some rationalization of the call centres, but in the short term there should be few job losses. The main impact will be on retraining call centre staff in the use of a new order-processing system. Redefinition of some job roles will have to be undertaken by personnel departments and negotiations may need to be undertaken with employee organizations on grading issues.

Internal departments

The personnel departments throughout ICANDO Chemicals will be critical to the success of the project. They will need to make sure that changes in staff take place as smoothly as possible. New job roles, job losses, and relocation of key staff will need to be planned and managed throughout the project. There will also be considerable pressure on recruitment of IT-related staff.

The warehousing and distribution departments will need to be involved in the planning of the new distribution scheme. This will involve new procedures, as well as changes to warehouses and distribution.

The call centres will have a substantial role to play. They will be at the forefront of the implementation. It will not be viable to switch the whole operation of ICANDO Chemicals overnight. Training the call centre staff in the new system will take each member of staff out of operation for 5 days, and with 500 staff in 18 call centres throughout Europe, this is going to need considerable planning.

The training departments are going to be involved in a variety of activities, from training staff to use the new computer system, and organizing training of IT staff on new tools and techniques.

Stakeholder overview

Again, this is a huge project. There will be many stakeholders. The management team will have a considerable task to manage all the complex relationships. Table 4.3 shows a small fragment of the stakeholder analysis needed for a project of this type. This would be backed up by a substantial report describing the stakeholders and their expectations.

4.7.2 GOALS

The primary goals of the system are:

1. To increase profitability of the chemicals business by
    1.1 Providing a homogeneous ordering system for all European clients
    1.2 Reducing stock holdings by supplying orders direct from production
    1.3 Allowing Europe-wide optimization of production
    1.4 Removing internal competition for customers
    1.5 Removing wastage through stock reduction
    1.6 Removing warehouse capacity and the related operating costs
2. To achieve the first installation of the revised ordering system within one year.
3. To complete the roll-out of the system and the restructuring of the business within two years.

4.7.3 INFRASTRUCTURE

The ordering system is a replacement, and will use new equipment and software. The system will need to interface to existing production control systems and accounts systems. An existing production planning package will be adopted to cover production optimization for European operations.

Table 4.3 Stakeholder analysis for the ICANDO Chemicals system

Stakeholder category	Role in project	Project implications	Actions needed
Main board	Provide funding	Will be seeking value for money	Agree budgets. Monitor expenditure
	Monitor and review	Regular reviews of progress, expenditure and risks	Establish regular steering group. Present project plan and costings, progress and risks
Employee representation bodies	Consultation on restructuring and implications for staff	Affects speed and cost of roll out	Discussions on restructuring Agreement on restructuring
	Representation of staff interests	Impact on staff morale and motivation	Keep staff briefed, and ensure that restructuring is fair and acceptable
Customers	Purchase chemicals	Need to advise customers of implications	Sales team to be briefed so they can brief customers
	Switch to web ordering	Need to consult customers on acceptability and requirements	Engage in requirements analysis Enrol some customers in beta testing
IT department	Develop system and deploy	Crucial that this is successful	Adopt sound project and development methods Select appropriate software and development tools
	Resource development and deployment	Appropriate recruitment, retention and management needed	Recruitment campaign Competitive employee package
	Purchase equipment, software; install and test	Crucial that this is timely and effective	Adopt professional purchasing approach Develop supplier relationships, and ensure good quality contracts

4.7.4 SWOT CURRENT SITUATION

Strengths
1. ICANDO are established in the market, and have a good reputation for delivery and quality of goods
2. Good distribution network
3. Loyal and dedicated staff
4. Parts of the business are at the leading end of efficiency in the market

Weaknesses
1. There is a high cost of warehousing and distribution compared to the market leaders
2. Customers are unable to link their systems to ICANDO's for automatic ordering

Opportunities
1. The best practices in the high performing part of the business can be used to improve the rest of the business
2. Large amounts of cash can be released if the warehousing and distribution is optimized to the best in the business

Threats
1. The ICANDO Group board is demanding higher profitability from the European Chemicals operation, or it will consider restructuring and possibly selling off large parts of the business.
2. Competitors are moving to e-commerce solutions and could take a good part of ICANDO Chemicals' market share.

4.7.5 RISK REGISTER

The initial risk register will be very high level. This is an enormous business project, and will generate substantial risks. The ones indicated in Table 4.4 would be a small list that need to be considered at project inception. The board and senior management would track these risks regularly, and adjust actions as appropriate.

Table 4.4 Risk register for ICANDO chemicals

Risk	Severity	Likelihood	Owner	Action
Progress is too slow for the company to recover its market performance	High	Medium	Main board	Regular appraisal of project progress
Employee relationships could lead to blockages on development and roll out	High	High	Personnel director	Tracking of personnel issues in each country, with due notice and proper and considerate management of staff reductions
Skills shortage in the IT market	High	High	IT director	Setting of recruitment and retention process and policies
Failure of the order taking system would cripple the company	High	Medium	IT development team management	A careful roll out strategy to uncover initial risks and minimize effect of teething problems. High reliability equipment and networks in a secure environment, plus rapid disaster recovery plan

4.8 ICANDO Site Safety

4.8.1 STAKEHOLDERS

Sponsors
The site safety application is funded out of research and development. The ICANDO group set aside a budget for R&D, and this is controlled by a Research Board. They budget the expenditure on a two year planning cycle. The funds are shared among different business sectors, and allocated to different categories of research. IT is one category, and one of the Research Board directors holds the budget for the IT category. Groups in the business sector can bid for a project.

For the site safety application, the safety auditors in central office put in a bid for a project that will cover the equivalent of one research scientist for a year. The sponsor examines the bid, and it is rated sufficiently highly to be funded.

Users
The users of the ICANDO site safety system would be engineers and planners involved in the design or alteration of storage sites. Auditors may also use the system.

Suppliers
This is a small-scale investigation. There is unlikely to be a great deal of direct supplier interest in this. The research team will be looking for possible tools to help them solve the problem.

Employee agencies
There are no employee impacts of significance. Engineers are used to using computing packages and it is not expected that there will be any problem in getting them to use the package.

Internal departments
There is little organizational impact of this particular project, at least while it remains an R&D project. Even if it develops into a full product, then the impact will be localized to the site engineering offices and the audit departments.

Stakeholder overview
There are relatively few stakeholders in this project. If the project steps out into a commercial development, then additional stakeholders might be considered, such as the software development organization that takes the product to market, and potential purchasers outside ICANDO Oil. An overview is shown in Table 4.5; this will not be very extensive, and might be used as part of the project justification documentation.

4.8.2 GOALS

The goal of this project is to determine the viability of producing a system to aid site engineers in the design of safe sites. If the evaluation is successful, the goal of

Table 4.5   Stakeholder analysis for the site safety system

Stakeholder category	Role in project	Project implications	Actions needed
Research board	Fund and monitor project	Ensure value of project, and monitor results	Proposal and project review through normal research procedures
Central services audit team	Proposers of project	Will be keen to monitor project and adopt any successful result	Need to be engaged in analysis and design Need to be involved in evaluation
	Providers of expertise	Must be engaged in development	Programme of interviews and acquisition of technical documentation
Site engineers	Final users of system	Will determine ultimate acceptance	Need to be engaged in analysis, design and evaluation

a production system would be to reduce incidents and increase the overall safety of the sites managed by ICANDO.

4.8.3   INFRASTRUCTURE

All engineers have access to a PC. The main restriction therefore is that the system needs to be proven on PC software. It is not considered viable to supply specialist hardware for this particular application.

4.8.4   SWOT ANALYSIS

This is a highly technical and speculative R&D project. The arguments for this sort of project tend to be less thorough. However, some justification would be needed, as competition for research money is considerable.

Strengths
1.   ICANDO has a good reputation for safety
2.   ICANDO safety standards far exceed all national standards

Weaknesses
1.   Audits regularly uncover minor infringements
2.   Site engineers have to read and learn substantial sets of guidelines when designing sites

Opportunities
1.   An automated tool could add to the quality of ICANDO safety procedures
2.   Safety is not considered a competitive area, and a successful tool could be marketed to other companies

Threats
None identified

Table 4.6   Risks for the ICANDO site safety system

Risk	Severity	Likelihood	Owner	Action
Site engineers will not adopt such a tool willingly	High	Medium	R&D team	Need to engage real site engineers in design
A fault in an automated tool could be counted as negligent by a court of law	High	Low	R&D team	This will be a prototype system in the first place. Development of a working system will need to follow strict quality standards

4.8.5 RISK REGISTER

Again, in a project like this, the monitoring of risks is usually minimal. The risks in Table 4.6 might be monitored at project reviews.

4.9 ICANDO Retail Petrol Promotions

4.9.1 STAKEHOLDERS

Sponsors
The ICANDO UK Retail Marketing department has a substantial annual budget, reviewed annually by the ICANDO UK board. They manage their own IT expenditure, and this covers a substantial amount for systems in the retail outlets themselves. The marketing manager is proud of the market share the company has, and he believes it is largely due to the loyalty programme. He is therefore willing to spend a considerable sum on improving that loyalty programme, and he believes that the best way is to exploit the Internet.

Users
The users of the system will primarily be the retail customers of ICANDO UK. They will be interacting with the system over the Internet, and possibly through wireless access. Call centre staff are also likely to use the system, to assist with queries and deal with problems.

Suppliers
As with ICANDO Chemicals, there will be a large interest in this from suppliers once the project is announced.

Employee agencies
There is no expected reduction in call centre staff or any planned reorganization of the call centres. Staff may need to be trained on some new aspects of the system. Employee agencies need not be involved.

Internal departments
The main impact will be in the call centres and the promotions departments. New literature will need to be produced when the new system is launched.

Stakeholder overview
See Table 4.7.

Table 4.7 Stakeholder overview for the customer loyalty system

Stakeholder category	Role in project	Project implications	Actions needed
Marketing manager	Provide funding	Will be seeking value for money	Agree budgets. Monitor expenditure
	Monitor and review	Regular reviews of progress, expenditure and risks	Establish regular steering group. Present project plan and costings, progress and risks
Marketing team	Promote Web site	Impacts effectiveness of Web site	Develop promotion Monitor impact
Customers	Use Web site	Needs to be very user-friendly and beneficial	Employ best design and implementation skills
IT manager	Ensure timely delivery	Late delivery will impact effectiveness	Assign high priority to project
	Ensure quality of delivery	Quality will significantly impact effectiveness	Assign best available skills to project Adopt quality assurance and monitor carefully

4.9.2 GOALS
The goal of the system is to improve customer loyalty by providing better access to the loyalty scheme over the Internet.

4.9.3 INFRASTRUCTURE
ICANDO UK has an existing Internet infrastructure and various Web sites. There is capacity to host the software. The loyalty system is already supported by an IT system, used in the call centre, and the Web facilities will need to utilize that system.

4.9.4 SWOT ANALYSIS

Strengths
1. The ICANDO customer base is sound and loyal
2. Customers make substantial use of the loyalty scheme
3. The quality of the loyalty scheme is considered good

Weaknesses
1. There is no Web access, and competitors already have a Web site

Opportunities
1. Web delivery of the product would enhance its position in the market place

Threats

1. Competitors are launching Web sites, and could take some of the market

4.9.5 RISK REGISTER

See Table 4.8.

Table 4.8 Risk register for the customer loyalty system

Risk	Severity	Likelihood	Owner	Action
Poor quality site would deter rather than attract custom	High	Medium	IT Development Manager	Use of an established Web design company with a track record. Ensure best skills available for integration with base system
Too slow to market, and the competition will gain ground	High	Medium	IT Development Manager	This will be a priority project, with resource guaranteed
Customers may not be aware of or wish to use the Web site	High	Medium	Marketing Manager	Develop launch promotion

REVIEW QUESTIONS

1. **What is a stakeholder?**
2. **Why consider stakeholders other than the users?**
3. **Give some examples of different types of stakeholder.**
4. **Why define goals?**
5. **Why is it important to consider infrastructure at the outset?**
6. **What is a risk?**
7. **What are the analysis tools introduced in this chapter?**

EXERCISES

1. A major competitor to ICANDO Chemicals announces the release of a Web-based ordering system. How does this impact the SWOT analysis?
2. ICANDO central IT services announce a major restructuring. How would this impact the risk analysis for the ICANDO Chemicals system?
3. Add call centre staff to the stakeholder analysis for ICANDO Chemicals. Consider their role in using the proposed system, and their experience of operating a call centre.
4. Add the warehouses to the stakeholder analysis for ICANDO Chemicals. Consider the change in operations.
5. Add production to the stakeholder analysis for ICANDO Chemicals. Consider the changes needed to take orders direct from production instead of from stocks.
6. A major accident occurs at an ICANDO storage site. How might that impact the SWOT analysis for the site safety system?
7. Add the R&D team to the stakeholder analysis for the ICANDO site safety system.

8. A senior manager in central services challenges the validity of the site safety system, suggesting that the money is better spent elsewhere. Adjust the risk register to reflect his challenge and the effect it might have.

9. Sales figures are released that show that ICANDO UK retail has had a dip in sales, and a competitor with a new Web-based loyalty system has had a rise in sales. Adjust the SWOT analysis accordingly.

10. Add the call centre staff to the ICANDO UK retail promotion system stakeholder analysis.

11. The leading Web design company that ICANDO UK plans to use for its design of the loyalty system goes into receivership. Adjust the risk register accordingly.

12. The senior managers for ICANDO Oil Trading are sceptical about the development of a workbench system. They cite late delivery of IT systems in the past, and they believe that the current systems are adequate. They object to the cost. Some of the traders are keen for improvements to some of the IT systems, and to have fewer screens. They also want better communication. Some middle managers are concerned that they have difficulty tracking risk at busy times. Develop an argument to support the development of a trader's workbench, using a force field analysis and SWOT analysis to support your arguments.

13. Create a stakeholder analysis for the ICANDO Oil Trading Workbench.

14. Define the goals of the ICANDO Oil Trading Workbench.

15. What infrastructure will the ICANDO Oil Trading Workbench need to incorporate or interface with?

16. Create a risk register for the ICANDO Oil Trading workbench.

Software Development Life Cycle

IN THIS CHAPTER YOU WILL LEARN:

1. The stages of the software development life cycle
2. About the waterfall and iterative approaches to software developments
3. Some methods for controlling iterative developments

Large IT projects are complicated, and even small ones are more complex than at first you might think. It is hard for the novice to understand this complexity. Writing a simple program as an exercise for a programming class seems difficult enough. When the messiness and obscurity of a business have to be taken into consideration, when there are dozens of conflicting opinions, and when the size of the development requires tens or hundreds of people to contribute over a number of months or years, then the whole task of producing a working system can seem unbearably difficult.

Much of the complexity comes from not having a clear idea of what the overall software development process is. In this chapter we shall look at the overall process to try give you a road map with which to locate yourself when you find yourself in the middle of a software development project. When you think it through logically the stages of software development are pretty obvious, and not that far removed from the stages of development of any artefact.

We shall look at the stages of software development, and at how the work can be made to flow through these stages. Just as with any type of manufacture, there are many ways of organizing a production process. Likewise, different types of product suit different types of organization. Also, different levels of risk impose different levels of rigour and checking on the process.

Every development process will go through the stages that we are talking about, either explicitly or implicitly. When I first started my IT career, I worked as a programmer/analyst and I undertook everything from requirements analysis through to testing, deployment and maintenance. I would probably not have recognized the boundaries between some of the stages. Computer systems were much simpler then. Nowadays it would be rare to find someone spanning all these activities, and there are good arguments for splitting some of the roles out to maintain quality; for example, it is bad practice generally to allow someone to test their own work without additional tests from someone else. On the other hand, the greater the number of people involved in software development, the more problems can be introduced by poor communication.

There is an end-to-end argument in the software development industry about the staging of development. At one extreme is the staged method approach, with lots of intermediate products, typified by the Unified Process (Jacobson *et al.*, 1999). At the other extreme are lightweight methods such as Extreme Programming, where there are very few stages and very few intermediate products. In reality, most practical developments sit somewhere in the middle, perhaps leaning a little in one direction.

What this book is aiming at is understanding, not prescription. Therefore we shall look at a fully staged development process, not far removed from the Unified Process (though hopefully a little simpler and more accessible for the novice). This maps out the jungle more thoroughly. If you, as an explorer in the future, feel that it is possible to take shortcuts that you can justify, then you may fold some of the stages together, and maybe miss out some of the intermediate products. A mature developer knows when to take shortcuts and when not.

5.1   Stages of the Software Development Life Cycle

As a butterfly must have transformed from egg through caterpillar and chrysalis, software must pass through a series of stages known commonly as the software development life cycle. These stages are usually stated as:

- Requirements analysis
- Systems analysis
- Design
- Implementation
- Testing
- Deployment
- Maintenance

Every development goes through these phases, whether it is done formally or not, consciously or unconsciously. Each stage requires input from the earlier stages and produces outputs for later stages. These inputs and outputs can be large, detailed documents, or they can be ideas in a developer's head. The half-hour spreadsheet that you develop to solve some tiny accounting problem actually goes through all of these stages, even if at lightning speed. It is also a continuous loop as the product at the end of development triggers ideas and proposals for new software, much as a butterfly lays eggs.

The phases are not necessarily done one after the other, as we shall see. They can be overlapped and done in parallel. Problems in later stages often mean that you have to go back to earlier stages. We shall discuss later in this chapter the various ways projects can negotiate these stages to make sure that they come out at the end with credible software.

We shall now briefly discuss the stages, in terms of their purpose, the inputs to the stage, the outputs of the stage, and the methods employed in the stage. The rest of the book will elaborate on these, explaining in detail what the various products of the stages are and how they are constructed.

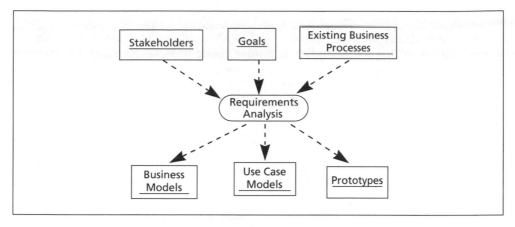

Figure 5.1   Key inputs and outputs of requirements analysis

5.1.1 REQUIREMENTS ANALYSIS

Purpose

Requirements analysis determines the needs and expectations of the various stakeholders from a system, producing a description of what the system should do in language that can be understood by all stakeholders, and upon which agreement can be reached.

Requirements are split into two types. There are functional requirements, which state what the system does, such as how it processes an order. There are equally important non-functional requirements, such as how the system performs in terms of reliability, number of people using it, and the quality of the interface.

Figure 5.1 shows the key inputs and outputs of requirements analysis, described below.

Inputs

Requirements analysis will use existing business processes, and the goals of an organization as its primary input. This is a 'soft' process, in that it is there to discover the purpose and behaviour of the system that is to be developed. It can be a messy process, and it is often overlooked or underdone in new developments. Failure at this stage is hard to detect until very late in the development process.

Outputs

The primary outputs are business models and use case models that define the functional requirements of the system and statements on non-functional requirements. Business models define the context of the system to be built. Scenario analysis can be used to detail the business processes. Use case models specify the external behaviour of the system to be built and how it fits into the business. There may also be prototypes, developed as part of requirements, that are used to clarify with stakeholders the behaviour of the system.

Methods
Workshops and interviews are used to gather the inputs. Feedback is a key factor in the success of this stage, and stakeholders need to have access to the various products of this stage. Reports and presentations are used to formalize the feedback and form a basis for agreement.

5.1.2 SYSTEMS ANALYSIS

Purpose
Systems analysis fully defines the behaviour of the computer system and how it interacts with the business environment, filling in the details of the requirements model in terms that are understandable by the developers.

Figure 5.2 shows the key inputs and outputs of systems analysis, described below.

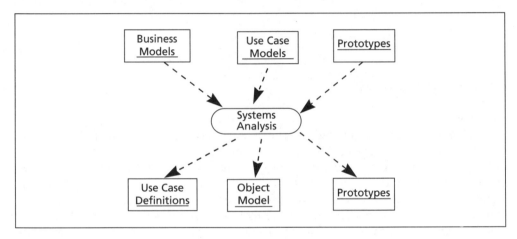

Figure 5.2 Key inputs and outputs of systems analysis

Inputs
The business models, use case models and prototypes from the requirements analysis will be used, together with detailed knowledge of business operations from potential users and managers of the system.

Outputs
Systems analysis will produce fully specified use cases and a detailed object model that specifies the information that the system will hold, together with the way that information will be used. More detailed prototypes may be used to obtain feedback from stakeholders on the system functionality.

Methods
Interviews and workshops can be used to gather information about how the system should operate, and the detailed information it needs to process. Scenario analysis can be used to structure the use cases and gather detail. Prototyping can be used to identify the data that needs to be used and how people will use it.

5.1.3 DESIGN

Purpose
Design defines how the system will operate and decomposes the system into manageable parts that can be developed and deployed, producing an architectural overview of the system and a mapping of the use cases onto the architecture.

Figure 5.3 shows the key inputs and outputs of the design process, described below.

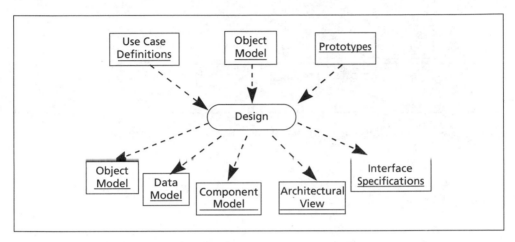

Figure 5.3   Key inputs and outputs of the design process

Inputs
The primary input is the set of use case definitions and the object model from the systems analysis stage, with any prototypes from the earlier stages.

Outputs
The primary outputs are an object model, including object collaborations to support the use cases, grouping of objects into components, interface specifications for users and between components and external systems, and data models for the storage of information in databases.

Method
A key stage of design is the definition of the overall architecture of the system. The individual use cases are then worked through, and the object model and object collaborations are worked out from the use case specifications. The architecture of the system will define the general structure of the collaborations.

5.1.4 IMPLEMENTATION

Purpose
Implementation produces the system as a set of components, integrating new parts of the system into previously constructed parts of the system and testing the components according to the specification produced by the design.

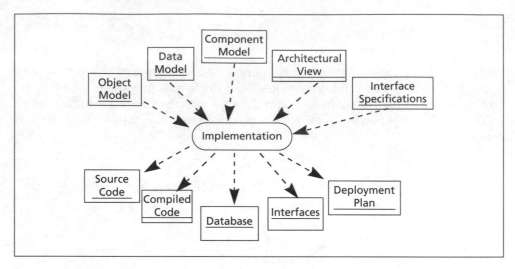

Figure 5.4 Key inputs and outputs of the implementation process

Figure 5.4 shows the key inputs and outputs of the implementation process, described below.

Inputs
The object model, object collaborations, interface specifications, architecture definition and data models from the design stage.

Outputs
Source code, compiled components integrated into the complete system, and a deployment plan.

Method
The object model can either be wholly translated by programmers, or part-translated by CASE[1] tools and completed by programmers, into working code and database definitions. The implementation team is normally responsible for testing that individual components meet the specification provided by the design.

5.1.5 TESTING

Purpose
Testing makes sure that the system that is developed meets the stated requirements, both functional and non-functional. It provides feedback to the development team on the quality of the product, allowing them to make corrections.

Figure 5.5 shows the key inputs and outputs of the testing process, described below.

1 CASE stands for Computer-Assisted Software Engineering, denoting a set of software tools that help in the analysis, design and construction of computer systems.

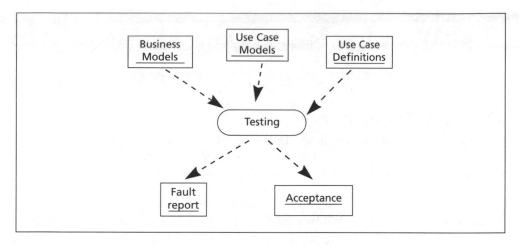

Figure 5.5   Key inputs and outputs of the testing process

Inputs
The constructed system is obviously needed, along with the business processes from the requirements stage, the use case specifications from the systems analysis stage, and any statements on non-functional requirements.

Outputs
Fault reports to be fed back to earlier stages for correction of the analysis, design or implementation. Successful testing will result in an acceptance of the system for deployment.

Method
The requirements models are the primary input to testing. Use case specifications and business processes are used to produce test scenarios. The test scenarios state the inputs and expected outputs. Special tests may be used to estimate non-functional requirements, such as scalability and reliability.

5.1.6 MAINTENANCE

Purpose
Maintenance keeps the system operational and in line with needs. A fine distinction needs to be made between minor changes that constitute maintenance and fresh developments that extend the system considerably; maintenance is a term often used to cover substantial further development.

Inputs
Bug reports and change requests.

Outputs
Modified analysis, design and implementation.

Method

A help desk is usually used as the front line for capturing operational problems. These are dealt with in a variety of ways, depending on the severity. Enhancements may be minor, or be treated as parts of the later development of the system.

5.2 The Waterfall Approach

Many software development books talk about a 'traditional' approach to systems development, where each stage of the software development life cycle is completed in turn, known as the 'Waterfall' approach. The metaphor suggests that it is difficult, if not impossible, to go backwards and make changes in the earlier stages development. The development project rushes headlong downstream, like a raft on a whitewater rapids adventure, with imminent shipwreck at each stage of the journey.

A formal system is introduced to 'sign off' each of the stages, and the next stage cannot progress until the earlier stage is signed off. Figure 5.6 illustrates the development over time.

This has a number of effects:

- Requirements can change during the lifetime of a project, so that what is delivered may already be out of date. If the first delivery of a product is a long time after requirements analysis, then it is very likely that the requirements will have changed.
- It is hard for implementers to determine what some of the reasoning was behind the analysis and design if it was done a long time earlier, particularly if the analysts have moved on. A long slow process has the ability to lose information.
- The motivation for such a process is largely defensive. The people who sign off the stages are blamed for shortfalls in the stages, not the people who worked on the stages.

In fact, few successful developments have ever followed this approach. I have only seen this attempted once in my career, quite recently, and it was an abject failure. There are few circumstances where this approach is appropriate. In practice, the waterfall method is rarely used, and probably hardly ever was. It should

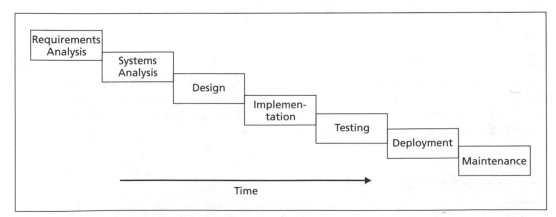

Figure 5.6 The waterfall life cycle

only be considered where the requirements are likely to be static over a long time frame, as in some engineering applications.

There are some particular situations where the deployment of a system has to be done in one single phase. Examples would be the replacement of a stock exchange trading system, where a phased implementation is practically infeasible. However, this does not mean that the earlier stages have to be regimented in a waterfall approach, and any project manager who is forced into a 'big bang' deployment would be very foolish not to have had a vast number of trial and test deployments beforehand.

5.3 The Iterative Approach

Iterative development is in fact the method most commonly used, either officially or unofficially. In this approach, only some of the requirements are fully worked out before the systems analysis is started. This is then taken through design, implementation and testing. The advantages of this are that parts of the system are delivered early. If requirements change, things are not set in stone. Developers can be used much earlier. Feedback on the delivered system can be used to improve later stages.

Most approaches today follow some iterative scheme, and in practice probably have done for most successful systems that were ever developed. The iterative process is commonly drawn as a spiral, as in Figure 5.7. Here the project begins with requirements gathering, and progresses through the stages; following deployment more requirements are gathered, using feedback from the earlier stages.

Figure 5.8 shows a more typical approach, with the stages more overlapped. For a very large project, teams may be working in parallel on lots of different aspects.

Iterative development is no guarantee of success, and it requires very careful management. I recall once, in a project that was going nowhere fast, a business

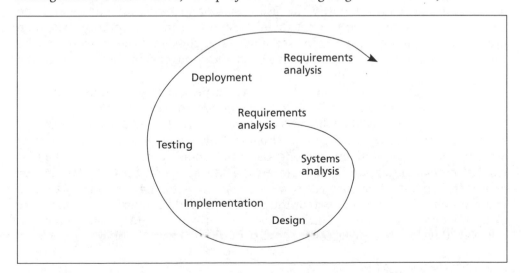

Figure 5.7   Depiction of the iterative approach as an expanding spiral of development

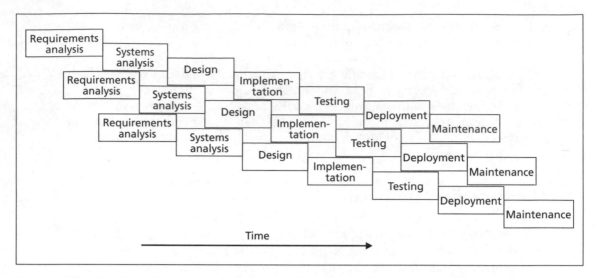

Figure 5.8 The iterative approach in terms of stages

colleague asking what 'iterative development' meant, and the quip reply was 'going round in circles', which she thought very appropriate. The spiral has to expand, and the system grow in functionality and quality.

5.3.1 ITERATIVE METHODS AND USE CASES

The core of iterative development is the notion of the use case. A use case is the smallest unit of useful functionality as far as a user is concerned. At the beginning of a project, it is important to make an early attempt to identify the use cases in the system, without fleshing them out in detail. Once that is done, a priority can be set on the use cases, and the most important ones can be developed first. The requirements phase will fully identify the use cases for a particular phase, and the systems analysis phase will detail them. Design and implementation will then produce a system that supports the set of use cases chosen. If the use cases can be used alone, then the system can be deployed and some early benefit given to the users.

Figure 5.9 indicates how progress through a project is undertaken. The use cases for the project are identified, U_1, U_2, U_3 and so on. This selection is not set in stone, and may be revised as the project progresses. A phase aims to implement a set of use cases, say $U_1..U_n$ for the first phase. This results in a set of objects that are grouped together into components that can be deployed: C_1 to C_3 for the first phase. These are integrated and deployed as a release: R_1 for the first phase. Later phases incorporate more use cases, which may make changes to earlier objects and therefore the components that they are composed into, and introduce more objects which may add to existing components or generate new components. In this way, development progresses.

5.3.2 CONTROLLING ITERATIVE METHODS

The core to successful management of a project is the selection of appropriate use cases, and the management of their progress through the development.

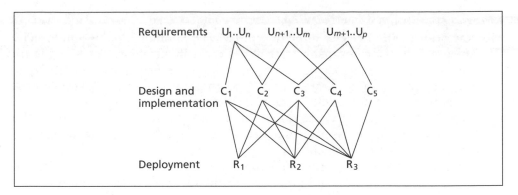

Figure 5.9   The tracing of use cases through the stages in iterative development

Estimation is far from an exact science in any software development, and the key to the process is a flexible planning approach. We shall now consider some methods that are appropriate. An excellent source of these methods is the Dynamic System Development Method (DSDM).[2]

The DSDM method is based on the principle that it is impossible to get a perfect system, and that any development is going to involve continued enhancement and extension. It breaks a project down into manageable phases, and provides a means for prioritizing those phases and organizing resources to complete those phases. Instead of contracting to deliver a specific amount of functionality in a phase, DSDM recommends that you decide on the resource that you can expend in a phase, and a fixed period in which to carry out the phase, and aim to achieve as much as is possible in the phase.

The core ideas are the notion of charter, which is the plan of the phase, Moscow prioritization, and time boxing. We shall now look at those in some detail.

The 80/20 rule

The famous 80/20 rule says that 80% of the benefit comes from 20% of a system. If you think of your trip to McDonald's, then ordering a routine meal results in quick service, but ordering a fish burger that hardly anyone orders results in a wait. McDonald's applies the 80/20 rule to good effect, maximizing the rate at which it can serve customers.

Computer systems are best developed like that. The most common problems are the ones that you need to deal with first. For example, if a call centre regularly gets queries about billing, but infrequent requests for a change of service, then implementing the billing enquiry use cases first makes sense.

So, when prioritizing, it is important to look for the use cases that give most benefit for the earlier phases. This has various advantages. It gets a usable system out of development quickly. It also allows for adaptation to changing needs.

---

2 http://www.dsdm.org/

Moscow prioritization

Moscow prioritization groups use cases into Musts, Shoulds, Coulds and Won'ts. The Musts are the use cases that have to be delivered in the phase. The Shoulds are those use cases that are expected in the phase, but the world does not end if they are not delivered. The Coulds are the use cases that it would be nice to implement if there is time or resource left in the phase, but no-one will cry if they are not delivered. The Won'ts are the use cases that definitely will not be delivered in the phase; it may not be necessary to state these, letting the rest of the known use cases to be considered Won'ts implicitly.

The phase should be planned with enough resource and time to complete the Musts and Shoulds. If there are problems, or the estimation has been too tight, then there is still a reasonable chance that the Musts will be achieved. If the estimation has been too generous then there is an opportunity to implement some of the Coulds.

Project estimation is a difficult subject. Early stages tend to be wildly out in their estimation. It is better to be conservative and have few Musts and lots of Shoulds and Coulds in the early stages. As a project progresses, estimation becomes more accurate.

Charter

Instead of specifying precisely what is to be delivered in a phase, a charter lists the use cases that are intended for development in the phase. The aim is to implement, as far as possible, the use cases chosen for this phase. Unlike a specification, it is acceptable to implement only some of the use cases, and to push use cases on to later phases. It is a statement of intent, rather than a commitment to provide.

Some traditionalists find this a difficult approach to accept. It often requires a culture change in an organization to accept a flexible delivery. It is important to communicate this with stakeholders, to ensure that their expectations are realistic.

Time boxing

Phases are controlled by time boxes. A time box says that you have (say) three months to work on a phase. During those three months, the use cases for the phase are worked on in priority order. Towards the end of the phase, effort is concentrated on completing what is possible. The implemented use cases are then tested and, if appropriate, deployed. Then the project can move on to the next phase.

The phase commences with a brief initiation where the planned use cases are reviewed. The Moscow prioritization is checked and understood. The bulk of the phase involves development of the use cases. There may be problems that arise during the development that mean a review of priorities. At the end of the phase, there is a consolidation of the work done, and a review of what has been achieved. Those use cases that are incomplete or not even attempted are put into the planning for the next phase.

5.4 Project Management

DSDM and the Unified Process focus mostly on the actual software development. The stance that this book takes is that software development is part of a project that requires general project management. Therefore we will take a slightly broader view.

Project management is a key skill that is generic, though project managers need to know software development to be effective. Good project managers are like proverbial hen's teeth. They need to be able to face senior managers credibly, and to motivate the project team. It is a balancing act that requires considerable experience and good interpersonal skills.

There are many project management methods available. The prime one that has gained ascendancy in the UK is PRINCE, which stands for Projects in Controlled Environments (see Projects in Controlled Environments, 2001). This provides a focus on projects that looks outside the actual work of the project team and concentrates on the procedures and processes that link the project into the environment. DSDM aims at this, but focuses more on the development cycles.

5.5 ICANDO Bulk Chemical Ordering

The ICANDO Chemicals system is a replacement for the diverse existing systems throughout Europe. This presents a particular challenge, in that it will not be possible to run the new ordering system alongside an existing system. There will need to be an overnight replacement of a system for a particular market.

The IT managers know the risks of non-iterative development, and therefore they propose a series of internal releases, to be put through rigorous quality assurance. They decide to focus on one market and aim to deploy in that one market once the system has been thoroughly tested and passed all acceptance criteria. They will operate the system for a period before rolling out the system in other markets.

The initial requirements analysis determines a set of essential use cases that must be implemented for a usable system. There are a number of desirable use cases and other use cases. These are indicated in Table 5.1. The 'must have' use cases will be the minimum that could be released for operation, but ideally the first release should incorporate the 'should haves'.

The project breaks the development into smaller iterations, with three iterations covering the 'must haves' and two covering the 'should haves'. These

Table 5.1 Moscow prioritization for release of the system

Priority	Use cases
Must have for release	User validation, customer identification, order taking, stock reservation, production reservation, delivery scheduling, order amendment, order cancellation, credit checking, customer registration, contract definition, delivery confirmation, delivery rescheduling, discount calculation
Should have for release	Order overview, production optimization, delivery optimization, customer contact history, web ordering by customer, Web amendment by customer, web order tracking by customer
Could have for release	Special offers prompting, call transfer
Won't have for release	None identified

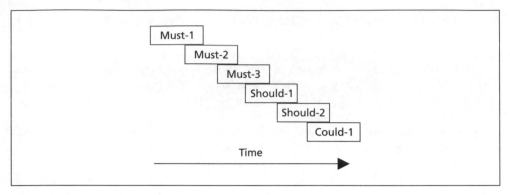

Figure 5.10 Organization of the iterations

iterations have their own Moscow prioritization. They are time-boxed at 3 months each, with the iterations overlapping in time, as indicated in Figure 5.10. The aim is to achieve all the musts and shoulds in the first 12 months, but the system will be deployable if only the musts are achieved.

5.5.1 CHARTER FOR ITERATION 1

The aim of this iteration is to get all of the user validation (log in etc.) and customer registration implemented. There will inevitably be new use cases determined to supplement the key use cases identified. A Moscow prioritization for the iteration is given in Table 5.2. The motivation for this is that without the ability to register customers and manage users the system is effectively unusable. These are also fairly straightforward use cases, and as the first iteration is usually a substantial learning phase it is advisable to keep the use cases as simple as possible.

The iteration will run for three months, and all the use cases will have been tested within the iteration. The iteration will cover the requirements through analysis, design and implementation to the testing of the use cases.

Table 5.2 Moscow prioritization for the first iteration of the ICANDO chemicals system

Priority	Use cases
Must have	User validation, user validation, customer identification, customer registration
Should have	Contract definition
Could have	Credit checking
Won't have	Order overview, production optimization, delivery optimization, customer contact history, Web ordering by customer, Web amendment by customer, Web order tracking by customer, special offers prompting, call transfer, order taking, stock reservation, production reservation, delivery scheduling, order amendment, order cancellation, delivery confirmation, delivery rescheduling, discount calculation

5.6   ICANDO Site Safety

The site safety system is small in scope, even if it contains a considerable amount of technically difficult development. The project is split into two iterations. The first will cover the drawing and definition of a site, and the second the definition and application of guidelines. The elapsed time for the project is 6 months, and therefore it is decided to time-box each iteration at 3 months.

5.7   ICANDO Retail Petrol Promotions

Speed to market is essential for this application. It is not considered viable to release anything other than a system that can take customer orders, as indicated by the Moscow prioritization in Table 5.3.

Table 5.3   Moscow prioritization of the use cases for the first release of the Customer Loyalty system

Priority	Use cases
Must have for release	Customer registration, customer validation, browse catalogue, order goods, schedule delivery
Should have for release	Email promotions
Could have for release	WAP enabled access, SMS messaging
Won't have for release	None identified

5.7.1   ITERATION 1

The first iteration will be the definition of the interface. This will be a complete Web site, but without the actual application logic. This is to be done in two weeks. It breaks the rule that development should be done use case by use case, but for Web development this is common practice. Once the Web has been designed and approved, then the use cases can be implemented in turn.

5.7.2   ITERATION 2

The second iteration is to enable customer registration and validation. This will be required in 6 weeks. It is hoped that browsing the catalogue will also be possible. The Moscow prioritization is given in Table 5.4.

Table 5.4   Moscow prioritization of second iteration of the retail promotions system

Priority	Use cases
Must have	Customer registration, customer validation
Should have	Browse catalogue
Could have	Order goods, schedule delivery
Won't have	Email promotions, WAP enabled access, SMS messaging

REVIEW QUESTIONS

1. What are the stages of the software development life cycle?
2. What is the purpose of requirements analysis?
3. What is the difference between functional and non-functional requirements?
4. How does systems analysis differ from requirements analysis?
5. How does design differ from systems analysis?
6. Of what value is testing to the development team?
7. How does the waterfall approach differ from an iterative approach?
8. What is a use case?
9. How are use cases used in iterative development?
10. What does DSDM stand for?
11. What does Moscow prioritization mean?
12. What is a charter?
13. What is the 80/20 rule?
14. What is a time box?

EXERCISES

1. Assuming that the musts and shoulds, but not the coulds, for the first iteration of the chemicals system are achieved, produce a charter for the second iteration that covers order taking, stock reservation and delivery scheduling as musts or shoulds.
2. Produce a set of candidate use cases for the site safety system. Produce a charter for the first iteration.
3. Produce a set of candidate use cases for the Oil Trading Workbench. Produce a Moscow prioritization for the first usable release. Propose an iteration schedule, and suggest suitable time boxes for the iterations. Produce a charter for the first iteration.

CHAPTER 6

Managing the Process

1. **The role of the organization in software development**
2. **A description of different organization types, and how these types influence development approaches**
3. **About typical roles in the development of software**
4. **About how software development is managed**
5. **Why projects fail**

Organization is the bedrock of software development. Good organizations tend to succeed with almost any tools or technology, and bad organizations will make bad work with the finest tools. That does not mean that there is a particular type of organization that is destined to succeed. There is no perfect organization, and radically different organizations can succeed equally well at the same task.

A lot of the arguments about Best Method, Best Language and so on stumble over a lack of understanding of organizations. I have worked with small organizations with developers who think that only if they used UML, a particular method, the latest CASE tool, or Java, then all their software development problems would go away. What they never realize is that the big organizations are having the same debates, even though they have some of the things the smaller organizations desire. The truth is that different technologies, different management methods and different skill pools are appropriate for different organizations and circumstances – this is hardly profound, but it sadly has to be pointed out.

In this chapter I will not prescribe a management approach. We have now considered the software development life cycle, and considered it a natural staging for the production of software, even if some of the stages are hidden and informal. What I hope you will get some understanding of is that there are certain types of organization, and that the methods used need to fit the organization.

We will begin by looking at different organization types. Then we will look at some typical roles. How each organization type applies each role is not really something that can be covered in a brief introductory text. Finally, we will look at how our three case studies would organize themselves for the production of software.

6.1 Organization Types

Charles Handy, in *Gods of Management* (Handy, 1995) describes four characteristic types of management culture. Each will succeed in its own way, though each will be better at some tasks than others. These cultures tend to attract certain types of people. The cultures are not always obvious at first, and in practice a real organization will be a mix of cultures.

Understanding the type of culture will help in determining the appropriate and acceptable style of development. It is no good putting together a strong role-based software development organization in a company that operates a club culture – it will not survive. Recognizing the type of culture you are in can help in achieving goals and avoiding unnecessary conflict.

6.1.1 ROLE-BASED CULTURES

Role-based cultures tend to be large and well-established. They break processes down into constituent parts and schedule work through the parts. People and groups specialize. Formal agreements are put in place, with regular official meetings and standard means of communicating between parts of the organization. These organizations are good at repeating tasks. Many mature IT systems are managed in this way. Teams are well-defined, and the work tends to get done according to schedule. On the downside, hierarchical organizations are not good at starting new and radical ventures, nor at producing things quickly under pressure.

Role-based cultures are fond of the 'organization chart', such as that in Figure 6.1. One of the first things a manager in a role-based culture does to indicate his role is to whip out an organization chart and say where he fits, who his boss is and who reports to him.

Role-based cultures will align their development into well-defined sections. There will be a project office responsible for planning and resourcing, a business analysis section, a systems analysis section, designers, developers or programmers, database teams, testing teams, and a help desk. There will be managers for each of the key role areas, and project managers that steer projects through the

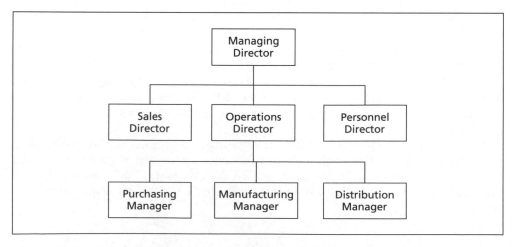

Figure 6.1 A typical organization chart in a role-based company

phases. The Unified Process seems to encourage this style of organization, though to be fair to the Unified Process, it defines roles that could be utilized in other styles of organization.

6.1.2 CLUB CULTURES

Club cultures have a strong central figure. This individual surrounds him- or herself with like-minded individuals and gives them great responsibility, but also expects results and loyalty. Anyone falling foul of the culture is soon moved away from the centre or out of the organization altogether. There is little by way of formal control, and communication is swift. Small software houses tend to operate like this. This type of organization is swift to respond to situations, and can take a vision very quickly to realization. However, they are subject to the whim of the centre, and quickly lose their way if the core of the organization breaks down.

You can recognize a club culture by the way a manager will introduce his team. There will be an emphasis on individuals and personalities. Names rather than roles will be used, and the senior staff will be referred to by name. Often staff will have grand titles on their business cards, but it is largely who they are and not where they sit that counts.

Club-based cultures will tend to have none of the regimentation that role-based cultures have. An individual will tend to take on many roles in an IT development. Formal documentation will not tend to happen, and decisions will need to be undertaken quickly. Explaining in a club culture that you cannot deliver a solution to a problem in a given time frame because you will need to go through all the stages methodically and update all the analysis and design models is likely to get short shrift; either you get in there and fix the code, or you look for another job.

6.1.3 TASK CULTURES

Task cultures centre on a particular task. They focus on results and will change and adapt their internal organization to achieve their goal. Clear role boundaries are not defined. Once the task is over, they want to move on. Task cultures are full of highly skilled individuals who are able to work in teams. They are expensive but effective. IT consultancies and research organizations tend to be task cultures. They are usually invited in to solve some particular problem. On the downside, task cultures lose interest when a problem is solved, and a product or service moves from the creative phase to maintenance.

You can recognize a task-based culture because the staff, including the managers, are always talking about problems and solutions. They are usually quick to assimilate new situations and to come up with ideas. There is less respect for personalities than in a club culture, and little respect for roles.

Task-based cultures will use whatever works. If modelling with UML helps to get a better solution, they will do it. If hacking the code directly works best, they will do that. Results count above process. Because the culture recruits achievement-oriented individuals with high skill, they will often produce very good results, but they will be patchily documented and difficult to maintain.

6.1.4 EXISTENTIAL CULTURES

Existential cultures are filled with professionals who work largely as individuals. Typical examples are solicitors, barristers and doctors. The specialism of the individual is prized, and the organization is there to feed the individual. Managers in these environments tend to be lower status than the individuals they manage. Universities tend to operate like this, though modern pressures are pushing them more towards a role-based culture. There are few IT organizations based on this model.

Existential cultures tend not to develop software, except as a means of extending professional skills. If you are considering a Ph.D. you might find yourself in this culture, but mostly you will be working as an individual honing your talents, not as a member of a team producing a product.

One of the problems for undergraduates, when they move into industry, is that the cultures they have grown up in are largely existential, and they have little direct personal experience of the other types of culture. As students, they have mostly acted as individuals, and the vast majority of the work they have undertaken has been as an individual rather than as a team. Some educational environments try to add some notion of teamwork to their programme, but for the most part students are out to develop and prove individual talent, at least in IT disciplines.

6.1.5 MIXING CULTURES

Few organizations are pure in their culture. Role-based organizations will often tolerate or even promote different forms of subculture. For example, a task-based research group is often established, and some of the marketing may be based on a club culture. Club cultures will often mature into role cultures as the organization develops. Sometimes a club culture will set up role-based subcultures to manage the routine long-term work.

What is the relevance of this to software development? Firstly, different cultures are going to tackle software development in particular ways. They cannot hide from the fundamental software development process, but how they operate it will differ considerably.

Knowing the culture you work in and your preferences is important. I have spent most of my career in task-based cultures (research and development, and consultancy) that were part of larger role-based cultures. I have also spent a fair amount of time in existential cultures (university research). Recently I joined a club culture that I did not recognize at first. I was soon rubbing shoulders with senior managers, but I was bewildered by what I considered to be hasty and highly risky decisions. Objecting to the decisions soon moved me out of the central core, and I survived barely two years.

Understanding cultures does help on choice of method. The Unified Process is much more aligned to role-based organizations than to any other. In fact, most model-driven methodologies are likely to find their home in this type of culture. Task-based cultures will cherry-pick the models and parts of a methodology. Club cultures will adopt whatever method is favoured by the centre, but high formality is not likely to be welcome. Extreme programming, and a number of other lightweight methodologies, are aimed at organizations that are much more delivery-focused and are likely to fit better into club cultures and task-based cultures rather than role-based cultures.

The ICANDO Oil organization is mainly a role-based organization, as most organizations of that size and complexity tend to be. The ICANDO Chemicals development would be formally structured. However, the site safety application is developed by the research group that is task-based, and the retail promotions system is for a club-based subculture where the marketing manager's whims rule. The decision-making and control in each case is likely to be very different.

We shall now look at some ways of organizing IT projects, and the roles that people may undertake. These will focus on role-based organizations, for two reasons. Firstly, they are easier to describe. Secondly, once you understand a role, it is easy to assimilate the function of that role into other organization types.

6.2 Steering Groups

For large-scale developments, there needs to be some high-level group that takes responsibility for setting the goals of a project and providing funding. These are commonly known as steering groups. For some projects and some organizations, the steering group will be an existing group of managers – either the board of a company, or some regular committee of managers. Sometimes, for a particular type of project, a special steering group will be set up.

The steering group sets the primary goals of the project. These goals may change over time, as either the market changes or the reality of the project development shows different limitations or possibilities. The dialogue about goals will be within the group and with the project management of the project.

The steering group controls the funding of the project. Usually this will be based on regular reporting of progress, and there will be a phased releasing of funds. Money is released to achieve agreed objectives. The cost–benefit modelling that is tackled in Chapter 7 will be important for the approval of the project and the ongoing tracking of progress.

The steering group monitors the high-level risks of the project. That projects fail is a fact of life. Sometimes this is internal to the project, through bad management or because there was inherently a risk in the technology. Sometimes the reasons lie outside the project, such as a downturn in business activity or a shift in the organization's goals. The steering group is responsible for stopping projects that are no longer viable.

Role-based organizations will usually have established management and committee structures that will take on the responsibility of steering groups. The choice of committee will depend on the size and the importance of the project. For ICANDO Chemicals, the project is of such importance that the ICANDO Chemicals board is to act as the steering committee.

Club cultures will either have the central figure acting as the steering group, or the central figure will set up a steering group of selected individuals. For ICANDO UK Retail Marketing the marketing manager sets up a team including himself, his finance manager, his IT manager, and the business manager for retail promotions.

Task-based cultures are less prone to setting up formal steering groups themselves, but they are usually part of (or working for) a larger culture that will establish a steering group. Consultancies delivering for a client will report into the steering group set up by the client. For ICANDO's site safety application, the research organization has a six-monthly meeting of senior managers from research and from operational business units that review the progress of projects.

6.3 Project Management

An individual is usually assigned the role of managing the project. The project manager will report to the steering group, and be responsible for coordinating all the parts of the project. The key role of the project manager is to make sure that the project is planned, that resources are in place to carry out the project, that risks are identified and addressed, and that deliverables arrive on time.

The role is one of continual negotiation. In a role-based organization this will be more bureaucratic, involving regular planning and progress meetings with the managers of the various groups. Individual groups may well be working on a number of projects, and there will be conflicts on resources from time to time. Also, work will need to be scheduled and slips in delivery dealt with.

In task-based organizations, the project manager will tend to be much more embroiled in the process, probably gathering much information directly from individuals. In club cultures the project manager is likely to be part of the inner circle and will be given freedom to organize the project as he or she sees fit.

6.4 Other Roles

Steering groups and project managers are likely to arise in some form in all organizations. The following roles are typical for role-based organizations. In a task-based or club-based organization the roles may be merged or in some rare cases eliminated.

6.4.1 PROGRAMMER

A programmer takes a design and constructs parts of the system, using various development tools and languages, such as Java or Visual Basic. They will work primarily from the class diagrams and the sequence diagrams, together with any interface prototypes that have been devised. They also find it useful to refer to the use case documentation.

6.4.2 DATABASE ARCHITECTS

A database architect is responsible for the underlying database tables, and all things to do with maintaining a secure and reliable database. This is a key specialism that is usually factored out separately from the design team. They will use the output of the design team and work closely with the programmers. They concern themselves with normalization and making sure that transactions are reliable and that procedures are in place to back up and recover data.

6.4.3 SYSTEM ENGINEERS

When the system is constructed, it needs to be deployed, firstly into a test environment and ultimately into the user environment. System engineers will be guided by the architects, programmers and database architects in the deployment of the system. They are responsible for the reliable operation of the system, the security of the system as a whole, and day-to-day administration tasks, such as backing up databases.

6.4.4 TESTERS
Usually programmers will 'unit test' their own work. That is, they make sure that their piece of work is reliable and meets the specification. However, it is not good practice to rely on developers to test systems. Testers will work from the business process definitions and the use case definitions to construct a test strategy that exercises the system in a realistic way. They then execute the tests and produce fault reports.

6.4.5 HELP DESK OPERATOR
Once a system is operational, things inevitably go wrong. This might range from simple things, like a user forgetting a password, through to a program giving a wrong result or even the system not working at all. Organizations usually have a help desk as the first point of call. The help desk operator logs a problem when it is reported, then finds someone to solve the problem, tracking the problem until it is resolved.

6.4.6 MIDDLE MANAGEMENT
A large project will be broken down into teams controlled by managers. These managers will be responsible for parts of a project, such as the business analysis or the design or the implementation. They will look after the day-to-day issues in their team and coordinate with other teams. They work with the project managers to schedule work and agree deliverables. Often a team may work on a number of projects at one time, and the manager will assign her resources according to priorities.

6.4.7 ARCHITECTS
Architects are responsible for the overall structure of the system, and the tools used to construct it. They will talk a great deal with the designers, making sure that parts fit together. They are usually highly experienced designers that have considerable talent in structuring systems. Normally they would be part of a design team, taking a lead role in the design of projects, and monitoring the quality of the designs produced.

6.4.8 BUSINESS ANALYST
Business analysts work with people to understand how a business operates. They will produce process maps to overview a business area. They will use scenario analysis, to identify primary and alternative paths in a business process. They will provide workflow descriptions of processes using activity diagrams. They will identify the use cases to support an existing or proposed business process. They will often produce test plans for the system.

6.4.9 SYSTEMS ANALYST
Systems analysts are concerned with how a system works within the business. They will work out the details of the use cases, using scenario analysis to determine the primary and alternative paths for a system to operate. They will outline the interfaces, perhaps working with a developer to produce a prototype of the interfaces. They will often get involved in determining the data required in the system, and may produce some high-level class diagrams.

6.4.10 DESIGNER

Designers are responsible for taking the work of the systems analysts and mapping it onto the architecture. They determine the objects to drive the system and the details of the screens, and make architectural adjustments with the architects. Their output is a specification of what has to be constructed.

6.5 Why Projects Fail

IT projects do fail, and you will indeed be fortunate in your career if you do not become involved in a major failure. Large IT projects are major undertakings with lots of people involved. There are risks in any human venture of such a scale and complexity. On the other hand, provided you survive, witnessing project failures is one of the most educational processes that you can experience, as long as you can step back and learn from the experience; growth through trauma is not to be recommended, but trauma without growth is wasted. Experience of failure gives a sense of realism, and helps you avoid these failures in the future.

The statistics on project failure are frightening. Some sources quote IT failure rates well in excess of 50%. The effects of failure are frightening too. I have worked in three organizations where massive redundancies have come about through IT project failures, with job losses both within the IT departments and elsewhere, and in one case I lost my job too. I recall recently a young colleague, barely three years out of university, with sagacity beyond his years wielding the second severance package of his brief career.

The UK Office of Government Commerce (2001) cites a number of causes of project failure that we will examine below. It is notable that these are primarily organizational failures, not technology failures. Usually a development team with adequate skills, clear direction, and sufficient time will produce a working system that meets needs.

6.5.1 DESIGN AND DEFINITION FAILURES

When someone authorizes a multi-million pound project, you would think that they would clear on what they are getting. Alas, it would be nice if that were true. Many projects, not just in IT, are poorly defined at the outset. Lack of definition comes from not providing clear goals and clear deliverables prior to authorization. Often a project is authorized on minimal information. The project as it evolves then produces a series of disappointments, leading it into repeated crises and ultimately cancellation.

Over-ambition is a common problem. To engage the various stakeholders, a great deal is promised. Lots of stakeholders have high expectations and become a problem to manage. The shortfall in deliverables and/or delay in achieving them again lead to disappointment and probable cancellation.

Over-distant end goals with no intermediate deliverables and/or review points can cause the project to deviate, or make it prone to cancellation. There is no reality check built in to long projects. It may seem obvious that a project should revisit its goals endlessly and do a frequent reality check. In large projects this can be a problem, and when political feuds start it is difficult to keep the project on track.

6.5.2 DECISION-MAKING FAILURES

Management by committee, with consensus required on detailed project decisions leads to indecision and drift. Clear goals need to come from the sponsor, and the project manager needs authority to implement them as she sees fit. 'No decision' in a project is usually the worst decision, because a bad decision teaches the project team while no decision results in drift and argument.

6.5.3 PROJECT DISCIPLINE FAILURES

Milestones can be set too far apart, and slippage is not managed. With too few milestones it is impossible to track progress. Plans can be constructed that are based on deadlines that people do not believe reflect reality, so they are not taken seriously. Missed deadlines are explained away, and deliverables get shunted further and further towards the end of the project. The prospect of failure is not acknowledged until someone in a senior position notices and initiates an investigation that ultimately cancels the project.

In lengthy projects requirements can change. If there is no mechanism for acknowledging these and re-steering the project, they may get tagged on as changes at the end of the project. Ultimately the project may deliver to the original goals, but not to the revised goals.

Risks are often overlooked or minimized. These can cause unnecessary delays or failure to deliver parts of the project. Contingency planning can be omitted or not applied to problems as they arise. The project then delivers only a partial solution or misses a critical deadline.

All of these are symptoms of weak project management. A project manager with inappropriate experience or skill will allow these problems to arise and not take action.

6.5.4 SUPPLIER MANAGEMENT FAILURES

Selection of suppliers is critical. Often the suppliers are chosen on inappropriate grounds. Systems are often very dependent on the quality of supplied components or tools, and that includes the quality of the supplying organization. Too often suppliers are chosen on the glitz of their marketing and not on the quality of their products, services and support. Too little time is spent scrutinizing suppliers at the procurement stage. Inappropriate linkages with suppliers can cause significant problems, either by suppliers being kept out of decision-making or suppliers becoming too involved in decision-making.

6.5.5 PEOPLE FAILURE

A key potential problem in any project is the disconnection between the project team and those for whom the project is being developed. This leads to an 'us and them' situation. Project staff can produce what they think their client needs. Clients become detached from what is realizable and expect too much.

Some project teams have a culture of hiding problems and explaining away risks. There is a habit of stumbling backwards into the future, and not anticipating problems before they become major issues. An opposite problem is one where everyone is crying wolf all the time, and project managers become deaf to the endless complaints.

6.6 Risks

As we have discussed before, software development is a risky activity. Risk needs to be acknowledged at all levels of the project, and procedures must be in place for dealing with risks. From the most senior member of the project team through to the most junior, there must be a collective responsibility to highlight risks as they occur, and to take action promptly to relieve them.

The modern approach to dealing with risk is to use iterative development. Applications are developed in small stages, and regularly integrated into a full product. Wherever possible, interim products are deployed. This has the effect of flushing out problems quickly instead of storing them up for months and years.

The other approach that we discussed earlier is the notion of a risk register. A risk register allows any project team member to raise risks that they identify. Risks need to be assessed in terms of their seriousness, and someone needs to be assigned to take action to minimize or ideally remove the risk.

Risks need to be an agenda item on project meetings. Deferring dealing with risks is not to be recommended. Managers need to chase risks, depending on severity.

6.7 Planning

Organizing the resources for a project is a complicated activity. Usually a planning tool is used. An understanding of the dependencies in a project is needed. Any piece of development will need to go through all the stages of the development process.

Good planning depends on accurate estimation. This can be problematic in the early stages of a project, as there is often no basis for estimating how long it will take to construct a piece of software without experience. Development often hits unforeseen obstacles. An iterative approach allows the calibration of the estimates for later phases.

Planning needs to take into consideration resource conflicts. It is unlikely that the flow of work into and out of teams is smooth. Analysis will arrive in batches. Testing teams will have short but intense periods of work on a project. Usually if you lay all of the activities end to end in the order they take, the elapsed time will be considerably longer because the intermediate stages are working on other things. The larger the project, the harder estimation is.

Without a plan, a project is like a small boat adrift in a large and menacing ocean. Every member of a team needs to know the overall plan, and their role in it. The project manager needs to check progress against the plan regularly and to adjust the plan accordingly. Major deviations to plan need to be raised with senior management, as these can seriously impact the value of the project.

6.8 Managing iterations

Iterative development needs very careful management. There needs to be a prioritization process to guide each iteration of the development. Then the iteration needs to be established and prioritization of use cases within the iteration needs to be agreed. Finally, a plan for the iteration needs to be produced.

As the iteration progresses, tracking of the plan will indicate how far down the prioritized list of use cases the team will achieve. Towards the end of the iteration, a decision is needed on what will be delivered. Work on use cases that cannot be delivered in the iteration needs to be suspended, and all effort focused on delivering complete use cases.

Once an iteration is complete and fully integrated, there needs to be a review on what is achieved. This will evaluate the success of the iteration, and provide input for the later iterations. Incomplete use cases will need to be incorporated in future iterations.

6.9 ICANDO Bulk Chemical Ordering

ICANDO is a long-standing, well-structured organization, with a central IT department used by all the companies. This project is to be implemented by the central IT department. The IT teams and staff are used to substantial developments. It has adapted over the years to changes in technology and method. It has an organization for the IT department, as indicated in Figure 6.2. The groups are really skill pools, and when a project is commissioned a project manager is allocated from the Projects group. Fluid teams are constructed for the execution of the project, drawn from the skill pools.

Thus, though the organization is a classical hierarchical one, the execution of projects is task-based. Each project will be assigned an architect who is responsible for the overall design, and designers will be drawn from the architecture team.

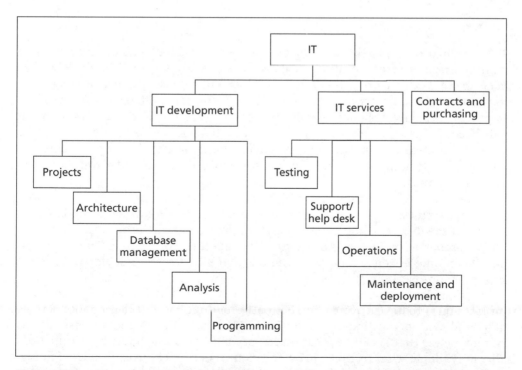

Figure 6.2   Organization of the IT department for ICANDO Chemicals

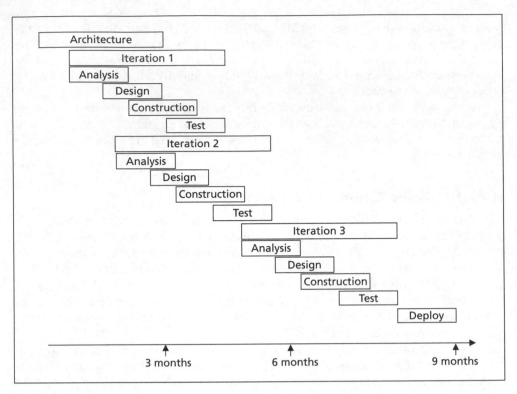

Figure 6.3 Outline project plan for the first deployable system

An initial project plan is drawn up that can provide a deployable system in three months through three iterations. This is shown in Figure 6.3. The decision has been made to run with two parallel development teams, running on staggered iterations. Within an iteration, analysis, design, construction and testing overlap. In practice, the involvement of analysts will go on throughout an iteration, but it will become less towards the end of the iteration. Likewise, designers will be involved throughout, but will peak in activity about the middle. Programmers will peak in activity in the second half, and testers will only be needed towards the end of an iteration.

There is an architecture phase which kicks off the development and runs well into the first iteration. In practice, further architecture work would be undertaken as part of the design of all the iterations, but the start of the project will involve a large number of major decisions that will shape the application. The iterations have been time-boxed at 3 months, and the goal is to achieve a deployable system inside 9 months.

The first deployable system is unlikely to be one that is used in anger. The project aim is to have a system in 12 months, and the target functionality is to be delivered within the first five iterations. The criticality of the success of this system means that it will be scrutinized very hard once the 'must have' functionality is available. User testing will be undertaken in a mock-up call centre. Simulations of full order taking will be carried out to establish usability and acceptance.

The board is acting as the steering group. Monthly board meetings have called the project manager in to present the progress. The IT director has taken a particularly active interest, and meets with the project manager and the IT development manager every week. At the weekly meetings the risk register is reviewed, and critical risks are reported up to the steering group. On successful completion of each iteration, the IT director has insisted on a demonstration.

The design and definition of the project are clear. The organization is well established, with a good track record of delivery, and it is used to facing up to difficulties. Good supplier management is in place, with a contracts and purchasing group. The company employs motivated and dedicated staff that work towards clear goals. There are few organizational blocks to delivery.

6.10 ICANDO Site Safety

The formality of a research project is usually much less than the formality of a development project. The most important thing is to have clear goals, milestones and deadlines. The work is undertaken by two R&D developers, who cover all the analysis, design and construction. A project leader oversees the development, and reports into quarterly research board meetings. The developers will test the releases. Acceptance testing and evaluation are to be carried out by the audit group and selected site engineers.

6.11 ICANDO Retail Petrol Promotions

ICANDO UK does not have a substantial in-house development team. It has a small IT projects team, with skilled project managers and support staff. Development is usually subcontracted, either to the ICANDO Group's IT development team or to software houses. In this case, the development is undertaken by a software house with a proved track record in e-commerce development. The software house chosen is involved in the detailed planning of the project, and it works to an agreed schedule of internal and external releases.

The aim is to get to market as soon as possible. A development schedule is agreed that can deliver minimum functionality inside 4 months, ready for beta testing with selected customers. Once the beta testing is complete, the product will be released with a major promotion. The outline project plan is shown in Figure 6.4.

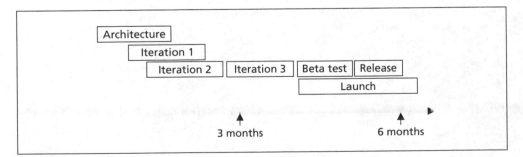

Figure 6.4 Outline project plan for the retail promotion system

The first iteration is agreed to be a complete development of the user interface, without the underlying application logic. This is common practice for Web development. The application logic is to be developed in two iterations, that each cover analysis, design and construction. These will both be completed by a small team of three developers who will cover the role of analyst, designer and programmer between them. They will test the product themselves before release, and the ICANDO project manager has arranged for internal testing by ICANDO staff.

The launch will be a lengthy process. There will need to be literature prepared. It is decided to do a phased launch by mailshot. Thus, instead of every customer being able to use the site from the day it is released, the user base will grow. This will allow the development team to iron out teething troubles without there being too huge an impact on the customers if there are problems.

REVIEW QUESTIONS

1. What are the different organization types described in this chapter?
2. Why is it important to understand organization types?
3. Which organization type likes to structure the organization very tightly and assign people to slots?
4. Are club cultures likely to insist on rigorous modelling and careful following of a process?
5. Which culture is most focused on results?
6. What is the purpose of a steering group?
7. How might you prevent design and definition failures?
8. Why is it important to be clear and explicit about risks?
9. How does iterative development help planning?
10. What do you do with a use case that you do not complete in an iteration?

EXERCISES

1. Modify the bulk chemicals project plan to incorporate the extra two iterations for the 'should have' use cases, targeting a deployment after 12 months.
2. Produce a plan for the site safety system, based on two iterations.
3. The trading workbench is approved, and it is decided that the ICANDO central IT department will undertake the development. There must be a workable release within 6 months, and enough implemented to convince the sceptical trading management team within 4 months. Produce a project plan.

CHAPTER **7**

The Cost–Benefit Model

IN THIS CHAPTER YOU WILL LEARN:

1. About the impact of IT projects on key financial measures
2. A way of estimating costs of software development
3. A way of estimating benefits of software development
4. How to construct cash flow models
5. About the pitfalls to avoid in cost–benefit analysis

An essential measure of success for most projects of any size in any organization is financial. The goals are often not obviously financial, but most organizations work within tight financial boundaries. Even if the goal of a project is improving some quality aspect of a business, this is usually done within tight financial constraints. Alas, everything can be reduced to a financial impact, though the financial impact is not usually the only factor in a decision. Projects that cost more than they save are, however, on a dubious footing. Mr Micawber never followed his own principle that income of a pound and expenditure of less than a pound meant happiness, and expenditure of more than a pound meant misery; as a result he was forever under pursuit from his creditors, and alas many IT projects follow his fate.

Consider the example of a state-funded health service. The goals of the organization are not financial, but to maximize healthcare provision and its quality. If there was a proposal to provide a new appointments handling system, then this would have to be weighed against a number of other projects, as there are usually more projects than funding available to carry them out. The trigger for a proposed new system might be a string of complaints from staff and patients. The cost of a replacement system, however, might be enough to provide a new scanner for diagnosis. How could you decide which to fund? On the face of it the scanner can save lives and the appointment system could not.

Suppose, however, that the existing appointment system has the following problems:

- It is difficult to reschedule appointments when a consultant is absent for sickness reasons.
- Appointments are changed overnight on a batch run, and sometimes there are mistakes that need more overnight changes.
- Because of the batch update, it is almost impossible to schedule an appointment for the same day. Staff will sometimes manage it with some cunning and telephoning round to check on cancellations at clinics.

The net effect of the above system is that between 5% and 10% of appointments are missed, and at least half of that can be attributed to inflexibility of the appointments system. With 50 consultants in the hospital, there is a reasonable argument that with a better appointment system the hospital could improve the effectiveness of the consultants by 3%, the equivalent of hiring one and a half more consultants. In addition, a consultant needs the equivalent of 1.5 nurse support staff, so there is an argument that it will improve nurse effectiveness by the equivalent of over two nurses.

Now the benefits of the system can be measured financially in terms of the cost of employing the extra consultants and nursing staff. There may be no direct financial return from the project, but it can now be positioned with other projects in terms of tangible and measurable benefits to the hospital.

Any project of any size needs some form of benefit derived, and usually this needs to be measured financially as well as in other ways. This chapter will look at ways of identifying the financial benefits of IT projects, with some simple guidelines on how to structure the cost–benefit model and what pitfalls to avoid.

7.1 Return on Capital Employed

One of the key financial measures for a company is the return on capital employed. There are indeed many financial measures, but this is a high-level one that is affected by any IT project. Let us look at what this measure is.

The capital in a company is everything that has been bought to make the company operate. All of the equipment, all of the stock ready for processing, all of the goods ready for delivery to customers, the trucks, the offices, the office chairs, the PCs on people's desk, the air conditioning in the computer room – all of these count as capital. Usually somewhere in the financial system there will be a monetary value placed on them, right down to the staplers and pencil sharpeners. Finance systems can usually give you a quick statement in monetary terms of the capital employed.

Clearly, the bigger a business, the more capital is likely to be employed to enable it to run. Unlike households, most businesses do not like having too much capital employed. The more money that is tied up in capital, the less effective the company is considered to be. It is easy to see why. If I came to you and asked to borrow €1000 to set up a business, and I would return €100 a year as your return on investment, you might think it a good idea. However, if I chose to set up a business that that needed €2000 to give the same return, you might prefer to put the money in a savings account.

Organizations have income, known usually as revenues, and expenditure. The name of the game is to make sure that revenues meet expenditure over time, and ideally for many businesses that revenue exceeds expenditure. Revenue is obtained mostly from sales of goods or services for companies, or through direct funding for public organizations such as schools and hospitals. Expenditure is everything that is paid for, including salaries and purchase of raw materials. Profit (or loss if negative) is obtained by taking expenditure from revenue. Governments usually tax this gross profit, so that the amount left for reinvestment or payment to shareholders is usually a good bit less.

A key measure is the percentage of profit relative to the amount of money invested in the organization. We thus end up with an equation known as the return on capital employed:[1]

$$\frac{\text{Revenue} - \text{Expenditure}}{\text{Capital Employed}} \times 100$$

Organizations differ in relation to their goals with this equation. Companies tend to want to maximize this equation, so they want to increase revenue, reduce expenditure, and reduce capital employed. That way they improve profitability from the amount of money invested in the company. Public bodies often have their revenue fixed, and are constrained to keeping expenditure in line with revenue. However, they still need to note this equation because by reducing expenditure in one area they can increase it in another. Likewise, if they can reduce the amount of capital employed, they can often use the sale as revenue and increase expenditure (albeit sometimes temporarily).

Now, all IT projects involve expenditure and usually an increase in capital employed. Thus, to have an impact on the overall return on capital, they need to do one of three things. They can reduce expenditure in another area, or they can increase revenue in another area, or they can reduce capital employed in another area. Any major IT project that does not do one or more of these is probably not worth doing at all.

7.2 Identifying Costs

There are some obvious costs to an IT project. These include the following:

- Development staff costs
- Equipment costs
- Consultancy costs
- Training costs
- Recruitment costs
- Software licenses
- Hardware and software maintenance
- Testing team costs

There are some hidden costs that are not always obvious to the IT team, but which are usually obvious to the managers in the business using the IT. These include:

- Training of users
- Overhead charges from the help desk
- Disruption to work when systems are down
- Disruption to work while users are gaining experience
- Redundancy costs if there is a reduction in staff
- Salary increases if there is a change in responsibility levels for staff using the system

---

1   There are dozens of financial measures used to assess the performance of a company. This is just one. However, it is one of the most overreaching.

- Office space to operate the system.
- Other restructuring costs, such as decommissioning offices, warehouses or plant

These costs do not all appear at once. The IT costs are usually incurred up front, with chunks for licences, and the business costs at the end.

7.3 Identifying Cost Reductions

Cost reductions in businesses come in many forms. The most frequent area for identifying cost reduction is in staff costs. IT tends to be used widely to improve the performance of staff, allowing them to do more work. If an individual can do more, unless there is an increase in the amount of work to be done, then fewer individuals are needed.

An example in a call centre might be that customers frequently request additional statements to be sent to them. It might be that the way the call centre handles this is for the customer service representative (CSR) to print off the invoice, put it in an envelope and put it in the post. If this takes five minutes, and typically a CSR does this six times in a day, providing a facility for the additional copies to be printed with the overnight batch run would save half an hour per CSR per day, and in a call centre with 50 staff this could represent the work of over three CSRs. The cost saving would be the cost of employing three CSRs.

Another area for cost reductions is in reducing wastage. High stock levels of perishable materials can mean that there is frequent writing off of damaged or degraded stock. Supermarkets over the last two decades have optimized their supply chain to such an extent that perishable goods are on the shelves almost as soon as they arrive. In fact, supermarkets have rather cleverly achieved a situation where many of the goods you purchase have not been paid for when you hand over your cash. We shall see an example of the effect of this later when we consider the ICANDO Chemicals example.

Another cost reduction area is in reducing office space, or changing the type of office space to lower cost facilities. Banks have been actively seeking this over the last two decades. A telephone service is cheaper to provide because the cost of out-of-town office space is cheaper than high street branch costs. An Internet bank is even cheaper to support, not counting the savings in direct personnel costs.

Ensuring that cost reductions are actually achieved is important. If the justification for a call centre modification described above just means that the staff have a lighter load during the day, then the project has failed to meet its target, and the effort could possibly have been better spent elsewhere. Of course, reducing staff load need not mean redundancies – they may be given other tasks to undertake or have less need for overtime or be reallocated to another part of the business.

7.4 Identifying Revenue Impact

Revenue impact is much more difficult to assess. This is usually the area of highest risk. The large explosion of interest in Internet businesses has been caused by the possibility of companies establishing new revenue streams. Because of the relatively low marginal cost of a transaction on the Internet, large potential revenue streams attracted a lot of investment. When the revenue streams failed to materialize, the companies were unable to meet their basic costs and failed dramatically.

For established businesses, revenues change marginally over time, but marginal changes can have a dramatic impact on a company's profits. A 1% drop in revenue with no corresponding fall in expenditure can tip a company from healthy profit into loss. Likewise, a marginal increase in revenue with a smaller increase in costs can improve profitability significantly.

In our examples, it is the ICANDO Retail area where an increase in revenue is used to justify the project. This is very much based on the intuition of the marketing management, backed up with some knowledge of the effect of such promotions with other companies.

7.5 Identifying Capital Impact

The prime area for reducing capital is usually in keeping stocks low. This has been one of the major successes of businesses over the last two decades. Keeping high stock levels means that you have to pay for raw materials and hold on to finished goods or work in progress for a long time before converting it to income. High stock levels require space, which also ties up capital, and incurs costs of staff that are required to manage it.

The perfect factory has its raw materials delivered the day they are needed, and finished goods delivered straight to the customer from the end of the production line. Unfortunately the world is not such a straightforward place, and there will need to be some storage. There are risks too. If raw materials do not arrive, production can stop, and if there is a drop in purchases for a period then either production would have to slow down or there would need to be some stockpiling.

Another source of capital reduction is in better management of cash. Most companies now arrange to pay their suppliers on the last possible day, and to get invoices out immediately they deliver goods. This may sound officious, but if a company delivers €1,000,000 per month in product then they will have €50,000 cash for every working day they can bring forward the invoicing.

Other capital reductions can come from making business more efficient. Staff reductions result in a reduced need for office space. Reduction in stock means a reduction in warehousing. Delivering direct from manufacturing reduces warehousing, transport and loading/unloading costs.

7.6 Cash Flow Models and Cost–Benefit

Part of the business planning for an IT project involves producing a cash flow model. This means that the organization can arrange appropriate funding and also see that the project provides some financial benefits. Table 7.1 shows a typical high-level cash flow model, expressed in thousands of euros. This is based on a simple system introduction into a call centre that aims at an improvement in efficiency that can reduce staff levels, and it takes a year to develop. Note that there is a high initiation cost and a high deployment cost. Though the quarterly net benefit to the organization from the project will be €133,000 (taking routine costs from savings), the project at one point will have a net overdraft of €366,000,

Table 7.1   A simple cash flow model

	Q1	Q2	Q3	Q4	Q5	Q6	Q7	Q8
Costs								
Development staff	20	20	20	20	10	10	5	5
Equipment	40			60				
Consultancy	5	5	5	5				
Training	10	2	2	2				
Recruitment	10							
Software licenses	20			50				
Hardware/software maintenance		2	2	2	5	5	5	5
Testing team		4	4	8	4	2	2	2
Training of users				20	10	3	1	1
Help desk charges	2	2	2	2	5	5	3	3
Disruption	1	1	1	5	10	2		
Redundancy					50	20		
Staff costs					5	5	5	5
Office space	3	3	3	3	2	2	1	1
Other restructuring costs					5	10		
Total	111	39	39	177	106	64	22	22
Benefits								
Stock reductions								
Other capital					5	5	5	5
Staff reductions					150	150	150	150
Revenue								
Total	0	0	0	0	155	155	155	155
Cumulative costs	111	150	189	366	472	536	558	580
Cumulative benefits	0	0	0	0	155	310	465	620
Net worth of project	−111	−150	−189	−366	−317	−226	−93	40

and it is a year after deployment before the project breaks even, and two years after development starts.

This would be a small project in IT development terms. However, the cost profile would not be unusual. Table 7.2 shows the breakdown of direct IT and non-IT costs over the two-year period. The business costs are substantial. For many projects the business costs will substantially outweigh the IT costs.

The cash flow that we have used above is a very simple one. There are more sophisticated ones that take into account inflation and costs of borrowing. We have not, for example, considered the cost of the overdraft or borrowing to cover the average increase in debt over the two-year period. It is not the intention here

Table 7.2 Distribution of costs between IT and non-IT

Development staff	110
Equipment	100
Consultancy	20
Training	16
Recruitment	10
Software licenses	70
Hardware/software maintenance	26
Testing team	26
Total IT Costs	**378**
Training of users	35
Help desk charges	24
Disruption	20
Redundancy	70
Staff costs	20
Office space	18
Other restructuring costs	15
Total non-IT costs	**202**

to get into details of accounting practices, but to give you a sense of the economics of projects.

7.7 Some Warnings

Many projects do not have much by way of cost–benefit analysis done at the outset. This often serves the vested interest of those people who want the project to run. However, a cost–benefit analysis does not mean that the project is viable, as there are lots of ways of fudging the figures. Some useful warnings are listed below.

Overlooked or missed costs

I remember one recent project where the system was developed and it was realized that the PCs in the call centre would need replacing to deploy the system as the ones installed were not fast enough and did not have enough memory. Replacing 60 PCs completely demolished the cost–benefit model. No-one thought to check. This may seem careless, but there will be inevitable oversights, hopefully not as drastic as this. A wise planner will put in a contingency line of up to 10% of costs.

Phantom benefits

A lot of projects are justified on the improved efficiency of staff. Though the argument is valid, the effect is often just to make life easier for staff. The only way that the benefits can be realized is to reallocate staff or get rid of them. Getting rid of staff is, thankfully, often a last resort for many companies, though they may do it in a more kindly way by simply freezing recruitment until enough people have left of their own free will. Thus, simple staff efficiency improvements need to be challenged. I have heard it cynically said, with more than an element of truth behind it, that if all the staff reductions from all the cost–benefit analyses of all the projects were added up, many companies should be operating with a negative number of staff.

Very recently I was involved in the performance testing of a system that had been justified on the reduction of call times in a call centre by about 20%. When we timed the different aspects of the call, the actual time spent on keying into the system and waiting for a response on some of the calls was less than 20% of the time of the call. As the non-system aspects of the call, such as introduction and discussion, were not changed by the system, the targeted benefits were physically unachievable.

Minimized risks

New technology brings risk. If a key piece of technology takes much longer to develop, then this can push the deployment and the reaping of benefits out considerably. Salespeople and IT staff are not renowned for flagging risks when they are trying to get a project off the ground. It is usually in their interests that the project is approved, and there is a natural tendency to hide anything that will block the approval.

Broken hockey sticks

For a while I was bemused to hear the regular use of 'broken hockey sticks' among information system planners. It was simply explained. Most projects have a cost model that can be drawn as in Figure 7.1, where there is a period of increasing expenditure, followed by a period of recovery of that expenditure, and then a happy and profitable period where the full benefits of the projects are reaped.

However, it was realized that most of the hockey sticks were broken, sometimes before the benefits were achieved sufficiently to meet the costs. A key problem was the length of the projects, and the fact that business changes often meant that systems needed replacing before their benefits were fully realized. Thus a system

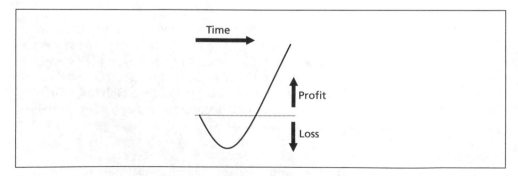

Figure 7.1   A hockey stick cost–benefit model

that is entirely justifiable if it has a five-year lifespan may be totally unjustifiable if it has a three-year or shorter lifespan.

7.8 ICANDO Bulk Chemical Ordering

The scale of the project is substantial, but not untypical of many large IT projects. The cash flow model in Table 7.3 is expressed in thousands of euros. Looking at the cumulative costs and benefits, the project will be €12 million overdrawn before the benefits start to arrive in the fourth quarter. Despite substantial stock reductions, in the fifth and sixth quarters, it is not until the seventh quarter that the project has a net benefit. Once the project has stabilized in the eleventh quarter, the quarterly benefit to the company will be €4.5 million. The bulk of the worth of the project of €117 million in the three years will come from stock reductions, and the ongoing benefit will arise from reduced costs in stock management (e.g. fewer warehouses).

Looking at the total costs of the project by category, in Table 7.4, about €19 million is attributable to IT and €29 million to non IT costs. This is not unusual for large system deployments. Restructuring a business and introducing new systems is a massive organizational change.

There are a number of factors that have been left out of the model. Firstly, there has been no revenue projection. It is hoped that by offering better service, such as Web-enabled ordering, more clients may be taken on board and revenues increased. However, this is speculative and not necessary to justify this project.

Secondly, the system is a replacement for existing systems that have a cost of operation. There will be a decommissioning cost associated with these, but the ongoing operating costs can be offset against the operating costs of the new system. Given the size of the project, this is considered small enough to overlook at the initial planning stage.

7.9 ICANDO Site Safety

The site safety system has benefits that are extremely hard to measure. This is true of many safety systems. The R&D team estimate, based on experience of previous applications that have been commercialized, that the development of a production system would be about €1.5 million. The cost of the R&D project will be €300,000. Thus, on a pure cost–benefit scale, the system would have to save €2 million to be argued as commercially viable.

Safety budgets tend to be set by the company, and projects prioritized within that budget. The justification for the site safety system is that one incident on a site could cost tens of millions of euros in damage and compensation. Given that one such incident typically occurs every three to five years in a company the size of ICANDO, the system would have to demonstrate that it would significantly reduce the likelihood of an incident.

The judgement on how effective a production system would be is dependent on the success of the prototype. The cost of €300,000 is deemed reasonable for the company to produce the prototype.

Table 7.3 Cash flow model for the Chemicals project

	Q1	Q2	Q3	Q4	Q5	Q6	Q7	Q8	Q9	Q10	Q11	Q12
Costs												
Development staff	1000	1500	1500	1500	1000	1000	500	200	200	200	200	200
Equipment	500	250	100	2000	2000	1000	1000	500	100	100	100	100
Consultancy	100	100	100	100	100	100						
Training	10	10	5	5	5	5	50					
Recruitment	20	10	10				5					
Software licenses	50	25	10	250	120	120						
Hardware/software maintenance		75	75	100	100	100	100	100	100	100	100	100
Testing team		10	10	40	40	20	20	20	20	20	20	10
Training of users				50	50	50	50	50	20	20	20	20
Help desk charges	10	10	10	50	50	50	50	20	20	20	20	20
Redundancy					1000	1000	1000	1000	1000	500	100	100
Contingency	500	500	500	500	1000	1000	1000	1000	1000	1000	1000	1000
Other restructuring costs					5000	5000	2000	1000				
Total	2190	2490	2320	4595	10465	9445	5775	3890	2460	1960	1560	1550
Benefits												
Stock reductions					10000	10000	30000	30000	30000	15000	0	0
Other operating reductions					2000	2000	5000	5000	5000	5000	5000	5000
Staff reductions					500	500	1000	1000	1000	1000	1000	1000
Revenue												
Total	0	0	0	0	12500	12500	36000	36000	36000	21000	6000	6000
Cumulative costs	2190	4680	7000	11595	22060	31505	37280	41170	43630	45590	47150	48700
Cumulative benefits	0	0	0	0	12500	25000	61000	97000	133000	154000	160000	166000
Net worth of project	−2190	−4680	−7000	−11595	−9560	−6505	23720	55830	89370	108410	112850	117300

Table 7.4   Total costs by category for the Chemicals project

Costs	
Development staff	9000
Equipment	7750
Consultancy	650
Training	45
Recruitment	40
Software licenses	575
Hardware/software maintenance	1050
Testing team	230
Training of users	330
Help desk charges	330
Redundancy	5700
Contingency	10000
Other restructuring costs	13000

7.10 ICANDO Retail Petrol Promotions

This project can only be justified on revenue, as there are no obvious cost reductions. There is no plan to remove the existing call centre and paper catalogue. The UK retail market for fuel is over 20 billion litres a year, and ICANDO has 5% of that market at approximately 1 billion litres. Profit is approximately €0.02 per litre, that is €20 million. Surveys suggest that ICANDO may increase its market share by between 1% and 3% per year with a good Web-based loyalty scheme. At a conservative estimate then, the increase in profit would be €200,000.

The cash flow for the project is shown in Table 7.5. Using the conservative estimate for revenues this would break even at the end of two years. The marketing manager makes a judgement that the revenue increase is pessimistic, and is likely to be nearer 2%, and on that basis decides to proceed. A fixed price contract with the development company is agreed, and the license costs and internal costs are well understood. Therefore it is considered a low risk in terms of costs.

REVIEW QUESTIONS

1. What are the elements of 'Return on Capital Employed'?
2. Why is return on capital employed an important consideration in project initiation?
3. Are all the costs of an IT project related to IT?
4. What are the key areas for cost reduction that can be targeted in an IT project?
5. Why is revenue impact difficult to assess?
6. Why is the capital impact of a project important?
7. What does a cash flow model tell you?
8. Why might people minimize risks when they are planning a project?

Table 7.5   Cash flow for the Web-based loyalty system

	Q1	Q2	Q3	Q4	Q5	Q6	Q7	Q8
Costs								
Development contract	30	30						
Equipment		40						
Project management	10	10	5	5	5	5	5	5
Software licenses		20						
Hardware/software maintenance			10	10	10	10	10	10
Testing		2	2					
Contingency	5	5	5	5	5	5	5	5
Total	45	107	22	20	20	20	20	20
Benefits								
Revenue			20	40	50	50	50	50
Total	0	0	20	40	50	50	50	50
Cumulative costs	45	152	174	194	214	234	254	274
Cumulative benefits	0	0	20	60	110	160	210	260
Net worth of project	−45	−152	−154	−134	−104	−74	−44	−14

EXERCISES

1. The retail loyalty system has missed out the costs of the promotion in the cash flow. Assuming this costs €30,000 in quarter 3, adjust the cash flow accordingly. How long now before it breaks even? Double the revenue increase (taking the marketing manager's estimate of a 2% increase in turnover). Now how many months does it take to break even?

2. The marketing manager for the retail loyalty system has sold advertising space on the Web site at a rate of €10,000 per quarter. Add this in to the cash flow model. What effect does that have on the time to break even?

3. For the trading system, there is an argument that the improved risk management could reduce losses on bad trades by €2 million a year. This is based on hard evidence of traders who took on more risk than they were allowed and which management did not spot early enough. In addition, the market information might improve trades by €2 million a year. There would be 20 traders' workbenches needed, and IT services would charge €8,000 a year for each workbench to supply and maintain. Total development costs are estimated at €700,000, including licenses and testing. Produce a cash flow analysis for this project. Is this a financially viable project? Is the speculative improvement in trade necessary for the justification?

ANALYSIS

Reader's Guide

Analysis is a broad term, covering the investigation of businesses and the definition of a system for use within a business. It relies heavily on the construction of models, using notations such as the Unified Modeling Language. In this section we cover the range of analysis from business modelling through to the definition of systems functionality using use cases.

If your interest is in the definition of system functionality, rather than the detailed design, then you should examine this section in great detail. If your prime interest is in actual design and construction (e.g. you are a programmer), then it is still very useful to study the methods and notations here, as they are the primary means of communicating with developers. If your interest is primarily management, then understanding business modelling will benefit you in assessing costs and benefits, and how to manage the development and deployment of IT systems in a business.

Chapter 8: Business Modelling

This chapter introduces modelling notations and methods for recording how a business operates or plans to operate. UML activity diagrams are introduced in some detail.

Chapter 9: Requirements Analysis

This chapter looks at the definition of detailed requirements for an IT system, using UML use case diagrams and use case descriptions.

Chapter 10: Buy, Build or Adapt

This chapter introduces the options for buying packaged IT solutions and a method for utilizing business analysis models in the selection of suitable IT packages.

Chapter 11: Object Concepts

This chapter introduces the ideas of object orientation and the UML notation for recording objects.

Chapter 12: Systems Analysis

This chapter introduces methods and notations for defining the behaviour of systems in great detail.

Business Modelling

1. The importance of the business context
2. A method and notation for mapping out business processes
3. UML activity models and their use in describing business processes
4. Business objects and some UML class notation
5. Elementary UML statechart modelling

In this chapter we are going to comprehensively cover a method for outlining a business in terms of the business processes that it follows. As with everything outlined in this book, the choice of techniques and the rigour with which they are to be used depends very much on the purpose and organization that is undertaking the development. If the development project is for a new business area or a new client, then a comprehensive business analysis is very important. If the development is for an established business area, and the development team are familiar with that area, then a less rigorous approach might be more sensible. The size and scope of a system also determine the level of business modelling needed; smaller systems development can be carried out with little or no business analysis, as the risk and cost of failure are relatively small.

The techniques discussed here will result in models that have a number of potential uses. The most obvious one is as input to the systems analysis stage of a bespoke development. However, businesses very often choose to use packages, and these models can be used as input to a package evaluation exercise (see Chapter 10). Understanding business processes is also essential for the development of accurate cost–benefit models (see Chapter 7). Figure 8.1 shows the relationship between business process modelling and the stages of cost–benefit modelling and systems analysis. The key outputs of business process modelling are business process definitions (including a process map) and a business object model that in turn are used by later stages.

We shall use UML activity diagrams as a way of describing business processes. We shall also introduce some elementary object modelling as a way of understanding the business context. UML, however, is only a partial solution to recording a business analysis, and we will introduce some additional notations and conventions along the way. The range of models that can be used to describe a business is unlimited. It is more important at this stage that you gain an understanding of business modelling than a full understanding of all the possible models that can be used and all the subtle details of the modelling notations. At

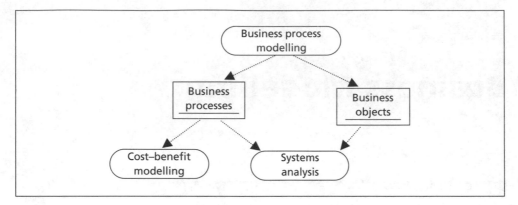

Figure 8.1   The primary models output by business modelling and their input into other software development processes

the end of the chapter we will discuss other models that might be considered here, and as you gain experience and understanding of the notations you might bring them into the business modelling phase. Modelling is about communication, and the choice of model is the one that provides the best communication; in this chapter I have chosen a workable and generally sufficient set of modelling methods and notations for business analysis.

The stages that we will describe in this chapter are indicated in Figure 8.2. The first step is to derive an overall map of the business processes. This gives an overview of the business area that is to be modelled, and where ultimately we plan to introduce a new IT system. Then the relevant business processes will be analysed using scenario analysis. This will capture a great deal of detail about the business process, and structure it in a particular way. From the scenarios we will produce business workflows that can be described using UML activity diagrams. We will

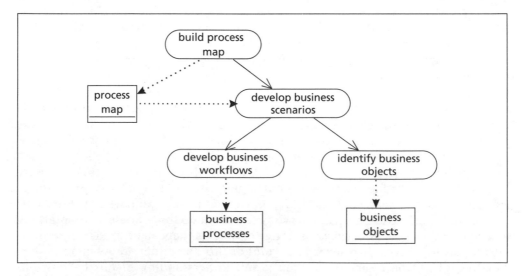

Figure 8.2   The stages of business modelling

also produce a business object model that identifies some of the key entities in the business environment.

There are many approaches to modelling businesses. This approach is loosely based on the SELECT Perspective method (Allen and Frost, 1998), with elements gleaned from a diverse set of sources. Business modelling to this level of detail is not often included in analysis and design methods, and in practice many organizations will omit this stage or carry it out in a limited fashion. This can lead to omissions later in the development process that emerge at the testing or deployment stages. The approach described corresponds to the Unified Process, and we shall discuss the relationship with the Unified Process later, though it does not clearly describe a process for business modelling.

8.1 The Importance of Understanding Business Processes

A common question when analysing a business environment is 'Why are you asking all of these things that are not directly to do with the system?'. There are many replies. Most importantly, to understand a system you need to understand the environment in which it sits. If you do not, you are likely to produce a system that does not do the job properly. Many computer system developments have failed because they forgot this simple fact.

Discussing the business environment is the basis on which an analyst should be agreeing a system specification with a client. Clients are unlikely to know much about computer systems development, but a great deal about their business and the workflows in it. The quality of the dialogue between the analyst and the various stakeholders in the system determines to a large extent the quality and comprehensiveness of the end product. Mistakes made at this stage are very costly, not only in the cost of rework to rectify the mistake, but also in terms of lost opportunities and damaged reputations. The dream is to get the system right first time, an ideal that is rarely achievable, but there is much to be said for not getting it too wrong first time round.

Some methods approach systems analysis by identifying the users of the system and determining the functions that they wish to perform on the system. The first stage would be to catalogue the potential users and identify how they would use the system. This is a workable approach, and one that the analyst might want to consider as either an alternative or as a complementary approach to the one recommended here. Business analysis is then done implicitly, and inevitably some understanding of the business context is gained. The approach we are adopting is more general than that, and begins by focusing on the business area, not on systems use.

The method contained in this chapter will allow you to present back to a stakeholder a comprehensive description of the environment in which the proposed system will sit. All of the diagrams and notations here should be shown to stakeholders, and agreement reached that they are accurate and comprehensive. As we move further into the analysis and design process, the notations become more complex and further removed from routine business operations.

A key question is how much time and effort should be spent on this stage. There is no fixed answer. It is not a stage that needs to be completed before later stages can start. When one area of a business is modelled, systems analysis for that area can begin in earnest. Feedback from systems analysis may trigger more business modelling. The business model is a living, evolving entity that is never set in stone. Most of the models described here can be elaborated in a matter of days, or at most weeks, but they will continue to be changed and added to throughout the development process.

Throughout business modelling, a vocabulary will be built up of the business domain. Clear descriptions will be captured of aspects of the domain, and the analyst will gather information in the form of sample documents that will be invaluable at the systems analysis stage. The drawings and analysis documents that are produced need to be backed up with the samples of documents from the business.

8.2   Building a Business Process Map

One of the first things an analyst needs to ask is 'Where am I?', or more particularly 'I am building a system, so what type of business is this fitting into?'. We shall now look at building a 'big picture', a map of the processes in a business. This is particularly important for agreeing the scope of a system. It is better to be clear at the outset which business areas a system is intended for. Often a system has a much wider impact than the commissioning business area, because business processes are interlinked and information is regularly exchanged between them.

Analysis proceeds from high-level woolly concepts to more concrete ideas; we shall see this happening over and over again as we proceed. A process map may look to be very abstract and possibly not too useful at first. Analysts often want to get on with the use case definitions. Developers want to get straight on and build the system they are employed to construct. Before you roll up your sleeves though, you should really be looking at the landscape. The further down the development cycle you are, the harder and more costly it is to rectify mistakes.

A good analyst has a 'good helicopter'. That is, she can rise up to view the countryside, then land to solve problems on the ground. Analysis proceeds like that, taking a mile high view of the world one day, worrying about the fine details of how someone is going to enter information into a system the next, then rising above the landscape again.

Process mapping is a mile-high view of a business. Scenario analysis which we meet next is definitely ground-level. The process map will not be set in concrete. It will evolve and be refined over time. It does not have to be rigorously accurate – it needs to be comprehensive rather than precise. The important thing is that by looking at the process map of a business a reader can get a quick overview of the scope and activities of that business.

One of its key roles is to act as a catalogue or table of contents of the business processes, and ultimately of the system use cases that sit within the business environment. From the process map, we shall be choosing processes to flesh out. Then from the processes we will be identifying system use cases to define the system functionality and its interaction with the environment.

8.2.1   A THREE-LEVEL BUSINESS PROCESS MAP

A business process is a logical grouping of events which can be agreed as a fundamental element of a business. It provides some meaningful and well-defined service. It can take place over a long or short period of time, and it may be made up of sub-processes. A rigorous definition is not really possible, and processes vary considerably from business type to business type.

Although some implicit ordering of processes may emerge as we build a process map, the intention is to describe a whole business area as a set of processes without concern about the order or the interactions of the individual processes. The number of processes varies. For a small operation, these might number tens, and for a large business there may be 200 to 300.

These processes will be grouped on no more than three levels. Experience shows that more fine-grained breakdowns are counter-productive and get into too much detail. The high-level processes will be gross processes that cover a wide area of business activity, and are made up of more focused processes.

The top level should be no more than about 10 high-level processes. These processes should span the whole of the activity of the business. This is a good discipline as it focuses the analysis into really understanding the key aspects of the business. For ICANDO Chemicals, these activities may be:

- PLAN – develop and monitor the tactical and strategic plans of the company; determine investment requirements, high-level resources and time-scales; monitor progress; evaluate performance; monitor risks and opportunities.
- BUY – all purchasing activities and the recording of these activities including payment; covers trading as well as established supply contracts; tracks quality and value of purchases.
- SELL – all selling activities and the recording of these activities; includes marketing in all forms; covers order taking, distribution and revenue collection.
- MANUFACTURE – all manufacturing activities and the recording of these activities; covers production planning and warehousing; includes transport between warehouses, plant and depots.
- DEVELOP/DECOMMISSION – all construction and decommissioning of plant, warehousing, offices.
- FINANCE – monetary flow and control activities; includes investments, bank account management, investor reporting, legal reporting.
- RESEARCH – all research activities covering product and process development.

It can be seen that at the abstract level these are very gross divisions of the company's behaviour, which may be considered too obvious and simplistic. However, experience shows that it is easy to obtain broad agreement on these. There may be substantial debate on the top-level breakdown. There is no 'right answer' and a good breakdown, not a perfect one, is what is needed.

The process map is intended to hide organizational structure, and simply to describe the functionality of the organization. Processes may be implemented in many different ways, sometimes even within the same company; for example, there may be many types of manufacturing plant within a company, producing different goods or producing the same goods in different ways. Having obtained the common abstraction it is possible then to map it back onto organizational structure.

The importance of the omission of information flow and time considerations cannot be overemphasized. There is rarely any disagreement on what an organization does, but there is always disagreement on how it does it. Flows can be added later, once functionality has been agreed. This is the point at which abstract processes are converted to concrete processes that a company carries out.

This approach is commonly known as abstraction. Abstraction picks out particular details for a particular purpose. An abstract model is easier to manipulate, and provides particular insight. We shall be using abstraction in lots of different ways throughout the analysis and design process. Computer scientists are fond of the term *abstraction*, with good reason, though often it is used in a more focused way. Think of abstraction as rising in the helicopter above the landscape and seeing common patterns.

The second level of the process map breaks down into finer detail each of the first level activities. Again, this is a logical grouping, and any temporal or informational links are implicit or coincidental. A second-level breakdown for the SELL activity of ICANDO chemicals might be might be:

- NEGOTIATE CONTRACT – all activities involving negotiations and setting up of contracts with a customer.
- TAKE ORDER – all activities relating to order taking
- DELIVER GOODS – all activities relating to delivery
- ACCEPT RETURNS – all activities relating to return of unwanted or unsatisfactory goods
- INVOICE CUSTOMER – all activities relating to invoicing
- ACCEPT PAYMENT – all activities relating to acceptance of payment

Finally, the second-level activities can be broken down into third-level groupings. A third-level grouping for the INVOICE activity for ICANDO Chemicals might be:

- Identify goods delivered and accepted
- Price goods
- Apply discounts
- Print invoice
- Issue invoice

Practical experience of trying to break down to four levels shows that it is very difficult to gain agreement, and becomes much more related to how a business operates rather than what it does. Sometimes, for a small business area it is only reasonable to break down to two levels. If the processes at the lowest level are becoming such that they are becoming meaningless on their own, then perhaps the detail at this stage is too great and should be left to scenario analysis.

Once the details of the process map have been agreed, they can be drawn up in a single hierarchy that outlines the overall business. Figure 8.3 shows the detail that we have produced so far for ICANDO Chemicals. You can imagine that for ICANDO Chemicals this could expand to maybe 200 or more processes. However, it should be possible to collate them on a single sheet of paper.

Having obtained agreement on the third level of the process map, it is possible to describe each activity in some detail. For a manufacturing company, such a description can take up many hundreds of pages. However, the principal value of the process mapping approach is its conciseness and brevity. Detailed descriptions are at times either too vague or too prescriptive, and we will not be recommending that in this book. However, for some purposes, such as software tendering, it is

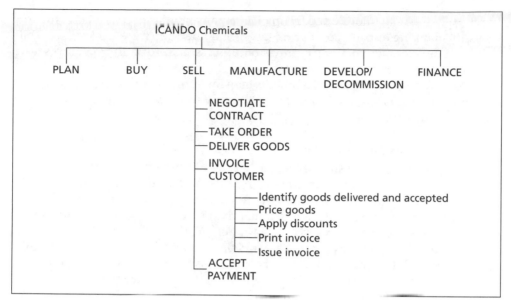

Figure 8.3   A process map showing all levels of the processes defined so far

vital to elaborate on activities for a third party to understand. We shall discuss the level of detail that is appropriate as we look at the case studies at the end of the chapter.

8.2.2   THE USES OF A BUSINESS PROCESS MAP

It can be seen that a process map is in some sense simplistic, and it leaves out a lot of detail. However, experience shows that there is considerable value in the process of constructing such a model. The following benefits have emerged:

- It is possible to construct the model with business personnel, without consideration of the operation of computer systems, or indeed any consideration of software design issues.
- Agreement is easy to obtain up to three levels.
- Summarizing a business in such a way, which can usually be printed on a single sheet of A4 paper, provides a framework for discussions which is manageable.
- The process map clarifies terminology.
- The model can be constructed in two or three days using personnel with a high-level view of business operations.
- Although it is a systemic view of a business, it can be understood easily by anyone with very little introduction.
- It builds consensus and emphasizes areas of commonality.
- By focusing on function rather than organizational structure, it can be used as a basis for discussion in business process re-engineering, and it can build a bridge between software functionality descriptions and business organization descriptions.

I have used these maps extensively over ten years, and has found them both easy to develop and apply, and effective for the groups with which I have worked.

I first used one ready-developed by an oil company, and used it as a basis for strategically mapping out and comparing large integrated software packages. I facilitated the development of a care-provision process map for a European research consortium, and they used this extensively as a basis for reporting and system definition. More recently I used a process map for a software tendering process for customer service packages. The approach is easy to teach and apply, for both IT and non-IT professionals.

8.2.3 CONSTRUCTING A PROCESS MAP

The development of a working process map can be carried out in a very brief space of time. A small team of business managers and experts can be used to outline the process map. The following workshop approach has proved to be successful.

A facilitator is needed who understands the process map concept. A group of business managers and/or experts are gathered. A series of workshops are scheduled over a short space of time. Each workshop should last no more than half a day, and should focus on one level of the model, say the establishment of the top-level processes, or the establishment of the second-level processes for one or two of the top-level processes, or the establishment of the third-level processes for one or two of the second-level processes.

At the start of each workshop, the facilitator needs to briefly describe the notion of process mapping, highlighting the following:

- it is aiming at gathering a high-level view
- interaction between processes is not to be considered
- a perfect process map is not achievable, and a working breakdown of processes is important

The workshops need to be rigorously time-boxed. The facilitator needs to record the list of processes and produce a brief summary of the individual processes. There will be considerable discussion about individual processes as members of the workshop make explicit their understanding of the business processes. There is often a good deal of surprise as people explain what goes on in a process, and there can be a lot of clarification of terminology.

The facilitator should not provide input into the decisions. A business expert is not usually a good facilitator. The facilitator needs to arbitrate and get the group to reach agreement. If she imposes too much on the group, and overrides the group, then the result will be less valuable and will lose the buy-in of the participants.

I facilitated the development of the social care process map discussed earlier in a period of two days. It needed to be done intensively, as the experts came from a number of European states and could not travel regularly. Over the two days we identified over 150 processes, and the experts clarified a number of areas of terminology.

8.3 Business Scenario Analysis

8.3.1 SCENARIOS

Scenario analysis is an apparently simple process that has considerable power in breaking down a complex problem into manageable parts. This will form the basis for both business process analysis and use case analysis. This is not directly supported by UML, but scenarios will be merged later into business workflows that can be described by UML activity diagrams.

The approach used is to break any process down into simple sequences. By collecting them in a disciplined way, it is possible to gather a considerable amount of detail. Do not be deceived by the apparent naivety of the approach. After a while you will get used to analysing situations by looking for primary and alternative paths.

A scenario is a sequence of events or actions. Computer systems and businesses can be viewed as collections of sequences of events. These sequences interact with each other. What makes the world look frighteningly complex is that there are endless numbers of possible scenarios in even the simplest systems. Buying flowers in the local flower shop can, when you think of it, be undertaken in a large number of ways – you might go to the shop or order over the telephone; you can pick the flowers yourself or get the assistant to pick them; they may be wrapped in different ways; they might have a greetings label attached; you might pay by cash, cheque or credit card; you might take the flowers away or have them delivered.

There is no way we could list all the possible scenarios in a business. What we need is to collect some representative scenarios and organize them. Once we have systems that can deal with some of the scenarios, we will find that they themselves develop very complex behaviour and cope with a much broader range of scenarios.

Here is a simple scenario for making a cup of tea:

1. Fill kettle
2. Boil kettle
3. Put tea in teapot
4. Pour boiling water
5. Wait for two minutes
6. Pour tea into cup
7. Add milk and sugar

Not everybody makes tea like that. Some people make the tea in a cup with a tea bag. Some people do not wait the full two minutes. Some people do not take milk and sugar. If you were designing a system to make tea (a bit far fetched), then you would have to consider a number of scenarios.

Here is a scenario for someone ordering a product from an Internet store:

1. Go to Web site
2. Browse catalogue
3. Choose product
4. Give delivery and credit card details
5. Submit order

Now this sort of scenario can vary endlessly. A customer might go back and choose several products. A customer might deselect a product. Credit card details may not be correct. There would be thousands of scenarios. However, you cannot gather scenarios forever. So we need a method of gathering some representative scenarios. To analyse a system, we will look for scenarios, but in a particular way.

8.3.2 THE 80/20 RULE

It has almost become a cliché to say that '80% of effort goes on 20% of activity', sometimes known as the Pareto[1] rule. There is more than a semblance of truth in this. Consider the following:

- Most of the transactions at a bank till are fairly swift, but a small number take four or five times the effort from the clerk.
- The majority of journeys to work are straightforward, but a small number take twice as long and cause a lot of disruptions.
- Usually when you leave home things are where you remember them, but the times that something is out of place cause panic and delay.

This is very true of computer systems development. Most of the effort in developing computer systems focuses on dealing with things that might go wrong or things that are unusual. If everyone typed accurately the right information into a computer system, then most of the development of computer systems would be much easier. But they don't. So you have to consider what might go wrong as well as what can go right.

There are some interesting conclusions from this general rule. Firstly, to cater for the majority of cases you can probably devise a business process or build a computer system fairly quickly. If you can identify the majority case, then there is a big benefit in doing this. Leaving the difficult cases until later is often sensible. Also, people are much better at dealing with problems than computers, so it is sometimes sensible to omit from your computer system a lot of the difficult things at first and leave them for people to do.

There are an infinite number of things that can go wrong in even simple businesses and computer systems. You will never design the perfect business or the perfect system from the outset, so what is really needed is a way of building good systems that can be extended. Perfection is often the great enemy of achievement. We are going to approach the analysis of processes to find out how they work the majority of the time. If we structure the analysis properly, and later find something we missed, it should be a straightforward action to accommodate the variance.

What we are going to do now is look at a way of applying this rule to the analysis of a business process, and later we will use it for analysing use cases for system development. We will look for ways of satisfying most of the people most of the time, and do this as cost-effectively as possible.

8.3.3 THE PRIMARY PATH (OR THE HAPPY PATH)

When you are analysing an activity, you can usually identify a path that is most commonly used, with a few variances. This is known as the primary path, or sometimes figuratively as the happy path. The primary path is the one that is used most of the time. If you can identify that, then you can satisfy the majority of the users of a process.

---

1 Vilfredo Pareto (1848–1923) was an Italian economist who noted that 20% of Italian people owned 80% of the country's wealth, and went on to postulate that a small number of causes are responsible for a large proportion of effects in a ratio of about 20:80. The rule has been adapted and extended, and is commonly known as the 80/20 rule.

McDonald's make use of this. Most people want a popular burger, fries and a drink. So they keep a fair stock of the popular burgers and fries. To keep things flowing they make the weirdo who wants the fish burger wait more often than not. They are dealing with the primary path as efficiently as possible. This way the queues are kept generally small, and only a small number of people have to wait, even at busy periods.

The primary path in a bank for someone cashing a cheque would be:

1. Customer presents cheque
2. Clerk checks signature
3. Clerk checks details
4. Clerk checks account balance
5. Clerk counts money
6. Clerk files cheque

For most people cashing cheques, this is normal. Of course, at each point something might go wrong. The signature might be missing, or the teller might not have enough notes of the right denomination. But maybe 95% of the time, this primary path is what is executed. So, if we were analysing what happens in a bank, then we would look for the primary paths of the transactions first.

Looking for primary paths first cuts down complexity. It stops 'analysis paralysis' where analysts get too wrapped up in the detail and forget that at the end of the day they have to deliver a working system, not a perfect system. So we will develop our systems from hereon in by looking for primary paths first, and worrying about the alternatives and problems later, sometimes much later. It makes use of the 80/20 rule, as the majority of processes follow the primary path, but the primary path usually takes only a fraction of the time to define and implement.

8.3.4 ALTERNATIVE PATH

Once you know the primary paths for a system, you can look for alternatives. These are things that might be subtle changes to the routine. Let us go back to our tea-making example.

1. Fill kettle
2. Boil kettle
3. Put tea in teapot
4. Pour boiling water
5. Wait for two minutes
6. Pour tea into cup
7. Add milk and sugar

By finding a primary path like the above, we can start to worry about things that might be different. For example, the kettle might already have enough water in it. This would be a simple thing to deal with — just go on to the next step. A bigger problem might be that the kettle does not boil. Then you have to look for reasons why the kettle did not boil. Was it switched on? Is there a power cut? Is the kettle broken? A lesser problem might be that someone likes very weak tea. So at step 5 you might only wait 30 seconds.

Note that by defining the primary path you have provided yourself with an interesting checklist to look for alternatives. Once the primary path is developed, you can ask at each step what the alternatives are.

The next question is what you can do with alternatives. The answer is usually to try to return them to the primary path as quickly as possible. Let us take the Web ordering scenario:

1. Go to Web site
2. Browse catalogue
3. Choose product
4. Give delivery and credit card details
5. Submit order

Let us look at Step 4. The credit card details may have an error in them. Now we could let the Web site take erroneous credit card details and let someone in the back office deal with it, say by phoning the customer. Or we could put in a check to make sure that the format is correct. That check could throw up an explanation to the customer and ask them to re-enter the details correctly.

The general rule is, if at all possible, to return an alternative back to the primary path. That way, the primary path provides a backbone or structure to the analysis. Sometimes, but usually rarely, the activity has to be abandoned.

You can use a simple numbering notation to record primary and alternative paths, as illustrated in Figure 8.4. Step 2 has one alternative, numbered 2.1. Step 4 has three alternatives, numbered 4.1, 4.2 and 4.3.

Primary path
1. Go to Web site
2. Browse catalogue
3. Choose product
4. Give delivery and credit card details
5. Submit order

Alternative paths
2.1 Catalogue database not available
  ● Put up error screen, apologizing to customer and asking them to check later.
4.1 Credit card details invalid so:
  ● Put up error screen explaining problem
  ● Ask customer to re-enter details
  ● Re-check details, and if OK, continue to Step 5
4.2 Credit card details invalid after second attempt
  ● Abandon transaction
4.3 Postcode does not match address line
  ● Put up error screen explaining problem
  ● Ask customer to re-enter details
  ● Re-check details, and if OK, continue to Step 5

Figure 8.4 A process analysis using primary and alternative paths

Now we are beginning to see the 80/20 rule in more detail. The alternatives will take up the bulk of the process definition, although they are actioned only a fraction of the time.

8.3.5 EXCEPTIONS

Exceptions are alternatives that are usually more drastic. An alternative is something that routinely happens, but not as often as the primary path. Exceptions are things that are rarer and require different levels of recovery. The best discrimination I have found between an alternative and an exception is that an alternative allows you to reach a goal but through a different route, whereas an exception results in a goal not being achieved.

An example might be in the Web ordering system that someone submits a fraudulent credit card. The response to that might be to accept the details and the order, but instead of issuing goods the police would be advised. Less dramatic might be the catalogue database being down, which we considered as an alternative above. In both cases, the goal of achieving a sale is not met.

The debate about what constitutes an alternative or exception is often a difficult one. At the end of the day though, it does not matter too much, as the process for dealing with them is the same.

8.3.6 THE BASIS OF AN ANALYSIS PROCESS

The ideas we have discussed above are simple, but powerful. We shall be applying the ideas of primary and alternative path analysis to two important areas for constructing models.

The first area will be to look at the business processes where we want to develop a computer system. The scenarios there will be business scenarios and involve activities of people, departments and computer systems. It is important to collect and organize these scenarios before developing the computer system. That way the analysts understand a lot about how a system is to be used.

The second area will be to look at the 'use cases', which are the points in a business process where the system is to be used. We shall use primary and alternative path analysis to open up the dialogue between computer systems and their users.

In both cases, we shall approach a complex situation by doing the following:

1. Finding what are the key activities (use cases or business processes)
2. Defining a primary path for each activity.
3. Using the primary path to look for alternatives.
4. Adding alternative paths, and wherever possible, returning to the primary path.
5. Using the primary path and alternative paths to identify exceptions.

Remember this sequence. It is your 'analysis primary path'.

8.4 Business Modelling With Activity Diagrams

Here we are going to look at a way of recording business processes using UML activity diagrams. By doing this an analyst will gain an understanding of the structure and dynamics of an organization. This understanding should be shared and clarified with all the stakeholders in the system development, from the sponsors who pay for it through to the people who will use the system. It is on the basis of this understanding of the business environment that the requirements for the system can be developed.

We will consider the basics of UML activity diagrams in this chapter. Activity diagrams are a variant on statechart diagrams, which we will consider thoroughly in Chapter 12, where you will meet a richer syntax for the transitions and the activities themselves; for business analysis, the level of detail in this chapter mostly suffices.

Earlier we looked at producing a process map. We then looked at gathering the key scenarios for business processes, using primary and alternative path analysis. Now we shall merge these scenarios into an activity diagram to describe the business process. The method is very straightforward, and involves working through the scenarios and overlaying the individual paths onto a single activity diagram for a process.

8.4.1 ACTIVITIES

An activity is a task in a business process (or other process, as discussed later). This is a small chunk of meaningful work. Examples might be:

- Printing an invoice
- Making a change to an order
- Contacting a customer about an unpaid bill

Business processes are made up of a number of activities linked together to form a workflow.

Activities are where the work gets done. They can be short or long. A business activity to manufacture a car might take many hours or days. Big activities can be broken down into smaller activities. Manufacturing a car could be broken down into manufacturing the chassis, then assembly of components.

Activities are drawn as lozenge shapes with the name of the activity inside, as in Figure 8.5, which shows an activity to print an invoice. The name needs to be a descriptive phrase indicating the goal of the activity. The details of an activity can be recorded separately in a text document.

Figure 8.5 The UML notation for an activity to print an invoice

8.4.2 TRANSITIONS AND EVENTS

Work flows from activity to activity. We show this as an arrow between activities. Figure 8.6 shows a simple transition from printing an invoice to sending an invoice. This is an automatic transition that takes place once the work of an activity, in this case Print Invoice, has completed. We shall see later that there can be multiple exits from an activity, triggered by events.

Businesses respond to events. Either something happens outside the business and a workflow is initiated, or something happens inside the business to trigger a

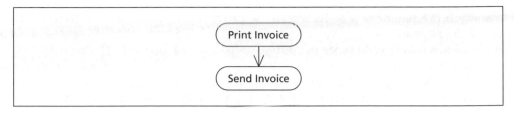

Figure 8.6   A simple transition from one activity to another

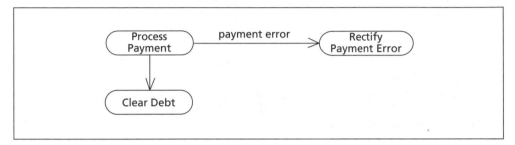

Figure 8.7   A transition triggered by an event interrupting an activity

workflow. Events are the driving force for businesses, and indeed any system that you are likely to examine, be it a business, a piece of electronics or a computer system.

What we are doing in business modelling is tracing an event through a business. An event triggers an activity. When an activity runs it has a normal completion that can trigger another activity. An activity can also be interrupted by another event, and the workflow can follow a different route out of the activity. Figure 8.7 shows an example where the Process Payment activity is unable to complete because there is some error with the payment. Either the cheque is not signed, or the bank refuses to make a payment for some reason, and we have grouped these specific events together under the name payment error. The event is written next to the arrow describing the transition that it triggers.

Once you have an event, you can trace it through by asking the simple question: 'What happens next?'. There will be many possible paths through a workflow, representing the many scenarios that it supports.

8.4.3 STATES

A state is an activity where nothing happens. Sometimes a business process is stuck waiting for something to happen. A customer order may be waiting for stocks to arrive at the warehouse. A payment process may be waiting for a customer to pay. We record states as round-cornered rectangles. Figure 8.8 shows

Figure 8.8   A state in an activity diagram

a state in the payment process where the process is waiting for the customer to make the payment.

There are two special types of state to help denote a process. The start state is the initialization of the system, and there is normally only one on a diagram. An end state denotes an end to the process. Sometimes there is more than one end state. Start states are drawn as black circles, while end states are drawn as black bullseyes, as shown in Figure 8.9.

8.4.4 BUILDING A WORKFLOW FOR A BUSINESS PROCESS

Now we have the basic building blocks for putting together a flow diagram of a business process. This is a key first stage in determining where computer systems will be used. By examining the workflow, we can make decisions on whether that activity needs computer support, say by providing a system to record payment or sending a reminder letter.

Figure 8.9 shows part of the business process for requesting and receiving payment from a customer. Note that the Wait For Payment state has two exit events: one for the normal course of events and one for the alternative where the customer does not pay on time. The Issue Reminder activity follows the rule of returning to the primary path, in this case waiting again for payment to arrive. The Process Payment activity has an event that can trigger an unusual exit when there is some error with the payment; it also has an unlabelled normal exit. Again,

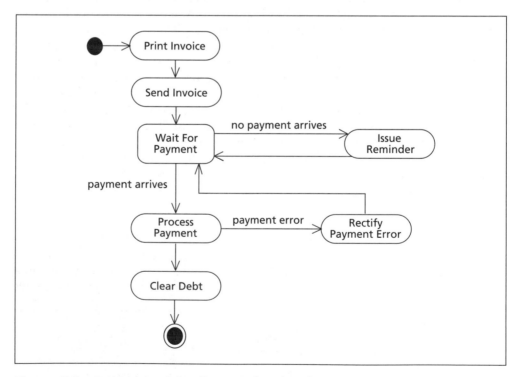

Figure 8.9 A simple activity diagram showing the process of obtaining payment

the alternative is returned to the primary path, this time to an earlier stage in the primary path.

8.4.5 SWIMLANES

An extra feature of activity diagrams is a swimlane. This is used to denote some business area where activities take place. A swimlane is a column on the activity diagram with a heading indicating the business area. Figure 8.10 shows an activity diagram with two swimlanes representing the IT department and the finance department. Printing an invoice, sending an invoice and sending a reminder have been allocated as tasks for the IT department. Processing payment, clearing debt and rectifying a payment error have been allocated as tasks to the finance department.

8.4.6 DECISIONS

We have seen that activity diagrams can take alternative routes dependent on an event triggering an exit from an activity or a state. Sometimes an alternative route is determined by some condition. To show this, a decision point is placed on the diagram, shown by a diamond shape as in Figure 8.11. The transition takes an alternative path dependent on a condition written in square brackets next to the exit path. The conditions can be written in English or a more formal language.

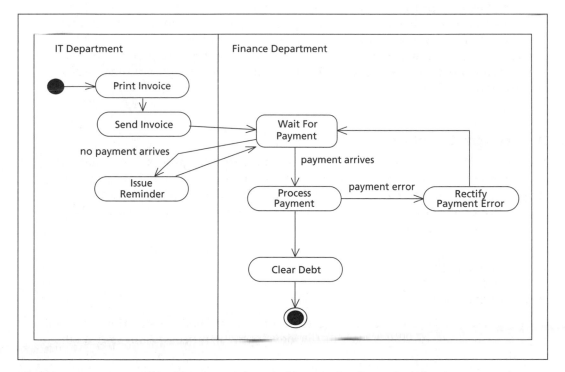

Figure 8.10   An activity diagram with swimlanes indicating which business areas carry out the activities.

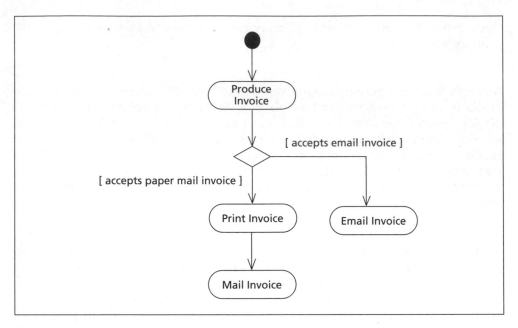

Figure 8.11 A simple example of a decision

8.4.7 STAKEHOLDER INVOLVEMENT

Building business processes like this allows you to talk at length with your client, checking that you understand what the system is you are building. You can then start to examine where in the business process a computer system might be needed, and both how and why it is used. Activity diagrams are perfectly acceptable for showing to all stakeholders. These should form a key part of the business requirements analysis.

8.5 A Process Catalogue

Now that we have a range of models, namely a process map, process scenarios and activity diagrams, we can organize these into a process catalogue. The process map provides an overview, and the catalogue is the detail. There will be an entry in the catalogue for each process of relevance to the system development. Each entry will contain the following.

- Primary path
- Alternative paths
- Exceptions
- An activity diagram

In addition, it is often useful to gather some additional information and to provide a linkage to later stages in the development process. Thus, we might include:

- Goal of the process (what it should achieve if everything works out)
- Necessary preconditions that must be met before the process can run

- Criticality of the process
- Business actors involved in the process
- System use cases that support the process (to be added during the systems analysis stage)
- Documents from the business area that provide insight into the business processes

8.5.1 BUSINESS PROCESS RE-ENGINEERING

We have now covered a very powerful set of models for analysing a business. The same models can be used to model a proposed business. One of the key activities of management is the reinvention of business processes. This is often known as business process re-engineering or business process redesign (BPR for short).

The introduction of new IT systems almost always involves some aspect of business process redesign. One prime example arising today is through the use of the Internet for customers to make orders directly, rather than through some agent. The reasons for doing this are to reduce costs or improve the service to customers. There is also a significant movement to use the Internet for business-to-business transactions, say by the automatic transfer of orders and invoices between the computer systems of different organizations.

Business analysis is often a basis for business process re-engineering. This can be done with no IT component considered. The workflow models we have produced in this chapter can be used for estimating business improvements. We shall look at some simple examples in the next chapter.

8.6 Business Objects

A big change in the way systems development is undertaken began in the mid-1980s. The ideas stem back to the early days of computing, but new languages were emerging that talked about 'objects' rather than 'programs and data'. The pace of change in the practice of information systems development since then has been considerable, and it is the norm to see new projects written using the notion of objects.

The basic idea of objects is very simple. The world is made of objects. Just open your eyes and ears – they are out there: bank customers, students, cats, elephants, cars, balls of string, atoms, molecules, tubs of ice cream, Madonna, stars, bureaucrats, Robin Hood. The world is built of objects. Objects are built of smaller objects, and so on *ad infinitum*. Objects combine to make bigger objects. We live in an object-oriented world.

Object modelling consists of looking for objects and inventing objects. The first objects that are considered are representations of things in the real world, such as customers, suppliers and contracts. Of course, there has to be some boundary. Even looking up from this book you can see more objects than you could reasonably list, and we shall be looking at the right way to find objects later.

Objects do things, and objects have things done to them. The 'doing' parts of an object are called operations. Objects also have information about themselves. The information about an object is held in things called attributes. Later, when we move on to systems analysis, we shall consider operations and attributes in great

Figure 8.12   The UML notation for an object or class

detail. At the level of business modelling, we need only note that objects have some state, and that they can be changed by actions on them.

Objects are drawn in UML using a rectangle with the name of the object inside. We shall see later that this rectangle can have a number of compartments, but for now we shall just consider the name of the object. (Strictly, this notation is for a class, but we shall explain the distinction between a class and an object later.) Figure 8.12 shows the UML notation for a customer object.

Object modelling is, at its simplest level, very straightforward. The trick comes in knowing what objects are appropriate – some of this comes with skill, but we shall include some guidelines. As we move on through systems analysis and design, we shall begin to devise special types of object. The skill of a designer is in knowing how best to choose objects and to make them cooperate.

The first stage of analysis is to look for objects in the real world, such as customers, orders, warehouses and stock. These are often known as 'domain objects' or 'business objects'. These can be related to give a picture of the environment in which the system is to be built. A common guideline for identification of objects is to examine documentation looking for nouns and considering the nouns as candidate objects. Once systems analysis begins the domain objects are given more detail. Design will add further detail and link them to system objects such as computer screens and transaction controllers.

Objects can be related. The relationships between objects are often very important. Figure 8.13 shows a customer object is related to an order object, and an order object is related to an order line object. The numbering on the relationship indicates that one customer can be related to zero or more orders, and one order

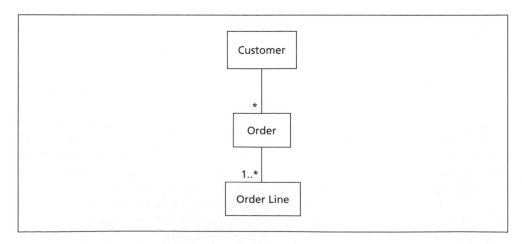

Figure 8.13   Showing relationships between objects in UML

has one or more order lines. An order must have exactly one customer and an order line must have exactly one order.

Later, we shall examine a much richer range of relationships. For the purposes of domain modelling we can stop here, though some of the richer notations might be useful occasionally.

The primary advantage of a business object model is that it gives a clear understanding of the relationships in the business environment. These relationships will often be reflected in some internal objects in the computer system to be built. Capturing these relationships at the business analysis stage allows the analyst to build a more complete picture of the environment in which the system will reside.

Figure 8.14 shows how we can place objects on activity diagrams, using an example business process for order taking. It is sometimes useful to illustrate where objects are created and manipulated in a business process. Business processes often change the state of an object. On an activity diagram, a state can be indicated under the name of the object in the rectangle used to represent the object, written inside square brackets. In this example the Take Order Details

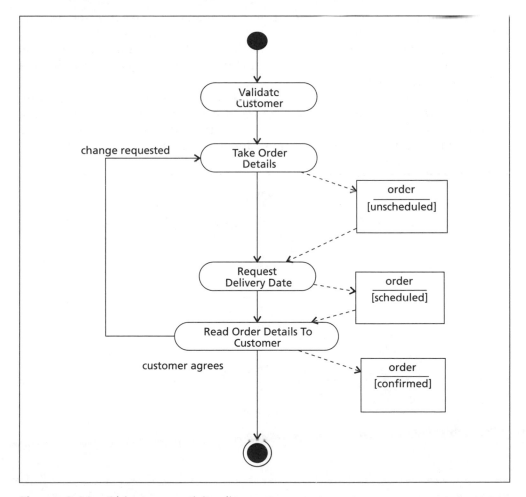

Figure 8.14   Objects on activity diagrams

activity creates an order that is as yet unscheduled, and the state is written as [unscheduled]. The Request Delivery Date activity will add a delivery date to the order, leaving it scheduled. After Read Order Details To Customer, if the customer accepts then the order becomes confirmed. Note that the order object is not necessarily a computer order – this business process would work just as well if the order were recorded on paper.

8.7 Elementary Statechart Modelling

We have seen already, in the previous section, that objects can have a state. We shall be looking later at how we can represent states using attributes. At the business modelling level, a more abstract notion of state is useful. For some of the objects, it is useful to model their behaviour in terms of state transitions. We met the idea of state in an activity diagram. That is where the process described by the activity diagram is awaiting some event before continuing. The notion of state of an object is similar. The object is in some state until an event moves it to another state.

Figure 8.15 shows a simple statechart model for an order object. After creation it is unscheduled; it then has a date added and is scheduled. The customer will then confirm that it is acceptable. It will then be delivered and invoiced, and finally, when it is paid for, the order will no longer exist. This is a single shot life cycle. Objects may oscillate between states.

Figure 8.16 shows a more complicated statechart diagram for a customer account. Here, specific events that take the account between states have been written alongside the lines that indicate the transition between states. The account starts with an open event. It immediately goes into a 'zero or credit' state,

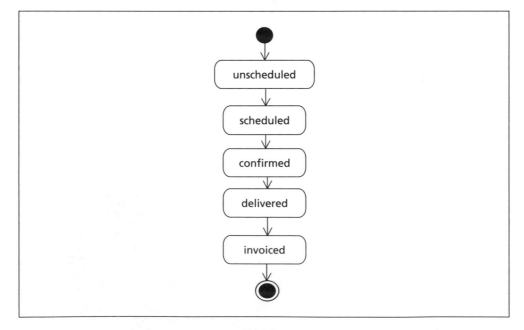

Figure 8.15   A simple statechart model for an order

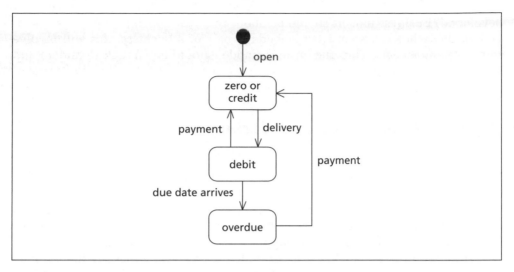

Figure 8.16   A statechart model for an account

as the customer has taken no deliveries. On a delivery, it goes into a debit state until payment arrives. If the due date arrives before payment, then the account goes into an overdue state. It can move from the overdue state to zero or credit once a payment is made.

Statechart models need not be drawn for every object. They are useful for describing more complex behaviours. We shall look at statechart models in more detail when we look at systems analysis and design.

8.8 The Unified Process

The Unified Process includes business process modelling and domain modelling as part of requirements analysis. The business process modelling notation is the business use case notation introduced above, and the domain modelling is based on the object modelling notation. These models are then used as the input to the development of use case models for the system, which is considered the next and most substantial part of requirements analysis. The Unified Process approach is fundamentally the same as the one described here, but less prescriptive and detailed.

8.9 Further Models and Notations for Business Modelling

The activity modelling described above is much more comprehensive and detailed, and can include specification of the activity behaviour and parallel flows. However, the level of detail needed for business modelling is probably as much as is included here. Object modelling incorporates operations and data, and it may be useful to capture data at this stage in the objects. We shall later meet sequence and collaboration diagrams. Very occasionally these are of use, particularly when describing complex interactions between parts of a business.

You need to beware, however, not to make the business model too detailed, and not to bring into the business model the details of the system that is to be developed. Business models should be about the way a business operates. Inevitably today when a system is an embedded part of a business, this will involve some system aspects. Thus the business model should be enough to understand the business for the purposes of describing the way a system fits into the business, and no more.

8.10 ICANDO Bulk Chemical Ordering

8.10.1 BUSINESS PROCESS MAP

ICANDO Chemicals want a new system to improve the sales process. In particular, their business plans imply much tighter integration between sales and manufacture. By special discounting structures for advanced orders, it is planned to increase the number of deliveries direct from the production line to reduce transport warehouse costs and the locking up of valuable working capital in stocks. Therefore the process map has been extended to cover the processes in manufacturing as well as sales. Figure 8.17 covers a representative set of business

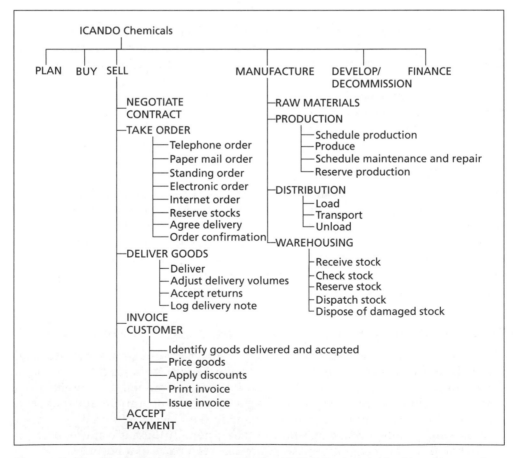

Figure 8.17 The business process map for ICANDO chemicals, focusing on the aspects relevant to the new sales order processing system

processes. The plan, buy, develop/decommission and finance processes are prob ably not relevant to the development. In practice, ICANDO Chemicals would prob ably develop and maintain a comprehensive process map of the whole business for other purposes.

Having constructed the process map, a description of the processes needs to be kept. To do this comprehensively here would not be of great value. However, we shall consider some of the processes that are particularly interesting.

SELL/TAKE ORDER/Reserve stocks

During the taking of any order, stock needs to be reserved. This can either be from the warehouse or from production. If there is a production run scheduled at a suit ably nearby plant with surplus stock in the delivery window, reserves should be made from production. Otherwise, the reserves should be made from the nearest warehouse. The reservation of stock may be changed by the operations manage ment team at any time from production to warehouse or the other way, and excep tionally a change of delivery may be necessary.

SELL/DELIVERY/Adjust delivery volumes

For many chemical deliveries, the quantity is metered at the delivery point. Usually the customer will gauge the delivery, and there will be a gauge on the delivery vehicle. The reason for this is that volumes can vary slightly. Also, it is sometimes the case that the customer has not completely exhausted their stock and only has storage for part of the delivery. Delivery vehicles also make multiple drops, and sometimes the remaining quantity on the vehicle for the final drop is not up to the order. The actual quantity delivered is written on the delivery note, and signed by the customer and driver. These quantities are the ones that need to be invoiced.

SELL/TAKE ORDER/Electronic order

This is a new process that is planned. Using secure Internet technologies, a customer's purchasing system can link directly with the ICANDO Chemicals ordering system. This requires a special contract to be in place and for suitable security features to be available. An investigation is under way, and ICANDO is participating in sector-specific development of XML-based interchange standards.

8.10.2 BUSINESS SCENARIOS

From the process map above we would then identify the processes where the new ordering system was to be applied. A scenario analysis would then take place for each of the processes. We shall elaborate a selection.

SELL/TAKE ORDER/Telephone order

Primary path
1.   Customer telephones call centre.
2.   The agent takes customer number and validates the customer on the system.
3.   Customer provides order details and the agent enters them on the customer order form on the computer screen.
4.   The customer provides a requested delivery date.

5. The system then validates the order and establishes if the delivery can be made on that date. The system may offer a preferred alternative date that the customer can accept or reject.
6. The agent reads back the details of the order.
7. The customer agrees.
8. The call is closed.

Alternative paths

2.1 The customer number is rejected by the system. The agent checks the number with the customer. If there is no mistake noted by the customer, then the call is transferred to the sales team that can deal with the problem.

3.1 A product order code is supplied that the system does not recognize. The agent cross checks with the product catalogue to make sure that the customer has not got the code wrong. Once the correct code is found, continue as before. If not, the customer may need to be transferred to the sales team at the end of the call.

3.2 The order may exceed the customers credit limit. The agent can ask the customer to reduce the order, or can transfer the call to the sales team if the customer wishes to increase the credit limit.

5.1 The system cannot offer a suitable date for the customer. The customer cancels the order. A note is issued to the sales team to contact the customer and for them to try and obtain the order, say by offering a preferential discount.

6.1 The customer notes that something is wrong with the order. The agent corrects the problem and then re-reads the order to the customer.

Exceptions

2.2 The system is unavailable, so the agent writes down the request on paper and continues the process when the system comes back online.

SELL/DELIVERY/Adjust delivery volumes

Primary path

1. Note meter reading on delivery vehicle (set to zero if appropriate).
2. Note meter reading on receiving vessel (set to zero if appropriate).
3. Discharge product from delivery vehicle into receiving vessel.
4. Note meter reading on delivery vehicle and calculate volume delivered.
5. Note meter reading on receiving vessel and calculate volume delivered.
6. Check that the two readings are no more than 2% out of line.
7. Obtain signature from customer accepting delivery.

Alternatives

6.1 Two readings are more than 2% out of line. Calibration checks to be requested on the meters. Note made of discrepancy and customer asked to sign.

Exceptions

7.1 Customer refuses to sign. Driver to contact the depot for instructions.

SELL/TAKE ORDER/Electronic order

This is an interesting example in that it is a business process that is fully automated. There might be an argument to defer this to the systems analysis stage. However, despite the fact that such a process is fully computerized by its nature, it is a business process, and we have chosen to model it as part of the business model.

Primary path
1. Customer enters purchase request on their own system.
2. Customer's system issues electronic purchase order to ICANDO Chemicals' system.
3. ICANDO Chemicals' system issues an acknowledgement to the customer's system.
4. A check is made that there is a contract for the customer.
5. Security checks made to ensure that this is really the customer.
6. The product request is checked to make sure that it is a legitimate order from stock supplied to the customer by ICANDO.
7. The delivery date requested is checked against possible delivery.
8. Stock is reserved.
9. Delivery is scheduled.
10. Confirmation of order sent to customer's system.

Alternatives
  6.1 The order contains a product that is not on the catalogue. A decline is sent to the customer's system with the reason 'product not recognized'.
  7.1 The order cannot be met on the dates offered in the order. A decline is sent to the customer's system with the reason 'delivery date not achievable'. A suggested alternative delivery date should be included in the decline message.

Exceptions
  4.1 There is no contract for this customer. A decline is sent to the customer's system, with the message 'no contract in place'. The request is referred to the sales team, who will check the problem and rectify it.
  5.1 The security check fails. No decline is sent. The details of the request are passed on to the sales team, who may escalate the problem if there is concern that there may be some fraudulent attempt to make an order.

8.10.3 BUSINESS WORKFLOWS

Having defined the business scenarios above, we can now compile them into workflows using UML activity diagrams. You will note that there is sometimes some information that is difficult to transcribe. Therefore, the scenarios should be included with the business model – the workflows provide an overview.

SELL/TAKE ORDER/Telephone order

Figure 8.18 shows the workflow for the telephone order process. This covers all the alternative paths. The exception is not really covered by this diagram, as basically the process cannot start if the system is down. The exits to the process may in fact be entries to another process; for example, into a sales process after the transfer of the call.

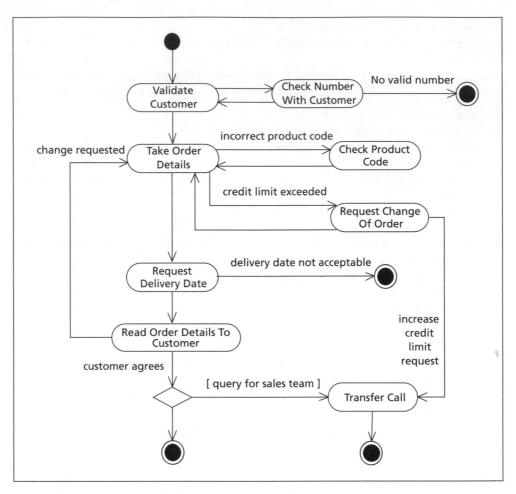

Figure 8.18 Workflow for the telephone order process

Goal of the process
To achieve a successful order for the customer.

Necessary preconditions
Customers must have a contract in place before making an order, and not be suspended for any reason.

Criticality of the process
This process is essential to the operation of the business. Manual ordering can take place in emergencies, but lack of computer support in this area would involve considerable business disruption and ultimately failure of the business.

Business actors involved in the process
Customers, call centre representative.

SELL/DELIVERY/Adjust delivery volumes

Figure 8.19 shows the workflow for adjusting delivery volumes. Note that the exit if the customer refuses to sign will invoke some other process. The noting of the discrepancy would also include requesting checking of the calibration of the meters.

Goal of the process
To achieve an agreed delivery at the customer's site.

Necessary preconditions
The delivery vehicle must have a working meter with a calibration certificate before it leaves the depot.

Criticality of the process
If this is not carried out satisfactorily, it can lead to customer disputes and possible loss of revenue.

Business actors involved in the process
Customer's goods inward, delivery agent.

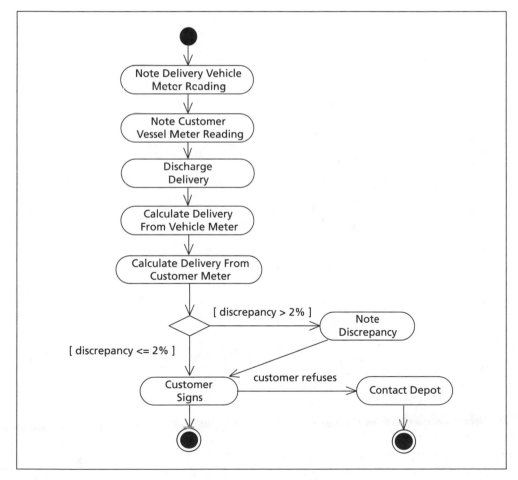

Figure 8.19   Workflow for adjusting delivery volumes

SELL/TAKE ORDER/Electronic order

Here we are using swimlanes to indicate where the work takes place. This is useful in this case because a number of actions have to be taken by the customer. Note that the process has a number of potential exits, each in the customer environment. One is an acceptance of the order, which the customer will probably just record. The others are declines of the order, where the customer may wish to take some different action.

Goal of the process

To achieve a successful online order for a customer without manual intervention from ICANDO.

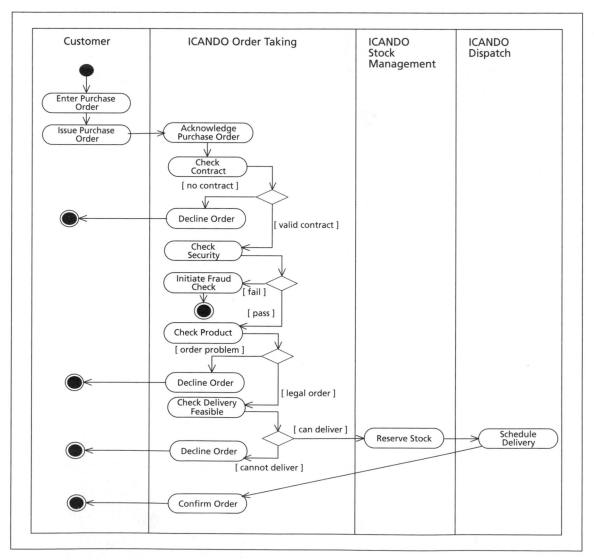

Figure 8.20   Workflow for electronic ordering

Necessary preconditions
Customers must have a contract in place that covers electronic trading before making an order, and not be suspended for any reason.

Criticality of the process
The process can fall back to telephone ordering, though there is a cost and reputation problem with this if it happens excessively.

Business actors involved in the process
Customer's purchasing system

8.10.4 BUSINESS OBJECT MODEL

Figure 8.21 shows a business object model. These are business entities that are of relevance to the processes that we have elaborated above. Clearly, there needs to be a notion of customer, and the business needs to keep some record of the customer either on paper or in a computer system. The customer has precisely one contract, and there is one contract per customer (a one-to-one relationship indicated by a line drawn between the objects). A customer can make a number of orders, but an order only relates to one customer (a one-to-many relationship, with 0..* written at the many end of the relationship). An order may be fulfilled by one or more deliveries, and a delivery may cover more than one order (a many-to-many relationship). Because an order might not be delivered (yet), the order is drawn as having zero or more deliveries.

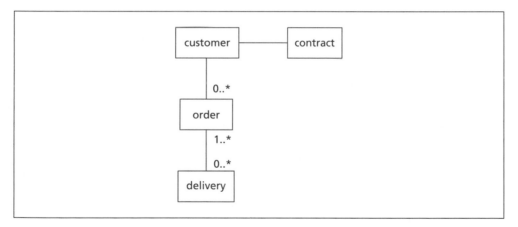

Figure 8.21   Business object model for ICANDO Chemical ordering

8.11 ICANDO Site Safety

8.11.1 BUSINESS PROCESS MAP

The site safety area is much more limited than the chemicals area. In fact, the process map here might well be a small part of a much larger process map under the ICANDO Chemicals Develop/Commission process. Figure 8.22 shows the process map for site safety as much as it is reasonable to break it down. Arguably the breakdown of the Modify Site process is too much for this stage of modelling.

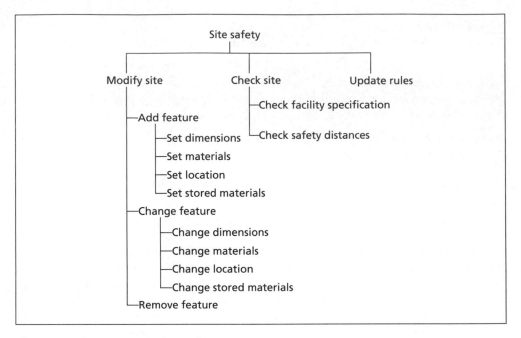

Figure 8.22 ICANDO site safety process map

8.11.2 BUSINESS SCENARIOS

Site Safety/Check Site/Check Safety Distances

Primary path
1. Choose a feature.
2. Choose a second feature.
3. Determine minimum straight line distance between features.
4. Look up in table that determines minimum safety distances between features of these types.
5. Report any infringement.
6. Repeat from 1 until all pairings checked.

Alternatives
 3.1 There is a firewall directly between the features, and a firewall is permitted, so measure the distance around the firewall instead of in a straight line.
 4.1 One or both of the features have a bund (earth mound to contain spillage) around them, so use the bunded distance, not the base feature distance.

Exceptions
 4.1 No table for features, so report an error and continue at 1.

8.11.3 BUSINESS WORKFLOWS

Site Safety/Check Site/Check Safety Distances

Goal of the process
To check and report on all the safety distances between all the features on a site.

Necessary preconditions
Regulations need to be available. A description of the site needs to be available.

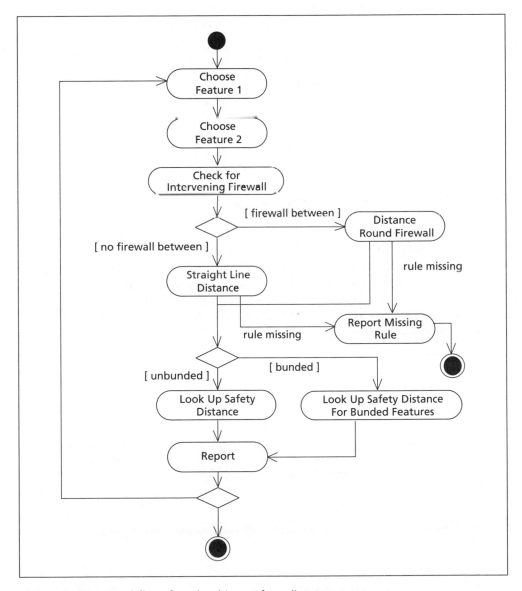

Figure 8.23 Workflow for checking safety distances

Criticality of the process
A safety audit needs to be undertaken before use of the site, and immediately after plans are made to change the site. Following a change, the site can be closed if the audit has not taken place.

Business actors involved in the process
Auditors (internal or external).

8.11.4 BUSINESS OBJECT MODEL

The site safety object model in Figure 8.24 does not look very exciting. A feature may have any number of rules associated with it, and a rule may apply to any number of features. We shall, however, see that the features and rules become much more interesting as we move through analysis and design.

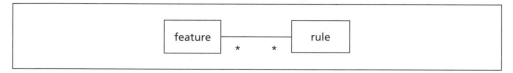

Figure 8.24   Business object model for ICANDO site safety

8.12 ICANDO Retail Petrol Promotions

8.12.1 BUSINESS PROCESS MAP

Figure 8.25 shows the process map for the ICANDO customer loyalty business. This is a subset of the overall process map for ICANDO oil. There is one contact point in the sales area – when a customer makes a purchase, points are awarded. The marketing process has tried to cover some of the ideas of the marketing manager, such as being able to email customers. Card administration and rewards are straightforward processes.

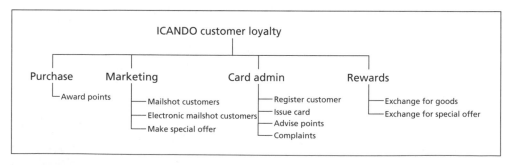

Figure 8.25   ICANDO customer loyalty process map

8.12.2 BUSINESS SCENARIOS

We shall examine two processes.

Card Admin/Register Customer

Primary path
1. Customer obtains contact details at retail outlet.
2. Customer calls the customer service department or visits the Web site or sends details by post.
3. Customer supplies contact details.
4. Customer is asked if they are willing for their details to be used for other offers.
5. A welcome pack, including a card, is ordered for the customer.

Alternatives
    3.1   Postcode and address do not match, so check with customer.

Exceptions
The contact centre or the Web site may be unreachable. There is nothing can be done – the customer must wait until it is available.

Rewards/Exchange for Goods

Primary path
1. Customer examines catalogue and chooses (paper catalogue or Internet catalogue).
2. Customer is validated.
3. Points value of goods deducted from customer balance.
4. Goods added to order.
5. Repeat from 1 as necessary.
6. Order confirmed with customer.
7. Order scheduled for despatch.

Alternatives
    1.1   Goods out of stock, so advise customer and resume at 1.
    3.1   Insufficient points, so advise customer, who can resume at 1 or exit.
    6.1   Customer cancels order, so reassign points and exit.
    6.2   Customer wants to change order. Can deselect goods and resume at 1, with points being returned to balance.

Exceptions
    2.1   Customer fails validation. Refuse transaction.

8.12.3 BUSINESS WORKFLOWS

Card Admin/Register Customer
See Figure 8.26.

Goal of the process
To register a customer with the promotion scheme and supply the customer with a card and welcome pack.

Necessary preconditions
None.

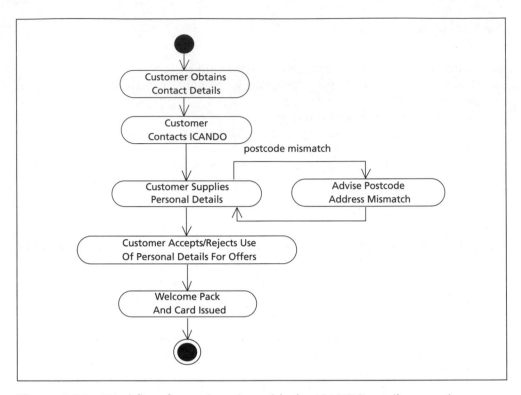

Figure 8.26 Workflow for registration with the ICANDO retail promotion scheme

Criticality of the process
It is important for reputation that this process works reliably. However, it will not impact the business greatly in the short term if it is unavailable.

Business actors involved in the process
Customers.

Rewards/Exchange for Goods
See Figure 8.27.

8.12.4 BUSINESS OBJECT MODEL
See Figure 8.28.

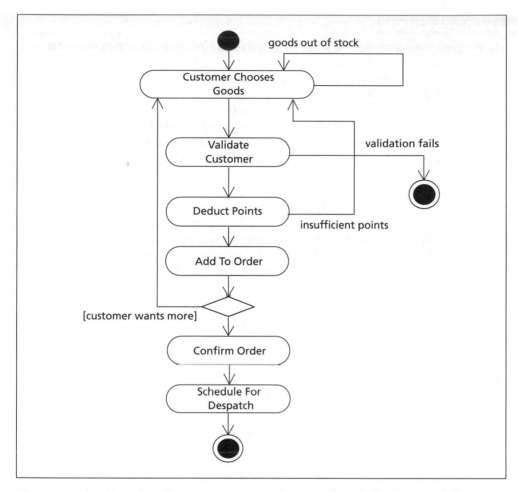

Figure 8.27   Workflow for customer ordering goods from ICANDO retail promotions

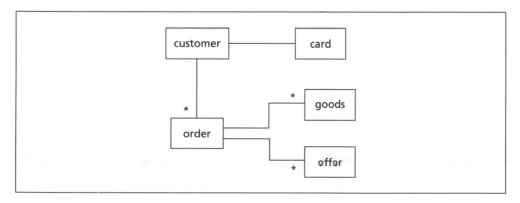

Figure 8.28   Business object model for ICANDO retail promotions

REVIEW QUESTIONS

1. Why should you spend a lot of time studying the business environment before beginning to specify a computer system?
2. What is a business process map?
3. What is a scenario?
4. What is the primary path for a process?
5. Why is the primary path sometimes known as the happy path?
6. What is the best way of dealing with an alternative path?
7. What is the difference between an exception path and an alternative path?
8. What is the basic analysis process?
9. What are UML activity diagrams for?
10. What is an activity in a UML activity diagram?
11. What is a transition in a UML activity diagram?
12. What triggers a transition in a UML activity diagram?
13. What is the difference between an activity and a state in a UML activity diagram?
14. What are swimlanes for in a UML activity diagram?
15. How are decisions placed in a UML activity diagram?

EXERCISES

1. Produce a process map for the ICANDO oil trading operation.
2. Produce a process map for the ICANDO/NeverShut retail outlet system.
3. Choose a process from the oil trading operation and produce a primary and alternative path scenario analysis. Produce an activity diagram to describe the process, and provide process catalogue entries for the goal, criticality, preconditions and business actors.
4. Choose a process from the ICANDO/NeverShut retail outlet system and produce a primary and alternative path scenario analysis. Produce an activity diagram to describe the process, and provide process catalogue entries for the goal, criticality, preconditions and business actors.

CHAPTER 9

Requirements Analysis

IN THIS CHAPTER YOU WILL LEARN:

1. **About UML use case diagrams**
2. **About functional modelling with use cases**
3. **How use cases fit into business modelling**
4. **About non-functional requirements and a way of recording them**
5. **How to describe use cases**

At last we come to some 'computer' models! Everything we have met so far covers the business context, which is an important precursor to the development of use cases. The notations we have considered so far could have been used by the Ancient Romans to design their administrative systems. There has been a good reason for spending so much time on the context of the system. Use cases fit into business processes, and the best way of finding use cases is to understand those business processes. We shall also be looking at non-functional requirements that are an important aspect of system design, and you can only understand those if you understand the business context.

Requirements analysis is the stage at which the external behaviour of the system is initially defined, and linked into the business environment. It is the contract between the development team and the other stakeholders. By contract, I do not mean a written document, signed and witnessed, but an agreement (formal or informal) between all parties in a development – contracts do not depend on lawyers and finely written paperwork.

Figure 9.1 shows the key inputs and outputs of the requirements analysis activity. The stakeholders are going to be involved in the requirements gathering, and the analyst will use the information already gathered on stakeholders to plan the capture of the detailed functionality and other requirements. The business process map and business process descriptions will the the key starting point for identifying use cases, and will provide a lot of detail about the use cases. The output will be use case diagrams that group actors and use cases together, and use case descriptions that provide a detailed account of the way the system is to function. Prototypes of the graphical user interface (GUI) may be produced at this stage too.

We are going to centre requirements analysis on the notion of a use case. A use case is a 'meaningful interaction' with a computer system. If you have used the Internet to buy things, an example of a use case would be choosing something from an online catalogue, and another might be paying for the goods. There are

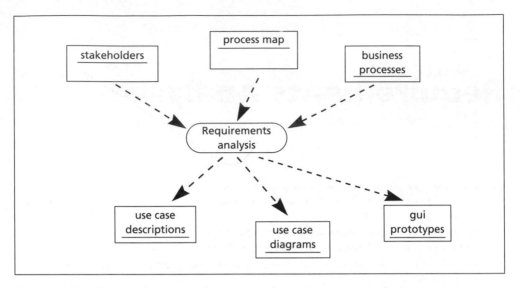

Figure 9.1 The key inputs and outputs of requirements analysis

various debates about the size and scope of a use case. We shall use the term to mean a transaction that can stand by itself and be completed in a single session with a computer system – a session with a computer system might invoke a number of use cases, some of them related to each other.

In fact, the notion of a use case is central to many leading development methods, such as the Unified Process. Development proceeds by identifying use cases, determining their interactions with the outside world, and then designing a set of objects to implement each use case. Systems analysis and design then becomes a process of 'use case elaboration', further refining the notion of a use case in terms that a developer can understand and translate into workable computer programs.

UML has extended the notion of a use case to incorporate the notion of a business process, discussed in Chapter 6. This seems to me to be a confusing notation, and not helpful. We shall not, for the rest of this book, consider a use case to be anything other than an interaction with a computer system.

Use case modelling is central to requirements definition and systems analysis. At the high level, a set of use case diagrams define the presentation of the system, and these are excellent tools for discussion with the stakeholders of a system, such as users and sponsors. At a more detailed level, use cases are used to fully specify the external functionality of a system, and are the starting point for designers, architects and developers involved in the construction of the system.

We shall be using scenario analysis, developing primary and alternative paths, to define the behaviour of use cases, in much the same way as we used it to define business processes. In fact, a use case is really just an automated business process, so that it is appropriate that the analysis method is similar. Thus, all the discussion of the 80/20 rule applies to the internals of use cases, just as it does to the mechanisms of a business process.

At the same time as collecting behavioural information, it is sensible to collect other project information about how a system is used. These are termed 'non-functional requirements', and they specify not so much what a system does, but the quality of the service it applies, such as how secure and reliable it is.

Use cases are a substantial part of the information required by developers to design and implement a system. We shall see later how we open up the scenario analysis using sequence diagrams and collaboration diagrams to further analyse the behaviour of the system and ultimately how the system is designed and constructed as a set of cooperating objects in a computer system.

Use case diagrams say 'what' a system does. The detailed analysis of use cases begins to say something of 'how' the system behaves in an environment. However, it does not say 'how' a system is structured internally to provide that behaviour. In computer system development you will frequently see this separation emphasized. Before you decide how a system works, you need to determine what it does first – a simple and obvious rule, but one so often forgotten, to many people's ultimate regret.

9.1 What Is a UML Use Case Model?

A use case model in UML consists of three key elements:

- **Actors**: people or things that use a computer system. An actor might be a clerk in a business, a manager, or even a customer accessing a system via the Internet. Other computer systems are also called actors. A banking system to which you send information might well be an actor in your system.
- **Use cases**: a use case is a meaningful piece of functionality provided by a computer system. It can be quite complicated. Examples would be printing invoices, accepting payment and ordering goods.
- **Relationships**: these are links between actors and use cases. Actors use use cases, and use cases can also use other use cases.

We draw a use case as an ellipse with the name of the use case underneath, as in Figure 9.2.

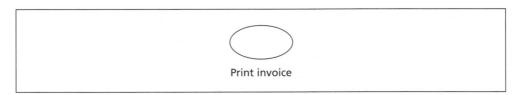

Figure 9.2 The UML notation for a use case to print an invoice

Sometimes the name is put inside, as in Figure 9.3 (overleaf).

The use case name is a concise, active description of the behaviour carried out by the use case, such as 'print invoice'. Do not write mini-essays to describe the behaviour of the use case – we shall use a more elaborate means for describing the behaviour in full. This is the sole notation for a use case in UML. All the details we shall use, such as primary and alternative path descriptions, are not part of UML: the language is very limited in this respect.

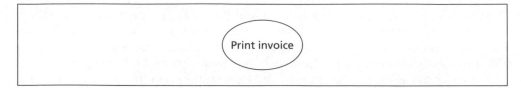

Figure 9.3 An alternative UML notation for a use case to print an invoice

Figure 9.4 The UML notation for an actor, an invoice clerk

An actor is drawn as a stick person, as in Figure 9.4. This is rather an unusual choice of notation when it is an external computer system, but you will get usèd to it. An actor is really a role, not a person. One person may use the system under many different roles. When finding actors, you are looking for the roles that people adopt, not the people or even the job titles, though job titles such as 'invoice clerk' are often descriptive of roles.

Relationships are drawn as lines connecting use cases and actors, as in Figure 9.5. This means that an actor uses the use case; in this instance an invoice clerk using some function to print an invoice. In any relationship there will be two-way communication. In this example, the invoice clerk may start up a screen that controls the print invoice, the system will prompt for a customer number, the clerk will provide it, the system will produce a list of items to be invoiced, the clerk will confirm, and then the system will produce the invoice.

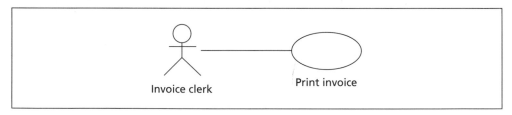

Figure 9.5 An association between an actor and a use case in UML

It is possible to use an arrow on the relationship, as in Figure 9.6. The direction of the arrow indicates who initiates the interaction, not the direction of flow of information. Usually in an interactive system it is the actor that initiates the dialogue, but it can be the use case. An example of a use case initiating an interaction would be when the system triggers interaction with another system, say to initiate a bank transfer.

A use case can use another use case. If you have a piece of well-defined functionality, it makes sense to reuse this wherever possible. There are two ways use cases can relate. The first is where a use case 'includes' another use case. In this case the

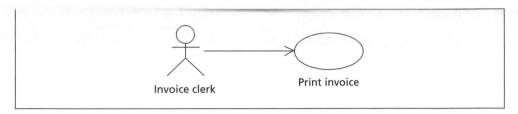

Figure 9.6 An association between an actor and a use case, indicating the direction of initiation

second use case is always invoked as part of the execution of the first. This is drawn with an arrow pointing to the use case that is included, with the label <<include>> tagged to the line, as in Figure 9.7. In this example, the order goods use case always incorporates a credit check. As a credit check is likely to be used in a number of places, it makes sense to split this out.

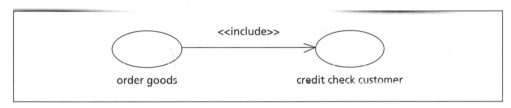

Figure 9.7 An includes relationship between use cases, where one use case always includes the behaviour of another

Sometimes a use case is only called occasionally from another use case. From the scenario analysis of the use case, this will often be to support an alternative path or an exception. We draw this with an arrow pointing the other way (yes, it is confusing at first, and no, I have never found a reasonable explanation) where the arrow points to the calling use case. So in Figure 9.8, the chase payment use case sometimes calls the issue warning letter use case, but not always.

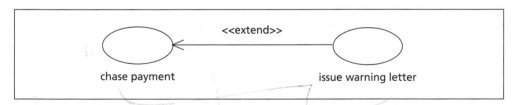

Figure 9.8 An extends relationship where one use case extends another use case, the extender being sometimes called by the extended

So now we have the building blocks for a description of a system's external behaviour. Let us look now at an application that manages payments for customers, as in Figure 9.9. A credit controller might be able to print invoices, chase payments, process payments, correct invoices, correct deliveries and register bad debts using a computer system. Part of chasing payment may involve

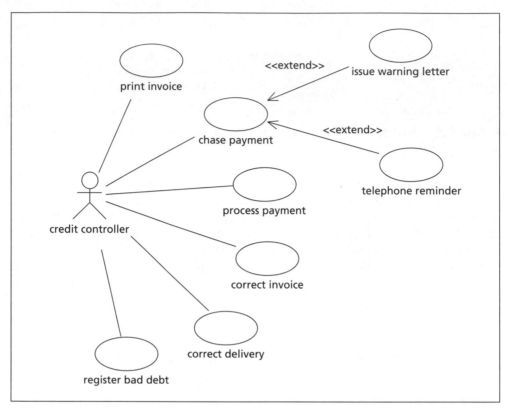

Figure 9.9 A use case diagram showing the functionality available to a credit control clerk

either issuing warning letters, where the computer system prints one off, or telephoning the customer, where the computer system provides a means of the controller logging the results of the conversation.

With a use case diagram like the one in Figure 9.9, you are getting a clear picture of who uses a system, and what they can do with it. You have also forced some decisions and provided some external structure to the system.

9.1.1 FINDING USE CASES

The first stage of analysis is to map out the business using:

- A high-level process map that breaks a business down into a simple three-level hierarchy of processes.
- Scenario analysis of business processes, using primary and alternative path analysis.
- Construction of business process workflows from the scenario analysis, described using UML activity diagrams.

Once you have a business process fully defined, you go around all the steps in the primary, alternative and exception paths asking the simple question, 'Is there a potential use of the computer system here?'. Sometimes you may need no system support in an activity in a business process, sometimes you may need just one use case, and sometimes many use cases are needed for a particular business activity.

You should now be beginning to see the a method of analysis emerging. It starts in the business arena, describing the business in some detail. Then it starts to think about where computer systems are used. The first thing to worry about is what the system does and how it fits in to the business, not how it does it in detailed technical terms.

Some methods approach requirements gathering by listing the potential users and considering the things they do. This is fine for simple systems. However, in my experience, simply determining the use cases from potential users of the system tends to miss out some important use cases in the first analysis. The key advantage of the approach using business processes for identifying use cases is that it forces the analyst to fully consider the environment of the system before making decisions about the system functionality. It also tends to produce a richer set of use cases in the first pass.

9.2   Non-Functional Requirements

You will regularly come across the notion of functional and non-functional requirements. Basically, functional requirements specify what a system does, and non-functional requirements say things about how well it does it. Use cases specify functionality, but they can also be used as a means of collecting and recording non-functional requirements too. We shall consider some of the typical non-functional requirements that might be imposed on a system.

Capturing the non-functional requirements at the use case definition stage is a good checkpoint. Different non-functional requirements may apply to different use cases; there may be different impacts of non-availability of a system for example. Non-functional requirements can easily be missed, but they can scupper the project after deployment. A system that is intended for a thousand users, but which works beautifully for only a hundred is no use.

9.2.1   SCALABILITY

The scalability of a system or a use case tells how many times this may be used at one go. This factor is something that has grown particularly relevant with the advent of Internet applications, where the potential concurrent users of a system can amount to thousands or, in extreme cases, tens of thousands. One company I know produces Internet ticket sales systems for major events, and they often have to produce a system that will sell many thousands of tickets in a few hours when some concerts become available.

The scalability requirement is going to affect the design and the implementation significantly. Hugely scalable applications will often need multiple processors to support them, and the designers will have to consider the need to distribute multiple processes. The architecture for a highly scalable application is more complicated than for an application that is only used by a small number of users.

Parts of a system can have different scalability requirements. The use cases that run for a credit control department may only ever have a small number of instances at any one time, as there is a clear physical limit on the number of people adopting the role of credit controller. Use cases in the same system that provide online ordering may need to operate for hundreds or thousands of concurrent users, depending on the application.

9.2.2 SECURITY

The data held by a company is precious. Few companies today could survive a loss of all their data. Moreover, the information that companies hold about their clients is sensitive, and disclosure could lose business or involve the company in litigation. The access to the system therefore needs to be secure.

Different levels of security are applicable, depending on the functionality. It is therefore appropriate to capture the level of security through use cases. Mostly a use case will be restricted to a set of users that are able to adopt the role of the actor officially linked to the use case. Designers will need to ensure that use cases work only for trusted users.

Use cases may involve the transmission of data over public networks. This has become increasingly the case with the growth of the Internet, not only for consumer to business transactions but also for business to business transactions. This introduces additional requirements to prevent the reading of information transmitted by third parties and fraudulent communications by third parties.

9.2.3 CRITICALITY

The criticality of a use case states how important that use case is. A company might be able to tolerate not running its general ledger for days or weeks, but if it cannot take and process orders for more than a day or so it can quickly get into financial difficulties and face loss of business from disappointed customers. Criticality therefore measures the impact of losing a use case.

Knowing the criticality, the designer or project manager can then build in means of quickly recovering a system so that a business can continue to operate. At the design level, data replication might be one strategy adopted to quickly recover from accidental loss of data. From an operations standpoint, companies also have disaster recovery plans to restore their core processes in the face of dramatic problems, such as a fire in a building.

9.2.4 FREQUENCY OF USE AND RESPONSE

How often a use case is fired is going to have a big impact on the design of the use case. A use case that fires once a day need not be too efficient. One that fires hundreds or thousands of times an hour needs to be as efficient as possible. Knowing the frequency of use helps designers and implementers know how much effort needs to go into optimizing the code.

The response time of some use cases is critical, particularly in real-time applications. There is an unwritten rule that interactive systems should respond in a couple of seconds maximum, but for a process control system a response might be required in milliseconds.

Optimizing code is a lengthy and expensive business. The maxim for design is not to consider optimization unless it is absolutely needed. Well-designed code should be reasonably efficient, but the tricks necessary to make systems respond rapidly require a high degree of skill and effort, and thorough testing.

9.2.5 USABILITY

The usability of a system is important in terms of its efficient deployment and the acceptability of the system. Usability varies from one type of user to the next. There are general guidelines for good user interface design, but there are no better experts on usability than the user community themselves.

Applications that are open to the public over the Internet need to consider the user who is not trained to use the system, and who wants to use it with the minimum of fuss. Developers of this kind of software soon learn guiding principles, such as that most Internet shoppers do not want to provide any information before they have browsed a catalogue and are ready to buy.

Applications that are used by skilled and trained staff often have different requirements. In a call centre, agents do not like using a mouse a great deal, and would prefer to navigate around the system using the keyboard as much as possible. They also like cluttered screens with lots of detail, and they like to memorize shortcuts to get around the system quickly.

The best way to assess usability is by prototyping of interfaces and careful beta-testing of products with representative sets of users.

9.2.6 RELIABILITY

My Ph.D. work was on the reliability of distributed systems. Looking at the complexity of modern systems, the fact that they work at all seems almost a miracle. That they tend to work, on the whole, reliably, is truly amazing. As with performance, building in reliability is expensive. Fortunately, today the mechanical and electronic aspects of systems are much more reliable than they were ten or more years ago. If not, the highly interdependent networks we have would fail too regularly for them to be useful.

Reliability covers availability, recovery from errors and accuracy. Of course, everyone wants systems that are 100% available and work properly all the time. However, lower levels of reliability usually have to be tolerated.

At the point of determining use cases, it is worthwhile discriminating between the use cases that need to be highly reliable and those that can tolerate a small amount of unreliability. An Internet bank, for example, will want to keep its account systems over the Internet online and accurate, but it may tolerate delays to internal reports. Critical process control systems often need some of their use cases to work to failure tolerances of once in a thousand years or better, and for there to be fallback routines on a failure to prevent catastrophe.

9.2.7 OTHER NON-FUNCTIONAL REQUIREMENTS

As you capture requirements, other non-functional requirements may occur that have not been anticipated in the above. Perhaps there is a need to access the system remotely for some use cases, or maybe the system has to function in a hostile environment. The potential list of non-functional requirements is endless.

9.3 Describing Use Cases

The high-level use case diagrams above are fine for a 'mile high' view of the computer system's behaviour. For many stakeholders, such as sponsors and managers, this will be enough. However, the analyst who thinks the job is done has a rude awakening. Once you have defined the use cases at the high level, a lot of work is necessary to open these up and define them in detail. It is now time to land the helicopter and work at ground level.

The notation we are following here is not UML. There is no prescription in UML regarding what information is recorded about a use case at this level. It is possible, as we shall see later, to use other UML diagrams to describe a use case, but the UML diagrams are lacking in some descriptive power.

Now we know what the system presents to the various users (or actors), we need to define in fine detail the 'how' of that interaction. Use cases are defined as detailed sequences of behaviour. The exact same process for opening up a business process can be used to elaborate a use case. You organize the sequences as primary and alternative paths. The primary path for correcting a billing problem for a customer by a customer service agent might be:

1. Enter the customer number.
2. Display the customer details (name and address etc.).
3. Check the customer's password and click on 'validated'.
4. Retrieve the last statement for the customer.
5. Scroll to the line item the customer is querying.
6. Agent decides to give a credit, so presses the 'credit customer' button.
7. Enter the credit amount.
8. Click on the 'confirm' button.

If we then look for alternatives, we might find that there is an interesting alternative to entering a credit amount, where the agent is not allowed to give more than a set limit, so an alternative might be:

   7.1   Credit amount over agent's permitted limit, so:
         7.1.1   Put up a screen asking for a manager's authorization code.
         7.1.2   Agent calls over manager.
         7.1.3   Manager enters authorization code.
         7.1.4   Code accepted, so continue to 8.

Detailing use cases in this way is essential to prevent vagueness later in the analysis and design process. This level of description is very suitable for showing to the users of the system.

Use cases are usually documented in a word processor. Using a set format for the use cases makes the collection and organization straightforward. A possible format for a use case is shown in Figure 9.10.

At the time of collecting the use case functional requirements from stakeholders, it is sensible to collect non-functional requirements as well. A well-designed use case format will provide a check list for analysts to make sure that the maximum information is collected. You may wish to extend the use case description to incorporate checks for the types of non-functional requirement that you consider important to the system.

An example use case description

Figure 9.11 shows a simple example of a use case description. In a real life application, these descriptions can run to many pages, covering lots of detail in the interaction and lots of alternatives.

Use case number:	Use case name:
Goal:	
Brief description:	
Actors:	
Frequency of execution:	
Scalability:	
Criticality:	
Other non-functional requirements:	
Primary path:	
Use cases related to primary path:	
Alternatives:	
Use cases related to alternatives:	
Exceptions:	
Use cases related to exceptions:	
Notes:	

Figure 9.10   A use case description format

9.3.1 ACTIVITY DIAGRAMS TO DESCRIBE USE CASES

The behaviour of a use case is sometimes complicated. To describe the behaviour graphically, you can use an activity diagram to draw out the primary and alternative paths. Sometimes a number of activity diagrams will be necessary to describe a use case.

9.4 Prototyping

A prototype is a quickly constructed demonstration of part of a system, to prove or illustrate a point. A user interface prototype is very valuable during requirements analysis for getting everyone in the project to visualize the way the system is going to work. These are very useful, and should be used regularly. There are many tools today that allow for quick construction of user interfaces. Internet tools are fine for a variety of purposes, as are simple PC database packages.

Prototypes should be quick and cheap to implement, and are done for a single purpose. They need not be done using the tools that will be used for the final delivery. Often the tools used for final delivery are too complicated for prototyping interfaces.

Prototypes should be thrown away when they have served their purpose. It is tempting to adapt them into the final product, but generally this is not a good idea.

Use case number: 99	Use case name: Browse Catalogue
Goal: Produce invoice for a customer	
Brief description: The customer will browse through the catalogue of shoes.	
Actors: Estimated 100 hits per day within 3 months, rising to 1000 within a year.	
Frequency of execution: Estimated 100 hits per day within 3 months, rising to 1000 within a year.	
Scalability: Up to 100 concurrent users expected	
Criticality: Very. Without the Web site available, the company is not selling.	
Other non-functional requirements: None identified.	

Primary path:
The following sequence is carried out for every customer on the sales ledger who has not been billed in the last month:
  1. Get sales items from the sales ledger.
  2. Get customer details from the customer file, covering billing address details.
  3. Get any credits that the customer has.
  4. Get discount details for customer.
  5. Print the invoice header.
  6. Print the line items on the invoice.
  7. Calculate any discounts.
  8. Apply any credits.
  9. Calculate and print the invoice total.
  10. Calculate and print the VAT.
  11. Mark items on sales ledger as invoiced.	

Use cases related to primary path: None	
Alternatives: 2.1 No customer details on customer file, so print an error message on a report. Do not mark the items on the sales ledger as invoiced. The message needs to detail the sales items that have been entered.	
Use cases related to alternatives: Invoicing error report	
Exceptions: None	
Use cases related to exceptions: None	
Notes: Created by Ken Lunn, 14 August 2001	

Figure 9.11   An example of a use case description

9.5 The Outputs of Requirements Analysis

You now have a very powerful set of tools to analyse a business and analyse how a system will support a business. The results of a requirements analysis are:

- A goal analysis
- A stakeholder analysis
- A business process map
- Detailed scenario analysis of the business areas where a system is being considered for development
- Activity diagrams to describe the business processes
- A set of top-level use case diagrams
- A set of detailed use case descriptions
- A set of user interface prototypes

The production of the requirements analysis is the time to get the stakeholders to agree. A business case will have been made before this. Some estimation will have to be done on how much the system will cost. So the requirements model is just part of the overall project model.

A use case catalogue will be developed throughout the requirements analysis, and this will be a substantial document. It is a living, evolving set of documentation that is essential for developers in the careful construction of systems.

9.6   ICANDO Bulk Chemical Ordering

The starting point for identifying use cases is the business process. We shall consider the telephone order process, shown in Figure 9.12. If we work through the steps in the process then we will come across candidate use cases. We can tabulate these as in Table 9.1.

There might be some debate as to whether Validate Customer should be a separate use case or just a step in the normal order-taking use case. As most calls into a call centre involve some validation of the caller, it makes sense to separate this out as an individual use case. The order entry use case then needs to have as a precondition that the customer has been validated.

The Check Product Code use case is more debatable. It may well be just a step in the Enter Order Details use case. We will keep it as a separate use case at this point, as there just might be some other call for it as a separate piece of functionality. If not, it should be merged back in as a use case step. As it is separated out, it will be an included use case for the Enter Order Details use case.

Table 9.1   Candidate use cases for the ICANDO Chemicals telephone ordering process

Process step	Candidate use case
Validate Customer	Validate Customer
Check Number with Customer	None
Take Order Details	Enter Order Details
Check Product Code	Check Product Code
Request Delivery Date	Assign Delivery Date
Transfer Call	Transfer Call

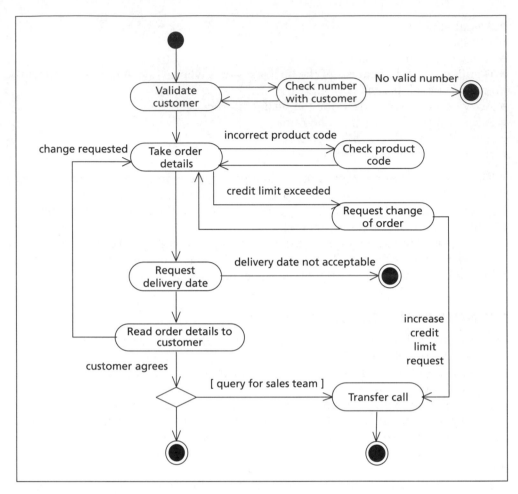

Figure 9.12 Workflow for the telephone order process

Assign Delivery Date again could be just a step. For the same reasons as Check Product Code, we will keep this as a provisional use case. There may be an option to leave the delivery date unassigned and for the date to be assigned at some other stage.

Transfer Call is a dubious use case. It might be nice if the system could transfer the current call to another desk with the customer's details. Some customer service packages have this facility. Again, it is decided to keep it, but to note that it may not be essential.

9.6.1 USE CASE DIAGRAM

We thus come to a use case diagram as in Figure 9.13. The role of the actor is as order taker. The separated out use cases for checking the product code and assigning a delivery date are linked as includes as part of the order-taking use case.

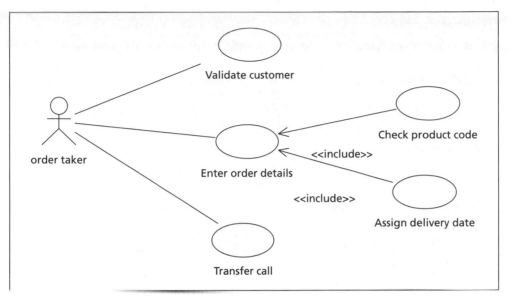

Figure 9.13   Use cases to support the telephone ordering process

9.6.2 USE CASE DESCRIPTIONS

We then complete use case descriptions for each of the use cases. Figures 9.14 and 9.15 are completed use case descriptions for two of the above use cases. As you can see, there is a good deal of information to gather. There is also a fair bit of creativity and design in terms of the process of defining the use case.

9.6.3 DISCUSSION

An application the size of the ICANDO Chemicals system would consist of hundreds of use cases. Some of these would be for operation in the call centre. Others would be for items such as management reporting. The process of defining the use cases and the descriptions would be lengthy, and the use case descriptions would go through a number of revisions before acceptance.

Careful cataloguing of the use cases will be needed, as well as cross-referencing back to the requirements. Careful control on the different versions of the use cases is needed, and for a project this large there would need to be some authorization procedure for the acceptance of a use case description prior to design and construction.

With a project of this size, even if a 'big bang' deployment is considered, the use cases, and the design and construction, need to be undertaken iteratively in small mini-projects. The overall map of the use cases will change in a small way as the project learns more about requirements. There will also be learning from the construction in terms of how easy or hard certain types of function will be.

Use case number: 33	**Use case name:** Validate Customer

Goal: Ensure that a customer is valid before other functions for the customer are carried out.

Brief description: This use case is applied whenever someone calls the call centre. It checks that there is a valid customer. Some calls may be handled without validation, but the norm for other use cases will be that this use case must have fired successfully.

Actors: any call centre staff authorized to deal with customer queries

Frequency of execution: The call centre takes approximately two thousand calls a day, and it is planned to take up to four thousand.

Scalability: The peak number of agents expected is 500

Criticality: This must run successfully for every call that involves orders or other customer service other than simple information. Therefore, highly critical.

Other non-functional requirements: None identified.

Preconditions: None

Postconditions: The customer number is recorded as valid for the duration of the call.

Primary path:
1. Customer supplies customer number and clerk types this in at the screen.
2. System responds with the customer name and address, and a unique password for the customer.
3. The operator asks for confirmation of the name and address and the password, and clicks a check box if the answers given conform to the data on the screen.

Use cases related to primary path: None

Alternatives:
1.1 Customer does not have a customer number to hand. The operator must ask the customer to find the number before proceeding.
2.1 The system cannot find a customer record for the customer number. A message is displayed to indicate this. The clerk must request the customer to check the number and if it is incorrect the use case can restart again at 1.
3.1 The customer cannot supply the name and address or the password. The clerk must close the call. The system must register the failed attempt to enable checks for fraud.

Use cases related to alternatives:
None

Exceptions:
If the system is unavailable, the clerk must take the name and telephone number of the customer, and call them back as soon as the system is back online.

Use cases related to exceptions:
None

Notes:
None

Figure 9.14 Use case description for Validate Customer

Use case number: 34	**Use case name:** Enter Order Details

Goal: Capture order details for a customer.

Brief description: Allows the clerk to enter the details of the order. Order details need to be checked against the product list, and to fit within the credit limit and contract of the customer.

Actors: Any call centre staff authorized to deal with customer sales.

Frequency of execution: The call centre takes approximately two thousand calls a day, and it is planned to take up to four thousand. Two thirds of these calls will be for orders.

Scalability: The peak number of agents expected is 500

Criticality: This must run successfully for every call requesting an order. Therefore, highly critical.

Other non-functional requirements: None identified.

Preconditions: The customer must have been validated.

Postconditions: The order must have been recorded, and a delivery date confirmed with the customer. A log entry is made on the customer contact details, indicating the order number if the order is completed, or a reason for abandoning the order if the order is not completed.

Primary path:
1. Customer supplies product code and quantity, and the clerk types this on the screen. This is repeated as often as necessary.
2. The customer requests a particular delivery date, and the clerk types this in. The system confirms this is acceptable.
3. The clerk reads the order and the delivery date back to the customer, who agrees.
4. The clerk hits the confirm button, and the system responds saying that the order has been accepted. The clerk thanks the customer and asks if there is any other service needed.

Use cases related to primary path:
1. Check Product Code
2. Assign Delivery Date

Alternatives:
1.1 Customer does not have a product code to hand, but does know the product name. The system should allow the entry of a product name instead of a product number, and then retrieve the product number.
2.1 The system cannot meet the requested delivery date, but offers a nearby one. The customer may accept the nearer one, or suggest a different date. This can continue until a mutually acceptable date is found.
3.1 The customer spots an error, and the clerk must change the detail.
4.1 The order exceeds the customer's credit limit, or includes a product not scheduled on the contract. This must be relayed to the customer, and corrective action agreed.
At any point, the order may be abandoned. This happens in a small number of cases. On exit, the clerk must choose from a set of reasons for abandoning the order, or write a reason for abandonment if there is not a prescribed reason.

Figure 9.15   Use case description for Enter Order Details

Use cases related to alternatives: 1.1 Check Product Code 2.1 Assign Delivery Date	
Exceptions: None identified	
Use cases related to exceptions: None	
Notes: None	

Figure 9.15 *(continued)*

9.7 ICANDO Site Safety System

The site safety system is very different from the chemicals system. The actual functions of the system are far fewer, and we shall have a smaller number of use cases. However, the use cases themselves will be more complicated. In analysing the business context of the site safety system, it is hard to find much in terms of business workflows. Therefore, instead of looking at the workflows, we can look at the process map to inspect for use cases; see Table 9.2. From this list, the use case diagram in Figure 9.16 has been devised.

Table 9.2 Processes and process steps and the supporting use cases for the site safety system

Process/process step	Use case
Add Feature	Add Feature, Move Feature
Set Location	Move Feature
Set Dimensions	Set Feature Details
Set Material	Set Feature Details
Set Stored Materials	Set Feature Details
Change Feature	
Change Location	Move Feature
Change Dimensions	Set Feature Details
Change Material	Set Feature Details
Check Site	Check Site
Check Facility Specification	Check Facility
Check Safety Distances	Check Distances
Update Rules	Load Regulations

9.7.1 USE CASE DIAGRAM

This is probably sufficient for the whole system. This use case map has been devised with some intuition as to how the system will operate. For example, the

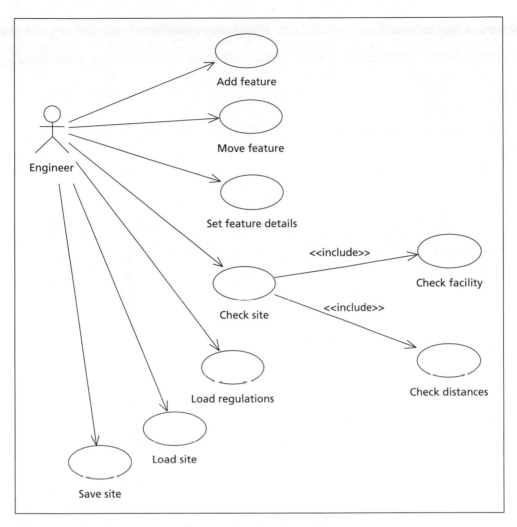

Figure 9.16   The use case diagram for the site safety system

use case to locate an object will probably involve dragging the object around the screen. The filling in of details will best be done by a form. Some experience suggests that a saving of the site details to disk and loading of site details from disk would be sensible in addition to the ones identified from the business processes.

9.7.2   USE CASE DETAILS

In elaborating the use case details, these have become a little more detailed in the descriptions in terms of how the system operates, as in Figures 9.17 and 9.18. The textual descriptions are not in themselves too clear without some screen defini-tion. The screen definitions need to be drawn up, and something like the defini-tion in Figure 9.19 should suffice at this stage. This shows a drawing screen with icons for the features on the left-hand side. A menu system is implemented on the

Use case number: 1	Use case name: Add Feature

Goal: To add a feature to a site.
Brief description: The engineer can add a feature by clicking on an appropriate icon for the feature, or by choosing from a drop down menu on the top of the screen.
Actors: Site engineer.
Frequency of execution: Each time a new feature is added or new regulations are added for a site.
Scalability: Not applicable.
Criticality: This can be done by paper and pencil if necessary.
Other non-functional requirements: None identified.
Preconditions: The site must have been created or loaded from disk.
Postconditions: The feature should be stored in the local repository.
Primary path: 1. Engineer clicks on an icon. The cursor changes. 2. Engineer drops the icon on the backdrop. 3. The system records the location of the object.
Use cases related to primary path: None
Alternatives: None
Use cases related to alternatives: None
Exceptions: None identified
Use cases related to exceptions: None
Notes: None

Figure 9.17   Use case description for Add Feature in the site safety system

top. To create a feature, the user clicks on an icon, moves to the correct place in the drawing area, and drops it on the background.

9.8   ICANDO Retail Petrol Promotions

For the customer loyalty system, we can take one of the processes and look for use cases there. Considering the steps in the Rewards/Exchange for Goods process, we might come up with the list of use cases indicated in Table 9.3.

Use case number: 5	**Use case name:** Check Distances

Goal: To apply the regulations and check safety distances between site features, reporting on any problems.
Brief description: The engineer will request the checking of the site by clicking on an icon or choosing from a menu.
Actors: Site engineer.
Frequency of execution: Each time a new feature is added or new regulations are added for a site.
Scalability: Not applicable.
Criticality: This can be done by paper and pencil if necessary.
Other non-functional requirements: None identified.
Preconditions: The site must have been created or loaded from disk.
Postconditions: A report of the safety distances is displayed.

Primary path:
1. Engineer clicks on the icon or chooses from the drop-down menu.
    For each facility
    2. The facility is selected.
        For each of the other facilities
        3. The second facility is selected.
        4. The rule base is searched for anything that pairs the two facilities.
        5. The distance between the facilities is calculated and compared with the rule restrictions.
        6. If there is a rule violation, the rule, facility details and distances are reported.

Use cases related to primary path: None
Alternatives: None
Use cases related to alternatives: None
Exceptions: None identified
Use cases related to exceptions: None
Notes: None

Figure 9.18   Use case description for Check Distances in the site safety system

Use case diagram

The resulting use case diagram is shown in Figure 9.20. This has been shown from the customer's perspective, interacting through the Web site. Note that the logic of

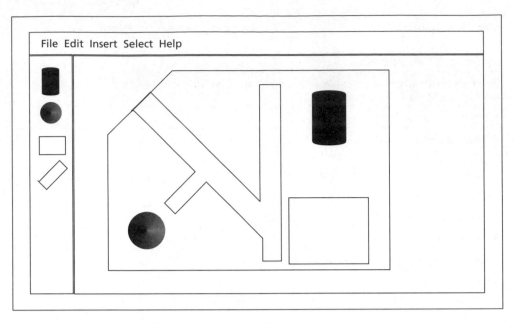

Figure 9.19 Layout of the site safety main screen

Table 9.3 Use cases for the process steps in the customer loyalty system

Process step	Use case
Customer examines catalogue and chooses (paper catalogue or Internet catalogue)	Display Web Site
Customer is validated	Validate Customer
Points value of goods deducted from customer balance	Adjust Points
Goods added to order	Browse Catalogue, Add to Order
Order confirmed with customer	Confirm Order
Order scheduled for despatch	Schedule Despatch
Goods out of stock, so advise customer and resume at 1	Check Stock
Insufficient points, so advise customer, who can resume at 1 or exit	Insufficient Points
Customer cancels order, so reassign points and exit	Cancel, Adjust Points
Customer wants to change order. Can deselect goods and resume at 1, with points being returned to balance	Adjust Points

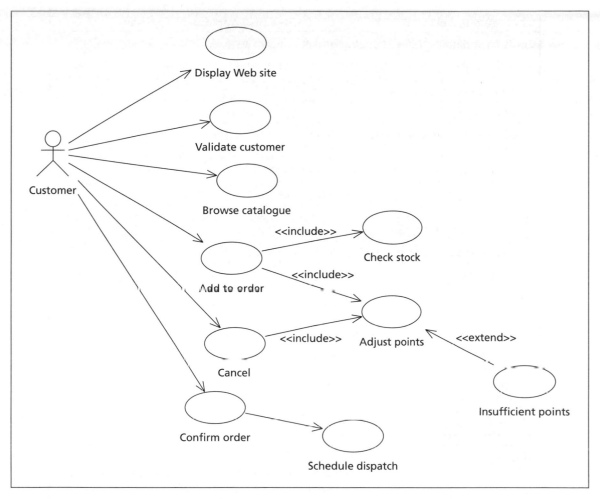

Figure 9.20   Use case diagram for part of the customer loyalty system

the operation of the interface has not been specified by this diagram. Some of that will come in the preconditions and postconditions of the various use cases.

Use case descriptions
See Figures 9.21 and 9.22.

Use case number: 7	**Use case name:** Add To Order

Goal: To add items to the shopping basket.

Brief description: When the customer has arrived at a particular item in the catalogue that she wishes to order, she clicks on the order button next to the item and the item is added to the shopping basket.

Actors: Customer

Frequency of execution: It is expected that the number of orders through the web site will rise to about 100,000 per year within two years of operation.

Scalability: Mostly there will only be a maximum of 100 people using the system at any one time, but if there are special promotions through email it might be reasonable to expect up to 1,000 users concurrently ordering.

Criticality: It will not stop the business if the system is unavailable, but it will damage customer loyalty if this happens too often.

Other non-functional requirements: None identified.

Preconditions: Customer must have logged in and been validated.

Postconditions: Item added to shopping basket.

Primary path:
1. The customer clicks on the order button next to the item on the catalogue page.
2. The system confirms that the product is in stock.
3. The system deducts points from the customer's account.
4. The system pops up an 'add to shopping basket' confirmation box.
5. The customer clicks OK.
6. The item is added to the shopping basket.

Use cases related to primary path: None

Alternatives:
2.1 The item is out of stock, so pop up an 'out of stock' message and quit the use case.
3.1 The customer has not got enough points, so pop up an insufficient points message and quit the use case.
4.1 The customer cancels the order, so quit the use case.

Use cases related to alternatives: Check Stock and Adjust Points.

Exceptions:
None

Use cases related to exceptions:
None

Notes:
None

Figure 9.21 Use case description for Add to Order in the retail promotions system

Use case number: 17	Use case name: Confirm Order
Goal: To confirm an order, create a record and schedule despatch.	
Brief description: Displays the shopping basket. The customer presses the confirm button. The order is created and despatch is scheduled.	
Actors: Customer	
Frequency of execution: As use case 7	
Scalability: As use case 7	
Criticality: As use case 7	
Other non-functional requirements: None identified.	
Preconditions: Customer must have logged in and been validated. There must be items in the shopping basket.	
Postconditions: An order is placed, and delivery is scheduled.	
Primary path: 1. Customer clicks on a button to confirm order. 2. The shopping basket is displayed. 3. The customer clicks on accept. 4. An order is created. 5. Despatch is scheduled.	
Use cases related to primary path: None	
Alternatives: 3.1 The customer wants to change the shopping basket, either by deleting an entry or changing the quantities ordered. Checks need to be made against points and stock, and the points adjusted accordingly. 3.2 The customer clicks on reject, or the page times out. The points deducted need to be re-credited to the customer.	
Use cases related to alternatives: Check Stock, Adjust Points	
Exceptions: None identified.	
Use cases related to exceptions: None	
Notes: None	

Figure 9.22 Use case description for Confirm Order in the retail promotions system

REVIEW QUESTIONS

1. **What are the primary inputs and outputs of requirements analysis?**
2. **What is a use case?**
3. **What is a non-functional requirement?**
4. **List some typical non-functional requirements.**
5. **Does a use case diagram specify the functionality of the system?**
6. **Are use case descriptions part of UML?**
7. **How can you link non-functional requirements to use cases?**
8. **How do you go about finding use cases?**
9. **What is an actor?**
10. **What does a relationship between an actor and a use case mean?**
11. **Does an arrowed relationship imply one-way communication?**
12. **What is the difference between an extend relationship and an includes relationship between use cases?**
13. **Does an actor correspond to a person?**
14. **What is the purpose of prototyping in requirements gathering?**

EXERCISES

1. In Table 9.2, the process step to remove a feature has been omitted. Add that step and a supporting use case. Produce a revised use case diagram to replace Figure 9.16. Then produce a use case description for the new use case.
2. Choose a process from the ICANDO oil trading system. Produce a list of process steps, and identify candidate use cases for each process step. Produce a use case diagram. Choose two use cases, and produce a use case description for each one.
3. Choose a process from the ICANDO/NeverShut retail outlet system. Produce a list of process steps, and identify candidate use cases for each process step. Produce a use case diagram. Choose two use cases, and produce a use case description for each one.

Buy, Build or Adapt

Before you build any IT system, it is important to consider whether it is appropriate to start from scratch, buy a solution, or buy part of a solution. Today the vast majority of business application developments utilize computer packages for part or sometimes all of their computer systems. The policy that most companies adopt today is to buy a package before building one. Only if the software package market cannot produce an adequate solution do they consider writing a software package. This has shifted the emphasis in many organizations away from pure development towards software integration with bespoke development primarily as a means of covering the gaps in the package market. The role of the IT developer in such organizations has changed in recognition of this.

In practice, most large organizations adopt a hybrid approach, using packages in some places and bespoke programs in others. They are also likely to have some well-established systems that could be replaced by packages, but where it is more economic to stay with the bespoke system and make changes to it where necessary. The challenge today is to make this mixed bag of software work coherently.

Most analysis and design texts focus on the construction of bespoke solutions. Hence the complaint that is commonly heard that object-oriented methods are only appropriate for greenfield applications. This is an understandable position to take, but it is wrong. If you were to commission an architect to build a major extension to an old building, you would not expect him to use the same technology as a medieval craftsman did. Just because a cathedral was originally designed with rough sketches and rules of thumb, it does not preclude the modern architect from using computer-aided design packages. Likewise, modern software development methods can be used as a way of enhancing existing systems.

UML models and other models that we have discussed so far can be used as part of the procurement process if systems are to be purchased rather than built. Business models can be used to scope where packages and bespoke developments fit in a hybrid approach. Often a package cannot meet all the functional requirements,

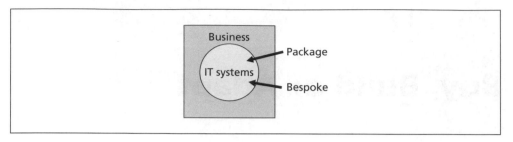

Figure 10.1   Fitting packages or bespoke systems into the business context

and it will be necessary to extend the package, when analysis and design methods that we will discuss later will come to the fore.

Figure 10.1 illustrates the issue of embedding systems in a business context, and shows the importance of understanding the business context before making the decision. It is the business requirements that determine the choice from a functional and quality perspective.

Packages come in many different forms. The simplest are single-function packages that solve a particular problem. For example, a common package in use today is one that looks up an address from a postcode. It has a well-defined function, and we might well incorporate the functionality as a use case that is included in other use cases as part of the requirements model.

The next level up of packages solves problems for a business area. An example would be the financial ledgers. All companies need to keep a tight track of money flows through the company. In the last two decades, hardly any company has written its own financial ledger packages. These packages are well defined, and often need little change to be adapted to a particular enterprise.

The largest form of package, known often as an Enterprise Resource Package, attempts to cover the majority of computing needs for a business. In reality, these are usually groups of tightly linked packages focused on different sectors of the business. Usually these packages come with some means of being adapted to cover gaps in the basic package.

No package solution, however, has achieved comprehensive coverage of a business sufficiently for any organization to simply unpack the package and go. There is always, it seems, some need for bespoke programming, either to add to the package functionality or to change some of its functionality.

The economics of packages are not straightforward. Licenses are usually costly, and much of the cost of deploying a package is the same as that of a bespoke solution. The cost of modifying a package is usually no less than the cost of building an equivalent bespoke feature. The reasons for choosing a package are often a mixture of quality, removal of risk of bespoke development, and speed of implementation.

If a package is not appropriate, then an organization needs to look at the software it already has. Usually that has an excellent control system around it for managing changes. Commonly this is known as legacy software, in a somewhat derogatory manner. However, the legacy usually works and has been adapted to an organization's needs over a number of years.

In recent years there have been a number of dramatic failures of replacement systems written using modern tools and techniques. Many a Cobol programming team has looked on with faintly suppressed glee as the great object-oriented project has collapsed with spectacular *Hindenburg* suddenness. To turn your back on a successful approach because it is not the latest method is folly in the extreme.

Some of the best successes in the e-commerce world have been hybrid solutions where a new Internet interface is grafted carefully onto a 15-year-old order-taking system. Judicious use of existing investments in IT is crucial to long-term success. Changing a computer system is not just about changing the boxes on people's desks; more often than not it is about changing the way people work, and that is costly.

Again, just as with packages, the notations and methods of requirements analysis can be used successfully. What we need to do in both cases is to define a boundary between the package or existing system, to define the new functionality, and to specify for the designers the way the systems can cooperate and share the tasks of the enterprise.

10.1 Packages and Procurement

Not long ago I had a dispute with some senior managers on the purchase of a package. They went along with what a supplier said their package did. It was very new and relatively untested. The supplier played a wonderful secrecy game, and convinced everyone that they had a unique proposition. My argument was that it was unsafe to buy something that was largely unknown without much more caution. The package was bought, and twelve months later the supplier refunded the substantial licence fee, but not until many crises had passed and a number of people had suffered damaged reputations, me included. Over lunch one day I told a senior manager of the supplier how amazed I was that my company had bought the package without more care, and I was told that rigorous assessment of packages was rarely done. Looking at their success at selling the same package to other large and reputable organizations, I began to realize he was right.

In jungle terms, this was a swamp. At one stage I was nostril-deep in it. In future I shall be much more sensitive to the squelching beneath my feet. However, it woke me up to a major issue. When it comes to buying computer packages, all the discipline of software development methods seems to fly out of the window. But there is a perfectly clear route through to assessing packages and selecting them that follows, to a large extent, all that is done in the development of requirements for bespoke systems.

Something that has amazed me is how little is written about software procurement when it is such a widespread activity. Amazon.com has barely half a dozen books listed under software procurement and nearly 3000 under software development. Maybe buying software is not sufficiently glamorous. In this dearth of written knowledge, a little of the process of procuring software is worth discussing.

10.1.1 SOME BASIC RULES FOR PROCUREMENT

Below are some valuable rules about purchase of software packages. Indeed, these can be applied to any IT purchase, be it software, hardware or consultancy. Though they seem common sense, they are often ignored.

Rule 1 – Know what you want

This may seem like a silly statement, but often at the inception of a project there is not a clear idea about what is needed. Package procurement should not start until a sound business analysis has been undertaken. Make sure you know the package market a little before you venture into talking to suppliers in some detail. Attend exhibitions, read information on the Internet, and gather as much documentation as you can about products before you start hinting that you are considering buying.

Rule 2 – Get the suppliers to work for you

Software vendors have huge budgets for sales. Most sales activities come to nothing. Of course, they will want to do the minimum they can to secure a sale, but if you are serious they will do a considerable amount of work for you. Clearly, this depends on the potential size of the sale, but if you are looking at a purchase costing tens or hundreds of thousands of euros, then there is no reason why the sales team should not be prepared to spend days or weeks answering your questions and supplying information in the form you want.

Rule 3 – Get the suppliers to talk in your terms

Suppliers have their own jargon. It can be impossible to map a package onto your business from the supplier's own documentation if you do not know the package in detail. Instead, it is better to get the supplier to show how their package fits your business by getting them to match the package to your defined business processes.

Rule 4 – See it before you buy it

Go and see someone who is using the package in anger. This again seems obvious, but a vast number of packages are bought on simple demonstrations. Demonstrations show functionality, but they do not illustrate issues such as scalability and reliability. Vendors usually have reference sites. There should also be a user group, and that user group should be a valuable source of information if you can gain access to it.

Rule 5 – Avoid paying for it before you know it will work

Unless you are 100% sure that the package will work, or the price is small, do not pay all of the purchase price until you are satisfied that the package will do the job it says it will. Either buy a small number of licences first, or agree a payment schedule based on successful deployment. Withholding money from a supplier is a good way of encouraging them to help you out quickly if a product problem arises.

Rule 6 – Don't buy from someone who will not be around for long

The supplier of a package will be needed to keep the package up to date. If the company who supplies the package is likely to disappear, then think twice about buying from them. An assessment of the stability and survivability of the supplier should be made before making a purchase.

10.1.2 REQUEST FOR INFORMATION (RFI)

A request for information is a formal request sent to a supplier to find out what the scope of their products is. It is a two-way communication process. The request is a statement of the organization's needs, in terms of functionality, and it asks questions about the quality of the supplier and its products. The response is the supplier's attempt to gain credibility. An RFI process usually involves lots of dialogue. An RFI might contain the following:

- A statement of the goals of the project intending to procure the system.
- A description of the business area where the system is required, perhaps described using business process maps and UML activity diagrams.
- Typical business scenarios that the package is expected to support.
- A statement of non-functional requirements, such as security, scalability and reliability.
- A request for financial and market information from the supplier, covering profitability and turnover, number of clients and number of licences sold.
- A request for reference sites.
- A request for prices, including maintenance charges and discount schedules for bulk purchases.

10.1.3 REQUEST FOR TENDER (RFT)

A request for tender is a more thorough document. The RFI will be sent to a broad range of potential suppliers. Once these are evaluated, a more thorough process of investigation is appropriate. At the end of it, the selected software should meet functional and non-functional requirements, fit into the technical architecture of the purchasing organization, and be supported by a cost–benefit analysis. Moreover, the supplier must be one that is reliable and that can support the package over the projected lifetime of its use.

The request for tender will repeat many of the questions of the request for information, but in more detail. More focus is required on the functional requirements, and the supplier should be asked to complete a rating of their package against the business requirements. At this stage, the purchaser should at least have produced a process map and scenario analysis of the business processes, and perhaps even a proposed use case mapping. A table such as Table 10.1 should be completed by the supplier. The supplier would be provided with the process names and a description of the process (probably the process scenarios). The module would be the supplier's product reference. The support level would be on some grade; the one I have found most straightforward is a Full/Partial/No support grade.

The request should also contain a request for a description of how the package would support some particular scenario. Table 10.2 shows a table filled in by a supplier to indicate how a package supports a process scenario.

Table 10.1 A process support table for an RFT

Process name	Module	Support level
Delivery	DVP023	Full support
Return of goods	DVP023	Partial support

Table 10.2 A process scenario rating table for package evaluation

Process step	Package support
1. Customer telephones call centre	Not applicable
2. The agent takes customer number and validates the customer on the system.	Module CC003 has full customer validation facilities to support this.
3. Customer provides order details and the agent enters them on the customer order form on the computer screen.	Module CC003 can be customized to support particular ordering requirements. Product details are maintained through the product suite PR001-PR0015
4. The customer provides a requested delivery date.	Module CC003 supports this if linked with distribution modules DS001-DS007
5. The system then validates the order and establishes whether the delivery can be made on that date. The system may offer a preferred alternative date that the customer can accept or reject.	As for previous step
6. The agent reads back the details of the order.	Not applicable
7. The customer agrees.	Not applicable
8. The call is closed.	Module CC003 will record the call details in the call log, with agent details. The order will be actioned.

The RFT document will supply blank tables for the supplier to fill in. We shall produce a comprehensive document for ICANDO Chemicals at the end of this chapter that can be used as a model.

10.1.4 DEMONSTRATOR PROJECT

Any major purchase of software should incorporate a demonstrator project. The demonstrator should tackle a serious part of the business activity, but not commit the organization to substantial expenditure on licenses, development or deployment. The demonstrator activity should not be long, perhaps three to six months maximum for large projects and much shorter for smaller projects. The demonstrator should be a reasonable sized sub-project that is going to be deployed and used.

The demonstrator is used to assess risk and recalibrate project plans and costings. In rare circumstances, it may cause a radical change in direction, say by causing the project to go back to the drawing board and find an alternative solution.

10.2 Package Software, Scoping and Gap Analysis

The Request For Tender information should be sufficient for the project team to assess the scope of a package. It would be exceptional for a package to cover all business needs straight from the box. The rating supplied in tables such as Tables 10.1 and 10.2 will provide a point for investigation to determine how much work is needed to modify the package or to add in additional components to make the package support the business.

A 'gap analysis' provides a list of items that the package does not support in relation to the requirements. This is the basis for decision-making on the choice of package, and for planning a package integration if it is selected.

10.3 Existing Software, Scoping and Gap Analysis

Existing software is a package. The only difference is that the organization probably knows a lot more about it than about other packages. It is perfectly viable to use the analysis tools outlined for packages to scope an internal system and to provide a gap analysis.

10.4 ICANDO Bulk Chemical Ordering – RFI

This is a sample from a typical Request For Information, based on the ICANDO Chemicals requirements. For a system this substantial and comprehensive, the document may run to fifty or more pages. Suppliers would normally invest a reasonable amount of effort responding to such a request, as the potential revenues are considerable. The purpose is to identify a short list of suppliers for a more detailed tender request.

10.4.1 INTRODUCTION

ICANDO Oil has consolidated its European bulk chemicals operations into a single operating company, ICANDO Chemicals. The restructuring has given opportunities for optimizing production and supply, rationalizing the various business units and improving quality of product and service. One of the cornerstones for achieving this will be a consolidated ordering system. The business currently has ordering systems implemented and maintained on a country-by-country basis. A phased replacement of these systems is required that can achieve, within a two-year time frame, a single European ordering system that will allow supply in any European state from any ICANDO Chemicals manufacturing unit or warehouse.

The timetable for decision-making will be

1. Issue of Request For Information – as dated on the covering letter.
2. Responses to RFI – plus one month
3. Short list of suppliers for tendering – plus two weeks
4. Issue of Request For Tender – plus two weeks
5. Responses to RFT – plus one month
6. Tender evaluation and selection – plus one month
7. Project initiation – plus one month.
8. Project demonstrator – plus three months.
9. Project development – phased over 12 months.

The schedule is very tight, but business requirements mean that a more protracted schedule will not be acceptable.

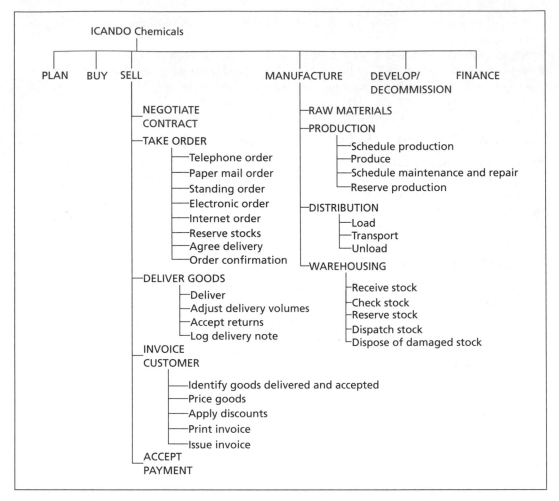

Figure 10.2 The business process map for ICANDO chemicals, focusing on the aspects relevant to the new sales order processing system

10.4.2 BUSINESS SCOPE

ICANDO Chemicals wants a new system to improve the sales process. In particular, we plan much tighter integration between sales and manufacture. By special discounting structures for advanced orders, it is planned to increase the number of deliveries direct from the production line to reduce transport and warehouse costs and the locking up of valuable working capital in stocks. Figure 10.2 shows a representative set of business processes. Additional details on the processes are provided in an appendix. The plan, buy, develop/decommission and finance processes are probably not relevant to the system, though we would be interested to know what your system offers in relation to these processes.

10.4.3 BUSINESS PROCESS SUPPORT

We have identified the following key processes that we would like the package to support. We would ask you to indicate how well your package will support these processes. Please supply product literature and indicate in your response which modules support which processes.

[Note that, in reality, this section would be very substantial, covering all the business processes where the package is being considered]

SELL/TAKE ORDER/Telephone Order
Figure 10.3 shows the workflow for the telephone order process. A more detailed definition of the process will be made available at the tender stage.

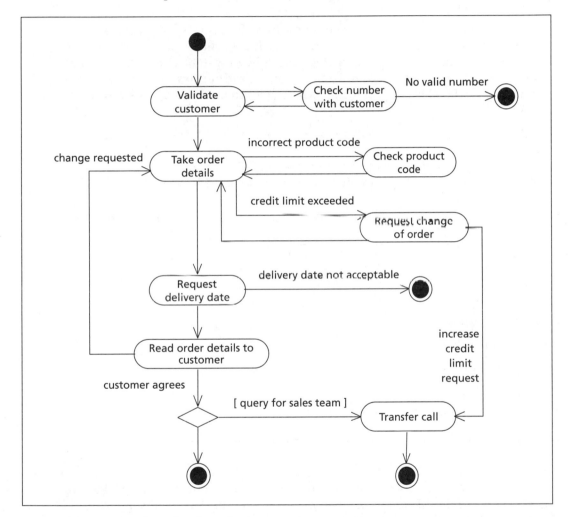

Figure 10.3   Workflow for the telephone order process

10.5 ICANDO Chemicals – RFT

This is a sample of a typical Request For Tender, based on the ICANDO Chemicals requirements. For a system this substantial and comprehensive, the document may run to hundreds of pages. Suppliers would normally invest a great deal of effort responding to such a request, as the potential revenues are considerable.

10.5.1 INTRODUCTION
As for RFI.

10.5.2 BUSINESS SCOPE
As for RFI, plus:

You are requested to address the overall business in terms of how your package would support this, and to address the detailed business processes outlined below. We would like you to complete the following table, indicating which modules of your package can be utilized to support the business process, and your estimate of the level of support for the package on the following basis (see Table 10.3):

- Full Support – all reasonable IT support is provided by the package for this business process.
- Partial Support – the package supports the process in part.
- No Support – the package has little or no support for this business process.

Table 10.3   The process support table for the RFI for the ICANDO Chemicals ordering system

Process Name	Module(s)	Support Level
PLAN		
BUY		
SELL/NEGOTIATE CONTRACT		
SELL/TAKE ORDER/Telephone Order		
SELL/TAKE ORDER/Paper Mail Order		
– etc. –		
MANUFACTURE/WAREHOUSING/Receive stock		
– etc. –		

10.5.3 BUSINESS PROCESS SUPPORT
We have identified the following key processes that we would like the package to support. We would ask you to indicate how well your package will support these processes. Please supply product literature and indicate in your response which modules support which processes.

[Note that, in reality, this section would be very substantial, covering all the business processes where the package is being considered]

SELL/TAKE ORDER/Telephone Order
As for RFI plus (Table 10.4):

Table 10.4 The process scenario rating table for the telephone ordering primary path for ICANDO Chemicals

Process step	Package support
1. Customer telephones call centre	
2. The agent takes customer number and validates the customer on the system.	
3. Customer provides order details and the agent enters them on the customer order form on the computer screen.	
4. The customer provides a requested delivery date.	
5. The system then validates the order and establishes whether the delivery can be made on that date. The system may offer a preferred alternative date that the customer can accept or reject.	
6. The agent reads back the details of the order.	
7. The customer agrees.	
8. The call is closed.	

REVIEW QUESTIONS

1. **What are the advantages and disadvantages of buying software instead of building it?**
2. **Is it cheaper to buy software rather than build it?**
3. **Is the process for buying software radically different from specifying software for construction?**
4. **What is an RFI?**
5. **What sort of things might you see in an RFI?**
6. **What is an RFT? How does it differ from an RFI?**
7. **What is a demonstrator project?**

EXERCISES

1. Produce a Request For Information document for the ICANDO Retail Promotions system, using the processes defined in the previous chapters.
2. Produce a Request For Tender document for the ICANDO Trading system.
3. Produce a Request For Tender document for the ICANDO/NeverShut retail system.

Object Concepts

1. **About the notions of object, attribute and operation**
2. **What a class is**
3. **About relationships between classes**
4. **About inheritance and aggregation relationships**
5. **How objects are grouped in class diagrams**

Object orientation has become the by-word for good software development practice. It is taught in the majority of universities, and the commercial world has taken on its mantle. Everything seems to be object-oriented. Even those things that should not be object-oriented have stolen the title in an attempt to gain from the kudos.

The computer industry has fads and fashions like any other industry. This particular fashion seems to have stuck, and this usually means that there is more than just a whim and preference behind it. There are lots of good software engineering principles behind the notion of object-oriented development, and there are a vast number of development tools and procedures to support it.

What does it mean, and why is it so important? Some of this goes back a long way in the history of computing. The first computer programs were a mish-mash of data and program, written in elementary computer languages known as machine code or assembler languages. These were difficult to produce. Very soon, however, programming languages were constructed that began to separate function and data. These languages grew in importance, power and comprehensiveness, as languages such as Cobol, Fortran, Pascal and C. They worked by taking in data, processing it, and outputting the data. They could be strung together to perform very complicated tasks.

The first great expansion of computing was in mass data processing. Orders were collected into long computerized lists. Overnight, these computerized order lists were transformed into delivery lists and delivery notes. Completed delivery notes were re-keyed into the computer, and overnight more long lists were transformed into invoices. And so the transformation went on, until finally the bank provided a computerized list of cleared payments that could be reconciled with the invoices by another overnight run. This was the heyday of batch processing, and it was an extremely efficient way of handling data. It is still in use today, and the majority of large businesses handle much of their sales processing in this way. Languages like Cobol are as efficient and effective at doing this as any other language, and arguably are better at the job than more modern languages like Java.

To build more complicated systems, however, the separation of data and processing became a block to productivity. The next generation of languages grouped processing and related data together. To produce the modern interactive systems you see today this was an almost essential step. Instead of dealing with lots of similar data in one go, systems are now expected to deal almost instantly with a set of related data on demand, instead of at some pre-scheduled period in the middle of the night. Imagine ringing a call centre, asking them to check a problem on your account, and them saying they would ring you back the next day when they had generated a printout.

Object-oriented languages first materialized in a form that a modern software engineer would recognize in about 1980. Smalltalk, a language first developed in the early 1970s, and a windowing system that looks remarkably similar to today's user environments, were released by Xerox. Since then, many object-oriented languages, such as C++ and Java, and windowing systems, such as the X Window System and Microsoft Windows, have emerged that are remarkably similar in many respects.

These languages and environments did not replace the batch systems, but complemented them. There is still a considerable amount of development using Cobol and similar technologies. The new languages and environments, however, facilitated a new style of computing that is the most evident to people, such as windowing environments and interactive systems.

Interactive systems can be written without the notion of objects, but objects are a more natural and productive way of developing interactive systems. An object is a well-defined grouping of data and processing that provides some clear service. A computer window is a prime example of an object; there is data describing its size and what it displays, and processing to allow it to change the display, accept information, and trigger other parts of the system to carry out tasks.

Two aspects of objects make them particularly useful for constructing systems quickly. Firstly, they can be linked together in a society to produce complex behaviour. Much of the design process we shall be considering will look at how this society can be organized to achieve a goal. Secondly, new objects can be derived from old objects, extending their behaviour. This is commonly known as inheritance. Thus, when a designer has produced a particular type of window, she can use that design as the basis for a new window with more behaviour.

A much touted feature of objects is that they are 'natural'. The argument is that within a computer system there are objects that correspond to real-world objects. Thus there will be a customer object to correspond to a customer in the real world. Then all the processing for customers and the data to represent customers are grouped together. This is, in fact, the way we will approach analysis. However, the construction of large-scale systems in this way is often infeasible, and we shall discuss the reasons why when we look at design. In fact, in most systems of any size, the notion of real-world entities such as a customer can be distributed widely about the system.

In this chapter we shall look at the key concepts behind object-oriented systems. Unlike the other key chapters in this book, it does not correspond to a stage in the development process. However, the concept is so fundamental from here on that it deserves separate treatment. You might note, however, that we have got a long way in the software development process without much of a need for objects, and that at this juncture you could well choose to go a different route with a development, and use non-object methods and implementation languages.

11.1 Objects

Objects are the building blocks of object-oriented systems. They are the smallest entity with significant behaviour. You might think of them as atoms or molecules, or the bricks in a building, or the parts of a car. They are made up of attributes that define their state and operations that define what they do or what can be done to them. Like atoms or bricks, objects are made of other bits, but the smaller bits have less value on their own.

The aim of an object-oriented analysis and design method is to identify an appropriate set of objects and to arrange them so that they can carry out tasks to implement use cases. This is what a builder does in constructing a house – a pile of bricks, tiles, timber, sand and cement is not much good until some organization is put into them.

Let us look at how an object is represented in UML. An object is drawn as a rectangle, as in Figure 11.1. The compartment is split into three parts. The top compartment contains the name of the object. This is always a noun or noun phrase that describes the object. The middle compartment contains a description of the data that defines the object. For this customer, we are storing the name, address and telephone number. These are called attributes. The bottom compartment defines the things the object can do. These are called operations. For this customer, all we can do is change the details.

Strictly, this notation is for a class. A class is a collection of objects that have the same name, attributes and operations, like all bricks of a certain type or all atoms of a particular element. Most people tend to use the words *object* and *class* interchangeably. An object is in fact an instance of a class, or for the mathematicians among us a member of that class. Fortunately, the context usually makes it clear whether we are talking about classes or instances. Designers are usually talking about classes.

There are additional compartments that can be added to the class notation. These are less common, and we shall not consider them in this book. For most purposes, you can think of an object as being defined by its attributes and its operations, and that a class is a blueprint for objects with the same structure. Instances of a class, the actual objects, vary by having different values in their attributes.

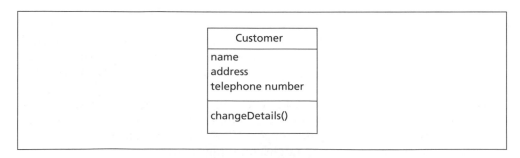

Figure 11.1   A customer represented in UML

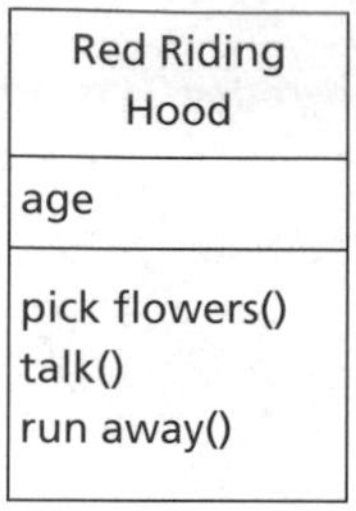

Figure 11.2   The UML representation of the Red Riding Hood object

The naive view of objects is that they are direct representations of real-world objects. In fact, they are a very flexible way of viewing real-world, or indeed fantasy-world, things. One of my favourite examples for teaching object concepts is the Red Riding Hood story – you can view the characters as objects, and there are lots of things you can describe about the relationships. In Figure 11.2 you can see a UML representation of Red Riding Hood. However, the notion of object is an abstraction. It is a simplification that removes much of the detail and formulates it in a particular way. A real Red Riding Hood (or Customer) is not a creature that hops from state to state in response to external stimulation of her operations, but a living autonomous creature with many aspects that cannot be fully written down or represented in a computer system.

Some early OO analysis methods began with object identification. By examining the various documents in the domain and conducting interviews, it is possible to find a vast number of objects. Then, by asking what information can be kept about the objects, and what can be done with the objects, attributes and operations can be defined. This is appealing at first and generates lots of candidate classes. Mostly, however, it generates too many classes and inappropriate attributes and operations; it is like a builder going and buying every possible brick he might use, and then spending his time sifting through them as he builds a house – he will build a fine house possibly, but end up with a lot of bricks left over, and probably spend more time than necessary. We shall be considering a more systematic way of identifying objects, attributes and operations. We will then look at a design process that produces additional objects that are a little removed from the real world.

11.2 Encapsulation

An important concept is the notion of encapsulation. We introduced objects as the smallest unit of meaningful behaviour within a system. All the information and behaviour of an object is defined within the object.[1] Strictly, the only way that an

---

1 In practice, most computer languages allow the querying and setting of some of the attributes without recourse to an operation. This is very much done to speed up the development of code. There are mechanisms for controlling how much of this is done in most languages, and some attributes can be completely hidden outside the object.

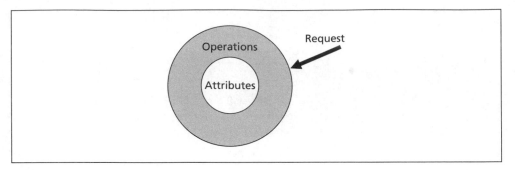

Figure 11.3 All requests on an object are controlled via the operations

object can be manipulated is through its operations. Figure 11.3 illustrates this, showing that any request on the object must be dealt with by the operations.

Encapsulation localizes activity. It means that the designer and implementer can carefully control the behaviour of an object, and if something odd is happening they know exactly where to look. In systems where processing and data are split, it can often be hard to trace where problems lie if the system is misbehaving.

Encapsulation leaves the designer free to choose the way data is stored inside an object. The behaviour of an object is defined by the operations. If the designer wishes to change the internal representation of an object, this can be done without damaging the role of the object, provided the operations are not changed in functionality or presentation. This has the advantage of allowing the development team to defer some decisions about implementation until quite late. For example, it might be sensible to use an array to store a small amount of information (say a set of menu options), but as that amount increases in size then the storage might be better in a database table.

At the core of the notion of object orientation is the representation of objects in this way. Object-oriented languages will keep all of the data and processing inside objects.[2] The trick is to make the objects cooperate, and this is done by one operation in an object calling another operation in a different object. To do this the objects need to know about each other, and they are linked by relationships.

11.3 Polymorphism

Computer scientists are wonderful at choosing complicated-sounding words to explain simple concepts. Polymorphism simply means that the two classes can use the same name for an operation or attribute without confusion. Because operations are not free-floating, but are bound to classes, there is never any ambiguity, and this is true of attributes as well. Figure 11.4 illustrates this, where a juggler

---

2 When we get to implementation we shall see that by necessity we have to keep data in structures that are not strictly objects. There are object-oriented databases that do allow this principle to be kept, but they are few and far between. In practice, most long-term data is stored in databases that are not object-oriented.

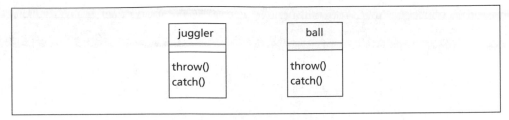

Figure 11.4 Illustration of polymorphism – two objects with operations with the same names but different meanings

has throw and catch operations that have quite distinctive meanings from operations with the same name on a ball.

This actually saves quite a lot of effort, and allows for more natural representations. It is very much as we would use words in the real world – we use the word *serve* as something you do with tennis balls on a tennis court and with soup in a dining room; the context defines the meaning (or we would have difficulties with tennis players working as waiters who are asked to serve soup).

11.4 Relationships

Objects only really become interesting and useful when you make them talk to each other. To do this, you define relationships between objects that need to talk. Think of a relationship as a line of communication. Once we have defined the relationships, we have the basis of building complex systems.

Let us look first at relationships between real-world objects. Any relationship between real-world objects can be modelled: customers order goods, clerks adjust accounts, cats eat canaries, dogs bite postmen, the woodcutter murders the wolf, cars run over little old ladies, employees work for organizations, patients visit hospitals, patients stay in hospitals. As part of our analysis we will want to record some of these relationships.

Once we start to design and build computer systems, we start to invent objects. We then need to relate them to other objects. So, computer screens need to talk to customer objects inside a computer system. The process of design is one of inventing new objects, breaking objects down into networks of objects and recombining them.

Our systems are societies of cooperating objects, as illustrated in Figure 11.5. To carry out a task, an object may do some work itself and then pass a request on to another object, which in turn will do some work and perhaps pass this on to another object, and so on. Part of analysis and design is identifying and defining these relationships. Objects can only communicate with each other if they have a defined relationship. In a large system, there may be thousands or tens of thousands of objects, all working simultaneously. They need to know about each other. We shall see during the discussion on implementation how we enable objects to know about their relations.

11.4.1 ONE-TO-ONE RELATIONSHIPS

In a one-to-one relationship, one object is associated with exactly one of its related objects. This is modelled by a straight line drawn between the objects, as

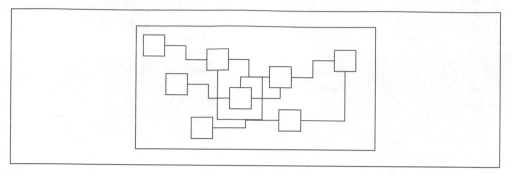

Figure 11.5 Computer systems are networks of cooperating objects

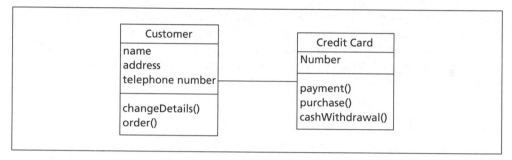

Figure 11.6 A one-to-one relationship

in Figure 11.6, where we are showing that we only allow a customer to have one credit card and a credit card to have one customer. The meaning of this is that the two objects can communicate, but using this relationship they can only communicate with each other. Thus when the order operation on the customer needs to pay for the goods, it might call the purchase operation on the credit card. Because the relationship is one-to-one, the purchase request can only go to the single credit card registered for that customer, and the purchase call on the credit card could only be from one customer.

If the relationship is one-way, an arrow is used to indicate the direction, as in Figure 11.7. This means that the Customer can call operations on the Credit Card,

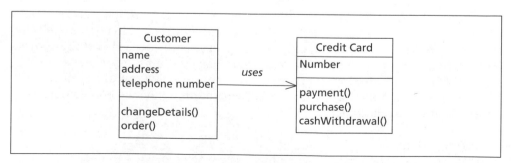

Figure 11.7 A unidirectional one-to-one relationship

but the Credit Card cannot call operations on the Customer. Sometimes it is useful to name the relationship, and the name of the relationship can be written along-side the line. In Figure 11.7 the relationship between customer and credit card is a 'uses' relationship – the customer uses the credit card. Where the relationship is obvious it is not necessary to name it. However, sometimes there is more than one relationship between two objects, and then it makes sense to label the relationship (e.g. a manager may supervise an employee and also evaluate their performance).

By indicating that such a relationship exists, communication can take place between the objects. This is done by an object calling an operation on another object. If the relationship is bidirectional, the objects at either end of the relation-ship can call operations on the other. If the relationship is directional then the calling of operations can only be in the direction of the arrow.

11.4.2 ONE-TO-MANY RELATIONSHIPS

Sometimes one object can be related to many objects. This is indicated by different marks at the end of the line. This is known as the multiplicity of the rela-tionship. The meaning of the notation is indicated in Table 11.1.

Table 11.1   The different multiplicity notations

Notation	Meaning
1	One at this end
1..*	One or more at this end
3..*	Three or more at this end
5	Exactly five at this end
*	Zero or more at this end
7..10	Seven to ten at this end

In a one-to-many relationship, the object at the one end of the relationship can communicate with many objects at the many end, but an object at the many end can only communicate with one object at the one end. If we were to change our rule about customers and credit cards, allowing a customer to order goods and purchase them with a number of credit cards, we would change the relationship as in Figure 11.8. Thus a customer can use many credit cards, but a credit card can only be used by one customer.

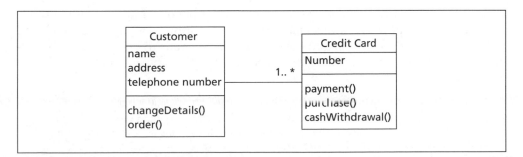

Figure 11.8   A one-to-many relationship

One-to-many relationships are commonplace, and are on the whole straightforward to deal with. They map very nicely into objects that can be implemented, and into data structures that can be held in a database.

11.4.3 MANY-TO-MANY RELATIONSHIPS

Many-to-many relationships are where one object at either end of a relationship can communicate with a number at the other end of the relationship. In Figure 11.9 we see that a truck can be driven by many drivers, and a driver can drive many trucks.

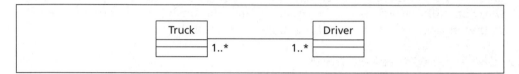

Figure 11.9 A many-to-many relationship

These relationships crop up from time to time, but they can be a nuisance when design and implementation take place, as each side of the relationship needs to be able to identify the list of objects at the other side. Often it is possible to find an intermediate object to split this relationship into two one-to-many relationships. In Figure 11.10 we have introduced a Journey object to show that the trucks are assigned to drivers for particular journeys. By doing this, we sometimes uncover additional information, such as that Journey needs a date.

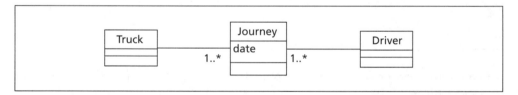

Figure 11.10 Removing a many-to-many relationship with an intermediate object

11.5 Inheritance

One of the key concepts of object-oriented development is the notion of inheritance.[3] It has several purposes. Often you will not need it, but when it is used it can provide very powerful and concise ways of describing complex situations, and reduce the amount of design and development that needs to take place. In particular, when a system is built using object-oriented languages, extending it by adding new object types is often easier.

---

3 Some methods view inheritance as a fundamental concept in object-oriented systems. For some aspects of implementation, it is very useful. In analysis, inheritance crops up less than you might expect. Because it is seen as a Good Thing, people sometimes go too far in the search for inheritance. Like other concepts, it is a tool that is useful, but good tools have specific purposes and should not be used for everything.

Often we will find that there are objects which have something in common. It is then useful to create an abstract object which groups together the common features, and to use inheritance to define the original objects. For example, consider our two fairy story creatures in Figure 11.11.

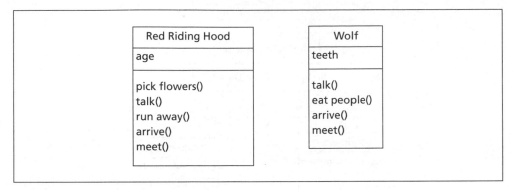

Figure 11.11   Two fairy story objects sharing common operations

Now we can see that they both have the same operations 'arrive' and 'meet' and 'talk'. We can therefore create an abstract creature that has the common operations. We can then draw the original objects grouped under the abstract object, as in Figure 11.12.

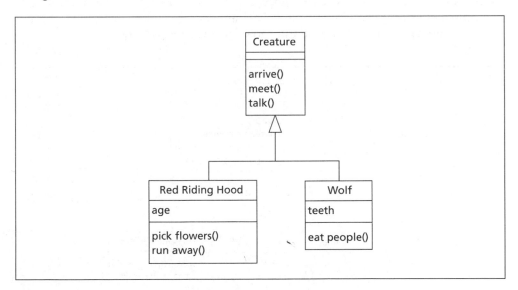

Figure 11.12   An example of inheritance

Inheritance means that the attributes and operations of an object are available in the specialized object below. The triangle in the diagram indicates inheritance. The point of the triangle indicates where operations and attributes are inherited from.

Let us consider more practical examples. Figure 11.13 shows employee and customer objects inheriting attributes and operations from a person object.

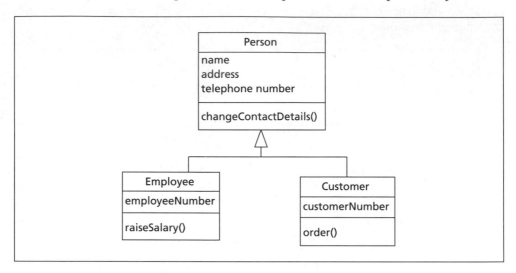

Figure 11.13   Inheritance from a common object

Inheritance can pass down an arbitrarily deep hierarchy. A slightly more complicated hierarchy is given in Figure 11.14, where we see two different types of employee: salaried and hourly paid. The name, address and telephone number and the employee number will be inherited by these employees.

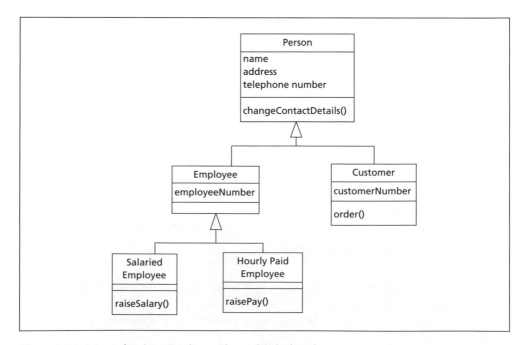

Figure 11.14   Inheritance through multiple levels

11.5.1 INHERITANCE AND REUSE

Inheritance is good for software reuse.[4] When new objects are created that are similar to other objects they can have many of their attributes and operations ready defined. Let us suppose we now introduce Grandma into our fairy story hierarchy, as in Figure 11.15. Here we get a Grandma who can instantly arrive, meet and talk. We could do the same with the Woodcutter.

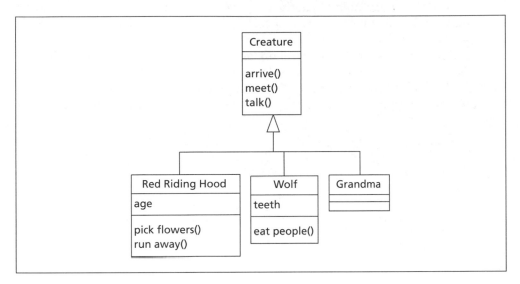

Figure 11.15   A simple example of reuse

It is now possible to buy or obtain ready-built class hierarchies written in object-oriented languages that can be extended in this way to produce a new application. When you use Java, you not only use a basic language, you also use a number of ready-made classes that you can inherit from[5] to produce working user interfaces.

Designing complex class hierarchies takes time, and good design requires experience. But the basic principles outlined above, with some intuitive guidelines, are the basis for the design of good, reusable designs. Reuse can be viewed from two directions. Components can be reused, which is a sort of bottom-up approach to reuse. Designs can also be reused. Both elements are important in the production of reusable software.

The notion of breaking the world down into hierarchies of types is not as old as the hills, but it goes back at least as far as the Ancient Greeks: all men are mortal, Socrates is a man, so Socrates is mortal. This approach is embedded in Western thought, and should be natural for most people to follow. Experience shows that

---

4 Reuse is the Holy Grail of the object-oriented world. Great crusades have been undertaken in its pursuit. At a practical level, reuse is a good idea to be encouraged. We shall discuss reuse at length later. However, use is more important than reuse, and alas too many projects get bogged down in the mire of reuse instead of focusing on the real issue of building something people can use.
5 Reusable class libraries have so far been more successful in the technical market than in the business application market. This is probably due to the world being more tightly defined in technical markets, and therefore there being more commonality.

describing things using hierarchies is an easy and comprehensive way of communicating both structure and functionality.[6]

11.6 Aggregation

We can make up objects out of other objects. This is known as aggregation. The behaviour of the bigger object is defined by the behaviour of its component parts, separately and in conjunction with each other. Figure 11.16 shows a simple example of a juggler. The diamond in the diagram indicates that one object is made up of another object. The numbers are indicative of how many parts there are. A juggler has two hands and two feet. He uses hands to catch and throw a ball. He may also kick a ball with his foot. By analysing our juggler object and breaking it down into component objects, we now have a better understanding of our object.

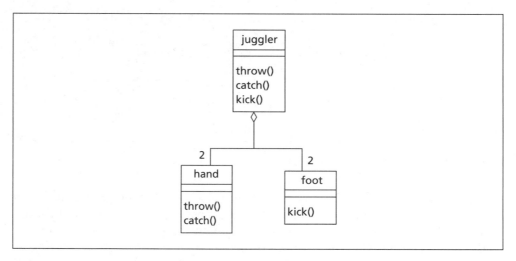

Figure 11.16   A simple example of aggregation

Hands and feet could be broken down into their constituent parts, say palms and fingers, soles and toes. However, that does not seem to help us to understand juggling, so the decomposition above is probably enough.

11.6.1 DELEGATION

The behaviour of an object that is made up of other objects is usually defined by the behaviour of the smaller objects. For example, to start a car, you start the engine. Thus the start operation on the car involves calling the start operation on the engine. This is known as delegation. The engine then will switch on the ignition system, switch on the starter motor, and then switch off the starter motor.

---

6 Early programming methods used a notion of top-down refinement that broke problems down into smaller problems in hierarchies. The programmer would continue breaking problems into sub-problems, and into smaller sub-problems, until the whole problem could be solved.

This is further delegation. To stop the car, there will be a call to stop the engine, which in turn will make a further call to switch off the ignition.

You may read elsewhere about the benefits of multiple inheritance. Most of the features of multiple inheritance can be simulated using delegation, with safer consequences. However, the arguments for and against multiple inheritance (inheriting from more than one parent) are lengthy and can be side-stepped for now.

11.7 Object Models and Class Diagrams

We now have the notation to describe quite complicated systems. The process of object-oriented analysis and design is one of elaborating an object model, increasing its detail and scope until enough is known to construct a computer system (if indeed that is what is wanted[7]).

Figure 11.17 is a simple model for the Red Riding Hood story (operations and attributes have been omitted for brevity, but could be shown). The Wolf eats Grandma. Red Riding Hood and the Wolf talk to each other. The Woodman kills the Wolf. Red Riding Hood picks flowers. All these relationships are one to one. Where the relationship is one-way, we use an arrow to indicate the direction. Red Riding Hood picks flowers, and this is a one-to-many relationship.

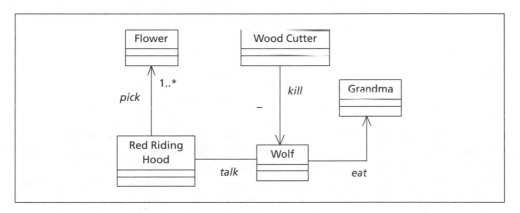

Figure 11.17   A class diagram for the Red Riding Hood story

Another example is one to describe patient referrals by GPs to specialists in Figure 11.18. A patient has just one doctor (GP), but may be treated by zero or more specialists. A specialist may treat zero or more patients and be used by at least one doctor. A doctor may use many specialists. Here we have left off directional arrows, as each party may need to initiate communication with another.

Figure 11.19 is a class diagram for a lift system. A floor has one or two buttons to call for lifts (one to go up, one to go down). A button may make a call to one of a

---

7   The end result of object modelling need not be a computer system. Jacobson (1995) describes object modelling as a way of modelling business, and I have worked with social scientists who have found object methods useful in modelling social and healthcare systems.

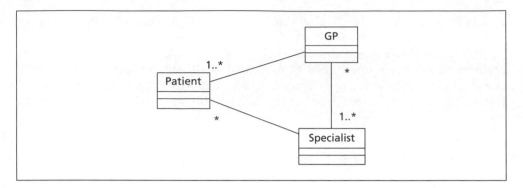

Figure 11.18 A simple class diagram to describe patient referrals

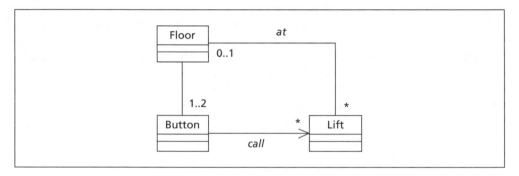

Figure 11.19 A class diagram for a lift controller system

number of lifts. A lift can be at one floor or no floors (i.e. be between floors), and a floor can have zero or more lifts at it. A number of lifts service a number of floors.

Figure 11.20 is a class diagram for a Web-based shopping system.[8] There is one home page and many product pages. There is one shopping basket page, which displays the contents of the shopping basket and allows you to change the contents of the shopping basket. The shopping basket itself is a separate object that will keep details of the products ordered. Once the customer submits the order, the shopping basket will create an order for the customer.

The class diagram (or set of class diagrams) is the principal output of an analysis and design process. The distinction between analysis and design is much greyer in object-oriented development. Essentially it is one of detail. Analysis usually omits concerns about how a system is to be constructed, and some of the objects may not be fully decomposed. Design may restructure the classes for a variety of implementation and software engineering reasons.

It is useful to think of the object model, represented in class diagrams during analysis and design, as the skeleton or framework of the system. It is vitally

---

8 Some designers do not like to represent interfaces such as windows in class diagrams. However, it is a perfectly valid representation, and if it adds clarity to an analysis or design then there is much to recommend it.

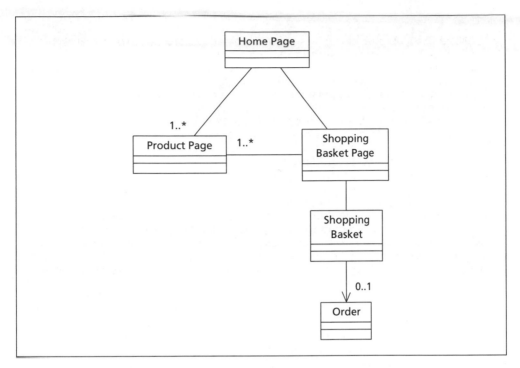

Figure 11.20   A class diagram for a Web shopping system

important to get the structure of this sound. We shall see how to add in function-ality later, which is like the muscles and vital organs within the skeleton. If the class structure is good, changes are generally much easier, and new functionality can be added fairly easily.

Devising good class structures is a skilled task that takes experience. Even the best analysts and designers produce poor class definitions from time to time. There are some good principles for structuring classes, as we shall see, but it takes a good deal of time before the novice can produce a good class structure quickly and easily.

11.8 ICANDO Site Safety

Typically, physical simulations have object models that correspond most directly to real-world objects. Therefore, for the purpose of this chapter, before we look at systems analysis and design, we shall look for some good examples of objects from the ICANDO site safety application.

One approach to object identification, preached in some simple methods, is noun-identification.[9] Textual descriptions are taken from the requirements docu-ments, and the analyst goes through and highlights nouns and noun phrases, as in

---

9 Personally I do not like noun-identification as a way of identifying candidate classes. My experience is that it results in a number of classes that are unnecessary and have to be pruned out. However, for systems such as the site safety system it may well be appropriate and not too problematic.

ICANDO has a number of chemical, petroleum and gas **storage sites**. A site must conform to rigorous **safety standards**. These standards specify the quality of **storage facilities**, and limits on the proximity of facilities to each other and to other facilities in the local environment. The reason is to prevent a **small hazard** from a **leak** becoming a **major hazard** causing a chain of **unpleasant events**. **Site engineers** are responsible for maintaining safety and specifying **changes** to the site. **Safety guidelines** are substantial **documents**. **ICANDO** have their own **company standards**, and there are often **local standards** as well. These **standards** change from time to time. Whenever a **site engineer** rearranges a **site** or adds a new **facility**, the **guidelines** need to be checked. Failing to meet **guidelines** is not only dangerous, it can lead to local **safety inspectors** closing the **site**. **Central services** have a **safety audit team** that visits **sites** as regularly as possible. They do find **infringements**, and often these are because the **site engineer** has misread **guidelines** or occasionally overlooked a **guideline**. They would like some form of **computer program** to help the site engineers maintain **safety standards**. The **IT research group** is called in, and they propose a **drawing tool** that allows **engineers** to quickly draw a **site**, including all the **storage facilities**, **offices**, **boundaries**, and **roads**. It will take **specifications** of each of the **facilities**. **Guidelines** will be read in, and the **site** automatically checked against the **guidelines**, with an **audit report**. On close **investigation**, it is determined by the **IT research group** that there are two **types of rule**. The first **type of rule** states the **materials** that must be used to construct a **facility**, specifying **qualities** such as thickness of **container walls**. The second type of rule specifies **minimum distances** between **facilities**, and the **distance** depends on the **facility** and the **capacity** of the **facility**. Some of the **distance rules** are complicated by the fact that **fire walls** and **bunds** (**mounds of earth**) can be introduced to provide a **barrier** that enables **facilities** to be located more closely to each other, and **distances** must be calculated differently.

The **IT research team** sketch out a suggested **layout** for the **interface** for the **system**, as in Figure 3.3. They suggest a simple **drawing facility** that allows the **site engineer** to draw up the **layout** of the **site**, and to fill in **details** of the **facilities** on the **site**. They can then upload the **guidelines** and check the **site**. The system will then flag any warnings about **problems** with the **site**.

Figure 11.21   Noun phrases highlighted as candidate objects for the ICANDO site safety system

Figure 11.21. These are consolidated into a list and considered as possible objects, as in Table 11.2. The list is then used to determine a basic object model.

Let us begin by grouping together some of the objects into inheritance and aggregation relationships. The first group of related objects we might consider are the various facilities on the site. Each facility will have a position and shape, and it will be possible to move them. This is represented by attributes and operations. How the position and shape are to be represented will need more consideration than we shall give here, but shape 'feels' like it might actually be defined by a class. By grouping all the types of facility under a class Facility, we arrive at a model as indicated in Figure 11.22. On looking at this hierarchy, questions already arise as to the details of the various facilities. StorageFacility looks to be a class that might be broken down into different types of storage facility, such as cylinder stores and bulk stores. Detailed systems analysis would begin to open that up. The hierarchy also prompts questions such as how the specific facilities

Table 11.2   Selection of objects from noun list

Candidate	Decision
Storage site	The system is to model aspects of the site, and it is likely that some representation of the site is needed, so keep as an object **Site**.
Safety standard	A safety standard is a collection of rules or guidelines. It is probably worth considering an object **Standard**.
Storage facility	There are lots of things that make up a site, including a storage facility. So consider an object **Facility**, and a special type of object **StorageFacility**.
Small hazard	The system is unlikely to be modelling leaks and hazards, so reject.
Leak	Reject, as for small hazard.
Major hazard	Reject, as for small hazard.
Unpleasant event	Reject, as for small hazard.
Site engineer	This will be a user of the system. If the system were to have some notion of user, then there might be a need to model the site engineer, but most likely there will not be such a need, so reject.
Change	This is something that is done to the site, rather than something that is recorded. Reject.
Safety guideline	There will need to be some storage of these, so keep as **Guideline**.
Document	This is a generic term, used to refer to safety guidelines. Reject.
ICANDO	The owner of the system. Reject.
Company standard	As for safety standard. Keep as **Standard**. Company could be stored as a value of an attribute 'source'.
Local standard	As for safety standard. Keep as **Standard**. Local could be stored as a value of an attribute 'source'.
Standard	Keep as **Standard**.
Facility	Keep as **Facility**.
Guideline	Keep as Guideline.
Safety inspector	Outside the system, so reject.
Site	Keep as **Site**.
Infringement	The system will need to report these, so keep as **Infringement**.
Computer program	The system itself, so reject.
IT research group	The creators of the system, so reject.
Drawing tool	The system itself, so reject.
Office	A special type of **Facility**, so keep as **Office**.
Boundary	A special type of **Facility**, so keep as **Boundary**.
Road	A special type of **Facility**, so keep as **Road**.
Specification	A description of a Facility, probably stored as attributes, so reject.
Audit report	A key output of the system, so keep as **AuditReport**.
Type of rule	Covered by **Guideline**.
Material	Attribute of **Facility**.
Quality	Attribute of **Facility**.
Container wall	Attribute of **Facility**.

Table 11.2 (*continued*)

Candidate	Decision
Minimum distance	Attribute of **Guideline**.
Distance	Attribute of **Guideline**.
Capacity	Attribute of **StorageFacility**.
Distance rule	Covered by **Guideline**.
Fire wall	A special type of Facility so keep as **FireWall**.
Bund	A special type of Facility so keep as **Bund**.
Barrier	A generic description of Bund and Fire wall, so reject.
IT research team	The creators of the system, so reject.
Layout	A description of the **Site**, so reject.
Interface	There will need to be some interface objects, but these will probably come out of the design. Wait until the design stage.
System	The system itself, so reject.
Drawing facility	A description of the system, so reject.
Detail	A generic term for the attributes of a facility, so reject.
Problem	A generic term for **Infringement**, so reject.

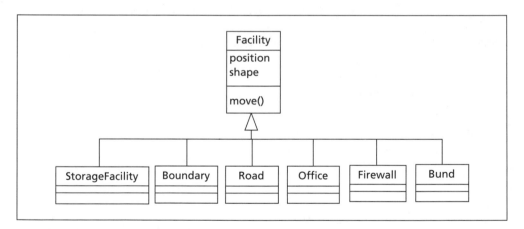

Figure 11.22 Inheritance hierarchy for facilities on a site

differ in terms of the details, which would be represented as attributes, and further analysis would prompt questions on these.

Now, considering the site, this is made up of a number of facilities. There might be a name and address to identify the site. We also know that the main aim of the system is to audit the site, and we can put an operation on to indicate that. We can use an aggregation relationship, as indicated in Figure 11.23. It is reasonable to assume that a site consists of at least one facility, though the multiplicity could be from zero to many to allow an empty site.

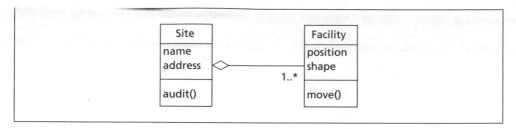

Figure 11.23   Representing a site as a collection of facilities

Looking at the standards and guidelines in Figure 11.24, we see that a standard is made up of a number of guidelines, and guidelines relate to facilities. The multiplicity of guidelines in a standard is many (arguably, as with facilities in a site it should be at least one, but the many has been used to show the slight difference in notation). A guideline refers to one or two facilities. It is not clear what the name of the relationship should be, but it should be fairly obvious what the meaning is, so the relationship is not labelled. Leaving out relationship labels is common.

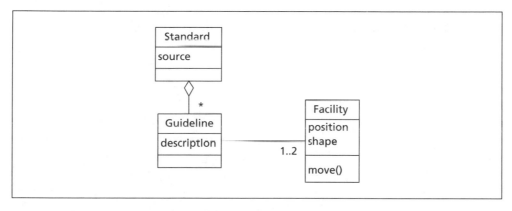

Figure 11.24   The guidelines and relationships in the site safety system

If we now look at the reporting, an audit report consists of a number of infringements. A site can have a number of audit reports. Each infringement relates to a particular guideline, and to one or two facilities. These are shown in Figure 11.25.

We now have a substantial object model, as shown in Figure 11.26. This would be a good basis for further systems analysis. Each of the objects could be examined for further attributes and operations. There will be extra objects put on through systems analysis and design to provide control and interfacing. The initial placing of operations, such as the audit operation on the site, is likely to change as the analysis and design progresses. However, we now have a good structure of the basic system.

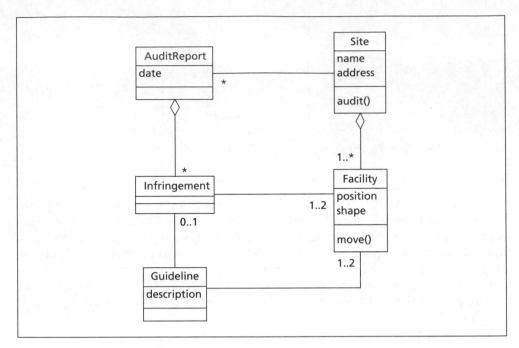

Figure 11.25 The audit report and infringements, related to the site facilities and guidelines

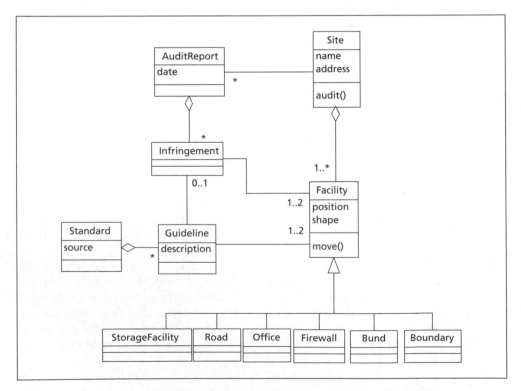

Figure 11.26 Initial object model for the ICANDO site safety system

REVIEW QUESTIONS

1. What are the three compartments in a UML class?
2. Where is data stored in an object-oriented system?
3. Where is processing done in an object-oriented system?
4. What does encapsulation mean?
5. What does polymorphism mean?
6. What is the difference between a class and an object?
7. What is an association?
8. What does a one-to-many association mean?
9. What does a one-to-one association mean?
10. What does a many-to-many association mean?
11. What is special about an inheritance relationship?
12. In an aggregation relationship, is there sharing of operations and attributes?
13. What does a class diagram consist of?
14. Do you produce only one class diagram for a system?

EXERCISES

1. On further analysis, it is determined that the storage facilities consist of cylinder stores, bulk liquid containers and bulk gas containers. Each store has a product type and a maximum quantity of product that can be stored. Gas containers have pressure ratings. Produce new classes, inheriting from the storage facility class. Add new attributes at appropriate levels in the inheritance hierarchy.
2. There are in fact two types of guideline. One guideline refers to a specific facility, and another relates to the distance between two facilities. Modify the guideline class to have two subclasses for these particular types of guideline, and put in direct relationships to facility(facilities) for these guidelines.
3. Shapes can be either simple rectangles or circles, or they can be sets of lines representing an arbitrary shape. (For this application, curved shapes are probably unnecessary, or they could be simulated by a small series of straight lines.) Produce an inheritance hierarchy showing the different types of shape, and showing the arbitrary shape as a collection of lines. Produce suitable attributes to describe the shapes. Then, instead of having shape as an attribute of a facility, link a facility to a particular shape using a relationship.

CHAPTER **12**

Systems Analysis

We are halfway through the book, and we now begin to analyse the system behaviour. In terms of project time-scales this is not unusual. IT projects are business projects, and the construction of a system is only part of the overall project. It is vital that the groundwork is done well in advance of defining the system. The effect of premature analysis and design can be a great deal of rework later on, or worse the production of a system that is inappropriate.

Of course, if the development is a relatively minor extension to an existing system in an established business, much of what we have gone through is overkill. However, that does not remove from the development team the responsibility of understanding the environment into which their system or subsystem is to be deployed.

Now we move on to the detailed elaboration of the requirements into computer-specific specifications of behaviour. This is the first point at which any notion of an object is essential. This stage focuses on the domain, and the necessary logical elements to support the domain. This will be a long and very detailed chapter, extending the notion of an object and introducing object interaction.

The inputs and outputs of systems analysis are shown in Figure 12.1. Use case descriptions and prototypes are the primary input, though the systems analyst may well refer to any of the previously provided documentation. The core of systems analysis will be driven by the construction of sequence diagrams that, in turn, are used to produce collaboration diagrams and class diagrams. Sequence diagrams use scenarios derived from the primary/alternative/exception paths in the use case descriptions to determine sensible networks of objects to implement the behaviour. These objects are recorded in class diagrams. Complicated classes have state models to further define their behaviour.

We will look a little at different types of object, and define a process for working through the use case descriptions to produce the key systems analysis outputs.

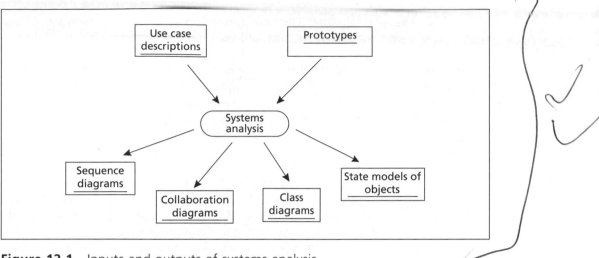

Figure 12.1   Inputs and outputs of systems analysis

12.1 Domain Objects

The early appeal of object orientation was the 'natural' way that objects can represent the real world, and some still preach that as a fundamental aspect. Objects are an abstract representation of things, and these things can be very broad. Some methods use the process of noun-identification to look for candidate objects; to find objects, simply look for nouns in the documentation in the domain or interview transcripts. This process is fine but crude, but it does illustrate well the point that systems can be thought of in terms of things in the environment.

This early idea came from the roots of object orientation in simulation, where computer programs were used to model real-world situations such as factories to determine how well or badly a design would work without going to the expense of constructing the real thing. The first cited object-oriented language was Simula, devised in the 1960s, where things in the real world had representations in the computer language, and behaviour in the real world was modelled as behaviour in the representations in the language. Simula was for simulating processes, and there needed to be a tight correspondence between the simulation model and the world it was simulating.

The nice thing about constructing systems with objects that correspond to things in the real world is that it is potentially much easier to understand the system. If we have an order processing system, everyone knows that there are orders, goods and customers. There should then be orders, goods and customers as objects in the computer system. Using the notion of encapsulation it is possible to find everything that orders, goods and customers do and can have done to them by examining the objects, attributes and operations.

The unfortunate truth, however, is that to construct systems that are maintainable, additional objects are necessary, and often it is necessary to break this ideal of encapsulation or at least re-define it. However, during the analysis phase, the notion of a strong correspondence between real-world objects and computerized objects is extremely valuable. The transformation from analysis through design will mostly retain these objects, but will introduce additional objects and rearrange some of the operations and attributes.

This leads to an important feature, known as traceability. If you know that there is a customer in the environment of a system, and that the system provides services for a customer, it is reasonable to look inside the system for a customer object and to identify the role of that customer object in the system. Traceability is important for debugging and maintenance. It allows developers to find their way around the system.

To some experts, this move away from 'pure objects' in systems is a heresy. However, Jacobson *et al.* (1992) distinguish quite clearly between designed objects and domain objects. There is a big distinction between the development of small scale or experimental systems and the construction of large systems that need to perform adequately and be robust and maintainable.

The purpose of the domain object model is to provide a vocabulary for fully specifying the behaviour of use cases. Jacobson *et al.* (1992) suggest the object name, the attributes and the relationships between objects are sufficient. In this way, behaviour remains in the use case descriptions.

In systems analysis, you are bridging between the world of the software developer, and the world of the business user. The foundations in the business world should have been set by the business process analysis and the use case analysis. The foundations that analysis needs to build on the developer's side are object definitions and interactions that can be translated into meaningful computer systems.

12.1.1 SOME MORE UML OBJECT NOTATION

UML has a notion of 'stereotype'. This allows you to extend UML with new building blocks that are an extension of existing building blocks.[1] Usually this is applied to classes, and new forms of class are defined that have special roles. Like ordinary classes, they have attributes and operations, but they are more focused in the way they are used.

UML has three distinct types of object stereotype, namely entity objects, boundary objects and control objects. Their roles in the analysis and design of object-oriented systems are quite distinct. An entity object is used mainly to model things that persist over time, and that the system will need to keep long-term information about. A boundary object is something that controls the interaction with the outside world, such as a computer screen. A control object is something that organizes complex behaviour that involves a number of boundary and entity objects.

The notation for an entity object is shown in Figure 12.2. It is possible to also show it with the stereotype label and the normal class notation as in Figure 12.3. The former has more immediate visual impact. Entity objects are long-lived, and

---

1 Some early object-oriented systems had the notion of flavours. There were vanilla objects, and you could mix in additional flavours to specialize the object. Stereotypes are a little like this, in that they take a vanilla concept such as a class and provide special types of class such as entity and boundary classes that are different flavours.

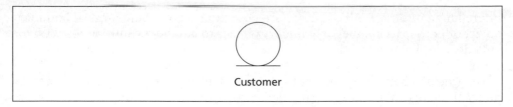

Figure 12.2   UML notation for an entity class

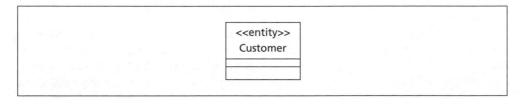

Figure 12.3   The UML notation for an entity class using a label to indicate the stereotype

they are often referred to as persistent objects. This usually means that at the implementation stage they have their attributes stored in database tables.

Database designers will recognize this stage as entity modelling[2]. It is precisely that. We shall see later how the entity objects are translated into database tables. Good entity modelling is crucial, and a good set of entity objects is a sound foundation for implementation.

Entity objects can have behaviour, implemented as operations. However, at the systems analysis stage it is arguably premature to start assigning operations. We shall defer this argument until later, when we look at some issues around design. However, it is often valuable to allocate attributes at this stage. Attributes are the data that need to be stored for the entities.

Boundary objects are drawn as in Figure 12.4. A boundary object defines the interface between the system and the outside world. This can be a computer screen, or it might be some other form of interface, such as an electronic

Figure 12.4   UML notation for a boundary class

---

2 To developers trained in database design, object-oriented modelling looks very much like extended database analysis. There is a very strong correspondence between the later stages of OO methods and database methods.

interchange interface. All use cases are going to involve some form of boundary object or perhaps a number of boundary objects to handle the interaction with the outside world. They are the facades that present the complex behaviour of use cases.

The role of a boundary object is to translate information supplied by actors into internal events that will be responded to by control and entity objects, and to present the response of these objects in terms that the actor can understand. For human actors this will usually be in the form of computer screens (or perhaps printouts), but for actors that are other systems this may be in the form of protocols.

Control objects are shown as in Figure 12.5. Control objects are there to mediate between a number of objects. For some use cases these may be unnecessary, as all the behaviour of the use case can adequately be supported by simple operations in the boundary and entity objects. However, there is often behaviour in a use case that involves coordination of a number of objects, and a control object acts as a mediator. We shall discuss the importance of this as we look at design.

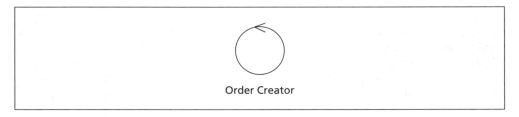

Figure 12.5 UML notation for a control object

Control objects do not usually persist for longer than the execution of the use case, and it is unusual to have any database representation of these. Very occasionally, the behaviour of a control object needs to be recorded for audit purposes, and there may be a requirement that introduces some sort of journal that can be represented by additional entity objects where the actions of the control object can be recorded.

12.2 Sequence Diagrams

Object-oriented systems are societies of objects that interact to carry out a particular function. Individual objects are pretty useless on their own. In a car, it is the steering wheel, steering column, steering rack, wheels and tyres, all acting in unison, that allow the car to turn a corner. Use case analysis has provided us with a very clear definition of the functions of a system. We now need to translate those functions into some set of objects and interactions that might be implemented in a computer system. Class diagrams, which we looked at in Chapter 10, do not define those interactions – they only define the paths along which those interactions take place. The class diagram is a road map. We need some way of describing journeys.[3]

During analysis, sequence diagrams are a way of tying together the sequences in the use case definitions gathered in the requirements stage with objects that will interact to support the steps in the use case. They are one way of describing a journey through the system. What we are going to do is to use a sequence diagram to either link in known objects, or to invent objects to support the use cases. A use case scenario represents a journey through the system and defines a sliver of the landscape. These slivers, merged together, will ultimately produce for us a complete map.

A sequence diagram is a two-dimensional diagram that documents a sequence in terms of the interactions between objects. Objects are arranged along the top of the diagram, and the interactions are listed underneath in time order going down the page. Those interactions start to tell us what the individual and group behaviour of objects is. The designer can then find ways of mapping this behaviour onto objects that can be implemented.

The process to be followed is to identify a set of representative scenarios from a use case, and to elaborate these using sequence diagrams. The set of scenarios should cover all of the alternative and exception paths through a use case. Those sequence diagrams can then be used to determine collaboration diagrams, which in turn can be used later to produce class diagrams.

Sequence diagrams are useful for analysis. However, they are getting to the level of complexity where it is difficult to have stakeholders view them, at least in detail. Sequence diagrams lead on to design. The initial sequence diagrams will not worry too much about fine detail, and miss out some important elements that need to be added during design. Design will use the sequences, but may need to add fine detail to the sequences and reorganize the objects.

You will probably find sequence diagrams the most challenging UML diagrams to understand. So far, most of the diagrams have been quite loose in their description, and as an analyst you can be quite free in the way you use them. However, sequence diagrams are very unforgiving. The best way of learning them is to read lots of examples and do lots of exercises.

Suppose that we have a simple scenario from an order-taking use case:

1. The sales operative takes the customer number and enters it on the screen.
2. The customer details are retrieved and displayed on the screen.
3. The sales operative checks that the customer details match those given by the customer, and ticks a confirm box.
4. The sales operative enters the order details.
5. The sales operative enters the delivery details.
6. The sales operative requests that the order is created.

Sequence diagrams group the objects that support a scenario along the top of the diagram, as in Figure 12.6. Here we have introduced a boundary object, Order

---

3   In fact, the process we are going to go through is one of deriving the road map from the journeys. From a large collection of sequence diagrams, the shape of the class diagram begins to emerge. As systems become more defined, the process starts to switch to finding routes through the existing class diagrams, and only adding in new routes when necessary.

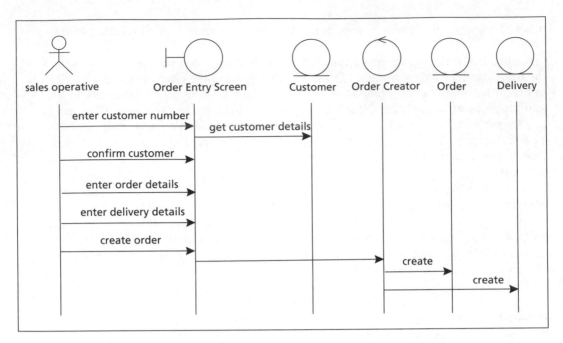

Figure 12.6   A simple UML sequence diagram

Entry Screen that will control all the interactions for this scenario. Once the customer number is entered, the order entry screen requests the details for the customer directly from the Customer object. The validation of the customer is done by the sales operative checking the customer details on the screen against the ones given by the customer (a password check might be done, if that is what is required). The next stage of taking the order and delivery details is done purely with the order entry screen; in reality, there may be extra objects involved if there needs to be a stock check or ordering from a pick list, but let's keep it simple for the time being. Then the order is created, and we have introduced an Order Creator control object to manage the creation of the order and the delivery; this may seem like overkill at this stage, as the order screen could have triggered the creations directly, but later we will see why this might be a good idea.

The vertical lines beneath the objects and the actors are timelines, indicating the history of the object, with time progressing downward. The arrows, which may go in any direction, not just right to left, indicate that there is communication between the objects. The arrow does not indicate the direction of communication – usually there is two-way communication, as with the 'get customer details' request, where the order entry screen needs information back from the customer object. The arrow does indicate which object initiates the communication.

This is a very neat linkage between the sequences of behaviour in the use case, and domain objects. In fact, this is one of the best ways of finding domain objects. If you brainstorm domain objects, then you tend to identify too many. This way, you obtain just the objects you need to describe the behaviour of the system, and no more.

We now have some simple guidelines for elaborating a use case.

1. Identify a representative set of scenarios for the use case, covering all of the alternative and exception paths.
2. For each scenario, produce a sequence diagram as follows.
3. Place the actor on the left-hand side.
4. Identify the boundary objects (there may be more than one), such as computer screens.
5. For each step of the scenario draw an interaction between the actor and the boundary objects.
6. For each interaction with a boundary object, determine whether there is a need to interact with another object (simple data entry rarely involves interaction with other objects).
7. If the interaction is with a single entity object, then create the entity object and service the request directly.
8. If the interaction is with a number of entity objects, then consider creating an intermediate control object to administer the communication.

Now this all looks very straightforward, but in practice each of these sequence diagrams can take many hours to produce. They often create a number of questions that need to be clarified with the stakeholders. More often than not the requirements analysis has left out some details of the sequences. This is not something to be concerned about – it is constructive work, cross-checking the requirements analysis. No analysis process runs smoothly from beginning to end. It is a messy, iterative process that is one of continual refinement and clarification.

One of the most effective ways I have found of carrying out the elaboration of use cases is to involve the business analyst that produced the use case definition and someone familiar with object modelling, perhaps even a designer. Rather than use a computerized tool to produce the sequence diagram, a set of sticky notes is used. The result can look something like Figure 12.7. The sequence of actions is written down the left-hand side, the candidate objects are written across the top, and the interactions are indicated with a cross. This is much more informal, and can allow very swift rearrangement. The problem with computerized tools is that sometimes they look too official. Once the sequence diagram is agreed, it can be drawn out neatly.

We shall be using sequence diagrams as the main link between use cases and objects. As we move through design, we shall see that the sequence diagrams allow you to add more and more detail, until it is possible to determine the details of the operations of the objects and derive the attributes. The sequence diagrams are quite a bit more sophisticated than the subset of the notation that we have introduced so far – we shall look at this in more detail when we consider design.

12.3 Collaboration Diagrams

Collaboration diagrams are another way of interrelating the objects that are complementary to sequence diagrams. Object-oriented systems provide their behaviour by objects working together. Individual objects only provide part of the behaviour. When objects work together, they can produce complicated and powerful behaviour. To do this, they exchange information and requests, and the

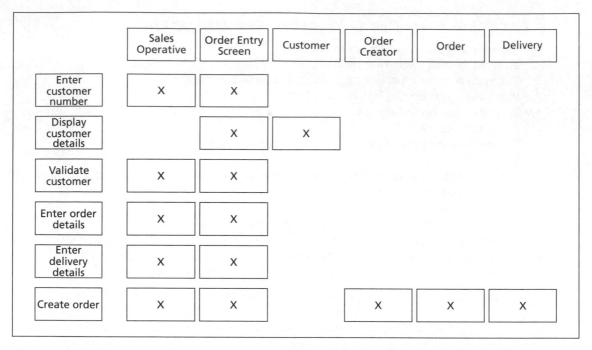

Figure 12.7   Using sticky notes to devise sequence diagrams

routes for these requests can be described using collaboration diagrams. In fact, the routes have already been defined in the sequence diagrams, but it is useful to draw these out in a different way, as shown in Figure 12.8. The advantage is that

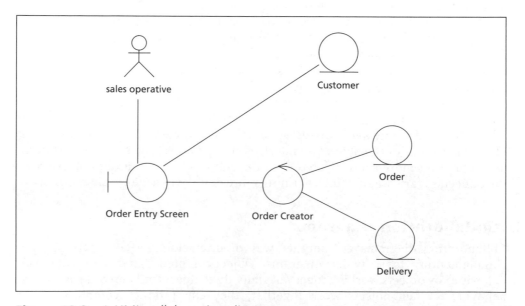

Figure 12.8   A UML collaboration diagram

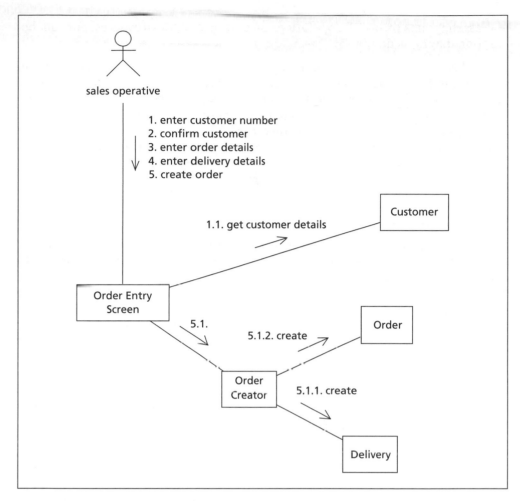

Figure 12.9   A collaboration diagram without stereotype displays but with messages

the lines of communication are much clearer visually. This can then be translated into a class diagram as we shall see later.

Collaboration diagrams look very like cut-down class diagrams. Figure 12.8 has used the stereotype icons and has no indication of the details of the interactions. In Figure 12.9 we can see the same interaction diagram with the objects drawn with rectangular icons and with the flow of messages drawn on the diagram, numbered to indicate the ordering. The key differences between a collaboration diagram and a class diagram are:

- The collaboration diagram shows the class relationships for a particular execution of the system, while a class diagram represents relationships for all potential executions.
- Collaboration diagrams can record message exchanges between objects, but class diagrams cannot.

- Class diagrams record the operations on objects and the attributes, but collaboration diagrams do not.

Overlay a number of collaboration diagrams, representing the various executions of use cases, and you can see a class diagram structure emerging, with the relationships defined. Consider the communications between objects on a collaboration diagram, and you can begin to identify operations that are needed on the objects to support the relationships. Investigate the information exchanged in the communications and you can start to see the attributes that the objects need to record. Design will take us down this road, and also cause us to examine the class structures.

12.4 Class Diagrams

Having determined the domain objects and the interactions, we can record in a class diagram some of the information about the data that is needed. Figure 12.10 shows a class diagram that mirrors the structure of the collaboration diagrams in Figure 12.8 and Figure 12.9. Two additional relationships have been added. It is not known at this stage whether a customer object will need to communicate with an order object, or a delivery object with an order object. However, as we enter the data that is needed it is clear that an order needs some linkage to a customer and that deliveries and orders need to be linked. Later we shall see that we may implement these links through references such as an order number and delivery number, but that is getting more towards design. Therefore links have been added to show that there is some relationship between order and delivery and between order and customer. Multiplicity has also been added, showing that a customer may have zero or more orders, and that a delivery can contain one or more orders. These are details that may need clarification with the business analyst.

We could start allocating operations to objects at this point. This is not recommended for a number of reasons. Firstly, we have captured the details of the interactions in the sequence diagrams, and there is an argument that this is sufficient for the designers to understand the system. Secondly, the designer may want to restructure the class diagram, and refine the sequence diagram accordingly. Architectural considerations will impact the structure of classes considerably.

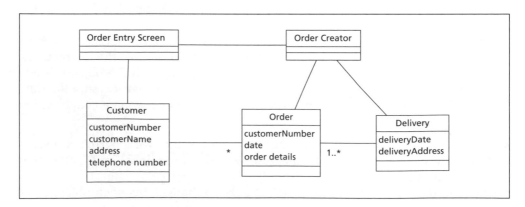

Figure 12.10 A UML class diagram

There will be decisions to be made about whether, for example, some of the operations should be implemented in control classes or in entity classes. These decisions are better left to the developers responsible for design and implementation. The principal information to capture in the class diagram at this stage is the data that needs to be kept in the form of attributes.

12.5 User Interface

One of the most powerful ways of engaging potential users and to clarify issues is to provide prototype screens. Figure 12.11 shows a prototype screen for the order entry screen we have been discussing at length in this chapter. A number of things come to light when you start to construct this sort of prototype. Firstly, it becomes a discussion point for the data that is to be collected. We might use this to go back to the customer object and refine the address attribute into its constituent parts. We also see that there is some notion of product, and it may prompt us to consider if we need a product object anywhere. Do customers know the product codes, and

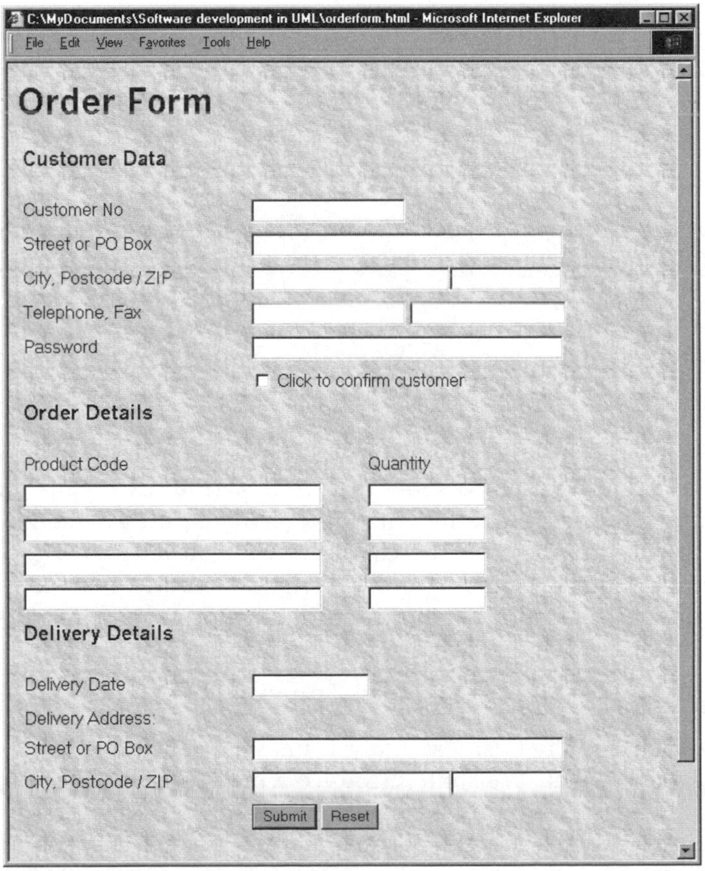

Figure 12.11 A prototype screen

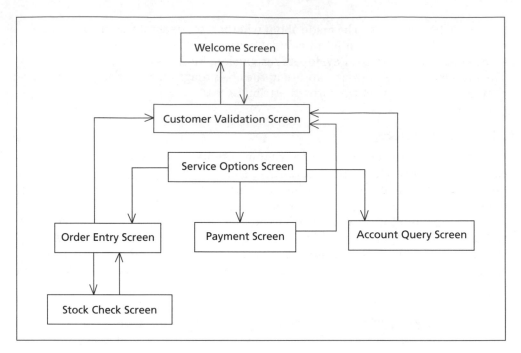

Figure 12.12 A simple screen organization

if not, might the system be expected to provide a list of product codes for order entry? Would the customer expect to have the price of the order fed back?

Again, as we push forward in the analysis and design process we see more questions being raised. Prototypes like this are tremendous tools for clarifying issues. They are now very quick and easy to produce with the right tools. The one in Figure 12.11 took a few minutes to prepare using an HTML editor, and could even be produced with an analyst or user present.

A map of the user interface is also useful. Screens are boundary objects, so a class diagram could be used to show the organization of screens. Figure 12.12 shows a simple screen organization. Attributes and operations are not shown, and the compartments for these on the classes have been left out. Associations are shown as unidirectional to indicate the navigation routes between screens. An arrow from one screen to another indicates that the former can invoke the latter.

12.6 Statecharts

We met statecharts in the business analysis phase. Their use in the systems analysis phase is very similar. We shall introduce a little more notation to add to the flexibility of their use. Two things need to be introduced. The first is that transitions between states have a little more syntax available. The second is that there can be nested states. (As activity diagrams are variants on statechart diagrams, all the notation below applies to them too.)

The full syntax for the label on a transition between states is

```
event-name(parameters) [guard-condition]/action
```

where event-name is the name of the event that triggered the exit from the previous state, parameters is a comma-separated list of values that are provided with the event, guard-condition is some condition that must be true for the transition to fire, and action is some particular action that must take place when the transition is fired. The guard condition and action can be expressed as simple English statements or in a programming language. The guard condition might also be expressed in OCL,[4] a more formal language defined as part of the UML standard. The action might also be expressed as an event trigger with the syntax

```
^target.event-name(parameters)
```

where target is some object that needs to respond to the event, event-name is the name of an event triggered by the transition, and parameters is a comma-separated list of parameters to be passed with the event.

Figure 12.13 shows a statechart diagram for a customer account. This shows that after the first delivery, the account goes into debit. From a debit state, a payment may take it into credit if the payment is sufficient to cover the outstanding balance. If the account is in debit, it is suspended when it becomes overdue. From suspended, it must be taken into a credit state. Deliveries when the account is in credit may take it into debit if the value of the delivery exceeds the current balance.

States may be broken down into substates. Figure 12.14 shows the states of a stock item. When it is in stock, it may be above or below the recommended stock level. Delivery to the warehouse or despatch from the warehouse will affect the stock level. When a substate starts, it normally starts at a start state and moves to

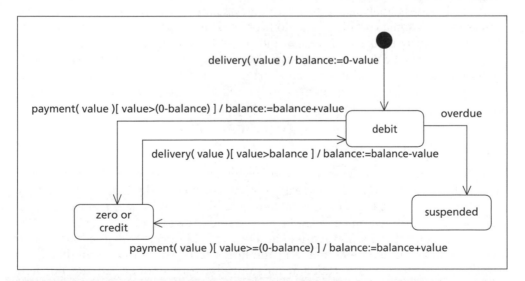

Figure 12.13 A statechart diagram for a customer account with events, guards and actions

---

4 OCL stands for Object Constraint Language.

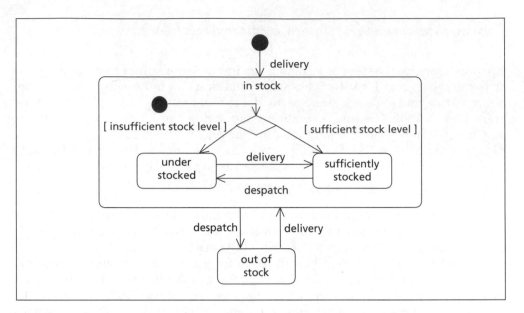

Figure 12.14 A simple example of substates in a statechart diagram

one of the other states. Here we have used a decision point (see activity diagrams) to determine which of the internal states it drops into. There is much more flexibility than this in the control of flow to and from substates, and if you wish to read more you can find a full description in Bennett *et al.* (2001).

As for business analysis, statechart diagrams are not used in systems analysis unless there is some complex behaviour of an object that needs to be considered. Systems analysis is likely to review and possibly extend some of the statechart diagrams developed during business analysis. Design may extend the detail a little further, and perhaps add extra statechart diagrams. The amount of modelling of this type is a matter of judgement, and the full notation may be used at the business analysis level for some application developments.

12.7 Brownfield Analysis

The above describes the analysis of systems for a 'greenfield' development; that is, where the system is new and there are few constraints on the implementation. In practice this is rare. Even for a so-called greenfield development, once the first deployment has taken place it can be considered brownfield.

The difference between greenfield and brownfield development is that a lot of decisions have already been made in the latter case. To add functionality to an established system means that you not only have to understand the business requirements, but you also have to understand the system that you are extending. Studies have shown that up to 50% of the cost of enhancing a system goes into understanding that system (Parikh and Zvegintzov, 1983).

If the system has been analysed and constructed using OO methods, there should be a ready-made class diagram available. For new use cases, it should be straightforward to search the established classes for classes to support the steps in the sequence diagrams. Where there is no appropriate class to support the use case, only then should a new class be introduced.

For systems where OO methods have not been applied previously, it is still meaningful and sensible to use the methods outlined in this book for analysis. Normally a system will have a database, and the database schema is in fact a cut-down object model. Database tables mostly store information about real-world entities, and are in fact implementations of entity classes. Thus you can proceed on the systems analysis by using sequence diagrams to tie in existing database tables, with new boundary and control classes, to implement a use case.

12.8 Analysis for Package Enhancement

Even the best packages are likely to need some form of enhancement for a business. Plug-and-play packages are rarely available. As part of the requirements analysis, some use cases will be identified that are not supported by the package, or that are only partially supported.

Packages often come with some 'recommended method' for customization. They may seem convoluted at first, but usually they will look something like the process we have been uncovering. Firstly you need to define the interactions in some structure similar to the use case definitions we have been using. Next, you need to define the interfaces. Then you need to trace the execution of the use case, and link it in to the interface with a series of interactions with pre-prepared components (perhaps objects, or some other computer representation), and if the components are missing there will be some procedure for defining and adding new components which will follow principles that we will discuss in the design stage.

12.9 The Essence of Systems Analysis

We have considered four UML notations above that are useful for describing the analysis of systems, namely sequence diagrams, collaboration diagrams, class diagrams and statechart diagrams. As with any other stage, it is a question of choice of tools, and it might be that occasionally you meet a need to use other notations, such as activity diagrams.

Systems analysis takes the development from the definition of business processes and the identification of use cases to support those processes, to the stage where designers and developers have a good and comprehensive model of the system's behaviour, the way the system needs to present itself to users, and what type of information is stored and retrieved by the system.

Keep clear in your mind that systems analysis is based on taking representative executions of a system and mapping them to an outline object structure. This is done by tracing representative scenarios from the use cases and working out detailed interactions between objects. This allows you to define the objects, and from the collaboration diagrams you start to get some idea of the structure of the object model and can begin to build a class diagram.

Do not expect systems analysis or design to be a one-off stage. There will be blind alleys, omissions and revisions. Systems analysis will uncover holes in the requirements analysis and involve clarification there. Design and implementation will uncover holes in the systems analysis. Testing will also determine missing or wrong systems analysis. It is a long to-and-fro exercise. You can treat it as a long series of frustrations, or accept that it is a continuous and sometimes messy learning process and enjoy the ride.

12.10 What Happens to Analysis Models?

When the analysis is complete, the design finished, and the system happily operational, what happens to the analysis models? They should, in principle, be the route for future modifications to the system. Often the analysis models can be the best guide to a system. So, in an ideal world, they would be kept and maintained along with the system.

Alas, I have rarely come across an environment where this is strictly maintained for long. Systems analysis is often the bridge across the river, but once the system is built shortcuts are taken to modification. Whether this is a good or bad thing is debatable. Much of this comes from a limited set of CASE tools, or badly integrated CASE tools that make it difficult to keep related documentation up-to-date. The other cause for neglect of analysis models is pressure of time.

12.11 ICANDO Bulk Chemical Ordering

12.11.1 REALIZATION OF THE VALIDATE USER USE CASE

Looking back at the requirements analysis, we see that we have already got a good idea of the operation of some of the use cases. Using the ideas developed in this chapter, we need to understand the use cases in more detail before we go on to design the system. Let us consider the use case for validating a customer, given in Figure 9.14. In the chapter on objects, we considered noun-identification as a way of determining objects. We shall now approach this in a more structured way, working through the different paths through the use case and creating sequence diagrams. We shall use the notions of entity, boundary and control object to give some structure to the object model.

The first step of the primary path is: customer supplies customer number and clerk types it in at the screen. This gives us the beginnings of a sequence diagram, as shown in Figure 12.15. This shows that we have a clerk (an actor) entering data using a welcome screen (a boundary object).

At this point it is unlikely that there need be any other objects involved, until the clerk does some sort of submit. This might be by hitting return after typing the customer number, or it might be by pressing a button. Whatever, we can extend the sequence diagram to incorporate the submit. This results in a sequence diagram as in Figure 12.16.

Now we need to consider the next step of the primary path: the system responds with the customer name and address, and a unique password for the customer. This implies the need for some object to store the name, address and password, and it would be sensible to group these all in a single object called Customer. This will be an entity object, because it is one that will need to persist, and it

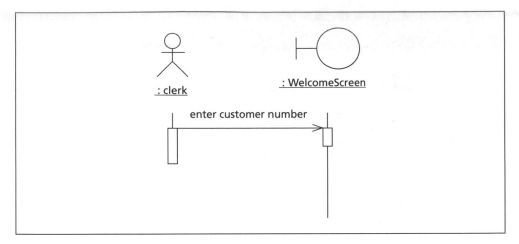

Figure 12.15   The beginnings of a sequence diagram, built from a use case scenario

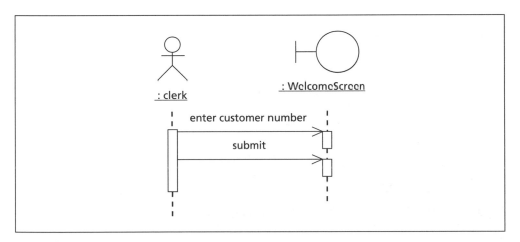

Figure 12.16   Further steps in the sequence diagram

corresponds very closely to a real-world entity, namely the customer. We might then come up with a sequence diagram as in Figure 12.17.

Now this is a reasonable first attempt at a sequence diagram. It has also told us that there is likely to be an entity object in the system of a class called Customer with attributes customerNumber, name, address and password. This would be drawn as in Figure 12.18.

This sequence diagram is fine, but we come to an issue when we reach the third step of the primary path, which says that the clerk clicks on a checkbox if the answers given conform to the data retrieved onto the screen. Now, the fact that the customer has been validated needs to be remembered as the operator progresses through the use cases. The Customer object might be used to keep that information, but that somehow does not feel right. The screen might keep the

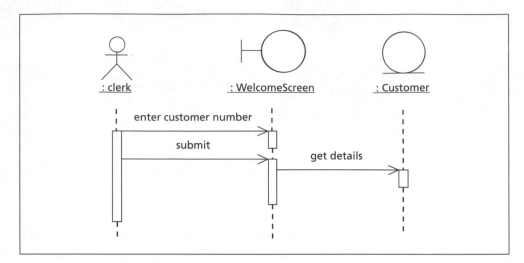

Figure 12.17   Further addition to the sequence diagram

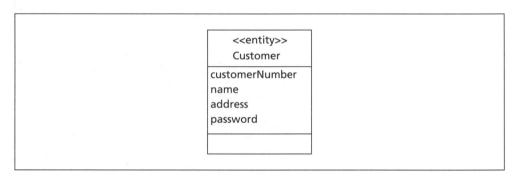

Figure 12.18   Entity object to store customer information

information, but as the query progresses we might have a new screen and destroy the validation screen. Looking back, we do have a construct that is recommended for consideration in any use case, namely a control object for that use case. If we route all requests through the control object, the control object can take the confirmation. We can then keep the control object available for the duration of the call. We end up with a sequence diagram as in Figure 12.19.

We now have quite an elaborate sequence diagram, and we have devised a reasonable structure for the operation of the system. We have a new class of objects – the Validation control object, as shown in Figure 12.20 – and it needs at least one piece of information stored as an attribute to determine whether the customer is validated or not. There are a lot of questions still to be answered, such as how the customer object is located, but many of these can be left to the designer.

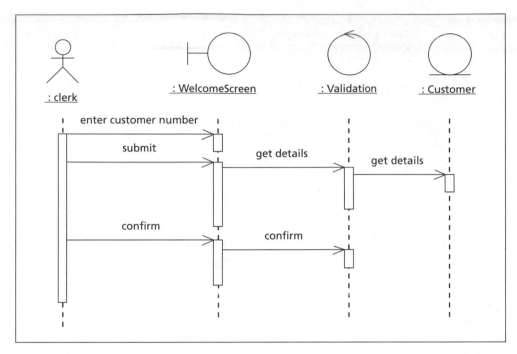

Figure 12.19   The final analysis sequence diagram for the primary path of the Validate Customer use case

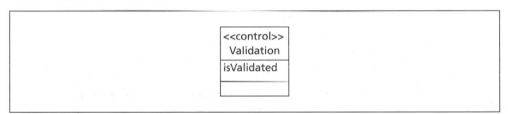

Figure 12.20   The validation control object

The sequence diagram can be redrawn as a collaboration diagram, as in Figure 12.21, that gives some sense of the structure of any class diagram that might need to be drawn.

Having worked through the primary path, we now need to explore the alternatives. Consider the third alternative, where the customer cannot supply the password or name and address. The system must record the attempt. This implies some sort of call log. It will be an entity object that needs to be stored. This will be created by the use case, as shown in Figure 12.22.

The additional object is likely to need to store the customer number, the time, the date and some note saying what happened. We would then have a class as defined in Figure 12.23. This object is likely to appear in lots of places, as call centres are usually required to log every call, whether there is an action carried out or not. The structure of the call log needs to be considered more carefully, and the systems analyst would almost certainly have to investigate by talking to various stakeholders.

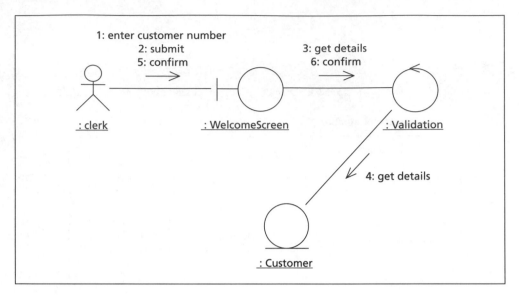

Figure 12.21 A collaboration diagram to show the structure of the system that supports the validate customer use case

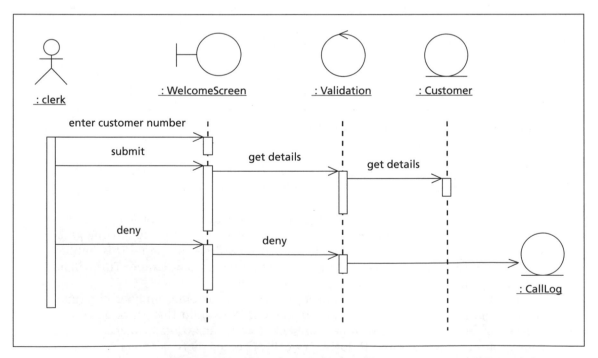

Figure 12.22 Sequence diagram to show the workings of the alternative in the Validation use case where the customer is denied

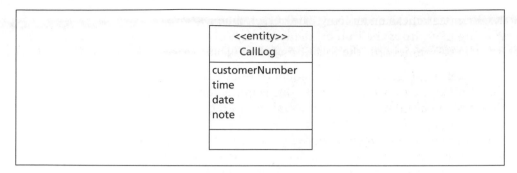

Figure 12.23   An entity object to store a call log

We now have a basis for the class diagram. It is common to show mostly entity objects on class diagrams, as they tend to be the ones with fairly static behaviour, though it is reasonable to show control and boundary objects (Figure 12.24). The relationship between a customer and a call log is one to many; there is no need to name it, as it is quite clear from the diagram what the relationship is.

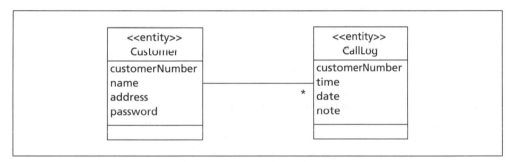

Figure 12.24   A class diagram for the entity objects supporting the Validate Customer use case

You can see from this process that systems analysis provides an incremental opening up of the use cases. It begins to identify some high-level structural behaviour. Through the identification of objects, it begins to elucidate the data that needs to be stored. It also challenges the definition of the use case and checks its validity. Systems analysis will generate a vast number of questions, which will require referral back to stakeholders for answers. We might, at this stage, be asking what other information might be stored about customers for validation purposes, and what extra might be stored in the log.

12.12 ICANDO Site Safety

12.12.1 REALIZATION OF THE ADD FEATURE USE CASE
Consider the primary path for the use case. This states that the sequence of actions is as follows.

1. Engineer clicks on an icon. The cursor changes.
2. Engineer drops the icon on the backdrop.
3. The system records the location of the object.

We can begin to construct a sequence diagram and devise objects to support this. Unlike the previous use case, this is quite detailed and technical in terms of the implementation. It is not unusual to get requirements as specific as this in technical domains.

We need to decide whether we are going to model fine-grained objects such as an icon, or model coarser-grained objects such as a screen. Firstly, this is an analysis phase, so concrete detail for implementation should be outside of scope. Secondly, very fine detail can often be left to the implementation phase. Thus instead of modelling icons, cursors and backdrop explicitly, we shall simply consider a screen. Thus we might make the first steps of our sequence diagram as in Figure 12.25.

Technically there will be lots of objects required to implement the above sequence, but it is not the analyst's job to decide those, nor is an analyst usually knowledgeable enough to decide. Different implementation environments will have different ways of achieving the same effect.

Now we have to decide what to do about the creation of the feature. The simple thing is to create a feature directly from the screen. However, the creation of the feature also involves adding it to the site. The transaction is a little more complex than might at first be thought. Thus we shall use a control object to manage the actions, as in Figure 12.26.

Thus the creation of the facility and the adding of the facility are managed by a control object. Some analysts would put the logic all within the Facility and Site objects or in the interface, and perhaps assign the creation of the feature to the Site object, or the addition of the Facility to the Site object.

The entity classes for Site and Facility are as devised earlier and shown in Figure 11.26 when we determined objects by noun-identification. The noun-identification process is a perfectly good way of determining objects. However, objects drop

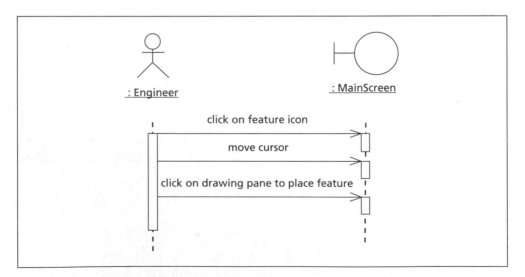

Figure 12.25 First stage of the realization of the Add Feature use case

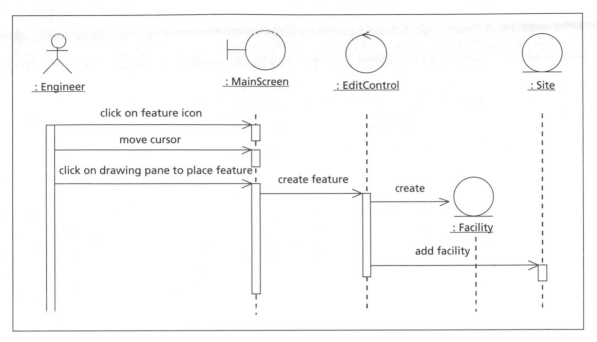

Figure 12.26   Analysis realization of the primary path for the Add Feature use case

out of the use case realizations. The advantage of using use case realization for identifying objects is that at the point of determination the precise role of the object is clear, at least in one use case, and there is less likelihood of determining objects that are unnecessary.

12.12.2 REALIZATION OF THE CHECK DISTANCES USE CASE

Looking at the primary path for the checking of use cases, we see a reasonably complicated definition of the logic, as follows:

1. Engineer clicks on the icon or chooses from the drop down menu.
   For each facility
2. The facility is selected
   For each of the other facilities
   3. The second facility is selected
   4. The rule base is searched for anything that pairs the two facilities
   5. The distance between the facilities is calculated and compared with the rule restrictions.
   6. If there is a rule violation, the rule, facility details and distances are reported

This is a somewhat more complicated process than we have met so far. There is a loop and a condition. The loop requires us to iterate around until every pairing of facilities has been considered. This is shown on a sequence diagram by surrounding the looped sequence in a box and putting a loop condition at the bottom right just outside the box. The condition is to create an infringement

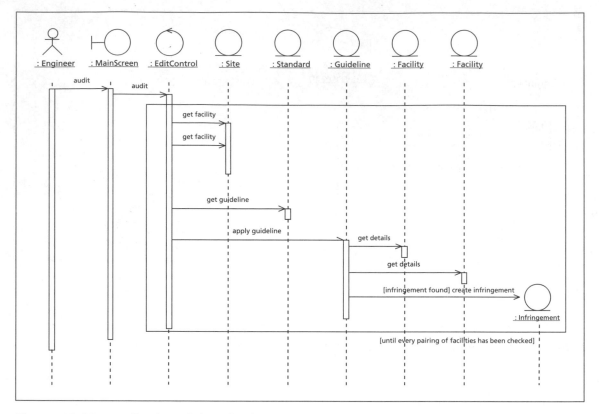

Figure 12.27   Realization of the Check Site use case

whenever one occurs. A condition is indicated in square brackets, showing that the sequence step fires only if the condition is true.

The resulting sequence diagram is shown in Figure 12.27. The edit control asks the site for two facilities, then searches the standard for an appropriate guideline. The guideline is then applied to the pair of facilities. If there is an infringement, an infringement object is created. The details of this matching and the pairing of objects will need much more analysis than has been shown here. This is quite a fiddly piece of code, and there will probably be questions raised during design that will need clarification, and further questions raised during implementation.

12.13 ICANDO Retail Petrol Promotions

12.13.1 REALIZATION OF THE ADD TO ORDER USE CASE
The primary path for the Add To Order use case is as follows.

1. The customer clicks on the order button next to the item on the catalogue page.
2. The system confirms that the product is in stock.

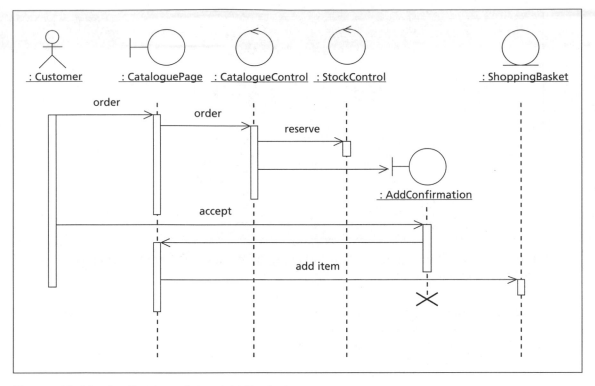

Figure 12.28   Realization of the Add To Order use case

3. The system deducts points from the customer's account.
4. The system pops up an 'add to shopping basket' confirmation box.
5. The customer clicks OK.
6. The item is added to the shopping basket.

This produces a sequence diagram as in Figure 12.28. There is a question about how the stock is structured. To cope with this, a StockControl object is introduced that will determine whether the stock is available and reserve it for the order. The realization of this we will discuss at length in the design section. The structure of the stock will be determined by further analysis. Almost certainly there will be a stock or product object that is accessed, and this will be implemented as a data-base table. There is a short-lived window that is popped up as a confirmation box. The shopping basket entity might well be broken down into shopping basket entries.

Looking at this, we might well have the beginnings of a class diagram in Figure 12.29. The control and boundary classes are not incorporated. This class diagram could be used by the systems analyst as a source of questions about things that need to be stored, over and above the obvious information.

12.13.2 REALIZATION OF THE CONFIRM ORDER USE CASE
The primary path for the Confirm Order use case is:

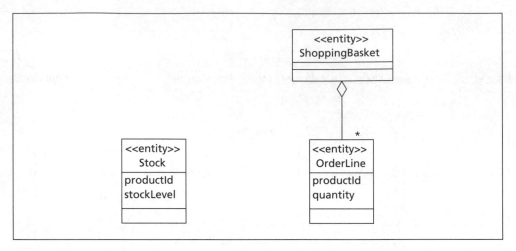

Figure 12.29 The beginnings of a class diagram to support the realization of the Add To Order use case

1. Customer clicks on a button to confirm order.
2. The shopping basket is displayed.
3. The customer clicks on accept.
4. An order is created.
5. Despatch is scheduled.

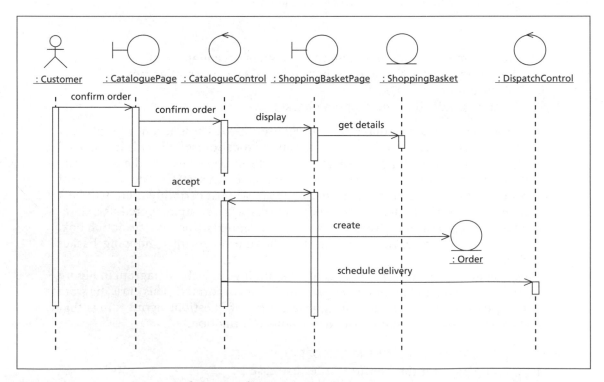

Figure 12.30 Realization of the Confirm Order use case

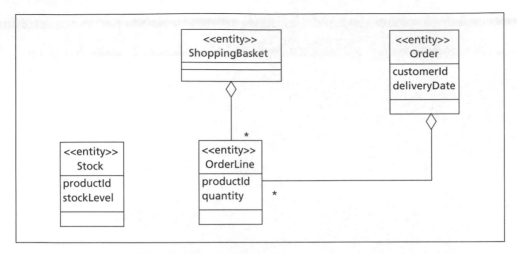

Figure 12.31   The developing class diagram for the customer loyalty system

This leads to a sequence diagram as in Figure 12.30. As before, there are lots of details to consider further. How is despatch organized, and what information will be needed? What information needs to be added to the order? Certainly the order needs to include some reference to the customer. These would prompt the analyst to go back and ask further questions. The class diagram starts to look like Figure 12.31.

REVIEW QUESTIONS

1. **What is a domain object?**
2. **What is an entity object?**
3. **What is a boundary object?**
4. **What is a control object?**
5. **What makes up a sequence diagram?**
6. **What are sequence diagrams used for?**
7. **How do you relate use cases to sequence diagrams?**
8. **What is a collaboration diagram?**
9. **What do statecharts show?**
10. **What is the difference between 'brownfield' and 'greenfield' analysis?**
11. **What are the primary inputs of systems analysis?**
12. **What are the primary outputs of systems analysis?**

EXERCISES

1. For each of the use case descriptions you produced for the exercises in Chapter 8, produce:
   (i)   a representative set of scenarios
   (ii) a sequence diagram for each scenario
   (iii) a collaboration diagram from each sequence diagram
   (iv) a class diagram

ARCHITECTURE AND DESIGN

Reader's Guide

This section assumes that the broad functionality of a system has been defined and agreed. It introduces more thoroughly the notion of objects and adds detail to the notations supplied in the sections on analysis. It also includes a brief introduction to database design, and ends with a chapter introducing the concepts of architecture with a description of modern architectures.

This section will be most useful to developers responsible for the detailed design and construction of systems. Some of the aspects of design will be of interest to analysts, but usually the complexity of design is not too important for analysts in their day-to-day work. Managers rarely need to understand this level of detail, but they may feel it important to know some of the elements of design.

Chapter 13: Design

This chapter introduces more detail to the UML notations used in systems analysis, and provides methods for fully specifying the functionality of a system so that it can be constructed.

Chapter 14: Database Design

This chapter looks at some specific aspects of design related to databases, introducing relational databases and concepts such as transaction, serializability and atomicity.

Chapter 15: Architecture

This chapter looks at the general issues of architecture, and at modern IT architectures.

Design

1. **More detail about classes, associations and sequence diagrams**
2. **How to specify operations**
3. **About additional types of class (factories) to manage creation of persistent information**
4. **About the notion of a component, and how components are composed to produce systems**
5. **A little about reuse and component-based design**

Systems analysis provides a comprehensive definition of the system's external behaviour, and a description of the gross structure of the system. It is like the provisional drawings and layout of a building. A good analysis team will have produced a description of something that is both usable and feasible to construct. The design team will need to take that description and provide detailed specifications of key parts of the system. In the construction of a building, the design team will worry about the quality and strength of materials, the specification of the load-bearing properties of beams and walls, and the way services such as electricity, networks and plumbing are routed through the building. A software designer is going to worry about how the functions are going to be distributed around the system, how storage is going to be managed, how parts of the system are to be structured, how the system is to be split into subsystems, how they communicate, how reliable the system will be, and what to do if disasters occur.

Systems analysts will mostly be focused on functional requirements, and provide a fuller description of what the system does. Designers must also consider the non-functional requirements captured during the requirements analysis stage such as scalability and reliability, as well as providing a description of how the functional requirements are to be achieved. They must initially define an architecture, and subsequently abide by the architecture and make changes to the architecture where necessary.

The role of architecture is paramount for designers. This defines the overall structure of the system in terms of the physical components, such as computers and networks, the softer components, such as databases and development environments, and the actual organization of the application software. Architecture needs to be considered before detailed design. However, in this book the architecture chapter comes after design, because the concepts needed to discuss architecture include those that are fundamental to design.

The output of design is a description of the system that can be transcribed by the implementation team into a working system. Many of the concepts we have met so far will be part of the output of the design process, but they will have been pushed to greater detail. In UML terms, you have met many of the basic concepts already, but we now need to consider them more comprehensively. We will also need some additional concepts, such as components.

In this chapter, we will look much more closely at objects, considering the fine detail. So far we have met them as a general concept. Now we need to know how operations and attributes can be specified. We will also look much more carefully at sequence diagrams, using them to define more tightly the interactions between objects; it is through the collaboration of objects that the design will provide the functionality to support the use cases. We will look at operation specification, which is where we need to flesh out the detail of what objects actually do. In the next chapter, we shall look at database design and the issues around that, as databases of some kind are almost universally used for the storage of persistent information.

The notion of a use case persists throughout design. Where systems analysis focuses mainly on the external behaviour of use cases, design focuses more on the internal behaviour of use cases. Use cases interact and interfere with each other. They do this through the underlying objects. Figure 13.1 illustrates this. Each use case depends on a number of objects collaborating, but those objects may form part of the collaborations to support other use cases. An example might be an order object that is used by a use case for taking orders, and by a use case to support delivery of orders.

Good design is not easy. There are some general principles that we shall talk about, but nothing beats experience for developing good designers. Talent is also needed, and many people struggle with the intricacies of design. Few people walk out of their degree courses with anything more than a limited talent for good design, and they will need to hone that talent as they work. The challenge has grown greater as systems have grown more complex and interdependent. Twenty years ago I would have claimed to have been a good designer of computer programs for most types of business application, when computer programs were mostly standalone and well-defined in function. Now, I would struggle in many settings to

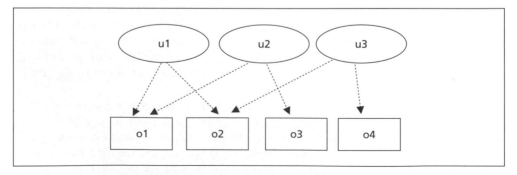

Figure 13.1   The interaction of use cases through objects

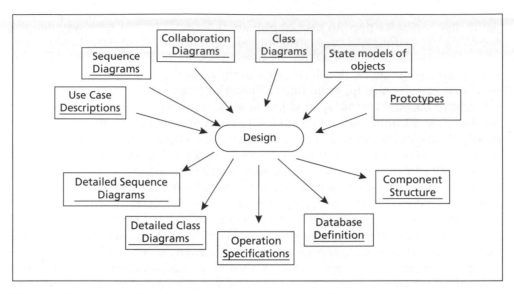

Figure 13.2   The primary inputs and outputs of design

produce good comprehensive designs for large, distributed systems. This should not deter you. Rather, it should show you that there are many challenges ahead and much to learn. No doubt the design of good systems will change as dramatically over the next two decades as it did over the previous two, with the emergence of mobile devices and new ways of delivering access to computing power.

Figure 13.2 shows the primary inputs and outputs of the design process. As with systems analysis, all previous documents will be available. The outputs from systems analysis, such as sequence diagrams and class diagrams, are given more detail. Database storage for data that needs to persist will be defined during design, and there will be a grouping of objects into components. The processing takes place in operations that will need to be specified in some detail. The objects will need to be distributed into some component structure, which will determine the application architecture.

13.1 Objects

The primary output of design is a set of objects described in class diagrams, related to each other, and organized so that they can implement the scenarios in use cases. Not only do they need to provide the functionality, they need to behave like good citizens and not interfere with each other in an unwanted manner. Keep in mind this idea of objects being members of a society, not discrete and separate entities. A designer is as much interested in good structures made up of objects as in the individual behaviour of objects.

Class diagrams are the map that use cases must adhere to in their execution, and in fact are often referred to as static models. You can think of use case executions as journeys through a landscape whose features are defined by the class diagrams that describe the system. Class diagrams are grown by repeated exploration of the paths that use cases need to take to provide functionality. For new systems, the use case elaborations will cut radical new paths, defining lots of new classes, operations, attributes and relationships. As systems develop, new or changed use cases mostly utilize the paths that have been defined, perhaps occasionally adding a new class or relationship, or adding to operations and attributes.

We have met the notion of an object as a meaningful grouping of data, called attributes, and things that can be done with that data, called operations. They are mostly drawn as rectangles[1] with (usually) three compartments.[2] Objects can be related in a variety of ways: through a special relationship known as inheritance where they can share common properties, or through aggregation relationships where an object can be composed from a number of other objects, or through associations that provide paths of communication between objects allowing one object to access the operations of another object. We have also met briefly the notion of a stereotype, where objects can be given specific roles such as entity and boundary objects, and can also have special notations to visually distinguish those roles.

We now need to look in more detail at the objects and relationships that can be defined before we move on to the details of design. These are part of the end goals of design, producing a comprehensive description of system behaviour in terms of individual objects and object interactions.

13.1.1 ATTRIBUTES

Attributes are where information is stored. So far, we have just named the attributes. At some stage, the detail of the attributes needs to be fully fleshed out. Ultimately the attributes will have to be implemented in some computer language, and all the details of the attribute worked out in full. UML allows a much more thorough definition of attributes than just naming them. The full syntax for an attribute definition in UML is:

```
visibility name[multiplicity]: type-expression = initial-value
```

visibility determines who can access the variable. So far we have said that a variable is not normally accessible by any other class. In fact, the visibility can be defined as in Table 13.1.

Table 13.1   Visibility of attributes

Visibility	Mnemonic	Meaning
+	Public	Any other object can view or modify this attribute if it can reference the object, and it can be inherited.
-	Private	No other object can view or modify this attribute, and it cannot be inherited.
#	Protected	No other object can view or modify this attribute, but it can be inherited.

---

1 We have seen already that sometimes a class can be drawn using an icon rather than a rectangle, as with control, boundary and entity classes.
2 There are additional compartments that can be used, but these are not common. See Bennett *et al.* (2001) for more information.

Table 13.2 Sample attribute definitions

Attribute definition	Description
`#balance: integer = 0`	An integer value called balance, set initially to zero, and not accessible to any object other than the one that it is defined for. It can be inherited.
`+postcode: string = ""`	A string value called postcode, set initially to a blank string, and accessible to any other object that can reference this object. It can be inherited.
`-name[5]: string`	A list of five strings called name, which are not initialized automatically on creation of the object. They are not available outside the object, and they cannot be inherited.

`name` is the name of the attribute, as we have used them in analysis.[3] `multiplicity` allows for multiple copies of attributes, effectively defining an array if `multiplicity` is more than one; if `multiplicity` is 1 then the square brackets and multiplicity are omitted. `type-expression` is a language-dependent expression to indicate the type of the attribute, such as string or integer;[4] the target programming language needs to be considered. `initial-value` is a language-dependent expression that can be used to give the attribute a value when the object is created. Table 13.2 gives some examples of attribute definitions.

In most object-oriented languages attributes may in fact be other objects.[5] UML allows the inclusion of other objects in an object on a class diagram using aggregation or relationships, but it is perfectly legitimate to use a type name that is a class defined elsewhere. When the time comes for implementation, we shall see that aggregation and other types of relationship sometimes require the incorporation of additional attributes to provide the associations.

Attributes are created when the object is created. Usually a class has an initialization operation called a constructor that sets up initial values for some or all of the attributes. Attributes may be modified by other objects or by the owner object, depending on the visibility. They can be accessed by the operations on the object, and may be changed by those operations. Attributes disappear when the object disappears, and often an object has a special tidy-up operation called a destructor that is called when the object is destroyed. In an object-oriented system, attributes cannot exist outside of objects.[6]

---

3 Many methods and organizations have naming conventions for attributes. UML does not specify any rules about naming.
4 UML has no definition of the fine detail of types. The designer needs to be aware of the target language. Fortunately, most languages have similar types for most of the values they can store, such as string or integer.
5 It is viable to use a class as a type in the definition of an attribute, and you will see this commonly in implementations. Suppose we had a class called Address; then it would be possible to define an attribute address: Address, that is, an attribute named address of type Address. Most object-oriented languages allow extension of their basic types (such as integers and strings) with user-defined types (usually classes). This has made object-oriented languages particularly flexible.
6 You will find limited exceptions to this rule in some languages, where there is some notion of a variable that is independent of objects themselves. In practice they are rarely used.

13.1.2 OPERATIONS

Operations are where the processing is done in an object, and in fact in a fully object-oriented system all processing is done inside operations. Operations may manipulate the attributes of the object and call operations on other objects, and if the visibility allows they may manipulate the attributes of other objects too. The object interactions we considered in the sequence and collaboration diagrams during analysis are implemented through operations.[7]

The first things we need to consider with operations are the operation signatures. This defines the precise format of the call to the operation and the information that is exchanged with the operation. The operation signature does not specify what the operation does, just the syntax of the operation. The definition of what the operation does will be considered later in the section on operation specification.

Operations take parameters, and can return values. The general syntax is:

```
visibility name (parameter-list) : return-type
```

We have implied so far that operations can be accessed by any other object. In practice it is possible to hide operations using `visibility`. Table 13.3 shows the meaning of the visibility rules for operations. `name` is the name of the operation. `parameter-list` is a comma-separated list of parameters with the syntax

```
kind name: type-expression = default-value
```

where `kind` is an indication of the direction in which information is passed, as indicated in Table 13.4, `name` is the name of the parameter, `type-expression` is a language-specific definition of the type of the parameter, and `default-value` is a language-specific expression to set the value of the parameter if it is not supplied. The `return-type` of the operation is a language-specific value that defines a return value; this is optional.

Table 13.5 shows some example operation signatures. As you can see, the detail can become very elaborate in terms of specifying the format of operation calls

Parameter types and return types may in fact be types of object, and in a UML design specification it is permissible to use class names as types. This makes object systems very powerful, and very expressive.

Table 13.3 Visibility rules for operations

Visibility	Mnemonic	Meaning
+	Public	Any other object can use this operation if it can reference the object, and it can be inherited.
−	Private	No other object can use this operation, and it cannot be inherited.
#	Protected	No other object can use this operation, but it can be inherited.

---

7 Object interactions can take place through event handling, and some object-oriented languages treat event handlers a little differently from operations.

Table 13.4 Parameter kinds for operation specifications

Parameter kind	Meaning
in	The parameter is supplied as input to the operation and is not updated by the operation.
out	The parameter is supplied to obtain output from the operation, and any value will be returned to the caller. Any value supplied by the caller will not be accessible to the operation.
inout	The parameter is supplied with a value as input to the operation, and will be set by the operation to return a value to the caller.

Table 13.5 Examples of operation signatures

Operation	Meaning
+setAddress(in address: string)	The operation called setAddress takes one parameter called address of type string that is used as input only. There is no returned value. The operation is visible to any object that can reference the object containing the operation. The operation can be inherited.
#setBalance(in balance:integer)	The operation called setBalance takes one parameter called balance of type integer that is used as input only. There is no returned value. The operation is only visible to other operations in the same object, and it can be inherited.
+getBalance(): integer	The operation called getBalance takes no parameters and returns an integer value. The operation is visible to any object that can reference the object containing the operation. The operation can be inherited.

The operation signature is basically the protocol for exchange of information between objects. The signature defines the precise shape of the data. However, the signature has no implication in terms of processing. We therefore need to further specify the operation in terms of what it does.

13.1.3 CONSTRUCTORS AND DESTRUCTORS

When a system is started, only a handful of objects exist in the system. These objects will have the responsibility of creating other objects. Objects, in turn, can create other objects, and so on until the system is a network of hundreds or thousands of objects.

When an object is created, there is usually a special operation called a constructor that is fired automatically on creation of the object. This is responsible for any initialization of the attributes, and may in turn create other objects; for example a constructor for an aggregate object may create all of its parts. In class diagrams it is not usual to show the constructor explicitly. However, if the initialization of an object is complicated, it may be desirable to make it explicit, and certainly we will have to specify the behaviour of the constructor.

When an object has finished its useful life, it often has some tidying up to do. A destructor operation is one that is called automatically when an object is destroyed. Again, this is usually omitted from class diagrams, but if there is complex behaviour it might be desirable to make it explicit. An example would be when an aggregate object needs to destroy its components. For example, an order object may have a number of order lines as aggregate parts, and when the order is deleted the order lines need deleting too; the deletion of the order lines can be done by the destructor of the order.[8]

13.1.4 ASSOCIATIONS

An association is a link between two objects that indicates a channel of communication.[9] If there is an association between two objects, then at least one of the objects knows about the other, and often both objects know about each other.[10] This basically means that one object can call the other object, or vice versa. A class can have an association with itself, meaning that one instance of the class can associate with another instance of that class; for example, a person class may relate to itself to define some relationship between persons.

The association link is drawn as a solid line connecting two classes.[11] The association has a number of adornments, as indicated in Figure 13.3. The association name is an optional description of the association, drawn somewhere near the centre of the association line. The association name gives some mnemonic description of the association.[12] If the association is obvious, it is better to leave the association name out. The optional role adornments are written at either or

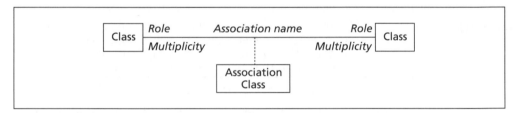

Figure 13.3 Associations with adornments

---

8 Many object-oriented languages have a notion of 'garbage collection'. Garbage collection looks for objects that are no longer used by the system and destroys them automatically. Garbage collection makes programmers' lives much easier. To get rid of an object in a garbage-collected system, all that is necessary is to simply get rid of any reference to it, and the language system will detect that it is no longer used. Garbage collection is quite safe, in that any object that is no longer referenced could not be found anyway; there is no danger of the garbage collector deleting wanted objects.

9 The association in class diagrams is more general than the idea of a relationship in entity–relationship diagrams. Class diagrams define lines of communication. Entity–relationship diagrams specify data linkages. As we shall see, associations often get translated into relations when the design considers databases.

10 When we consider implementation, we shall see that associations are implemented by putting attributes at one or both sides of the association. These attributes keep references to the objects at the other side of the association. In this way, the objects 'know' about each other.

11 You can have associations between more than two classes. These are shown by connecting the classes associated to a diamond. This notation is rarely needed in practice.

12 Optionally there can be an arrowhead (a black triangle) on the association name to indicate the direction in which the association name should be interpreted. See Bennett *et al*. (2001).

both ends of the association line to indicate what role the class plays in the association. Roles are used less often than association names. In fact, the association and the roles are often obvious from the two objects that are related. Multiplicity indicates how many instances of a class are bound into a particular association; if the multiplicity is omitted, it is assumed to be one. An association class allows you to supply attributes and operations for the association; association classes are relatively rare in practice, and it is usually possible to split an association and make the association class a normal class with two associations with the other two classes.

You can have multiple associations between two objects, as indicated in Figure 13.4, where a customer may have one invoicing address and one or more delivery addresses; roles have been used to differentiate between the different associations, according to the type of address. An object can also have associations with other objects in the same class, as indicated in Figure 13.5, where an employee may have a supervisor, a supervisor may have a number of supervisees, an employee may optionally have one counsellor, and a counsellor who is also an employee may counsel a number of staff; the associations have not been named, but multiplicities have been included.

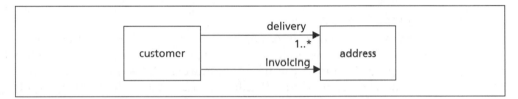

Figure 13.4   An example of two associations between the same pair of classes

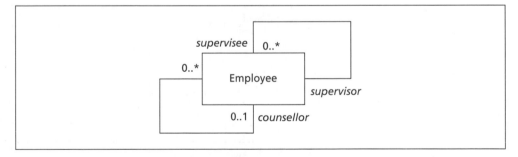

Figure 13.5   Example of multiple associations between objects in the same class

We have met the idea of association in analysis. In design we need to be more precise, and as we shall see we shall often decompose analysis objects into design objects. The role of the designer is to preserve and implement the functionality prescribed by the analysts through such transformations. Ultimately the associations are going to be implemented by attributes stored in either or both classes at the ends of the association, or by data paths in databases.

13.2 Sequence Diagrams

We use sequence diagrams in systems analysis as a way of opening up the use cases and describing their operation in some detail. From systems analysis we generate a good description of the external behaviour of the system, and some proposed objects that correspond to entities in the real world (entity objects), or to interfaces with the real world (boundary objects), or to complex interactions between objects (control objects).

Now we need to take these sequence diagrams further. There are two things we need to do. Firstly, we must consider the objects themselves. Are they viable objects for implementation, or do they need to be restructured in some way? Secondly, the interactions on the sequence diagrams need to be supported by operations. We will need to define those operations and the information that is exchanged by these operations.

We now need to consider a little more detail about sequence diagrams. We introduced them informally to support systems analysis. In design, we need to be more precise. Design is in fact a refinement of the systems analysis, adding detail to the way the system operates, and making key decisions about the internal structure.

13.2.1 LIFELINES AND FOCUS OF CONTROL

A sequence diagram consists of a set of object lifelines. The object is drawn at the top of the lifeline.[13] The lifeline is shown as a dotted line drawn vertically below the object. Time proceeds down the lifeline. Figure 13.6 shows a lifeline on a sequence diagram. The order of the lifelines on a sequence diagram is largely irrelevant. By convention, it is usual to arrange the interactions so that the arrows are mostly left to right, but that is not always possible.

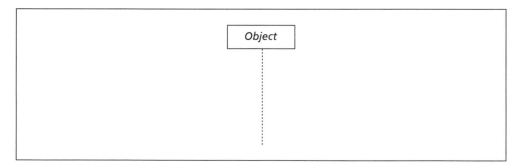

Figure 13.6   An object lifeline

During a particular execution of the system, the locus of control often passes into an object, implying that the object is carrying out some work. This can be shown on a lifeline by a bar, as indicated in Figure 13.7. The locus of control is initiated by some stimulus, as indicated in Figure 13.8. The object on the left has

13 UML allows you to draw sequence diagrams with the lifelines going left to right and interactions going up and down, but this is so rare, and so obvious when it is seen, that it has been omitted.

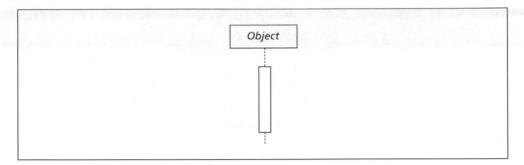

Figure 13.7 Locus of control bar on a lifeline

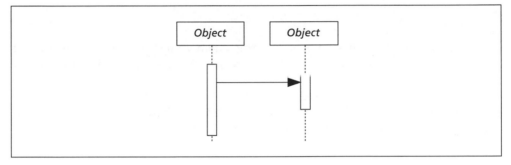

Figure 13.8 Initiating locus of control

triggered action on the object on the right. In this case, the object on the left remains active, as it has not completed its work until the call to the other object has completed; we shall also examine alternative ways of passing the focus of control.

Objects can create other objects, and this is shown on a sequence diagram by a stimulus pointing to the head of the object that is created, as in Figure 13.9, where the object on the left creates the object on the right.

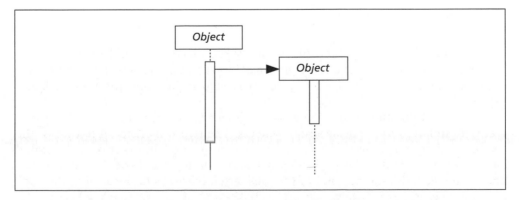

Figure 13.9 Showing an object creating another object

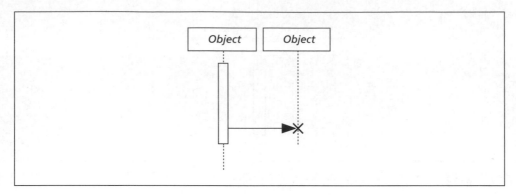

Figure 13.10   One object destroying another

Objects can destroy other objects, and this is shown by a stimulus pointing to a cross on the lifeline of an object, as in Figure 13.10, where the object on the left destroys the object on the right.

Objects may call trigger actions within themselves (say by calling one of their own operations). This is shown by a stimulus going back to the object lifeline and creating a nested locus of control, as in Figure 13.11.

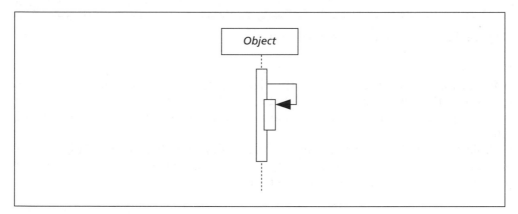

Figure 13.11   An object calling itself

Iteration, where a sequence of actions takes place over and over again, is shown by drawing a box around the group of interactions and writing a recurrence condition underneath the box. Figure 13.12 shows just one interaction being repeated.

Sequence diagrams thus have very powerful means of describing the creation, deletion and interaction of objects. The two-dimensional nature of the sequence diagram allows you to see very complicated interactions. As stated earlier, object-oriented design is mostly about creating good societies of objects, and sequence diagrams are one of the most effective ways of describing the society's behaviour.

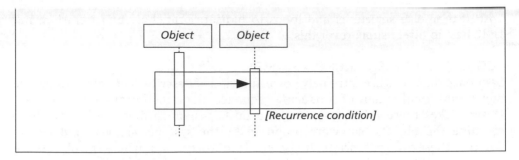

Figure 13.12   Iteration on a sequence diagram

13.2.2 MESSAGES AND STIMULUS

Stimulus can affect the locus of control in different ways. The arrowhead shows the type of stimulus. Table 13.6 shows the basic flow notations.[14] The procedural flow is the most commonly used one. This corresponds to one object calling an operation on another object and waiting for that operation to complete before progressing.

The branching and iteration notations of UML sequence diagrams are not particularly clear at times, and not all the current software tools support them properly. Often it is noted by *ad hoc* comments on the diagram. The best approach I have seen to this is to put pseudo-code down the left-hand side of the diagram,

Table 13.6   Message flow notation for sequence diagrams

Arrow	Stimulus	Description
⟶	Procedural or Synchronous	When the first object calls the second object, it suspends activity until the second object completes the request. When the second object loses the locus of control, the first one resumes.
⟶	Flat	This triggers the second object to start execution. Normally this is asynchronous, meaning that the first object does not wait for a return. However, it can be used if it is unknown whether or not the message is asynchronous.
⟶	Asynchronous	This triggers execution of the second object, and the first object continues without waiting for the second object to complete its task.
[c1] [c2]	Branching	Splitting the arrow into two or more branches means that more than one object might be called, depending on some conditions. The conditions are written in square brackets. If the conditions are mutually exclusive, this represents a branch; otherwise it shows potential concurrent execution of the called objects.

14 There is a dotted arrow notation to indicate return of flow of control. However, this is usually superfluous. For more information see Bennet *et al.* (2001).

with if-then-else structures and loops to indicate branching and iteration, but UML has no direct support for this.

13.2.3 CONSTRUCTING SEQUENCE DIAGRAMS

Sequence diagrams are extremely powerful ways of describing collaborations. We met an informal means of producing sequence diagrams for analysis purposes. Design takes these initial diagrams and pushes them further. Design needs to examine the objects that were proposed by the systems analysis and decide whether these are appropriate. It also needs to worry about where the objects are created and, if the objects are persistent, where and when they are stored in or retrieved from a database. Architectural considerations will determine the way objects are represented. The interactions between objects need to be precisely defined, and operations assigned to objects to support the interactions.

13.2.4 SOME DESIGN PATTERNS FOR INTERACTIVE SYSTEMS

A design pattern is a 'layout' of a design that is commonly used. Use of patterns has become a much-debated topic in software engineering. Some of the patterns that are discussed, such as those by Gamma *et al.* (1995), are complicated and beyond the scope of this book. However, we shall introduce some very useful patterns here for the structuring of systems.

If we look at our exploration of the expansion of a use case through the introduction of boundary, control and entity objects, we can see that the common pattern to an interactive system looks something like Figure 13.13. This is a pattern that is repeated over and over again in the design of interactive systems. A user will interact with a boundary object that is usually a screen. This interaction may in fact involve a considerable exchange of information, say in completing a form. The boundary object (or screen) will then request some control object to carry out a piece of work, say when the user presses a submit button. The control object will then delegate the work to a number of entity objects.

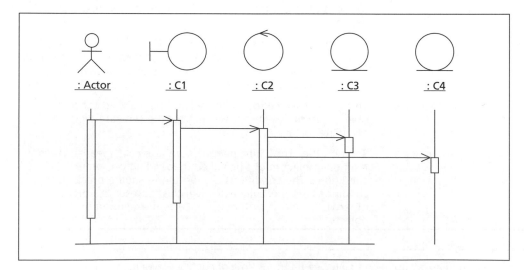

Figure 13.13 Standard design pattern for interactive systems

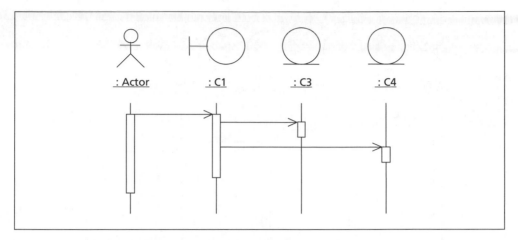

Figure 13.14   A simpler pattern for simple interactive systems

This corresponds to a three-tier architecture, which we shall discuss in detail in the chapter on architecture, with the top tier handling all the detailed interaction, the middle tier concerning itself with business logic, and the bottom tier with information that is long-lasting. This separation of interface, logic and basic information is one that has been prevalent in various forms throughout the brief history of software engineering.

A simpler pattern, used in some instances where the logic is not particularly complex, is shown in Figure 13.14. Many simple tools for the construction of small applications use this pattern. There are advantages in terms of speed of construction, but the disadvantage is that much of the business logic is buried in the interfaces or in the entity objects. However, in some cases where the business logic is straightforward, this type of pattern is viable.

The assumption so far is that objects are in fact already in existence. Designers have two issues to consider. One is that objects need to be created the first time they are needed. The second is that objects that need to persist (mostly entity objects) are stored in a database, and there are usually no instances of the object available for use without explicitly creating one; for example, a customer object is not likely to be kept live in the system, as it is only used from time to time, and if it were kept live then the system would need to manage many thousands of them. Thus there is a need to create active objects from database records for the duration of use case executions.

To do this, a common technique is to use 'factory' objects. These objects take responsibility for creating objects when they are first needed, and for transferring the objects to and from the database during their life. Figure 13.15 provides a typical pattern where a control object will trigger a factory object to retrieve information from a database and create an entity object. A real-life example would be when the user typed a customer number that was given via a control object to a factory object; the customer number would be used to retrieve a database record that would in turn be used to populate the attributes of a customer object. Once the object has been created in memory, the other objects can reference that object,

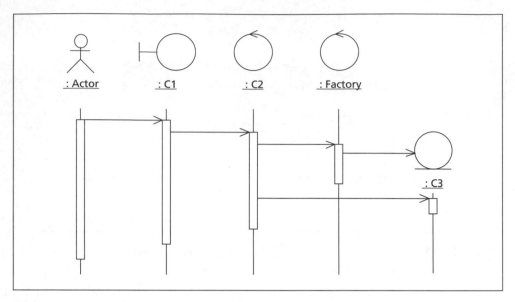

Figure 13.15   A pattern that shows the use of factories to instantiate objects that have been stored in a database

as in the previous two patterns. Finally, if the object needs to be returned to the database, the factory object can be called to transfer changed attributes back to the database and destroy the entity object.

Simple patterns like the above will get the designer a long way in the construction of systems. Later, when we have looked at databases, we will consider the factory objects in more detail, and consider some basic patterns for driving database interactions.

13.3 Collaboration Diagrams

Collaboration diagrams are an alternative way of showing object interaction. They are in fact semantically the same as sequence diagrams; they just show the flow of interactions in a different way. They look a little like class diagrams, but operations and attributes are not shown, and the message interactions between objects are shown. Figure 13.16 shows a collaboration diagram that illustrates the flow of messages from an interaction with an actor. The boxes represent instances of classes, and the lines indicate lines of communication that must be represented as associations in a class diagram. The messages are written adjacent to the lines, with an arrow indicating the direction of call. To indicate the order of calls, the messages can be numbered.

I find these diagrams less useful in practice, though some designers are fond of them. However, they do illustrate very clearly the idea that use cases are implemented as journeys through the landscape mapped out by the class diagram, and that the class diagram is constructed by firstly mapping out the journeys and then combining these journey descriptions together. Some CASE tools allow the

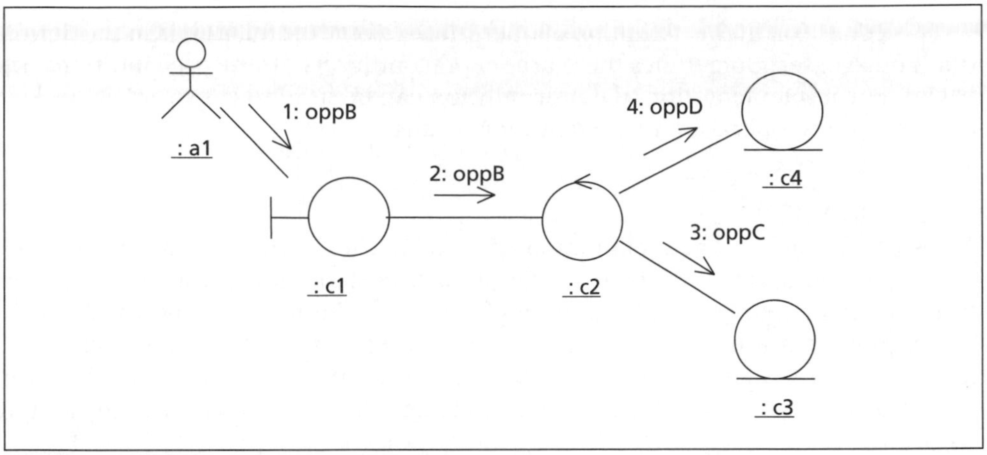

Figure 13.16 A collaboration diagram

automatic generation of collaboration diagrams from sequence diagrams, and this can be a useful step towards visualizing the shape of the class diagrams.

13.4 Operation Specification

So far we have defined the syntax of operation calls, specifying the information exchange. However, we need to specify the details of the operations. The level of formality and rigour needed to do this varies. At the simplest level, a textual description can be used. The formal methods school would like to use a mathematical description, and we will look briefly at the Object Constraint Language (OCL) later. Complex operations can be described by the UML diagrams that we have met so far, including activity diagrams and sequence diagrams. An informal approach, using something known as 'pseudo-code' is quite common, though this is not supported directly by UML.

13.4.1 PRECONDITIONS

We met the idea of preconditions in the specification of use cases. A precondition is a statement that must be true for a use case or an operation to legally fire. An example of a precondition on an operation to withdraw money from an account would be that the amount to be withdrawn did not exceed the credit available in the account. A properly constructed operation that is fired when the precondition is true will produce the desired effect. Calling an operation with the precondition false will not guarantee a result.

Preconditions can be described as simple English statements, or as mathematical statements in a language such as OCL, or statements in the target language in which the system will be implemented; UML permits any of these. The more rigorous the statement, the more time and effort usually goes into the preparation of it, but then less work is needed later to tighten up the definition for implementation.

A precondition in the definition of operations is very useful, as it is in the definition of use cases. Sometimes there are no preconditions, or the preconditions are trivial. For implementation, the precondition can be used to construct a check at the start of the operation to prevent illegal calls.

13.4.2 POSTCONDITIONS

A postcondition is a statement that must be true when an operation (or use case) has legally completed. As with preconditions, postconditions can be expressed formally in a language like OCL, or less formally in English or pseudo-code, or in the implementation language; again UML allows any of these. Postconditions need to record state changes made by the operation; for example, a withdraw operation needs to have reduced the available credit in an account by the amount withdrawn.

Postconditions can be used as the primary tool for specifying behaviour. In a formal methods environment, using mathematical specifications of functionality, the postcondition would state all the required changes by the operation. Sometimes this is known as design by contract, with the preconditions and postconditions determining the contracted behaviour of an operation.

13.4.3 PSEUDO-CODE

Pseudo-code is an old idea that has long been used for the detailed specification of computer systems. It 'borrows' the basic structures of most computer languages, such as if-then-else and loop constructs. For the designer, it is useful when there needs to be a detailed description of some processing, but where the other notations available are inappropriate or cumbersome. It would be over the top for designers to specify every part of the system with pseudo-code, as it would leave little creativity in the construction process and take an inordinate amount of time. However, it is a tool worth having.

UML does not support any notion of pseudo-code. This can be very limiting, because often, once details need to be considered, a textual description can be more concise and precise than a diagram.

Figure 13.17 shows some sample pseudo-code. As you can see, it is perfectly legitimate to mix some programming language constructs with English statements. Here SalesLedger might be a factory or other object that is designed to deliver a sequence of sales items, and getSalesItem may be an operation to get the next sales item. There is an implicit ordering that groups the sales items for customers together. The definition here is neither rigorous nor watertight. The aim is to convey the outline of the logic in an accessible way. More rigour and proper code might as well be developed by the designer, but often the detail is left to the implementer.

13.4.4 ACTIVITY DIAGRAMS

Activity diagrams are commonly used to specify details of operations. Figure 13.18 shows how you might specify the operation to print an invoice. The activities are then simple program steps. It is acceptable to put language statements as activity descriptions.

```
Print Invoice
SalesLedger.open
SalesLedger.getSalesItem
While SalesLedger.hasItems
   Customers.getCustomer(salesItem.customerID)
   Print the customer details on the invoice
   While salesItem.customer unchanged
     Print the current salesItem
     Add salesItem.value to total
     SalesLedger.getSalesItem
   EndWhile
   Print invoice salesItems total
   Apply customer discounts
   Calculate VAT
   Print amount payable
   Skip to next invoice
EndWhile
```

Figure 13.17   Pseudo-code to describe invoice printing

13.5 User Interface

The user interface is the most public aspect of the system. A naive approach to user interface design is to create one or more interfaces for each use case. This, however, provides a messy and complicated user interface. In practice, a use case often needs multiple screens in an interactive system, and quite often a number of use cases can be supported by a single screen. Figure 13.19 shows the relationship between screens and use cases.

There are two aspects to user interface design. The first is the overall structure of the interface, and the second is the layout and detail of the individual screens. The overall structure is best understood by acknowledging that screens are in fact objects, and thus a class diagram is appropriate to describe them. Figure 13.20 shows a small interface to an order-taking and tracking system. Directional associations have been used to indicate the paths that can be taken through the interface, and the attribute and operation compartments on the classes have been suppressed.

This fits in perfectly well with the idea of the class diagrams as being maps and use case executions as journeys on the landscape defined by the map. In this case, the map only shows user interfaces (which are boundary objects). Other maps will show entity and control objects.

The screens themselves need designing. Using UML to design the detail of these is usually overkill – using objects in class diagrams to represent buttons is carrying OO methods too far for most application development. The best approach by far is to draw out the screens, either by hand or through some tool. If the tool can provide some simple interaction so that potential users can play with the screens,

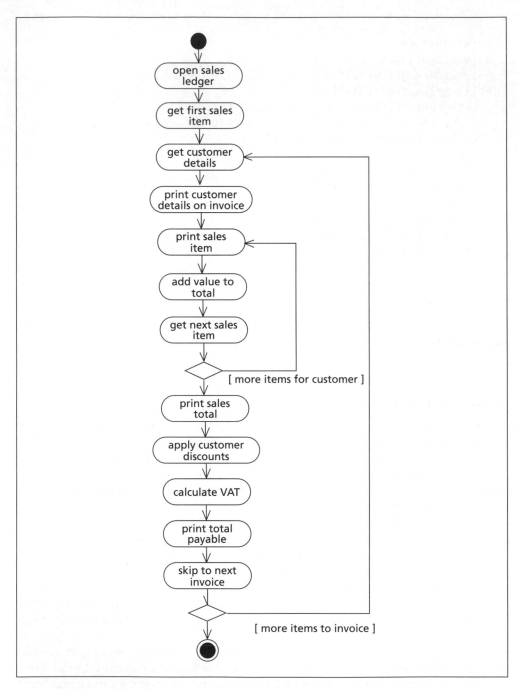

Figure 13.18 An activity diagram to specify operation logic

all the better. If the screens can be linked together to simulate the overall structure and navigation between screens, even better.

Good interface design is beyond the scope of this book. However, in most working environments, there will be some common standards defined. For most

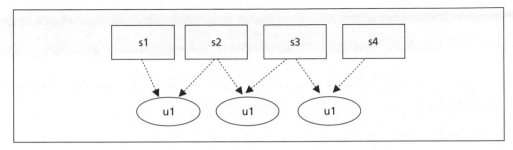

Figure 13.19   The relationship between screens and use cases

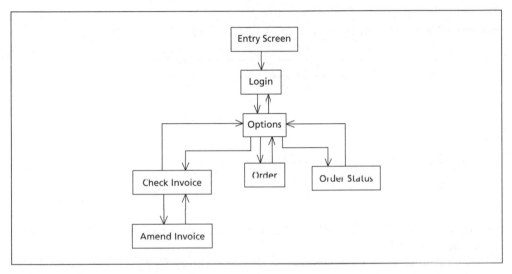

Figure 13.20   Class diagram used to show the layout of a user interface

brownfield development, the user interface structure will not be negotiable – it will have to conform to the structures and styles in place.

Some simple guidelines are worth following. Firstly, screens need to contain reasonably logical groupings of functionality, which is pretty obvious. Users like common tasks and frequently accessed information grouped together to minimize navigation. Too many screens can be an obstruction to ease of use. Users also like to know where they have been, and to have a clear route from where they are to where they want to be. Screens need to be consistent in look and feel. Help needs to be available. Feedback from the system needs to be meaningful. Expert users like minimal explanation and shortcuts. Novice users like plenty of explanation and are not able to use short cuts.

13.6 Components

A typical application is built out of hundreds of classes. These classes need to be grouped together for implementation. Components are groupings of objects for

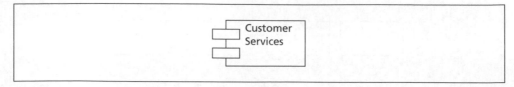

Figure 13.21 UML notation for a component

Figure 13.22 UML notation for an interface class

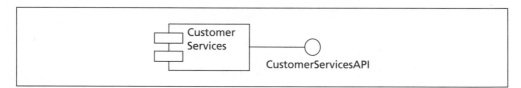

Figure 13.23 An interface class linked to a component, publishing the services of the component

implementation. Components in UML map onto physical implementations, such as Beans in Java.[15]

The UML notation for a component is shown in Figure 13.21. Objects in the design are assigned to the component. The component publishes an interface, and this is represented by an interface class which is drawn using the notation in Figure 13.22. Interface classes are a special type of class that have no inherent behaviour themselves, but which provide a route through to operations on other classes. The interface class for a component is drawn linked to the component as in Figure 13.23.

Once we have begun to group the classes into components for implementation, we can define the structure of the application in terms of the components and how they call each other. Figure 13.24 shows a number of components grouped together. The Accounts User Interface will be all of the objects that define the interface for (say) the accounts department. The Customer Services and Account Services will be the control and entity classes for the support of the use cases for the accounts department. The Database Services will supply transfer of entity objects to and from the database. The dotted arrowed lines represent dependencies, indicating that the objects in one package can call the objects in another package via the services published by the interface classes.

The process of defining components needs careful consideration. Two software engineering principles need to be taken into consideration – cohesion and

---

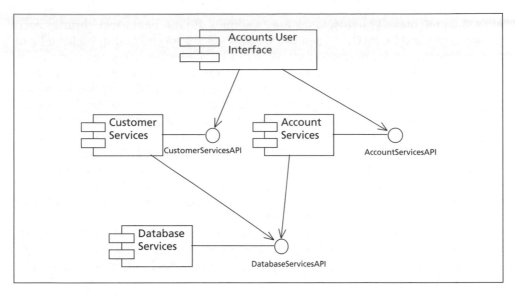

Figure 13.24 The organization of components to define the overall structure of the application

coupling. Cohesion is where a group of objects support each other well and have related functionality. Thus, all the control objects and entity objects for account management would be cohesive – they will tend to call each other, and to have related functionality. Within a cohesive group of objects there will be considerable interaction.

Coupling is the degree of interaction between components. Tightly coupled components have a high degree of interaction and dependence. Loosely coupled objects have a low degree of interaction. Tight coupling implies strong interdependence, and means that the components have lower standalone capacity.

Generally it is better to make the coupling between components low and the cohesion within components high. This makes for more maintainable systems. The components will be easy to comprehend because they are internally well defined. A large number of bugs within systems also come from interfaces, and keeping the interface interactions to a minimum is therefore desirable.

Of course, like any principle, there are exceptions to the rule. For example, it may seem like good cohesion to keep the boundary classes in the same components as their respective control and entity classes. However, because of the way systems are often deployed, it makes more sense to group a number of boundary classes into a component which will be deployed to one computer, and for that component to perhaps use a number of other components to service the interfaces that are deployed on other computers.

13.7 Reuse

Reuse is the holy grail for many software engineers, and there have been many crusades in search of it. Long, long ago, the idea of functions made programmers dream of constructing powerful systems out of pre-defined functions. Some success was achieved by this, and some examples are mathematical libraries such as those supplied by NAG.[16] Then came computer packages, and these have been remarkably successful in some areas, such as financial accounting and some types of order-processing and stock management. More recently came the idea of components, where systems could be built out of pre-defined components. Methodologies have been devised to generate software components that can be reused.

The economics of reuse need to be examined carefully before any strategy is adopted. If it costs three times as much to make a component reusable as it does to make it usable, and it costs half as much to reuse something as it does to use it, then you have to reuse a component more than six times to get any return on initial investment. Moreover, when a component is shared among many systems, the dangers of changing it are magnified – you might compromise a number of systems as well as the one you are working on.

Reuse should not be an end goal of software developers. If you can reuse things, then that is likely to reduce the cost of implementations. However, bad reuse strategies can be very damaging, and produce a great deal of useless or use-once code at high expense.

A good strategy is to aim for use before reuse. Once a system is up and running, then future systems may sift the system design for good parts to reuse. However, there is no free lunch, as the IT industry regularly rediscovers. The techniques below have their areas of success and their limitations. Consider them, and if they are appropriate for your application you may like to study them in more detail.

13.7.1 COMPONENT-BASED DEVELOPMENT FOR REUSE

A current strategy for producing reuse is to split the development stream into two parallel streams, as indicated in Figure 13.25. The first stream consists of

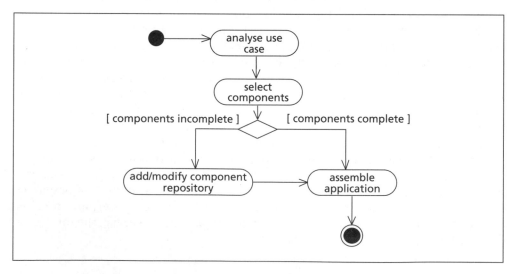

Figure 13.25   The workflow for component-based development

---

16 Numerical Algorithms Group: http://www.nag.co.uk/

component designers and developers. The second stream consists of application assemblers. Application assemblers take the use case definitions and look for pre-built components to assemble the application, with the minimum of code development. When an application assembler cannot find a suitable component, or the existing components need some extension, then the component development stream is provided with a request to provide new components or modify existing ones. Once these are available, the application assemblers build the system from the components.

The advantage of this approach is that separate development streams for applications are forced to consider reuse of components. The component developers are the prime custodians of reuse. The disadvantage can be slowing down the application development streams. In practice, it is likely that a small amount of development will go on as part of the application assembly.

An option with component-based development is the purchase of pre-defined components. This is a small but growing market. Mostly these are for technical purposes, such as graphics generation or bar-code reading. There are also specialist components for particular business sectors, such as the finance industry.

Components conform to particular technology standards, such as JavaBeans or Microsoft's component model. It is not usually possible to mix components from different technology platforms. Thus a key architectural decision, namely the technology platform, will determine the component architecture and the options for third-party supply of components.

13.7.2 Application Frameworks

A framework is a partially prepared application that is a common root to a number of applications. Typically it will make use of the inheritance facilities of objects. Consider a bank that has different types of customers. All customers have names and addresses, but the facilities available to customers vary by the type of the customer. We thus might produce a framework that contains the abstract view of customer, and then the various applications to deal with the different types of customer can inherit the common properties. Figure 13.26 shows a Customer object that would be part of the framework, and three types of customer, namely BusinessCustomer, CharityCustomer and PersonalCustomer, that inherit the

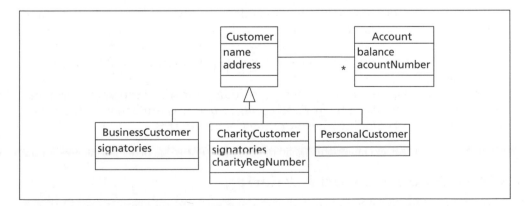

Figure 13.26 Use of a framework

properties of Customer, including the relationships such as the accounts of a customer.

The approach to application development using frameworks is for the development stream to inherit, wherever possible, from a framework object. Sometimes the development stream will consider an object, attribute or operation to be sufficiently general purpose to be incorporated in the framework, and they can promote them. Once an application is constructed, the framework team can examine the application for generic functionality that they can promote.

Frameworks are appealing, but to make serious use of them there need to be a number of similar applications being developed. Financial services development often has a high commonality of functionality that requires a little specialization. Application packages often make use of this idea, and the customization of a framework is the way packages can be adapted to local requirements; the advantage of this is that package upgrade is usually an integration of a framework that extends the existing framework, and which therefore minimizes disruption.

13.7.3 DESIGN PATTERNS

Patterns are a little more abstract in concept than frameworks. We have already met a couple of patterns when we were discussing the typical organization of interactive systems. Patterns are frequently recurring features, or abstract solutions to specific problems. A very simple example of a pattern would be the structure of an order, as in Figure 13.27. As a designer you will naturally pick up patterns as you gain experience, probably without consciously thinking of them as patterns.

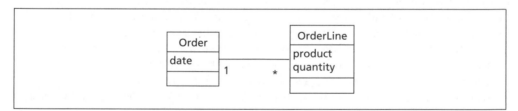

Figure 13.27   A simple pattern to show the typical structure of an order

With a framework, you embed your application code in the framework, and your new classes automatically get the behaviour of the abstract classes. With a pattern, you construct your code to look like the pattern, taking its structure and modifying it slightly. Thus, with the order pattern above you would copy and add to the structure.

Patterns have become a major research topic, and the academic world has become very excited about them. Catalogues of patterns are being built up, and current practice is beginning to explore the use of patterns.

13.8 ICANDO Bulk Chemical Ordering

Design means that we need to take the analysis and produce a description of the system that can be implemented in programming languages. Design progresses much as systems analysis docs, but pushing the detail further and further until there are classes that can be implemented. A good starting point is the sequence diagrams that have been devised in systems analysis.

The designer needs to work through the individual use cases and come up with some overall approach to the architecture. It is not a simple task, but one that will involve considerable invention and revision. The requirements of individual use cases will overlap and sometimes interfere with each other.

Only a brief taster of design can be worked through here. A design document for the ICANDO chemicals system would be more substantial than this book.

13.8.1 DESIGN FOR THE VALIDATE CUSTOMER USE CASE

We begin with the sequence diagram in Figure 12.19. This is not one that could be directly implemented in a programming language, for the following reasons:

1. We have not produced a description of the screen layout.
2. We have not determined how the customer object is going to be found.
3. We have not defined the information exchange with the objects.

If we take these in order, then the first thing we might do is devise the screen. In practice, this could not be done in isolation for this use case. There might be other information on the screen that supports other use cases or routes to other use cases. There is, however, enough to provide a definition of some of the fields that need to be available on the welcome screen.

The Welcome Screen might look something like Figure 13.28. There would be a field for the entry of the customer number, and a button to trigger the validation. The information needed back would be the customer name, the customer address and the customer password. The clerk would need to click on the Accept tick box to accept the customer as validated.

UML does not have any screen definition notation that would allow us to describe the screen as in Figure 13.28. The most we can do is produce a class definition, as in Figure 13.29. This shows the various fields represented as attributes, and the buttons and tick boxes as operations. How helpful this representation is

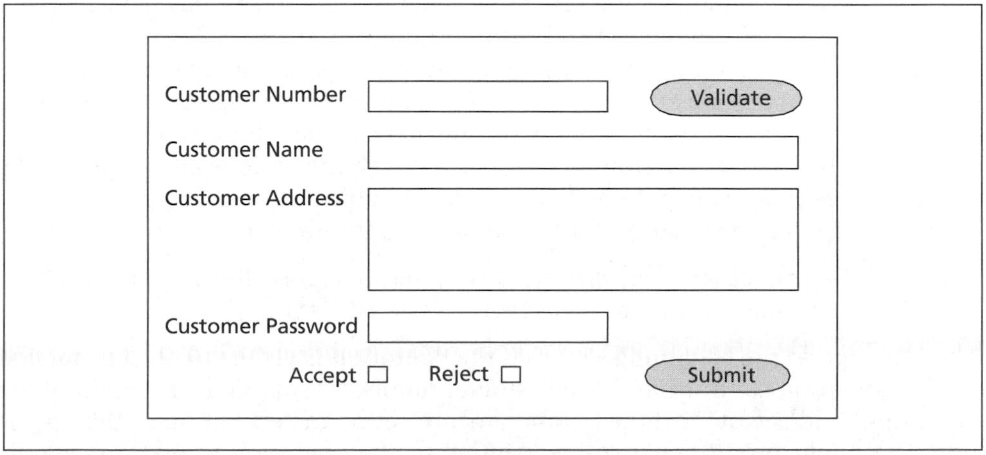

Figure 13.28 Layout of the welcome screen for the Validate Customer use case

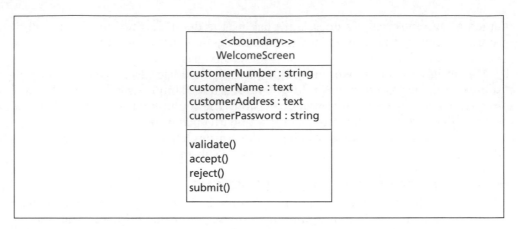

Figure 13.29   A UML representation of the welcome screen

can be debatable. One thing it has allowed is the introduction of typing on the fields. UML does not include particular types for the attributes, and these will be types in the target implementation language.

We can now consider the identification of the customer object. In a system of this type, the customer object is almost certainly going to be stored in a database. An individual customer object will not be live in the system for most of the time the system is running. Instead, an object will be created for the period of time it is needed. The attributes of the object will be kept in a database record, or a set of database records if the attributes are complicated. The common way of dealing with this is to introduce a special object, known as a factory, to construct the object from the data in the database. Thus, the first thing that needs to happen is that the validation control object will call a factory object to have the customer object created, and then the validation control object can access the customer object. We end up with a sequence diagram as in Figure 13.30.

The data factory is classed as a control object. There might only be one instance of this object, available to all objects within the system for the purpose of bringing objects out of the database and returning them there. We can now consider the design of the individual objects and the operations on them.

The Validation control object needs a validate operation that will take the customer number, request a customer object and return for display the customer name, address and password. We might thus have a class definition as in Figure 13.31. This definition will grow as we work through the various alternative paths and use cases that involve the Validation control object.

The full operation signature for the validate operation would be

```
+validate( in customerNumber: string, out customerName: text, out
customerAddress: text, out customerPassword: string)
```

The plus sign at the beginning says that the operation is visible to objects outside of the validation control class. The customer number is supplied when calling the operation, and the other three parameters are set by the execution of the operation. We might produce a small description of the operation in pseudo-code as follows:

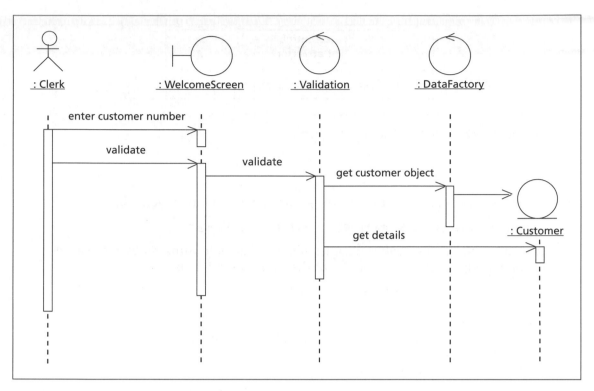

Figure 13.30 The addition of a factory object to create an object from the database

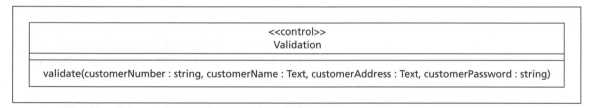

Figure 13.31 Class definition for the Validation control class

> Call the data factory operation to get a customer object for the
>   customer with the supplied customer number.
> Call the customer object, asking for the customer name, address and
>   password.
> Return, setting the customer name, address and password.

The data factory will need an operation to get the customer object. This would result in a class definition as in Figure 13.32. The data factory would have an operation for each type of object that needs to be retrieved from the database. Sometimes there may need to be a retrieval of a large set of objects (say all customers with a particular name), so that a lookup can be done if the customer has forgotten the customer number.

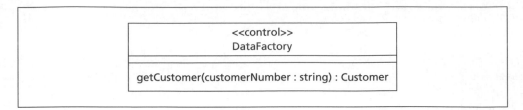

Figure 13.32 The DataFactory class definition.

The full operation signature for the getCustomer operation would be

```
+getCustomer(in customerNumber: string): Customer
```

It would need to be visible to other objects, and it returns an instance of a Customer object. The pseudo-code for the operation might be:

```
Retrieve the customer record from the customer table with the value
  of customer number as given.
Create a customer object.
Set the attributes of the customer object from the fields in the
  customer record.
Return the customer object.
```

Finally, we need to define the customer object itself. This would be as in Figure 13.33. For this particular use case, the customer number, name, address and password would need to be stored with the customer object. For other use cases, this would need to be extended to cover additional information, such as a credit limit for the customer.

As you can see, the design involves a considerable addition of detail to the analysis model. It needs some knowledge of the implementation environment, and it will often require further investigation to determine the detail that needs to be supplied.

The boundaries between analysis and design are not clear-cut. Some of the things we have discussed, such as the screen layout, might well have been determined by the systems analyst. Even if the systems analyst defines something, it is

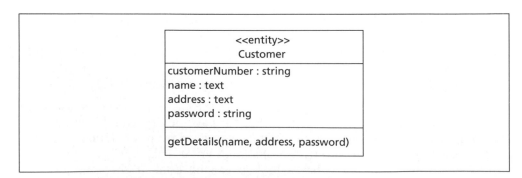

Figure 13.33 Class definition for a customer object

not set in stone, as sometimes the designer will suggest a different way of doing the same thing.

13.8.2 USER INTERFACE DESIGN

The design of the user interface is in part devising screen layouts for individual use cases. However, there is a need to consider the overall operation of the user interface. Thus, as screens are devised, the relationship between screens needs to be considered. As with anything in design, the screen organization needs to be fluid and to develop as the design progresses.

If we go back to the use case diagram in Figure 9.13, we might make a reasonable guess at a user interface structure as described in Figure 13.34. From the welcome screen, the clerk might go to the take order screen. From the take order screen, the check product code and delivery screens would be accessible. If, during the take order, there was a request to transfer the call, then there might be a one-way movement to the call transfer screen, returning ultimately to the welcome screen ready for the next customer call.

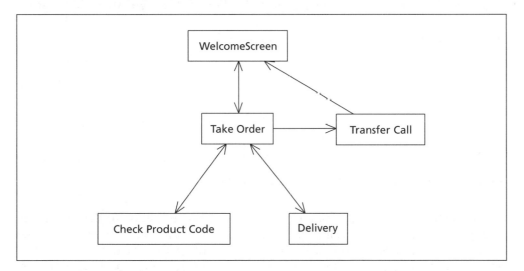

Figure 13.34   User interface structure for telephone ordering

13.9 ICANDO Site Safety

13.9.1 DESIGN FOR THE ADD FEATURE USE CASE

The clicking on an icon and placing of the facility on the drawing sheet is quite a complicated piece of programming that is very dependent on the implementation environment. The description of the environment would be quite lengthy, and is really beyond the scope of this book. We shall therefore look at the part of the use case dealing with the creation of the facility and the placing of it on the site.

If we look at the sequence diagram in Figure 12.26, the operation that we need to design is the one that places a facility in the site. Looking at the class diagram in Figure 11.27 we have already made a stab at the definition of a facility, and

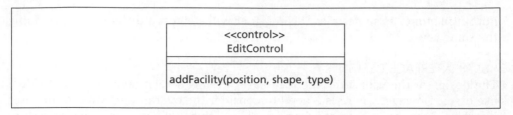

Figure 13.35 First definition of the edit control object

determined that it has a shape and a location. Thus to create the facility, the operation that does that will need to know the shape and location. It will also need to know the type of facility. Thus, our first version of the EditControl object might be as in Figure 13.35.

The addFacility operation needs to know the position, shape and type. The choice of types of the parameters needs to be thought through. Mostly a programming language will not have any explicit notion of coordinate, so we might have a need to create a coordinate class, as in Figure 13.36.

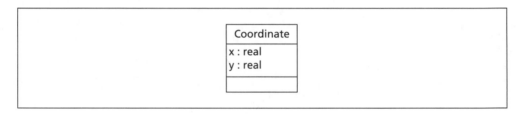

Figure 13.36 A class to represent coordinates

We might also create a (somewhat more complicated) class to define a shape (this is left as an exercise). The type of the facility will ultimately refer to a storage facility, a road, or whatever. It is unlikely that the part of the drawing tool that deals with the screen would need to know anything about the particular types of thing it is drawing, so it might pass on a string to indicate the type of the object that has been drawn. We thus come up with an operation signature:

```
+addFacility(in position: Coordinate, in shape: Shape, in type:
    string)
```

where Coordinate and Shape are to be defined as classes. All of the parameters are input to the operation and are not changed by the operation.

The logic of the addFacility operation might be described by pseudo-code as follows

```
Create a new facility object of the appropriate type (storage
    facility, road, office etc.) depending on the 'type' parameter.
Set the position and the shape of the new facility.
Add the new facility to the site.
```

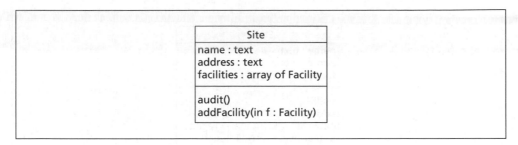

Figure 13.37 The revised Site class

The creation of the facility is fairly straightforward. The site will need a new operation to cope with the addition of a facility, and some data structure to keep the list of facilities. We thus might end up with a revised Site class as in Figure 13.37.

We are slowly getting to the point where it would be possible to program from these descriptions. Programming itself might query the design and offer different ways of achieving the same goal. Design is not a straightforward process, and requires frequent revision.

13.9.2 DESIGN FOR THE CHECK SITE USE CASE

The sequence diagram in Figure 12.27 needs no change in structure, as the objects are in memory for the execution of the use case. The challenge for this use case is in the binding of the objects together. We now have a new operation on the edit control object, resulting in a revised class definition as in Figure 13.38.

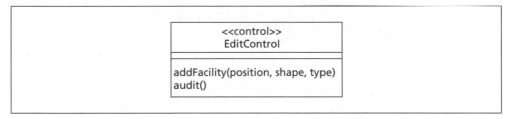

Figure 13.38 The revised edit control object

The first problem that presents itself is the pairing of the objects on the site. We need to devise some routine that pairs facility 1 with 2, 3, 4, and so on, then facility 2 with 3, 4, 5, and on until all have been paired. We thus might come up with the pseudo-code for the audit operation on edit as

```
1. Set a variable i to 1
2. Set a variable j to i+1
3. Check the guidelines for facility i and j
4. If j is less than the number of facilities, then add 1 to j and
   go back to step 3
5. Set i to i+1.
6. If i is less than the number of facilities, go back to step 2
```

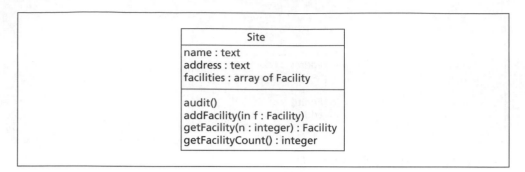

Figure 13.39 The revised site class

This will pair off each of the facilities and apply any guideline appropriate to the facilities. We need to be able to obtain the number of facilities on a site, and be able to get a facility based on a number (assuming the facilities are numbered 1, 2, 3, ...). Thus we might extend the Site class as in Figure 13.39. All this would translate straight into a programming language, apart from Step 3, which we need to consider further.

The guidelines are based on the safety distances between facilities, and the guideline depends on the particular type of the facility. Thus we need to search the standard for a guideline that refers to the two types of facility in question. Thus, on the guidelines we need an operation to get a guideline based on the two types of facility being considered. The Standard object may well be extended as in Figure 13.40 with an operation getGuideline. This needs to know the types of the two facilities that are to be checked, and a string has been used to describe the types. A guideline will be returned.

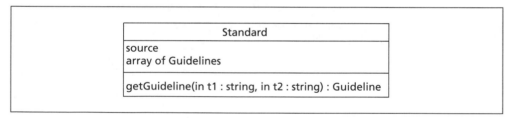

Figure 13.40 The revised standard object

Having got the guideline, it needs to be applied. The sequence diagram suggests that the application might be an operation on the guideline. This seems reasonable, as it is purely a local consideration for the guideline. Thus we might have an operation on the Guideline class to check two facilities, as indicated in Figure 13.41. The core of the rule is the minimum safety distance between two facilities, and the facilities are described as strings and the distance as a real number.

The check operation will return an infringement if the guideline is broken. The return value will be true if there is an infringement, and false otherwise.

We can now revise the pseudo-code for the audit operation on edit control to be:

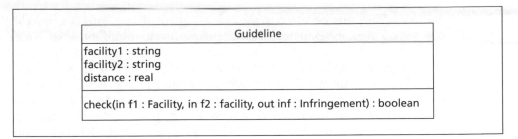

Figure 13.41 Revised guideline

1. Set a variable i to 1
2. Set a variable j to i+1
3. Apply the guideline for facilities i and j by
   3.1 get the facility types for facilities i and j
   3.2 get the guideline that applies to the two types
   3.3 apply the guideline to the two facilities
4. If j is less than the number of facilities, then add 1 to j and go back to step 3
5. Set i to i+1.
6. If i is less than the number of facilities, go back to step 2

This could all be translated into programming code.

This is all quite complicated. Technical systems tend to have the most complexity in the implementation, and the problem above is relatively simple. There would almost certainly be quite a lot of revision of the above design, even through the process of construction.

You should be getting the idea by now that the designer needs to work at a much finer level of detail than the analyst. The designer will often have to refer back to the analyst to ask for more information. The designer is also apt to miss detail that the programmer will require, and there will be questions fed back on the design. That does not excuse analysts or designers from providing the most comprehensive description they can. It is merely a fact of life in the process of developing computer systems of any complexity (or of any construction process, be it building or engineering).

13.10 ICANDO Retail Petrol Promotions

13.10.1 DESIGN FOR THE ADD TO ORDER USE CASE

This use case would be elaborated in much the same way as the previous use cases. However, it does have one challenging feature relating to the reservation of stock, and we shall consider that in some detail. The thing that makes this particularly challenging is that the application is run over the Internet with customers who may abandon the order for lots of reasons. However, if they make an order that is not fulfilled because the goods have been oversubscribed, there will be a disappointed customer.

Let us begin by adding an operation to the StockControl object. This is a control object that we set up in analysis to deal with all the issues surrounding stock. Now we have to provide some detail on how it will operate. The operation that we need is indicated in Figure 13.42. The reservation will clearly need to know the product, as indicated by the product ID, and the quantity. The sessionId is an Internet convention – when you use an e-commerce site and log in, it is usual to assign a unique session identifier that can be used to keep track of the activities for that session (we need not consider here how that is implemented). Basically, the browser will indicate the session whenever any request is made back to the server.

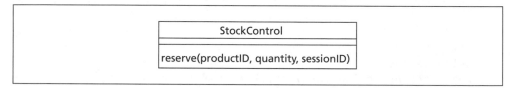

Figure 13.42 StockControl object

Internet applications will usually have a session object, which is effectively a control object. It will last as long as the user is browsing the Web site. If the user explicitly logs out or closes down the browser, then the session object will tidy up and disappear. If the user does not interact with the Web site for a specified period, say ten minutes, then the session object will automatically close down and take any action needed.

We can now look at the reserve operation on StockControl. The obvious thing is to keep a stock record for all products, and this might be a simple object as in Figure 13.43, with a productId and a quantity. Details of the product would probably be kept in another object. Now if, on reservation, we simply deduct from the quantity, then we remove the risk of over-ordering provided we ensure that reservation is not allowed if there is insufficient stock.

Figure 13.43 A Stock object

The problem comes when the customer does not complete the transaction by executing the confirm order use case in Figure 9.22. Then the amount of stock that was reserved needs to be returned to the stock record. The solution is to introduce an extra object to record the reservation, as shown in Figure 13.44. This will store the sessionId as well as the product and quantity reserved.

We can now put two operations on the StockControl object to commit the reservations for a session or to undo them. We thus end up with an object as in Figure 13.45.

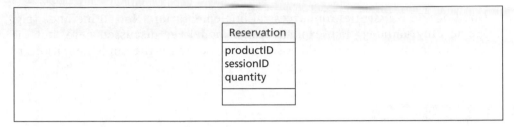

Figure 13.44   A reservation object

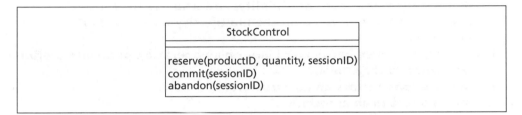

Figure 13.45   The revised StockControl object

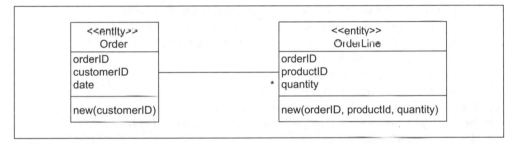

Figure 13.46   The class diagram for the orders

13.11 Conclusion

Design is a tricky area. It requires an understanding of the implementation environment as well as an understanding of the user requirements. Inexperienced designers are able to work on small parts of the system with clear guidance and a well-defined architecture. Good design, covering architectural considerations (see next chapter) takes a great deal of experience and skill.

The above examples should have given you some taste of the complexity that design involves. Different types of application present different problems. For example, the site safety system has complicated algorithms, while the other two systems described need to manage database transactions carefully.

Design is very much filling in the fine detail from the broad picture that analysis has provided. It needs to consider not just what the system does, but how it does it. It needs to concern itself with issues such as database integrity and recovery from disasters (big or small). It needs to worry about the shape of the data. For larger systems, the issues of reuse need to be addressed.

Good design is essential for successful implementation. Not all methods (e.g. Extreme Programming) use explicit design models as discussed here, but the underlying issues need to be addressed in the coding for the implementations to be successful.

REVIEW QUESTIONS

1. For an attribute, what is the UML specification for the type expression.
2. What are the three types of visibility, and what do they mean?
3. What does it mean if you omit the multiplicity on an attribute definition?
4. What are the three parameter kinds on an operation parameter definition? What do they mean?
5. What are constructors and destructors?
6. What is a role in an association?
7. How many associations can there be between a pair of classes?
8. Can a class have an association with itself?
9. What is a lifeline on a sequence diagram?
10. How is focus of control shown on a sequence diagram?
11. How do you show repetition on a sequence diagram?
12. How is branching shown on a sequence diagram?
13. What is a design pattern?
14. What is a precondition on an operation?
15. What is a postcondition on an operation?
16. What is pseudo-code and where is it used?
17. How might you show the structure of the user interface?
18. What is a UML component?
19. What is cohesion in a component?
20. What is coupling between components?
21. What are the approaches to reuse?

EXERCISES

1. Work through the design for the ICANDO trading system for the use cases you have defined.
2. Work through the design for the ICANDO/NeverShut retail system for the use cases you have defined.

Database Design

1. **The way databases are related to objects, and how to map persistent objects to database tables**
2. **About the notion of normalization for database design**
3. **How databases are queried in SQL**
4. **About transactions in applications**

So far we have been considering computer systems as made up of objects. When a system starts up, a society of objects is created that provide functionality to support use cases. Now we must embark on the strange facts of life of computer systems. Where do objects come from, and where do they go when the system is switched off? What are the birth and death of objects?

Many objects are transient. They are created for a short-term purpose, and they disappear. Computer screens, control objects, interfaces to other systems and factory objects can all be recreated each time the system is turned on or when they are needed. However, some objects, typically entity objects, need to be remembered between executions of the system. When you switch off the computer, you would like your customer records still to be there when you turn it back on again. The way we do this is to store the objects on a computer's hard disk.

There are lots of ways of keeping things on a hard disk. Relational databases are the most common, and this is the way we will be exploring in this chapter. Almost every business application today uses relational databases. It is possible to keep things in files, and thirty years ago this was the most common way of storing data, but this is tedious and rarely used for large scale applications. Object-oriented databases[1] have been around for over 15 years, but they have not gained ground over relational databases, and are generally not considered except for certain specialist applications.

Relational databases were invented in the 1970s and became popular throughout the 1980s until they became the almost universal first choice for storing large quantities of data. Databases existed long before then, but were a

---

1 An object-oriented database keeps representations of objects in the database that correspond to the representations in programming languages. They enforce encapsulation of data, and access to information is strictly controlled. This does lead to performance problems and lack of flexibility, and thus these types of databases have not caught on except in niche applications where they have features that are valuable.

little more cumbersome to build and search, and much less flexible. We shall be looking at databases in a very simple way. We shall not consider in detail the query languages, but focus on the structure of the database and how we can get objects into and out of the database.

A relational database stores things in tables, much like spreadsheet tables or tables in a book. These tables are sometimes known as 'relations', but mostly they are just called tables. They are very simple structures, and the elegance and power of relational databases lies in this simplicity. Each table has a fixed number of columns.[2] At first this seems a limitation, as something like a customer order might potentially have a variable and limitless number of fields. However, we shall get over these problems by breaking complicated data into simpler parts and finding ways of recombining those parts.

The rows in the tables are known as records,[3] and it is in records that we store objects. The elements in a record are known as fields, and they correspond to the attributes of the object that is being remembered by the record. The fields in a record are simple types, such as integers, strings and dates. Each column has a name, and this corresponds to the attribute name in the object that the table represents. Table 14.1 shows a representation of a relational database table that holds names and addresses – simple, is it not?

Table 14.1 A relational table

name	address
John Smith	25 Burgundy Drive
Imran Khan	14 Cheviot Lane

The question is: how we can store complicated data that represents real-world objects, such as customer orders with arbitrary numbers of data entries? The answer is to spread the information across a number of database tables, and to link the tables together. At first, it is difficult to see the benefit of this, as often the individual tables can look pretty meaningless, and it requires quite a lot of work to reconstruct them into a meaningful structure. Hopefully, however, you will see some good reasons for this as you read on.

Firstly, we need some 'hooks' in records to tie them together. These hooks are known as keys. A key is a field or set of fields that uniquely identifies a record in a database table. No two separate records in the same table are allowed to have the same key value. Quite often a field is invented to act as a key, such as a customer number. Keys are very important, as you can link records by storing the keys of one table in another table. Consider Table 14.2, which is a simple table for storing employee information (very simple: it just keeps names – in practice there would be many columns). A key, called 'employee number', has been invented. This means that we can refer to an employee by quoting the employee number instead of the name. This has some advantages. Firstly, it gets over the problem of two

---

2 Early databases, such as network and hierarchical databases, did not keep to this simple rule, and records could have repeating groups and be of variable length.
3 Some purists in the database world will call records in database tables 'tuples', for reasons best known to themselves.

Table 14.2 A simple relational table to store
employee details

employee number	employee name
123	John Smith
235	Imran Khan
432	Lauren Wu

employees with the same name. Secondly, the key is smaller and easier to store. If
you know the value of a key, you can interrogate the table to find the record that
corresponds to the key and examine all the data for that record.

So, now that we have a simple shorthand way of referring to information in a
record, we can use it in other records to refer back to the full information. Table
14.3 uses the key of the employee record as a shorthand to refer to the person who
has made the expense claim. Note that in this table we have an invented key called
'expense claim number', and this may be used in other tables to refer to the
expense claim. The 'employee number' column is the link back to the employee
table, and this is known as a foreign key. A foreign key is a value stored to refer to
information in another table.

Table 14.3 A simple relational table to store expense claims

expense claim number	employee number	amount
23	235	34.54
24	432	67.89
25	235	83.23
26	123	19.11

Special computer languages, known as query languages, are used to manipulate
data in databases. These enable the programmer to insert data into tables, to
retrieve data from tables, and to combine tables to produce new views of the information. One of the most common uses of a query language is to join tables
together. Thus we might join Tables 14.2 and 14.3 to produce a new table as in
Table 14.4. This 'joined' table would never be actually stored anywhere – it would
just be temporarily created for use in the system.

A database is a collection of tables. An application will have tens, sometimes
hundreds, and occasionally thousands, of tables. Each table can contain many

Table 14.4 A new table created by joining together two other tables

expense claim number	employee number	employee name	amount
23	235	Imran Khan	34.54
24	432	Lauren Wu	67.89
25	235	Imran Khan	83.23
26	123	John Smith	19.11

thousands of records. To get a sense of the enormous size of some of the databases that exist, consider your local telephone company. They will keep a record for every subscriber, and that may run into millions of records for some telephone companies. Then, for billing purposes, they need to keep a record of every call made by each subscriber, so that the telephone calls database table could have hundreds of millions of records just to record a month's calls. Think, too, of a credit card company keeping records for all transactions for all their cardholders.

Databases mean that we can store the information for a large number of objects. It would be unrealistic to activate all the records and convert them into objects when the computer is switched on – apart from being unnecessary, it would incur an awfully long wait. Thus we need to devise some way of creating objects from records on demand. Most instances of objects lie dormant in the database for the majority of time, then like summer butterflies they are given a brief chance to flit their wings when called upon by a use case, after which they settle back into their slumber until the summer sun shines on them again.

The way records are activated as objects is usually in response to a use case interface accepting some key. For example, when a customer calls a service centre they may give their customer number, which in turn will be typed into a screen. The customer number will be used to look up the customer record, and because the customer number is unique to each customer, it is a key in the database table. The customer number might also be used to look for the latest invoice information for that customer. While the use case is active, all relevant objects such as customer and invoice objects will be live in the system. When the use case finishes, the live objects will disappear. Any changes to information in the objects will be catered for by the use case writing back the information to the database.

Databases require a book in their own right, and you are well advised to look at some of the standard texts on relational databases, such as Connolly and Begg (2001). However, for completeness, we shall consider some of the key features of databases. We will not get into the detailed intricacies of query languages, or the fine issues of integrity, but we will say a few things that the general developer needs to know about. Most organizations employ specialists to manage the data, recognizing the importance of the data to the organization.

Another advantage of relational databases is that they come with powerful tools for *ad hoc* report-writing. Though object fans would have us think of everything as objects, it is usually quicker and easier to produce reports direct from the underlying data than it is to generate objects from the database records. The implication for the structure of applications is that there are usually two routes to the underlying data. The primary route is through an application that manages the data. The secondary route is through a query interface and report writer that allows fast production of management information. Figure 14.1 illustrates this, showing the database as the underpinning of applications and reporting.

This is contrary to the 'purist' object view, where all accesses to data are controlled through an object interface. However, purist views rarely work in practice, and the majority of applications will use databases in this way. A sensible compromise position is that the direct access to the database should only permit retrieval and not update, leaving changes to the data to be controlled by the application.

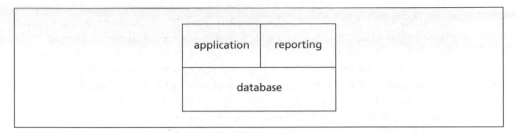

Figure 14.1   Basic architecture, with a database at the base and a mixture of application and reporting systems on top

We shall now look at some important aspects of database design. For more in-depth discussion of databases, you really need to read a book devoted to databases, such as Connolly and Begg (2001). The aim of the rest of this section is to allow you to link the more detailed database theory into object-oriented design.

14.1 Entity–Relationship Diagrams

An entity–relationship diagram is very similar to a class diagram, and can be viewed as a subset of a class diagram. Database designers use them extensively. The difference is that they represent database tables, not objects. There are no explicit operations on tables, just attributes. Typically attributes are not listed. Figure 14.2 is an entity–relationship diagram for a database to support order-taking.

Here we have used the UML convention for relationship multiplicity labelling. Some entity–relationship tools use different notations for multiplicity, but it seems senseless to use anything radically different from the UML convention if you are adopting UML for the design notation.

As stated earlier, not every object is stored, and thus we do not need to produce an entity-relationship model to support all the objects in the system. We do not normally store anything to remember boundary objects, as these are usually things like screens that are created on demand and only last a short time. We do not often store anything to remember control objects, though sometimes we need to keep a record of transactions. We almost always store entity objects, as these are the objects that typically model real-world things and for which the system is

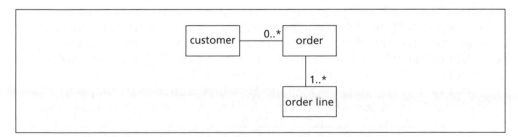

Figure 14.2   An entity–relationship diagram for part of an order-processing system

designed to keep some record. We also need to record relationships, and some relationships involve the definition of extra tables, as we shall see.

There is a subtle difference between the lines on an entity–relationship diagram that represent relationships between data, and the lines on a class diagram that represent associations. Relationships in E–R diagrams are about data navigation, and have no implication for message exchange. Associations in class diagrams define paths for communication between objects.

Any substantial application that requires storage will need an entity–relationship model defining. From this model, the database designer can produce a database schema for implementation of the data.

14.2 Database Implementation of Objects and Normalization

Now that we have a basic notion of what a relational database is, we can look carefully at the way we transform the objects that need to persist into database tables. This is a fairly straightforward process, though the rigours of relational database design may involve the further decomposition of objects.

Long ago, Ted Codd made a name for himself by defining relational databases (Codd, 1970) and a process of refining data to make these databases easy to use and manage. The process of refinement is called normalization. Normalization is the bane of many a poor undergraduate, though the basic concepts are very simple. Codd defined a large number of normalization steps, but only three are commonly used, and the rest are too complicated and esoteric for most people to concern themselves with.[4] We shall look at the first three normalization steps. Normalization can be treated very mathematically, but we shall be looking at an informal concept that is workable.

14.3 Storing Objects and Relationships

14.3.1 STORING OBJECTS

For the most part, storing objects is straightforward. The attributes of the object usually map to columns in a table. An object is stored as a row in a database table. Complications only arise if the attributes are complex in some way, say because they are objects. The trick then is to break the complicated attributes out into separate tables and link the tables together with keys.

The fun begins when we try to implement associations, which must be represented by relationships. Objects need to refer to each other. They usually do this by keeping attributes that somehow reference other objects. When objects are just held in the computer memory, quite often the programming language takes care of most of the worries. When objects are stored in a database, the linkages need to be more explicit. The designer then needs to invent special attributes to implement the links, and these will ultimately be the keys stored in database tables.

---

4 Database conferences used to be filled with many esoteric papers defining new normal forms, and discussing the mathematics of normalization. Such is the stuff that academic dreams are made on, but for most practical purposes these are not often used.

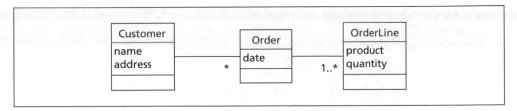

Figure 14.3   One-to-many associations to be implemented in a database

14.3.2 IMPLEMENTING ONE-TO-MANY RELATIONSHIPS

In a one-to-many association, one object can be linked to many objects. There is no easy way for the 'one' object to record the 'many' objects it is linked to. In a programming language it would be possible to keep an array at the 'one' end of the relationship. In a database, it makes sense to record the relationship at the 'many' end. So the table used to store the object at the 'many' end has an extra column (or set of columns) added to store the key of the object at the 'one' end of the relationship.

Figure 14.3 shows two one-to-many associations. The Customer–Order association is implemented by inventing a key (customer number) for the Customer and creating a Customer table as in Table 14.5. We would then store the customer number in the table that is used to store the Order class, as in Table 14.6, with a key to link back to the customer table. The order table has also got its own key, called order number, and this is used in the table used to store the OrderLine class, as in Table 14.7.

Table 14.5   Database table to implement the Customer object, with added key

customer number	name	address
10324	Briggs Metals	14 Iron Way
19875	Tonkeys Alarms	Unit 4, Bridge Park

Table 14.6   Table to implement the Order class with added keys

order number	date	customer number
4563	37130	10324
4565	37134	19875
4568	37135	10324

14.3.3 MANY-TO-MANY RELATIONSHIPS

Many-to-many relationships present a greater problem. To record the number of records linked to a table, some complicated data structure would be needed, and this is not permitted in a relational database. Therefore an additional table needs to be introduced. The additional table consists of pairings of the keys from the linked tables.

Table 14.7 Table to implement the OrderLine class with added key

order number	product	quantity
4563	5 mm screws	200
4563	5 mm washers	500
4565	6 mm bolts	300
4565	6 mm nuts	300
4568	20 cm plate	450

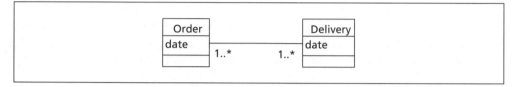

Figure 14.4 A many-to-many association

Consider the association in Figure 14.4, where an order can be fulfilled by a number of deliveries and a delivery may fulfil a number of orders. The order table may be as in Table 14.6 and the delivery table may be as in Table 14.8. A relational database does not permit arrays or any complicated structure to be a field. Therefore we need an additional table as in Table 14.9, which keeps pairings of keys from the Order table and the Delivery table.

Table 14.8 Table to store the Delivery class

delivery number	date
9234	37175
9235	37177

Table 14.9 Table to implement the many-to-many relationship between the Order class and the Delivery class

order number	delivery number
4565	9234
4563	9235
4568	9235

14.3.4 PROBLEMS WITH ONE-TO-MANY

Sometimes it is better to store a one-to-many relationship using a separate table, as if it were a many-to-many relationship. Consider the example where a salesperson is allocated to only one shop, which might be implemented as in Table 14.10. If there arise business reasons why an employee might not be assigned to a

Table 14.10 Table to represent an employee allocated to a shop

employee number	name	shop number
123	Mita Patel	14
126	Robin Cook	19

Table 14.11 Table to implement the one-to-many relationship

employee number	shop number
123	14
126	19

Table 14.12 The table for the employee with the key to the shop removed

employee number	name
123	Mita Patel
126	Robin Cook

shop (e.g. long term illness), then the shop number is not valid. One solution is for a null value to be entered in the shop number in the employee record. The alternative is to create a separate table for the relationship, as in Table 14.11 and to remove the shop number from the employee table as in Table 14.12. Then if a salesperson is temporarily not allocated to a shop, the record matching shop with employee is deleted, but the employee record remains.

14.3.5 ONE-TO-ONE RELATIONSHIPS

One-to-one relationships offer the broadest range of possibilities. The link can be made by putting the key of one object in the record recording the other object. This can be done at either side of the one-to-one relationship.

14.3.6 DATABASE SCHEMAS

It is rather slow and tedious to describe a database by drawing out the table structures. Thus we have a shorthand notation for describing the database structure. The structure of the database is known as a 'schema'. We describe a database table by writing the table name and then listing in brackets the fields (or columns) in the table, separating the fields using commas. We then underline the key. A simple ordering database might then be described in Figure 14.5.

14.4 Database Querying – SQL

Although we shall not consider programming languages in the construction phase, it is useful to understand a little about database query languages. For many years now, the Structured Query Language (SQL) has been a standard. It is a very

```
part(partNumber,partName,price)
customer(customerNumber,name,address,telephoneNumber)
order(customerNumber,orderNumber,date)
orderLine(orderNumber, lineNumber, partNumber, quantity)
```

Figure 14.5 A schema for a simple orders database

rich and powerful language for managing data in a relational database. We shall look at a few of the basic statements in the language.

Firstly, to create a table, we have a command CREATE which allows the creation of a table in the database with a number of columns or attributes. An example would be to create a Customer table as follows:

```
CREATE TABLE Customer (
    CustomerNumber INT,
    Name TEXT,
    Address TEXT
)
```

This will create a table with three columns. In an SQL database, each of the columns in a table has to have a simple type, such as integer or text string.

There is a simple command DROP to remove a table from a database. So, to remove the Customer table below you would use the command

```
DROP Customer
```

This removes the table and all the data.

Having created a table it is then necessary to populate it. This can be done with the INSERT command. To create a customer record in the Customer table we could use the SQL command

```
INSERT INTO Customer SET
    CustomerNumber = 12,
    Name = "Ken",
    Address = "School of Computing, Canalside West, Huddersfield, HD1
    3DH, UK"
```

This will create exactly one record with each of the fields set as illustrated.

Having got a table populated, there is a command SELECT to get data from the database. The simplest form is to get all of the data, as illustrated by

```
SELECT * FROM Customer
```

This will get every record from the Customer table. How those records are handled very much depends on the programming language being used.

Of course, getting every record from a table is not the only way. A slightly more complex version of the SELECT command will return a subset of records based on some constraint. For example to get the records where the customer name is 'Ken' the following command can be used

```
SELECT * FROM Customer WHERE Name = "Ken"
```

This will get every record where the name is 'Ken' – there may be more than one.

A further elaboration of the SELECT command allows you to get only some of the fields. For example, to just get the name and address of all records in the Customer table where the name is 'Ken', we would use

```
SELECT Name, Address FROM Customer WHERE Name = "Ken"
```

This returns records with just two fields with the customer name and address.

Finally, we need to be able to combine information from two tables. Suppose we create an order table as follows

```
CREATE TABLE Order (
    OrderNumber INT,
    CustomerNumber INT,
    ProductName TEXT,
    Quantity INT,
    Price INT
)
```

Then to pair up the products with the name and address of the customer who ordered the product we would use the SELECT command as follows:

```
SELECT Name, Address, ProductName, Quantity
FROM Customer, Order
WHERE Customer.CustomerNumber = Order.CustomerNumber
AND Customer.Name = "Ken"
```

This will return records for all orders made by all customers with the name 'Ken'.

14.5 Normalization

Producing a database can result in tables that do not behave very well. For example, you might end up storing the same information in two or more different places. Or you might end up deleting useful information when other information is deleted. There is a process of removing these problems known as 'normalization'. This sounds very technical, and the definitions are cumbersome. However, the basic idea when you understand it is very straightforward.

The ideas of normalization were developed by Codd in the 1970s. The principles have been around for much longer, but he formalized them and gave them a definition. There are lots of 'normal forms'. We shall only consider the first three, which are the most common and the most useful.

14.5.1 FIRST NORMAL FORM

A table is in first normal form if it has a fixed number of columns and if it has fields that are simple types such as integer, date or string. Though that sounds straightforward enough, entities in the real world are much more complex than that. As we have seen, an order might have lots of repeating information. Thus, to represent it, we might have to split the repeating information out into separate tables and link the tables with keys. Further, if an attribute is a complicated structure, such as another object, then we will have to split that out into another object too.

14.5.2 SECOND NORMAL FORM

Second normal form aims at simplifying tables in such a way that data is not stored more than is necessary, and that potentially useful data is not lost if records are deleted. Consider the table:

```
registration(studentNumber, studentName, courseNumber, courseName)
```

The fields studentNumber and courseNumber are together the keys on this table, so they are underlined. This is a perfectly reasonable table, as you can see who is registered on what course. However, it does present potential problems.

Firstly, studentName will be repeated for every course that she is registered on. This wastes space, and if the student name has to be change, then all of the relevant registration records need to be changed. The same applies to courseName too.

Secondly, if the only place that studentName and courseName are recorded is in the registration record, then if a particular student is not registered for any courses, then there is no record anywhere of her name, and if no student is registered on the course there is no record anywhere of the course.

We can remove these problems by 'normalizing' the table. The definition for second normal form says that 'every non-key attribute must be fully dependent on the key'.[5] That means that every bit of the key is needed to work out each attribute. If only part of the key is needed to determine the value of the attribute then it is not in second normal form and we need to split the table up.

Now if we look at studentName, we see that it depends only on studentNumber, and not on both studentNumber and courseNumber. Therefore studentName is not fully dependent on the key – it depends on part of it. So we take studentName out of the record, and put it in a separate table with the part of the key that determines it:

```
registration(studentNumber, courseNumber, courseName)
student(studentNumber, studentName)
```

This is a better structure for three reasons. Firstly you can now keep information about a student when the student has not been registered on a course. If a student is no longer registered you do not lose the student name. And finally, the student name is stored in only one place, so that it is easier to change the student name (you only have to change the one record) and there is less to store.

If we continue, we see that courseName depends on courseNumber, and so again is not fully dependent on the key. We do the same thing and split out courseName, and get some similar benefits for course information.

```
registration(studentNumber, courseNumber)
student(studentNumber, studentName)
course(courseNumber, courseName)
```

---

5   In fact, the full definition is a bit more complicated than this, as there may be a number of candidate keys for a database table. However, this is an introduction, and the full intricacies are left for further study.

Normalization thus increases the number of tables. However, in practice it normally reduces the amount of information stored in the tables themselves, and therefore the amount of space taken up on the disk.

14.5.3 THIRD NORMAL FORM

Third normal form sounds even more complicated when you define it, but it is very similar. As before, it is trying to remove the need to store information unnecessarily, and it makes updating the database easier.

A field is said to be transitively dependent on the key if it is dependent on a non-key attribute that is dependent on the key. To see what this means, we need to consider an example. Consider the following table.

```
order(orderNumber, orderDate, customerNumber, customerName)
```

Here `customerName` depends on the key `orderNumber`, but that is because `customerName` depends on `customerNumber`. This is called a 'transitive dependency'. So what we do is split out the `customerName` into another table, giving us two tables as follows.

```
order(orderNumber, orderDate, customerNumber)
customer(customerNumber, customerName)
```

Now we have the advantage that we can store information about customers with no current orders, and we only store the customer name in one place.

14.5.4 CONCLUSION ON NORMALIZATION

Normalization is done to improve the structure of the database. It is appropriate to do this at the design stage, as it is sometimes useful to feed this decomposition back up to the class level. Primarily it achieves the following:

1. It prevents storing the same information twice, by repeating the same information over and over again in a table or in multiple tables.
2. It makes updating easier, because information is usually stored in only one place.
3. It prevents accidental deletion of data, such as removing vital customer information when removing order information.

If there is a need to see the information in unnormalized form, query languages will permit this. They will combine the normalized tables together and present them back as unnormalized views. So SQL can reconstruct an unnormalized view of the data without changing the way it is stored.

The definitions of second and third normal form look more complicated than they really are. Once you have an intuitive grasp of the reasons for normalization and the steps to normalize, then it becomes automatic and straightforward. The process of normalization is to split tables down until the repeated storage of information is at a minimum.

14.6 Transactions, Journalling and Recovery

There is a little-discussed topic in many books on object-oriented analysis and design that will come as a great shock to many designers if they leave out consideration of it. It is to do with the notion of a transaction. Database specialists consider this in great detail, but the designer needs to be very aware of the need for proper transaction management, either through the database's built in transaction handling or by other means.

We have the idea of systems as networks of objects cooperating to solve problems. Unfortunately, as with all societies, there are frequent conflicts of interest. Two use cases executing at the same time may, if they are not designed properly, interfere with each other. Consider two use cases, one to deposit money into an account and one to withdraw it. They might implement the following steps.

Transaction 1: T1.1 Read the account balance
T1.2 Add the deposit amount to the balance
T1.3 Record the new account balance
Transaction 2: T2.1 Read the account balance
T2.2 Deduct the withdrawal amount from the balance
T2.3 Record the new account balance

Now all is fine, provided that the two transactions do not overlap and both transactions complete. However, if the transactions overlap, then you might get a sequence something like the following:

T1.1 Read the account balance
T1.2 Add the deposit amount to the balance
T2.1 Read the account balance
T2.2 Deduct the withdrawal amount from the balance
T1.3 Record the new account balance
T2.3 Record the new account balance

Now if you look carefully, you will see that the recording of the account balance for the deposit has been overwritten. Thus the deposit has been lost.

It is perfectly possible to construct scenarios where any two use cases that operate simultaneously on the same data will result in erroneous actions by the system if they are not controlled. When designing use cases that update information, various strategies need to be followed.

14.6.1 TRANSACTIONS

The notion of a transaction is common in the database world. A transaction is the smallest meaningful and coherent operation on a database. The property of transactions that databases try to maintain is that they either succeed or have no effect. A transaction that only partially completes leaves the database in a damaged state. For example, a transaction that transfers funds between two accounts that fails after withdrawing from one account before depositing in the other will effectively lose money (or at least lose the record of money).

Few computer languages incorporate the notion of a transaction, and the implementation is usually subordinated to the database. However, the designer cannot ignore the notion of a transaction, or the system that is constructed will allow for actions that compromise the integrity of the system.

Use cases are either single transactions or may be made up of a series of transactions. If the use case does not require the update of information, it is probably safe to ignore the issue of transactions. However, if the use case does update information, then the designer needs to prescribe how those updates take place.

14.6.2 SERIALIZABILITY

The result of any two transactions on a system need to be as if the two transactions happened in strict order, one after the other, even if the actual operation of the transactions overlap. This is known in database circles as the serializability constraint. If use cases are designed without consideration of this, then the system is seriously compromised.

The usual solution to this is some form of locking strategy. If a use case is going to update a record and use other information to determine the update, it needs to prevent other use cases from doing the same until the update is complete. Thus, when information is retrieved from a database, it is often necessary to lock that information to prevent other use cases from using it. When another use case comes across a piece of locked information, it can either wait for the information to become unlocked, or it can quit. The use case holding the lock can proceed in safety. When the work is complete, the lock can be released. Any use case waiting on the lock can then proceed.

You can think of locks as traffic lights. Whenever the paths of two use cases meet, one needs to proceed safely before the other crosses its path, or they will crash. However, a use can hold a number of locks, so that it can be holding up a number of use cases, which in turn might be holding up lots of other use cases.

Locking is a simple idea, but it does lead to problems. The first one is deadlock. Two or more use cases can sit waiting for each other to proceed. When this happens, one or more of them will have to back down, or parts of the system will be stuck forever. There are various strategies for dealing with this, which are mostly outside the scope of this book. One way is to have some sort of deadlock detection. Another (known as optimistic locking) is to leave all of the updates to the end of a transaction and make sure just before the writes that all the dependent data has not been updated by another use case; if another use case got there first, the use case rolls back.

Databases come with a variety of locking strategies. It is common to be able to lock individual records in tables, though some databases only implement table-level locking. Part of the design team's duties involves understanding the locking strategies available and implementing them accordingly.

14.6.3 ATOMICITY

Transactions need to be atomic. That is, they are indivisible in their effect. Either they succeed completely, or they do not succeed at all. An account transfer transaction must complete or have no effect. If the computer system fails in the middle of the transaction, or the use case has to be aborted for some reason, then any updates that the transaction has made must be undone, and any locks that the transaction has obtained must be released.

14.6.4 IMPLEMENTING TRANSACTIONS

The natural place for transaction handling is in the control object for a use case. When the use case reaches a point where a transaction must start, it will usually call a start-transaction operation on the database (or do this indirectly through a factory). From thereon, records need to be locked before they are accessed. Once the transaction is complete in terms of updating information, and the use case considers the transaction to be successful, then the transaction must call a commit-transaction operation on the database. The commit-transaction will secure all the updates in the database and release the locks. If the transaction is not to complete, the transaction can call an abort-transaction operation on the database that will undo any updates and release the locks.

If we consider our account deposit and account withdrawal transactions, you can see the added steps that need to be included as part of the design. The effect of the lock account on the second transaction to effect it would cause the transaction either to wait until the lock is released or, in some circumstances, to be aborted.

> Transaction 1: T1.1 Start transaction
> T1.2 Lock account
> T1.3 Read the account balance
> T1.4 Add the deposit amount to the balance
> T1.5 Record the new account balance
> T1.6 Commit transaction
> Transaction 2: T2.1 Start transaction
> T2.2 Lock account
> T2.3 Read the account balance
> T2.4 Deduct the withdrawal amount from the balance
> T2.5 Record the new account balance
> T2.6 Commit transaction

Databases have been carefully designed to ensure that integrity is maintained in this way. If a system crashes, the database will roll back any incomplete transactions before the system is allowed to resume. If a transaction is held open for too long, the database can abort it.

14.7 ICANDO Bulk Chemical Ordering

14.7.1 DATABASE DESIGN FOR THE VALIDATE CUSTOMER USE CASE

So far, we have found only one entity object that is likely to need a database entry, namely the customer object. So far, this is a very simple table, with the schema

```
customer(customerNumber,name,address,password)
```

The key will be customerNumber, and the table is already in third normal form; every attribute is fully dependent on the key, and there are no transitive dependencies. Thus there will be no need for further decomposition of the table. Constructing a customer object from a record in the customer table will be just a straightforward copying of the fields into the object attributes.

14.7.2 TRANSACTIONS FOR THE VALIDATE CUSTOMER USE CASE

The use case we have developed so far has minimal need for locking. The designer will need to consider a number of things when deciding a locking policy. The decisions will not be automatic.

The only database record we have considered so far is the customer record. One of the use cases might involve changing this record, such as changing the address or password. The serialization rule says that such updates should work as if they had happened 'atomically', and the norm would be to lock the record. The big question is whether the record for the customer should be locked for the whole call.

Firstly, the question arises whether a customer could be making two orders or other enquiries at the same time. If the answer is yes, then holding a lock on the customer record could wrongly prevent that. If the answer is no, then the a lock might be useful to detect some issue arising if someone is fraudulently trying to make an order.

In the case of a validation, the check is instantaneous, and the likelihood and significance of a change of address or password during a call is so minimal that the use of a lock seems unnecessary.

When looking at use cases that update the database, such as the taking of an order, locks would need to be considered. For example, if orders require reservation of stock, then a stock record might need to be locked during the ordering process.

14.8 ICANDO Site Safety

14.8.1 DATABASE DESIGN FOR THE ADD FEATURE USE CASE

The operation of drawing tools like the site safety system usually involves reading all the details into memory on startup, maintaining the in-memory version, and saving the modified versions back on exit. This is much the same way as most word processing systems work. It is unlikely that two people will be editing a site at the same time, and therefore all the issues about locking and so forth are ignored.

For a tool like this, saving data in files is often the option chosen. However, we shall assume that there is a relational database for storage. So far, there are two entity objects, facility and site, that need to be stored. Site is straightforward, except for the list of facilities. The database trick on this is to put a key on the site (siteId), and to place that key in the facility record so that all the facilities for a site can be found by searching the facility table for all records with a particular siteId. The facility record is a bit more complicated. Firstly there is the notion of a coordinate, and we can simply manage that by putting the coordinate attributes in the facility record. The shape presents more of a dilemma, and there will need to be a separate shape table or set of shape tables to deal with this, keyed on a value (this is left as an exercise). Thus we have schemas:

```
site(siteId, name, address)
facility(facilityId, x, y, type, siteId, shapeId)
```

We will most probably need extra tables for each of the particular types of facility, keeping specific information about that type of facility.

14.9 ICANDO Retail Petrol Promotions

14.9.1 DATABASE DESIGN FOR THE ADD TO ORDER USE CASE

The commit operation needs to be incorporated in the commit order use case, and the abandon needs to be incorporated in the cancel use case.

We have two entity objects that will need to be stored in the database, namely the reservation and stock objects. These will be simple and straightforward tables as defined by

```
stock(productID,quantity)
reservation(productId, sessionId, quantity)
```

We might produce a sequence diagram to describe the actions of the reserve operation, as in Figure 14.6. There will need to be access to the database through a database control object. To ensure that the operations for deducting from the stock record and creating a reservation record are atomic (i.e. they both complete or neither completes, so that no stock is lost), a transaction is used. The begin transaction operation on the database control will make all the other accesses until the end transaction operation apply locks as necessary.

14.9.2 DESIGN OF THE CONFIRM ORDER USE CASE

Considering the sequence diagram in Figure 12.30, we see that the bulk of the detailed design will be in the sequence of actions after the acceptance of the order.

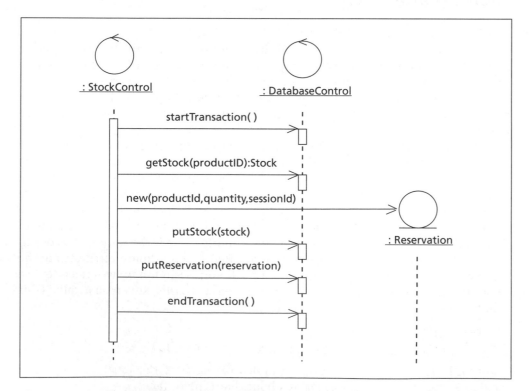

Figure 14.6 The implementation of the reserve operation on the StockControl object

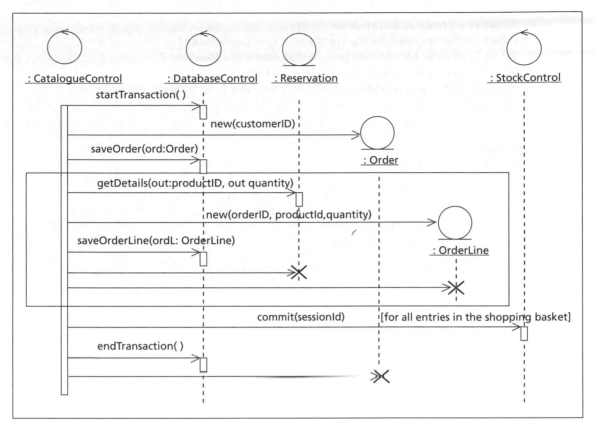

Figure 14.7 Sequence diagram to describe the operation on the catalogue control for accepting the order

This has been elaborated in Figure 14.7. Again, all of these have been wrapped in a transaction. The database control object will then lock each of the database records accessed until the end of the transaction. A new order is created, and then for each of the reservations made during this session an order line is created. The reservations, orders and order lines can be deleted once finished with.

We have two new entity objects, Order and OrderLine. These can be shown in the class diagram in Figure 13.46.

There will be two database tables with the following schema:

```
order(orderID, customerID, date)
orderLine(orderID,productID,quantity)
```

REVIEW QUESTIONS

1. How does an entity–relationship model differ from a class diagram?
2. What is a relational database?
3. What is a key in a relational database table?
4. What is a foreign key in a relational database table?
5. What is the purpose of normalization?

6. **What is a transaction in a database?**
7. **What is the serializability constraint on a database?**
8. **What is meant by atomicity in a database transaction?**
9. **How is serializability enforced in a database?**
10. **What is the main problem that can be caused by locking records in a database?**

EXERCISES

1. For the ICANDO trading system design produced in the previous chapter, produce a normalized database schema, and consider the need for transactions.
2. For the ICANDO/NeverShut retail system design produced in the previous chapter, produce a normalized database schema, and consider the need for transactions.

CHAPTER 15

Architecture

IN THIS CHAPTER YOU WILL LEARN:

1. **What is meant by technical architecture and application architecture**
2. **How modern architectures evolved**
3. **About modern technical architectures**
4. **About component-based and framework-based architectures**

Architecture defines the overall shape of the application. It is really the overview and structure, like the outline plans and sketches of a large building. From it you should see how everything is put together. Large systems without a clear architecture can become unmanageable. Without some access to the architecture of a system, through formal documents or word of mouth descriptions, making modifications or additions to a system is like trying to find an address in a strange town without a street map and without knowing the local language. Likewise, creating a substantial system without a clearly defined architecture is going to result in something with the characteristics of a shanty town rather than a shopping precinct or skyscraper.

Architecture is difficult to define. In doing so, in this chapter I am at risk of informed readers saying no, this is not what is meant by architecture, though their definitions would probably suffer the same response if they exposed them. The current job market is full of job titles with the word 'architect' in them, but that is largely a matter of fashion. I had the role 'technical architect' once, but it did not seem very different from the consultancy roles I had undertaken previously.

However, modern methods emphasize architecture – the Unified Process is 'architecture-centric'. They emphasize the need for an early architecture baseline, which will be elaborated throughout a project. This is no more than putting together a plan for the layout of the system. It will need to be adjusted as circumstances dictate, but a first attempt is important.

Architecture is really the first stage of design, though it is put here in the flow of the book because the concepts that we talked about in the previous chapter are the ones that need to be considered. Detailed design is what happens most of the time, filling in the overall architecture. Architectural design worries about the bigger picture, and takes some of the more strategic decisions.

Technical architecture is about computers, networks, tools, packages, databases and so on. It is the very gross framework into which the application will be fitted. It has a massive impact on issues such as the performance and scalability of the application. Lots of issues will drive the selection, from the application requirements, through the culture of the organization developing the system, to the market place where the technology is sourced. In this brief chapter we can only give a hint of the various options available.

Application architecture is about the way the application is divided up and fitted into the technical architecture. Most modern applications are distributed over a wide area, and there are many things to consider that will impact the performance and scalability of the system. They are viewed as layers of software components, with particular roles and responsibilities. In addition, the application architecture will need to worry about non-functional requirements, such as integrity, reliability and recovery.

This chapter will give a flavour of architecture. Fortunately for most developers, early in their careers architecture is defined by others, and they are filling in the details. It is the experience they gain in working with architectures that will make some of them good architects in their later careers. For most developers, architecture is something they need to understand rather than apply, as stonemasons needed to understand the shape of the cathedrals they constructed without designing them in the first place.

15.1 Modern Technical Architecture

Technical architecture is about the computers that run the application, the networks that link the computers together, and the languages and software that are used to develop and integrate the application. There are myriad choices to be made, and knowing what fits well with what is a daunting challenge. Technical architectures have evolved at a rapid rate, and it is worth reviewing that evolution to get some sense of how modern systems are structured and why.

It is always dangerous to generalize, but most modern architectures are three-tier architectures distributed over a number of servers and desktop PCs, linked using local networks and the Internet. The three-tier architecture conforms to the notion that we have discussed in the earlier design chapter, where the processing for a use case is split into three basic parts: firstly the user interface, secondly the business logic corresponding to control objects, and thirdly the data services corresponding to the entity objects.

The physical shape of this type of architecture is shown in Figure 15.1. The ubiquitous PC is used mainly for presentation, though for some simple applications the application services can be merged into the PC. The application server deals with most of the business logic for the application. The data server deals with long-

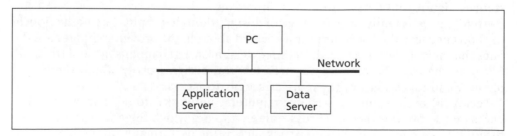

Figure 15.1   The basis for modern architectures

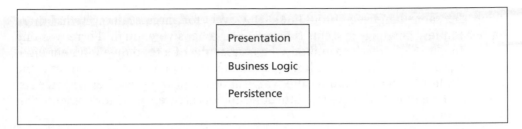

Figure 15.2   The logical view of modern architectures

term storage. The application server and the data server are often combined, though for large applications there may be a number of application servers and data servers. The network can be a local network or a wide area network, or often a mixture of both.

The logical view of this architecture is shown in Figure 15.2. The presentation layer handles all of the interaction with the user, and there may be elements of interaction through this with other systems. The business logic is where the core of the application runs. Persistence is usually a relational database.

When this architecture is extended to incorporate the Internet, it looks only slightly different, as in Figure 15.3. Here we have a Web server that is the primary point of contact for user interfaces. The PC will normally access the application through a browser, and the Web server will route requests through to the application server, which in turn deals with the data server. The network can still be a local area network, and not a wide area network such as the Internet.

This style of physical architecture is becoming more common even for internal applications within an organization. The ease of development and deployment of Web applications makes them very attractive for many applications. It still conforms to the logical structure of Figure 15.2, but the presentation logic is split between the browser and the Web server.

Network architectures do not, on the whole, need to concern the developer once the notion of a multi-tier approach has been accepted. Network addresses and interconnects are managed fairly seamlessly today. However, the interfaces between the various layers do need consideration.

15.1.1 SELECTION OF TOOLS (LANGUAGES, CASE TOOLS)
The physical architecture plays a large part in determining the software development tools. The ideal would be a single, consistent development environment,

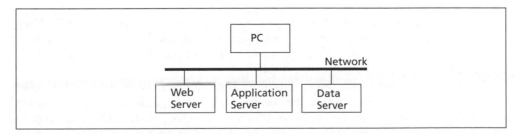

Figure 15.3   A modern architecture incorporating a Web server

using the same language throughout. However, for large-scale systems, there have been few language systems that are comprehensive enough. Forte was one environment that seemed to embody the philosophy of a total development environment, and Java has come a long way in that direction. The Internet and the World-Wide Web have muddied the water in terms of integrated environments, and even Java that can be executed through applets is rarely used for presentation over the Internet.

The choice of language and tools is usually split along the logical architecture layers; that is, for presentation, business logic and storage. The other driver in terms of language choice is skill availability. The best tool is not always the one that is easiest to maintain. It is no good having the most marvellous development environment if the developers are rare and expensive and prone to be snatched by your competitors.

There is an awful lot of technology snobbery around. If you want to ruin an evening, ask a 'language expert' what the 'best language' is. The answer is usually the one they know best. All languages have their advantages and disadvantages. Alas, the power and productivity of languages is often a function of their complexity, and hence overall cost to manage. And the language you are most effective in is the one you know, until you learn another.

Presentation languages

Presentation languages manage interactive interfaces. They are good at collecting data, presenting data, and providing some basic checking of information. Currently Visual Basic is very popular, as it is fairly easy to learn. More complicated languages such as Delphi and Java have their advocates, as they have more power and flexibility.

For Internet applications, the presentation language is almost universally HTML, even for applications where the business logic is written in Java. XML with style sheets is beginning to have an impact. HTML has the advantage of being simple and cheap. With the addition of a scripting language such as JavaScript, the interface can be programmed to undertake a fair bit of validation and add some sophistication. HTML interfaces tend to be simpler and easier to produce than is possible with other languages.

The criteria for selection are the suitability of the interface that the language can present, how it is to be deployed (e.g. over the Internet, through a browser, or as a fixed application in an office environment), the skill pools available, and cost.

Business logic languages

The choice of the middle tier languages is usually less constrained. Most languages that have some notion of an object can be used here, and non-object languages such as Cobol and C continue to be widely used. Java is gaining in popularity, and C++ has become well established.

The choice of business logic language depends partly on the interfacing language chosen, and partly on other issues such as how well the language sits in the operating system and the packages that interface well with it. More often than not it is a matter of history rather than anything else that determines the main programming language. At the risk of upsetting the various technophiles, I believe that the choice is more to do with pragmatism and the organisation's ability to manage the developers than with technical excellence.

The Internet is driving the use of languages such as Java, Basic and PHP, as these are languages that interface well with Web servers, but other languages such as Coldfusion and Python are popular. C, Cobol and C++ do not fit well into this environment. Again, it is pragmatism that will drive the choice.

Persistence languages and tools

Fortunately the Tower of Babel problem has not hit the database world. Almost universally the language of choice is SQL, and the database is relational. The choice of actual database is usually based on price and performance. Some database vendors also sell development environments that encompass the logic and presentation layers.

SQL provides a clear and consistent way of searching for data, selecting relevant parts for use, retrieving, saving and updating. The simplicity of relational databases is likely to keep this so for the foreseeable future.

Object-oriented databases first emerged in the 1980s, but never really gained a hold in the market place. They are to be found in niche applications where their special features are valued, or where there is additional functionality that makes them useful. Few developers would consider them for storage for large-scale application development.

Packages and components

Almost every application delivery today incorporates a substantial amount of purchased rather than developed software. Few sensible organizations would consider building a system that they could buy at a reasonable price. Purchased software can range from complete application solutions that need some customization through to small components to solve particular problems. These need to be fitted into the overall architecture.

An application package purchase is, in fact, an architecture purchase at the same time. It has a particular application architecture, and will run on prescribed technical architectures. The package will have prescribed means of customization that guide developers through updating the architecture. Customization will be very much filling in new or modified use case definitions in the existing architecture, rather than extending. The methods we have talked about so far may stop at the systems analysis stage or, if the package incorporates objects, more of the notations and techniques that we have described may be appropriate.

Large components that solve particular problems usually come with a defined application programming interface (API). The API is in fact equivalent to an interface object. The component can then be used within the overall design as a 'super object'. It will appear in component diagrams, and may appear in sequence diagrams that define how other objects in the design will interact with the component.

Smaller components may be used for particular purposes. Some languages, such as Delphi and Java, have spawned a rich market for interface components such as diary pages. These are considered much more by the implementation team as a quick means of implementing the design.

15.1.2 CONNECTIVITY AND MIDDLEWARE

Large applications are now assemblies of a number of components often built on a mix of platforms and in different languages. Getting these to communicate and cooperate is one of the core roles of architecture. There are basically three core approaches. The first is tight, real-time coupling of the systems, allowing one system to invoke immediate responses from another; an example would be in a call centre where a customer's bill needs to be brought up from the billing system for the customer service system. The second is a slower connection, where the components need to exchange information, but can wait while the other system takes care of it; an example here would be a mail order request that needs to be enacted within a day rather than immediately. The third is data exchange where information is grouped together and submitted in batches; an example would be despatch systems producing a daily or weekly submission for invoicing systems.

Real-time links

These can be implemented using a variety of techniques. The standard one is CORBA, specified by the Object Management Group. CORBA is a collection of standards for the publishing and calling of objects in a distributed environment. CORBA stands for Common Object Request Broker Architecture, which is a rather large and imposing phrase.

An Object Request Broker (ORB) is a connection between parts of a system that is defined in a platform-independent way. The exchange is through object-interactions. Two objects registered with an ORB can communicate, even if they are written in different languages. The objects can be anywhere, and the ORB takes care of locating objects, routing requests and returning results.

ORBs can communicate with each other, and they use IIOP, the Internet Inter-Orb Protocol, to do so. Thus objects bound to two different ORB's can communicate. Figure 15.4 shows in a simple way the communication between two objects on different platforms using CORBA. Obj1 is registered with its local ORB. To make a request to Obj2, it supplies an object name and request to the local ORB, which determines that the recipient Obj2 is registered remotely with its local ORB. The request is routed via IIOP to the local ORB of Obj2, which in turn calls Obj2. The response is routed back in the reverse direction.

CORBA has become the common standard, but there are proprietary solutions available. The principles are similar, but the details of the connections will differ. CORBA has a variety of services provided, such as encryption, that enhance the distributed environment.

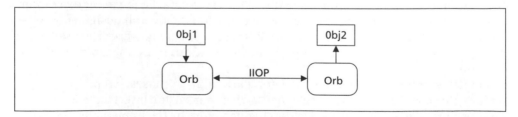

Figure 15.4 Object interaction in CORBA

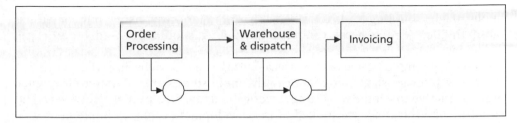

Figure 15.5   Subsystems linked by message queues

Message queues

Sometimes the system needs to pass information, but does not need to have a real-time response. When an order for some goods is taken, a message needs to go to the warehouse to select and despatch it, but it is not essential that it happens immediately. The warehouse system needs to pick up the message when it is ready, rather than to respond instantly.

This leads to a looser coupling of parts of the system. In this way, the order-taking subsystem can operate independently of the warehouse subsystem. The only requirement is that when a message is sent it needs to have guaranteed delivery. A commonly used middleware is message-queuing, though there is no standard as yet for this software.

Once a system has submitted a message to the message queue middleware, it can rely on it being delivered as soon as the recipient is able to take the message. The sender can check the status of the message (i.e. whether or not it has been picked up yet), but has no direct access to the recipient. When the recipient picks up the message, an acknowledgement may be sent back.

Figure 15.5 shows three systems linked by message queues. The order-taking system issues a message to the warehouse to despatch goods. The message goes into a queue that the warehouse system will pick up when it is ready. The warehouse system will likewise, once it has despatched goods and got the delivery confirmation back, pass on a message to the invoicing system to produce an invoice for the goods. The time that a message spends in a message queue may be milliseconds, minutes, hours or even days. The use of message queues is appropriate when there is no need for immediate response, just a guarantee that action will be taken.

File exchange

The loosest form of integration is exchange of files. An application such as order processing may store a number of requests on a file, and then periodically transmit the whole file. This is appropriate when there is less urgency in response. In the example in Figure 15.5, the exchange between the warehouse system and the invoicing system might be implemented by a daily exchange of files rather than a message queue if the invoicing only runs once a day.

Which method?

The method used depends mostly on the timing issues of response. Looser coupling generally leads to more robust and reliable systems that are easier to debug. Tight coupling leads to systems that are more responsive, but sometimes more fragile. As a general rule, loose coupling should be used before tight coupling.

A recent example I came across was a package vendor debating whether to link their new Internet shop component to the main stock control system. It seemed more attractive to get the shop to automatically deduct from stock. However, tight coupling like this, once we looked at the development effort to implement real-time stock deduction, was more costly and would reduce the online availability of the shop, as well as adding processing demands on the core stock management system. Instead, it was chosen to put a loose coupling in, exchanging an orders file and a stock level file every few hours. This meant that the shop could run without the stock control system being live.

15.2 Development Approach and Architecture

The organization needs to understand its overall approach to the development of systems. Different organizations have different needs. Software houses, package vendors and user organizations view software development very differently. The longevity, size and criticality of systems will determine how much investment is to go into making applications maintainable and reusable.

Package vendors have a vested interest in prolonging the lifetime of their packages before radical revision, and making them easy to maintain. User organizations cannot usually afford the same level of investment in reuse and maintenance, though they have a vested interest in these areas. Software houses produce to the customers' demands, but they are less concerned as organizations with these issues, except in so far as their customers demand them.

15.2.1 COMPONENT-BASED DEVELOPMENT

Component-based development aims at high reuse and formalization of reuse. Development is split into component development and application assembly. Use case elaboration is a process of selecting suitable components or specifying new or changed components, and then assembling these components.

The core to this is setting up a well-defined and properly managed component repository. Components need to be extended carefully to ensure that all previous uses of components are not compromised when they are changed.

Moving to a component-based architecture is a core strategic decision of a development organization. It increases the up-front cost of development, with the pay-off once components are repeatedly reused. It is a long-term strategy, not one to be undertaken lightly.

15.2.1 FRAMEWORK-BASED DEVELOPMENT

Framework approaches are an alternative to component-based approaches in the search for reuse. Common aspects of applications are grouped together in a set of related abstract classes. Architectural features, such as database access and factories, are provided as partial solutions in a set of abstract classes.

Frameworks are established by looking for abstract parts of applications. A framework needs to be managed in much the same way as a component repository. Application developers and framework developers need to work in tandem.

If an application developer needs a new object, attribute or operation, it can be submitted for consideration by the framework developers. If it is deemed common, then it is assembled into the framework. If not, it is a specialization of the framework.

For frameworks to be viable, there needs to be a high degree of commonality between a number of applications that are going to use the framework. Most customizable application packages are forms of framework, and those with an object concept will often use inheritance from core objects as a way of extending the package.

15.3 Developing an Architecture

At the beginning of the chapter we emphasized the importance of architecture, but also that few people are involved in the definition of it. For most developers, the architecture is given, and their role is to fill in a small part of the architecture. For adaptation of existing systems, or customization of packages, this is all that developers do. New systems, or major extensions to existing systems, will however, need a significant architecture step.

Architecture needs to be informed by the use cases. Considering architecture before there is a clear idea of what the system needs to do is an obvious folly. This does not mean that all the use cases need to be defined before the architecture can be defined, but it makes a great deal of sense to flesh out a set of architecturally significant use cases (i.e. ones that will place demands on the architecture) before detailed consideration of the architecture.

The first stage is to determine the technical architecture. The choice of computer systems, operating systems and networking will need to consider the demands the system is likely to place and the integration of the system with other systems. The languages and other development tools need to consider the type of system (e.g. Web-based) and the skill sets available.

The application architecture needs to consider the complexity of the system and the type of deployment. Simple systems in a local environment might be two-tier, with a lot of processing on the desktop PCs. Larger applications will probably have three layers, and Internet applications will need to consider the Web server(s) as part of the presentation layer.

15.4 ICANDO Bulk Chemical Ordering

The bulk chemical ordering system is business-critical. Without it, ICANDO Chemicals would rapidly cease to trade. This has huge implications for the architecture. Reliability and performance are essential. The system needs to be able to cope with the most drastic failures, such as the destruction of a data centre by fire. The maximum period of time that an outage could be tolerated would be no more than a week, and outages of even an hour could seriously disrupt business.

The need for an Internet interface into the application, for customers to make orders themselves, requires a choice of tools that incorporate browser deployment for some (if not all) parts of the application. This will constrain the chosen software.

There also needs to be integration of existing systems, such as production systems. Some of the systems will be established systems. The connection between some of the systems will be over a wide area network.

15.4.1 TECHNICAL ARCHITECTURE

The overall physical architecture will incorporate two data centres and a number of call centres spread over Europe, plus the manufacturing plants and warehouses. The need for high performance and reliability means that high bandwidth communication lines are provided between each call centre and each data centre, and the data centres are linked. This is shown in Figure 15.6. The plan is to be able to run with either or both data centres operational. The data centres will exchange information on a regular basis, so that one data centre can take over the whole load in case of a failure. The communication routes are arranged so that any part of the ICANDO system can route through to any other part by at least two possible routes. As a further backup, there is an arrangement with the telephony suppliers to use a public switched network in case of failure of the private lines.

Each site is connected to the Internet directly. This provides a further option for connecting sites, though the high level of communication between the sites will make the Internet infeasible for routine operation. The Internet connections provide flexibility and access to public systems.

It is decided that the ordering application must run as an intranet application with the call centres just having PCs with a browser. No local deployment of application code is permitted. The primary reason is one of being able to rapidly deploy new versions of the system. If copies of programs have to be distributed to hundreds of PCs for deployment, this can take a long time. Using Web server deployment, all that has to happen is to change the central servers.

Within the data centres, the physical architecture of the systems is made up of a number of application servers that operate the business logic, a number of Web servers that present the information to the call centres and customers, and a robust data server cluster, as shown in Figure 15.7. The computer systems are connected by a high-bandwidth local network. The network will be linked to the

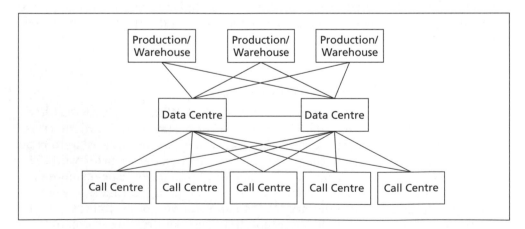

Figure 15.6 Overall physical connection between sites in the ICANDO chemicals system

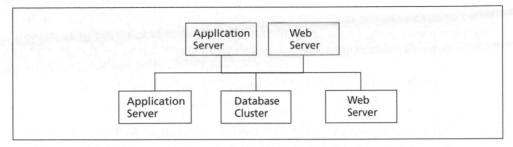

Figure 15.7   Internal architecture of the ICANDO Chemicals data centre

other data centre and the production and call centre sites by a private, high-bandwidth wide area network, and directly onto the Internet. The Web servers will deal with the presentation, and route requests to the application servers, which in turn will access information in the database cluster. Use of multiple Web servers and application servers is for both performance and reliability reasons.

15.4.2 TOOLS

Presentation languages
The current presentation language for the Internet is HTML. However, given that there might, in the future, be changes to presentation languages, it is decided that an intermediate layer of XML is used to link the business logic with the presentation. This will permit changing the presentation, or having two forms of presentation, without needing to change the underlying business logic. Thus the application will have a presentation structure as in Figure 15.8. The developers of the presentation layer will need to know the definition of the information to be exchanged through XML. The developers of the core application will then be able to work independently of the presentation format.

Business logic
The planned life of the application is over 10 years. The range of possible application development languages is vast, from Cobol, which has been around for almost half a century, to Java, which has been available for barely half a decade. Java is chosen for the following reasons. Firstly, it is highly portable, and will

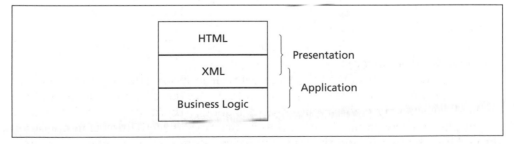

Figure 15.8   The organization of the presentation layer in the ICANDO Chemicals application

allow the change of the computer systems that it runs on. It also fits into modern middleware very well. There are many new components being developed in Java, and though it is relatively new it has sufficient penetration in the market to suggest that it will be around for a very long time. On the down side, it is relatively slow, but the decision is to spend extra on processing power to compensate.

Persistence

There is no consideration of any other storage technology than relational data-bases with SQL. For most projects of this size, it is an automatic decision. However, that does leave open a number of considerations in the choice of supplier. Different databases have different characteristics in terms of price, performance and reliability.

This application requires high performance and high reliability. This results in the choice of a system that can be 'clustered' (Figure 15.9). There can be a number of data server processors linking to the disks. This means that processing power can be increased to incorporate extra demands on the application. Application requests will be routed to the least loaded data server. Every write to a disk is done to two disks, which are kept in tandem. Thus if there is a failure on one disk, the second disk can continue to run and support the application while the first disk is repaired.

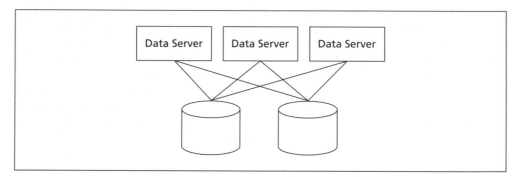

Figure 15.9 Clustering of the data servers for ICANDO Chemicals

Databases also keep a record of every update to the database, known as a journal. For additional security, daily backups are exchanged between the data centres of the databases, and every journal entry is sent directly to the other data centre. Thus if there were a total disaster at one data centre, the other could recover all of the transactions.

Packages and components

The order-taking parts of the system are not well supported in the package market in the style that ICANDO feels is appropriate. However, a number of parts of the application are very well supported. In particular, there are a number of sales ledger packages available. ICANDO has a variety of these packages in operation throughout the world, and the most appropriate one for the market is selected. One of the key criteria is that the database technology is compatible with the one used by the order-taking system, and that the database is accessible through SQL.

A variety of other packages are also incorporated for management reporting, production scheduling and so on. Choices are made based on a variety of reasons, from the functionality of the system to the compatibility with other components. Overall, the aim is to provide as much ready-made functionality as possible.

Connectivity and middleware

The connection between the data centre and call centres/customers will be the HTTP Internet protocol over the Internet. This is an automatic choice, given the style of application construction. The protocol runs very well over both the Internet and an intranet, with the intranet offering guaranteed performance.

Within the data centre, CORBA protocols are employed. Most of the exchanges will be in real time, and CORBA complements Java very well. The packages selected are CORBA-compliant, and this will enable easy communication between parts of the system.

For some information exchanges, such as the regular exchange of data between data centres, a simple file transfer protocol is adequate. The order-taking application is not required to run 24 hours a day, meaning that there are periods, such as overnight, where large quantities of data can be exchanged over the network.

15.4.3 DEVELOPMENT APPROACH

The application is planned to have a long life, with consequent maintenance. A policy of aiming for maximum reuse is adopted, and a highly structured way of developing is required. Therefore a component-based approach is chosen. This has the added advantage that some of the components can be sourced externally.

15.5 ICANDO Site Safety

The site safety application is very simple in terms of physical architecture. It needs to run standalone on a PC. This leaves the selection of development tools and storage technology. The primary objective is to prove the concept and determine whether the use of such an application is viable. If the concept is proved, then the application can be rewritten. The aim is thus to provide the application as quickly as possible, with the highest degree of functionality.

The research team has a long history of IT development, with a high degree of skill in the Smalltalk language. Java is considered, but the view of the research team is that Java is weaker on interactive development, and that their knowledge of Smalltalk will allow them to progress more quickly anyway. Smalltalk has embedded the split of applications into model, view and controller, as indicated in Figure 15.10.

This splits an application into three parts, in the same way that we devised entity, boundary and control objects. The model is a representation of the state of part of the application, usually relating to some aspect of the physical world. In this application, there might be a model to represent a storage facility. The view is the presentation of the model, equivalent to a boundary object, and in this application it might be the drawing of a storage facility on the screen. The controller manages changes to the model and interactions with the view, much as a control object might. Thus if the user changed the details of a facility through the view,

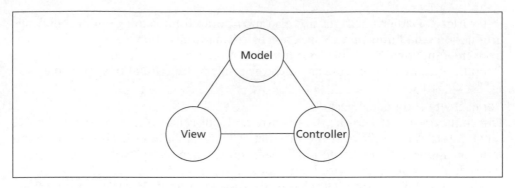

Figure 15.10 Model/View/Controller architecture of Smalltalk applications

then the controller would liaise with the model to make sure that the appropriate state change took place.

There is some debate about how to store guidelines and site descriptions. Though there is the possibility of using a database, and the initial design recommended that, after some consideration it is decided that storage will be done in files. Guidelines will be entered in a fixed format through a forms interface and written in a fixed format to a file. Site details will be written out into a fixed format file. The added complexity of a database for this application is not justified in terms of the increased time taken to develop it. However, if the proof of concept works, then a database might be a serious consideration.

15.6 ICANDO Retail Petrol Promotions

Though reliability and performance are critical aspects of the retail promotions system, they are not as business critical as for the chemicals system. There is also a greater constraint on funds, as the business benefit of this system is less clearly defined, and much smaller. Consequently, the system will be less robust.

15.6.1 TECHNICAL ARCHITECTURE AND TOOLS

This will be a straightforward Internet application. The presentation is to be in HTML. The Web server, application services and database will all run on the same computer. To cope with system failures, a second system is available for a rapid restore and reinstatement of the service.

The presentation must be in HTML. There is no expectation that the system will run for a very long time and need considerable revision, so the use of XML is not considered. One possible advantage of XML might be in interfacing with mobile technologies, such as WAP, but as the application is fairly simple this is ruled out.

The language chosen for the application is ASP with Basic. The reasons are speed of development and availability of support. There is little complexity in the application, and thus the drivers for other languages are minimal.

The database will be relational, and a relatively cheap system is chosen that can cope with the anticipated number of transactions. The cost of disk mirroring is not considered worthwhile, and the approach taken to recovery is for all transactions

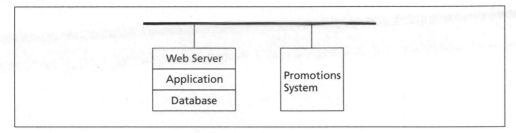

Figure 15.11   Physical architecture of the retail promotions system

to be recorded to a tape. If the system fails, then a new system can be restored by applying the journal to the latest backup, with an anticipated recovery time of about one hour.

The only package involvement will be the link to the existing call centre system. This is easily managed through calls to the database. The resulting physical architecture will therefore be very much as in Figure 15.11.

The connectivity will be very straightforward, with external access using Internet HTTP protocols and access to the Promotions system using the local area network protocols. There are no additional packages to consider.

REVIEW QUESTIONS

1. **What does technical architecture concern itself with?**
2. **When might you use a real-time link between parts of an application, such as CORBA?**
3. **When is message queuing appropriate for linking systems?**
4. **What effect does a component-based approach have on application architecture?**
5. **How does framework-based development affect application architecture?**
6. **What are the layers in a three-tier architecture?**
7. **How does a Web server impact on a multi-tier architecture?**

EXERCISES

1. Propose an architecture for the ICANDO trading system.
2. Propose an architecture for the ICANDO/NerverShut retail system.

CONSTRUCTION, TESTING AND DEPLOYMENT

Reader's Guide

Once a software system is designed, the task of construction and deployment takes place. Detailed discussion of construction is beyond the scope of this book – there are as many approaches as there are programming languages. There is a brief introduction to issues around construction, but no detailed instruction.

The chapter on testing is important to all developers and managers, and it is important for analysts to see the links between their work and testing and documentation. Deployment and construction are really of most interest to technical staff. Most of the issues discussed in this section are important to managers.

Chapter 16: Construction

It is not possible to go into the details of implementation in a particular language, but some issues about construction and the organization of teams to build software are discussed.

Chapter 17: Testing

This chapter thoroughly discusses how to test systems and interim products in systems development, linking the testing back to the original analysis.

Chapter 18: Deployment, Support and Enhancement

This chapter discusses issues around the deployment of systems, including the planning of deployment, documentation and training.

CHAPTER **16**

Construction

IN THIS CHAPTER YOU WILL LEARN ABOUT:

1. How construction is organized
2. Issues in implementing user interfaces, programs and databases
3. The importance of exception handling
4. Integration

Construction is the point at which all the pontifications of the analysts and designers have to be converted into something that actually works. Though most people think that this is where all the effort goes, in practice it is often much less than half of the effort that goes into the production of a system. The rest of the effort is taken up by analysis, design, testing and deployment.

Programmers are either the heroes or villains of the piece. They either produce something that works and is well liked, or they take the flak for poorly constructed systems. If the system is well designed and meets a real need, and they do their job properly, they ride into town with the plaudits of everyone. If the system does not meet needs, or is badly designed, then they are jeered. That is not to say that the developers of systems are blameless themselves, but they usually take a disproportionate part of the glory or the disdain, depending on the overall success.

The primary inputs and outputs of construction are shown in Figure 16.1. In a well-established environment, the developers will be given:

- a comprehensive set of use case descriptions
- use case elaborations in the form of activity diagrams, sequence diagrams and collaboration diagrams
- class diagrams
- operation specifications
- interface definitions
- prototypes if they have been used
- architecture definition

These should be enough for the developer to proceed to the construction of a system. The result is a set of components and an integrated system ready for testing.

Of course, design and analysis are not perfect, and there will need to be clarification of the information that is passed. The developers, as they write programs, will find holes in the design. There needs to be dialogue, as well as the handing over of analysis and design documents.

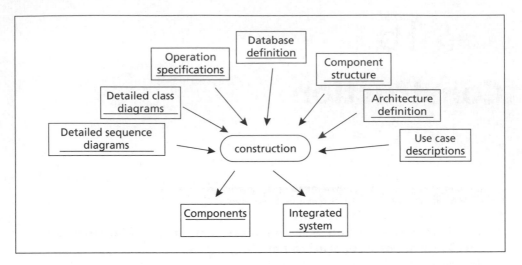

Figure 16.1 Inputs and outputs of the construction process

Not all developers will be lucky enough to receive well-structured designs in a defined notation. It is surprisingly common, even in large organizations, for developers to be given little more than essays describing system requirements. In circumstances like that, they would be well advised to go through an informal analysis and design process before committing to code. Project managers, in pressured environments, do not always see the need for interim models, and may view them as procrastination.

Construction very much depends on the organization, the approach to development (e.g. component-based), the technical architecture (particularly the development tools), and the application architecture. It is almost impossible to give anything other than a flavour of the construction process. It is certainly not the task of this book to consider languages and the details of construction in particular languages. At best, we can only obtain a flavour of what construction is like.

16.1 Organizing Construction

If the application is developed in a single language, plus a database, then the most common way of sharing out construction is by allocating use cases to developers. In this way, individual developers will be able to work reasonably independently. Database construction is usually separated out, as a specialist skill. Use case developers will produce the user interface, the logic and links to the database.

Figure 16.2 shows this organization, with individual developers working on sets of use cases, producing the user interface and the logic. There are usually fewer database developers, as most of the effort goes into construction of the logic. Developers will tend to work on related use cases, thereby minimizing the interdependence of their work.

This style of development is commonplace in timeshare applications (e.g. CICS applications). It is the simplest to organize and produces fewer integration problems and problems of cooperation between developers. However, it becomes less

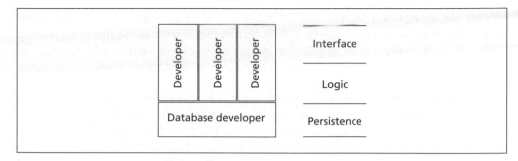

Figure 16.2 Organizing developers in a single language environment

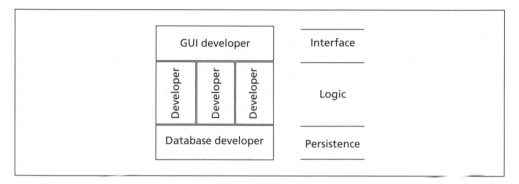

Figure 16.3 Organization of developers where the user interface language is different from the logic language

viable in environments where multiple languages are to be used, as the developer then has to be multi-skilled.

Where the user interface language differs from the logic language, a situation that is increasingly common today, especially for Internet development, the user interface is separated out. Figure 16.3 illustrates the organization of this. The use cases will be driven by developers who are working on the core logic of the use case. The GUI development is likely to be more straightforward, and fewer developers will be dedicated to that.

One advantage of this style of development is that the user interface can have a better and more consistent look and feel. For Internet applications, the development of the interface is a critical component that needs great care and attention, though it often takes up less time than the core application logic. The disadvantages of this are the increased amount of communication required and extra problems with integration.

Variations of the above will take place. I managed one development where the user interface was so complicated and the business services relatively easy that the use cases were shared among the GUI developers, who were supported by a smaller team of business service logic developers. There will also be variations to deal with situations where a package or a large component is to be integrated into the system.

Component-based development will have its own particular organization. Use cases will be allocated to individual developers or small teams and developed as above, but alongside the use case developers will be a component development team. The use case development will mostly be assembly from components, with a dialogue between use case developers and component developers to extend the components where necessary. A similar approach is needed for framework-based development.

As you can see, organization of the development team depends partly on development style and partly on the technologies used to implement the project. Each approach has its strengths and weaknesses, and it is not the subject of this book to explore them in any detail. The only comment needed here is that good communication within the construction team, as well as between the construction team and the other teams, is essential for success.

16.2 User Interface

The user interface is the public presentation of the system to the majority of its users. On its quality much of the success of the system depends. Analysis and design should have given a comprehensive view of the shape and functionality of the interface, and this will be particularly true if there have been prototypes developed.

It has become increasingly common to separate the user interface development from the application logic development. One of the drivers for this is the Internet, where HTML has become the dominant presentation language, and HTML has very limited capabilities for processing. The security structure of the Internet forces separation of presentation from information very rigidly, and therefore the user interface can do little more than provide data validation and very simple consistency checks.

In other areas of development, too, the separation of the interface from the application logic has become commonplace. This has arisen through the availability of environments that provide powerful interface generation but limited logic capabilities. Arguably languages like Visual Basic fit into this category, and there are many other proprietary languages and tools with similar or better capabilities.

Using HTML has distinct advantages in terms of deployment, but limits the amount of interaction possible. One way of enhancing the interaction is to use a browser scripting language, like JavaScript, that can undertake logical checks on data and improve the quality of the interface. HTML can also embed Java applets and similar plug-in technologies to improve the quality of the interaction. The constraint in Internet deployment is that any programming in the presentation does not have access to the local machine for storage or retrieval.[1]

Java comes with a comprehensive interface library that allows Java developers to provide a comprehensive interface. This is less colourful than HTML, but more powerful in terms of controlling the interaction. However, user interface development can be one of the trickiest aspects of Java.

---

1   The exception to this is the use of cookies, where a browser allows a Web page to write a very limited amount of information to disk in a protected way, and for other pages to read that information later. This is how many applications keep track of usage and of the user of the system after logging on.

Other languages come with proprietary interfacing libraries. For example, C++ has very limited input and output capabilities itself, and relies on proprietary libraries, such as Microsoft's, for the presentation logic. Much of the complexity of using languages comes in understanding the interface libraries. Another of the advantages of HTML in this respect is its relative simplicity.

16.3 Programs and Application Logic

The choice of programming language is huge. C++ has become dominant in many financial applications, and Cobol is still remarkably popular. Java is gaining in popularity. Though this statement is likely to be controversial in many circles, I do not think that object-oriented languages are an essential choice. Given an unlimited supply of developers, good project management, and little or no legacy software, languages like Java are to be preferred, and their object-oriented features are beneficial. Unfortunately the world is not overflowing with skilled OO programmers, management systems have been set up to deal with other development environments, and there are vast numbers of legacy systems written in Cobol. It is notoriously difficult to retrain programmers in OO languages when they have been programming for years in procedural languages like Cobol and C.

This leads to the question of what the big deal about OO languages is, and why we have been looking at OO methods. In fact, the implementation languages and the methods for analysis and design are largely orthogonal. The design will inevitably be influenced by the larger implementation environment, but many of the good design features, such as the separation of entity and control objects, ease the use of procedural languages in construction.

Leaving out the issues of user interfaces, programming is mostly about implementing control objects and managing entity objects. Control objects are the basic transactions, prompted by the user interface, to manage the entity objects. Entity objects, from a construction perspective, then become essentially active database entries.

Implementing in an object-oriented language will be very much along the lines discussed in the design chapter. Most of the design constructs will map neatly onto implementation constructs. There will inevitably be quirks of the implementation environment that need to be worked around, but mostly there will be a clear mapping between design objects and implementation objects.

Implementing in a procedural language will involve more work – the specification of the control objects is effectively a program or function specification. However, it is not viable for languages such as these to promote database entries into entity objects, and therefore the language will usually deal directly with the database through a language such as SQL.

16.4 Databases

Databases are used for storing information that needs to survive for a long time. In our approach to design, the database keeps the attributes stored in entity objects, and there is a correspondence between entity objects and database records, usually one-to-one. In an object implementation, databases can be accessed through 'factories' that deal with much of the management issues. Factories take a database record (or set of related records) and create an object in the programming environment. That object will have operations added to it, as defined in the programming language.

Database records are really very simple objects themselves. They have four operations – Create, Read, Update and Delete – endearingly known as CRUD. It is possible that the design team have acknowledged the implementation environment and specified the programs with database access explicit in these terms. If not, the implementation team will need to make the translation from the more abstract design.

16.5 Components

Systems are usually grouped into components for deployment, even if the approach is not 'component-based'. Objects are grouped together for implementation and compiled into components. These are then deployed throughout the system. Components communicate, either through direct calls to each other or through some protocol over a network such as IIOP.

16.6 Exception Handling

One of the least appreciated and most underrated aspects of system development is the handling of exceptions. Exceptions occur at points where the computer system is unable to continue functioning as planned. There may be design or implementation reasons, or it might be that part of the system is unavailable for some reason, such as a server being down.

When a fault is detected, an exception is raised. Some computer languages such as Java have built-in exception handling. In other languages, the exception handling has to be built in to the application. When an exception is raised, someone needs to be informed so that corrective action can take place.

When a part of the system fails to deliver to another part of the system, it cannot simply fall silent or return nonsense. It must tell the other part of the system that it has failed, and give some reason. One of the common ways of doing this is to allocate some code, say an integer value, to each type of error that the implementation team detects. A database matching error codes with text is then kept for diagnosis.

When a fault occurs in a system, the fault needs to be both notified to the requester of a service and logged somewhere. Notification to the requester is important so that the requester can take corrective action. Logging is important for later diagnosis of system faults.

A fault in one component will often trigger a fault in the calling component. That will in turn cause a fault in the component that called it, and so on, until either some software can correct the error or ultimately the fault manifests itself in a user interface. Then the dreaded error message appears. It is important that the message that arrives on the user interface has a complete trace available of all the errors that led to the final error. Otherwise, fault finding becomes tracing a needle in a haystack.

One of the most difficult projects I worked on involved a poor exception handling system. Parts of the package simply did not respond if a fault occurred.

Other parts, instead of notifying the requester, simply logged the fault locally. Diagnosing errors could involve trawling through a number of logs and trying to collate logged error messages. Added to that, the error messages were not coded, and were arbitrary text messages. Instead of simply reading an error code from a screen and looking it up, even a simple network failure could take hours to trace. The error reported on the interface was usually a time-out error, or an error saying that data was unavailable, and these errors were simply useless in themselves.

This is unfortunately not a rare situation, and a number of development teams have related similar problems. As systems are more and more constructed as distributed sets of components in multiple languages, the proper tracing of exceptions through the system gets harder and is more and more arbitrary. The problem is compounded when purchased components are integrated into the system, as they will come with their own exception handling procedures.

The only solution is for implementation teams to be disciplined and to plan the exception handling as part of their work. Project managers need to see this as a valuable part of the development team activity, or they will pay the price in testing and debugging costs – exception handling delivers no directly usable functionality, but it does provide integrity and better diagnosis that pays off in the long run.

16.7 Integration

In the end, it all has to be put together. Integration is the messy stage of making everything fit. The more components, and the more implementation technologies, the more problematic this is. Alongside testing, integration is one of the most heated activities in a development environment. It quickly finds out whether the parts fit together, and inevitably there will be problems.

The only advice about integration is to do it often. Test harnesses for components serve a useful purpose, but it is when components are bound together that the proof of the system functionality emerges. The engine, gearbox, steering, brakes, and electronics of a car may all appear to work perfectly individually, but it is only when you put them all together and try to drive the car that you know for sure that they really work.

16.8 Conclusion

A full treatise on construction would incorporate a detailed introduction to the programming environments available. That is way beyond the purpose and scope of this book. However, I felt it important to incorporate a brief chapter on construction in order to cover a few issues such as organization, exception handling and integration. Those who will become developers or are already developers will spend a great deal of time learning the complexities of the myriad development environments around.

The usual case study material and exercises are omitted from the end of this chapter. To produce adequate case study material that links back to the design would involve details that would assume too much knowledge of the implementation environments. However, you might like to try mapping the designs you produced from the previous chapter into working languages and environments that you know.

REVIEW QUESTIONS

1. For a single language implementation with a database, how might you organize development?
2. If the presentation language and the logic language are different, how might you organize development?
3. What are the advantages and disadvantages of HTML as a presentation language?
4. Is it essential to use an object-oriented language for the construction of the logic layer?
5. Why is good exception handling important?
6. Why is it good to integrate frequently?

Testing

IN THIS CHAPTER YOU WILL LEARN ABOUT:
1. **The different stages of testing**
2. **How to develop test plans**
3. **Organization of testing and feedback**

Testing is a Cinderella subject. Unlike Cinderella, however, testing teams do not often get to marry the prince, and they remain at the hearth, among the cinders, tidying up the mess of the ugly sisters and being abused by them. Yet testing is fundamental to successful project delivery. A good testing strategy will determine the success of a project. An under-tested product is going to cost more in the long run because faults will inevitably have to be fixed, and too many faults in a product will damage its reputation and perhaps cause substantial losses.

Testing is not unique to software development. All product development needs to incorporate a testing strategy, and the success of that strategy largely determines the success of the product. Testing starts upstream. In many ways the cost–benefit analysis we discussed at length in Chapter 7 is a form of test, making sure that the economics of the project is right before committing more resources to the development. Prototypes too are a form of test, checking that the analysis and initial design is appropriate. Reviewing use case descriptions also tests the analysis, to make sure it is in line with needs.

Testing, however, is usually meant as testing the final product: the computer system to be deployed. This is particularly important, as it is usually the last chance to make repairs before the system is released. However, if testing is left too late,[1] the costs of repairs can be enormous. Testing, like fine wine, is better little but often.

Testing works best if it is woven into the development process. It makes use of the information supplied by earlier stages in the development process to make sure that the process is on track. Imagine an ancient mariner who set an early

---

1 There is a fable about a famous Chinese healer who was asked who was the greatest healer. He replied that there were many healers like him who were called to treat the chronically sick and the dying. Sometimes they succeeded, and if they failed no one blamed them. They became famous among the lords and princes of the day, and they were much valued. The healer said he had an elder brother who could spot diseases as they arose, and treat them before they became chronic. This elder brother was popular in his local community. The healer's eldest brother could prevent illnesses arising, and no one knew him outside the family.

compass direction and then sat back and enjoyed the voyage while the sailors toiled to keep the ship in the preset direction. Winds, tides and currents would cause the ship to drift. As the weeks went by, the small accumulated changes could cause the ship to miss a continent and either land at the wrong place or perish in the waves. The mariner needs to check the position of the ship regularly, to monitor the sun and stars, and to adjust the direction to compensate for obstacles. Small, frequent adjustments are needed, and this needs continuous feedback. Too many projects, alas, share the fate of a lackadaisical ancient mariner, and founder sadly after an exciting but misdirected journey.

Testing is seen primarily as a veto over delivery. In fact, it is a feedback mechanism. Faults are found that have been caused much earlier in the process, and the tester needs a mechanism for feeding back the fault. The further back the feedback has to travel, the more costly it is. Finding that there is a validation fault on a field on a screen usually means that the error can be corrected within a few hours. Finding that insufficient information has been gathered to complete a process can involve analysts, designers and developers working for days or weeks to repair the fault.

The software development process that we have been defining has a number of key outputs. The primary aim of testing in the later stages is to make sure that the end product meets the functional and non-functional requirements of the system, and it will make use of the earlier documents to do this. We have produced early in the process two key sets of documents. The first is the set of business process definitions, and the second is the set of use case specifications.

Business process definitions are central to final acceptance testing. All systems are there to support a business process of some kind. Acceptance testing will walk through a business process, providing a system with sample data and checking the results. For example, if a customer order is entered, it is necessary to follow through the whole business process to make sure that the goods are taken from the warehouse and delivered, and that the invoice is printed (testing would not physically do this, but would simulate it).

Use case definitions are central to system testing and acceptance testing. Use cases define in detail the way the system interacts and behaves. A use case can be tested individually in system testing, or it can be tested in relationship with other use cases as part of acceptance testing.

Some non-functional requirements involve testing of a different sort, which can be difficult to devise. Scalability testing involves simulating the use of the system by a large number of users. Reliability testing can involve long runs of the system. We shall look at some of the issues separately for this form of testing.

Figure 17.1 shows the primary inputs and outputs of the testing phase.

17.1 Testing Requirements

I recently heard a prominent speaker state that the majority of faults arise during requirements, but are often not identified until testing or until operation. If you think about it, this is almost a truism. Although software developers are not miracle workers, on the whole they manage to produce in software a reasonably faithful representation of the requirements as they see them. Problems arise when the requirements are incomplete, wrong or badly expressed.

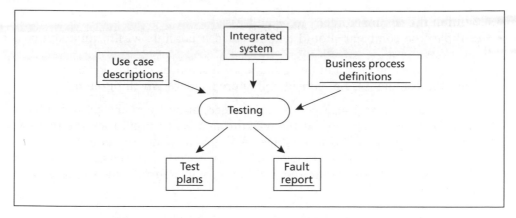

Figure 17.1 Primary inputs and outputs to the testing phase

Poor requirements can arise either through sloppy gathering of requirements or a poor way of recording them. We have focused on a fairly thorough documentation of requirements along the lines of business process definitions and use case descriptions. If the analysis team follow some methodical approach like this they are less likely to miss key requirements. However, they are bound to miss some, or someone is going to change their mind about something.

Various stakeholders have an interest in the requirements. The end users are one obvious category of stakeholder, as they are going to be the ones using the system. However, business managers have a role to play, as they are often pushing for changes in business processes that the end users may be reluctant to accept initially. The usual process is for a document describing the requirements to be published and delivered to the business managers for review. They will then be expected to sign off the requirements.

This is not a particularly productive way, as documents tend not to get read thoroughly. A better route is for the analysts to provide a structured walkthrough of the requirements analysis to groups of stakeholders, and to gather feedback from the walkthroughs. If user interface prototypes have been constructed, these can be incorporated in the walkthrough.

A structured walkthrough can take the following format:

1. The analysts present a business process, using primary and alternative paths.
2. Stakeholders comment on the structure of the process.
3. The analysts present a set of use cases that are designed to support the business process.
4. Stakeholders comment on the appropriateness of the use cases.
5. The analysts present each use case, using primary and alternative paths and non-functional requirements.
6. Stakeholders comment on the detail of the use cases.

The stakeholders' comments need to be recorded. They also need to be graded. Even the most thorough analysis will result in some comments. Comments can be graded on some scale such as:

- Essential: the comment needs to be addressed
- Desirable: the comment should be addressed if possible within time and cost limitations.
- Useful: the comment should be addressed if it requires minimal changes.
- Reject: the comment is not considered appropriate or worth pursuing.

The result of a walkthrough can be acceptance, provisional acceptance subject to minor changes, or rejection. If the walkthrough is accepted, then the requirements can be taken to the next stage, perhaps with minor modifications to respond to comments. If the walkthrough issues a rejection, the comments need to be reviewed and the revised requirements put through a further stage of testing by a walkthrough.

17.2 Testing Analysis

Systems analysis pushes the requirements into more detail, and describes the use cases in terms of domain objects. Stakeholders will have difficulty understanding many of the notations and issues involved in analysis. However, the analysis has to be handed over to the design team. This is an excellent checkpoint for the analysis.

The design team will have a good understanding of the architecture of the system, and their main role is to translate the analysis models into models that fit into the architecture. Designers and developers often have a much more grounded sense of what is achievable than analysts, and tend to work at a finer level of detail. The handover process should be one of careful scrutiny.

At this point the analysis team should have business process descriptions, use case descriptions, user interface prototypes and a domain object model to describe the system. The handover should be on the basis of use cases, and a suggested workshop would be as follows:

1. Analysts present the business processes and use case descriptions.
2. Designers/developers comment on them.
3. Analysts walk through each use case, following primary and alternative paths.
4. Designers/developers comment on them.
5. Analysts present user interface prototypes.
6. Designers/developers comment on them.
7. Analysts describe the domain objects and sequence diagrams they have developed for each use case.
8. Designers/developers comment on the domain objects and sequence diagrams.

Again, the comments need to be recorded and rated using, say, the Essential/ Desirable/Useful/Reject criteria described above. The analysis can be accepted fully or provisionally, or rejected.

Now you will be beginning to see that feedback is occurring. The types of problems that are likely to be uncovered through workshops like this are:

1. Identification of missing steps in the use cases.
2. Logical faults in the detail of the use case.
3. Information that cannot reasonably be stored or retrieved.

Table 17.1   A typical comments database

Use Case ID	Originator	Comment	Status	Action
3	User – Jim	No customer address on customer details page	Essential	Revise specification of interface
3	User – Tahara	Nice to see a summary of the customer balance on the customer details page	Desirable	Check with developers if easy to provide
3	Developer – Asif	May need a pick list from customer names if customer cannot remember customer id	Essential	Change use case specification, adding alternative path if customer does not remember customer number

A database needs to be kept of the comments, with a structure such as that in Table 17.1. There may be more fields necessary, such as who authorizes, date raised, date actioned and so forth.

As you can see, the use case is central to the testing process, just as it is during the whole software development process. A simple database in the above format, perhaps slightly extended, can be used to control the feedback process. It is then viable to ask questions such as: 'What are the essential comments for the use cases in this phase?'.

Databases like this need to be controlled carefully. I recall one database on a project I was reviewing that had grown to thousands of comments. Anyone was allowed to enter comments, and it became a buck-passing mechanism. Arguably there should only be entry to this database at key stages.

17.3 Testing Design

Design is getting further from the stakeholder in terms of accessibility, and many analysts will be uncomfortable with the level of detail and the concepts that are applied by designers. Design will take the simple sequence diagrams produced in systems analysis and extend them into specifications that can be implemented. Detailed object models will emerge that can be implemented. Final decisions will be made on the user interface and its operation.

Designers can test their designs with the systems analysts and with the developers who will be implementing the code. Once the design is complete, a workshop can be devised to which analysts and developers are invited. This should cover:

1. A description of the architecture of the system, including key object structures.
2. A brief description of the use cases that are being designed.
3. A structured walkthrough of the sequence diagrams and/or collaboration diagrams that map the sequences in the use case onto object interactions.
4. Details of the classes to support the use case, with attributes and operations.

5. Details of the operations in terms of parameters and any transformations expressed as pre- and postconditions.
6. Details of the database structures supporting the persistent objects.

At each stage, analysts and developers may feed back comments. Analysts will be primarily concerned that the design supports the requirements, and will need to check that all paths are covered in sufficient detail. Developers will be more concerned with logical consistency and the feasibility of implementation.

The comments can be added to the database, as indicated in Table 17.1. Again, a simple rating can be used. Comments are likely to be more detailed, and may need to be supplemented with additional information.

17.4 Unit Testing of Code

At last, we get on to the more traditional areas of testing. At this stage, some aspects of the final product have been constructed. Unit testing of code usually resides within the development team. Developers are responsible for undertaking testing of the components they are working on and for ensuring that they integrate with other components that they depend on or on which they depend.

It is not possible to be too prescriptive about this process, as much of the testing process will depend on the architecture of the system and on how the components are fitted together. The most painful testing situation I have been involved with had developers using two different languages, an unusual communication protocol, a database and an overly complicated link to a remote mainframe system. This meant that to test, three developers and three separate systems had to be lined up. A bug that took ten minutes to fix could take two hours to find with developers mostly waiting in that time, or filling in with other work.

For a reasonably concise description of classical test methods for testing software, see Pressman (2000). You may like to look there for ideas. However, common practice (for good or ill) is rarely so rigorous on unit testing.

A developer will normally test her work by putting together a simple test harness that feeds requests and reports on the responses. This test harness will cover a representative set of scenarios that are to be handled by the unit. The unit may be an operation on a class, a class itself, or a suite of classes, perhaps incorporating a database, to implement a use case. Usually there will be a debugging environment that will allow the developer to step through her code very carefully, examining inputs and outputs along the way.

Once a developer has satisfied herself that her work is complete and works to her satisfaction, the next stage is to integrate her work with other components. This will involve two or more developers working together to identify and rectify problems. If a single language environment is being used, this can be straightforward. However, increasingly multiple language developments are taking place, and two developers will often need to cooperate in areas where they do not have overlapping skills.

Ultimately, a developer will be satisfied that her work is sound and fits in with other people's work. It will normally then be set aside for system testing. However, the integration of other people's work may raise problems, and cause her to review the code and undertake further testing.

Occasionally it will be possible for another developer to test someone's work. In my first IT role, team leaders would run independent unit tests on code before it was released for system and acceptance testing. Systems were much simpler, with less complicated interaction. This is an ideal that may be worth striving for, but in practice this can be difficult. Usually it is left to individual developers to undertake their own unit tests, for the friction of integration with other components to uncover faults, and for system and acceptance testing to uncover the remaining faults.

Alongside testing, code reviews may be used to provide a check on the quality of code. Code reviews have many advantages. By making code reviews a key stage of development, individual developers are encouraged to produce readable code. This may not be the quickest way to get functioning code, but it pays off in the long run when someone else may have to maintain the code. It will also encourage documentation of the code with comments. Getting developers to explain code often forces them to scrutinize it more carefully and to spot errors themselves. Also, a fresh pair of eyes will often spot errors.

Code reviews can be informal, or formal. An informal review might be undertaken by a team leader before releasing code. A formal review might involve the developer presenting to a group of other developers with a minute-taker and a formal report produced at the end. Formal reviews would follow a structured walkthrough format, as described above, with the developer presenting the design and the code, and comments being made by the reviewers.

Extreme programming (Beck, 1999) takes a particular view of testing and coding. All code is written by two people, and they code from test plans. Developers write the test plans before they produce code. This sounds a little unusual at first, but it is really just a reorganization of roles and responsibilities. Extreme programming also has a step known as refactoring, where the code is revised according to various quality criteria.

This stage of testing is often the most diverse, and very dependent on the professionalism and quality of the development team. Time pressures can also impact the quality of the testing at this stage, and there is always pressure to release code as quickly as possible. However, the development team should be careful not to release code into the next stage of testing before they are sure that most of the problems have been rectified. Once the later stages are invoked, the game is out of the bag and mistakes are harder to hide.

17.5 System Testing

So, now you have an integrated system that the developers say matches the design, and the designers say matches the systems analysis, and that the analysts say meets the requirements of the business users. Does it? System testing looks at the whole system and exercises its functionality. It would be a foolish project that simply shipped the product on the say-so of the developers (though I know enough foolish projects that have done this).

System testing should not be undertaken by the developers who produced the system, though it is often useful to have some development expertise involved to verify certain state changes, such as making sure that data is recorded in the database. The purpose of system testing is to exercise all the parts of the system, making sure that it fits together and provides the promised functionality.

The first stage of testing is to produce a test plan. Surprise, surprise: the test plan is derived from the use case implementation plan. What is being done is to test the use cases that have been developed, both individually and as a cohesive whole. They system testing may cover all use cases developed to date, or only those developed in a particular phase and any that are tightly linked to that phase.

From the use cases to be tested, detailed test plans can be provided for the use cases themselves. This will involve deriving test scenarios that cover the various alternative paths through a use case, inventing data and determining some test that ensures that the use case has fired successfully. The test scenario should indicate the expected result, in terms either of data stored or output from another use case.

Using the detailed test plans, the system test team will then work systematically through all the use cases. As they do, they will almost certainly identify problems. These may be minor problems, such as data validation not working accurately, or more major ones, such as the interface not appearing.

With luck the testing team will be able to exercise all the use cases reasonably. As they work, they will keep a log of the problems they found. Each problem needs to be rated in terms of seriousness: say 1 for serious problems that must be fixed, 2 for problems where there is a work-around, and 3 for minor problems that can be accepted. A database of defects can then be drawn up as in Table 17.2. The actual description of the defect can often run into many paragraphs.

The defect log is likely to keep fields for comments from the development team, dates and a description of action taken.

Table 17.2   A simple defect log database

Use case ID	Test scenario ID	Tester	Defect	Rating
3	3.2	Aisha	The postcode on the address on the customer display does not appear.	2
3	3.2	Aisha	The customer validated tick box does not operate and prevents further execution	1
3	3.7	Josh	Customer details window is a bit too big and needs scrolling down to see all details. Nicer if more compact.	3

17.6 Non-Functional Testing

Functional testing is straightforward, if long-winded and time-consuming. Non-functional requirements are much more difficult to address. Some testing of these, however, needs to be considered.

17.6.1 SCALABILITY

Scalability is the property of a system to deal with the maximum number of transactions that it will have to undertake in a period, without failing or decaying in performance to such a degree that the system is unusable. This is a particularly difficult aspect to test, especially when systems might be used by thousands of users, as is the case with many Internet applications. Rather than give a specific set of rules, which would be difficult to devise, I shall relate an anecdote of a system that I had to test for scalability.

The application was a customized package meant to operate initially for 60 users in a call centre, and ultimately scale to over 2,000 users. The core application ran on a server with a link out to a remote mainframe system to access some information. Each user had a PC that was mainly dedicated to user interface management.

The package vendor was new in the market, and we were an early adopter. They had undertaken their own scalability tests on the package. This consisted of running a large number of processes up on the server, driving the application through many transactions. Reasonable estimates of individual user throughput indicated that the ability of the core application to cope with transactions would scale to several thousand concurrent users.

We tried a similar server-side simulation that certainly indicated that for 60 users there would be no problems. However, on deployment we found mysterious tail-offs after about 10 users were logged in. The vendor blamed our network, and naturally we blamed the package. In a complex environment with servers, networks, a mainframe and lots of PCs, tracing performance problems is almost impossible.

In desperation, to track the performance problem we set up a test run with a number of people logging on to the system in laboratory conditions, driving the system at about 5 times the normal throughput for a user. People logged on in stages, and when the 14th person logged on, the system almost ground to a halt. Setting up an experiment like this was costly in terms of people, so in order to trace the problem we had to find a different mechanism.

I asked a programmer to write a script on a PC that drove the server over the network with a logged in user. The script drove transactions at a parameterized rate, with randomized delays to simulate real users. We then borrowed as many PCs as we could and started the script off one at a time. When the 14th script started, the system started to stall. The CPU shot up to 100% utilization on the server, and the response time decayed dramatically.

Now we had a reproducible problem. Only when you can reproduce a problem can you trace it. The vendor was able to send in a consultant to examine the operation of the system. They traced the fault to a single module.

The key lessons from this are as follows. Firstly, simulations are not perfect. Even the best tests fail to uncover faults. In our case, it was not the number of transactions that scuppered the system, it was the number of people logged in, a fault that was hard to anticipate. Secondly, in a complex network environment it is almost impossible to diagnose live performance problems as they happen and to reproduce them. This leads to the need to set up experiments that are reproducible and simulate realistically the real environment. Thirdly, the cost of organizing people to drive systems is exorbitant. Some computer simulation of real human interaction will be necessary.

Every scalability test will be unique to the system that is being tested. The ultimate scalability test will be the users themselves, and we shall discuss deployment strategies that can control the risk of failure through scalability problems. When problems do arise, considerable ingenuity will be required by the development team to produce experiments that reproduce the problem and enable them to diagnose the fault.

17.6.2 SECURITY

The level of security needed on systems varies considerably. As more and more systems are exposed over public networks such as the Internet, security becomes more critical. Security needs to be built in to environments, but some testing of procedures and the system is wise. Some security testing can be built into system testing by getting the testers to attempt to access information that should be barred, or entering illicit information. For thorough security testing of critical applications, a specialist may be needed who knows the typical loopholes in systems and can apply that specialist knowledge; in practice, this level of testing is rarely needed.

17.6.3 RELIABILITY AND RECOVERY

Basic reliability of systems is the realm of systems engineers. However, the software developer has some responsibilities, and some of the testing below will consider this.

Functional testing will ensure a considerable part of the reliability of systems in that the data that needs to be stored will be ensured as accurate and complete. However, failures outside the scope of the software need to be dealt with.

The first class of failure will be from aborted transactions. Test plans need to incorporate tests to see what happens if a transaction is aborted. Perhaps the customer rings off in the middle of an order, or maybe the computer system or network crashes. It is important to make sure that the transaction recovers properly, and does not (say) result in unwanted items delivered to the customer or the customer's order getting completely lost.

The second class of failure will come from lost data. Computer disks can fail, or operations staff can accidentally delete data. Some tests need to be devised to cope with this. Databases usually have rollback and recovery mechanisms, and these need to be exercised during the testing to make sure that they work and recover all the data.

17.7 User Acceptance Testing

System testing is there to ensure that the system provides its intended functionality. User acceptance testing (UAT) is the final stage before deployment. User acceptance testing is usually undertaken by a team of individuals that have no direct connection with the development team. Either this will be a group taken out of the user community for the purposes of evaluating a particular system or, in some organizations that undertake a substantial amount of software development for their users, there may be a specific team set up to undertake acceptance testing.

UAT groups will devise their own test plans, again based on the business process and use case definitions, but also incorporating where appropriate their own knowledge of the business domain. In addition to functionality, they will concern themselves with usability, in terms of either ease of use or performance.

If the analysis, design and system testing have been effective, the number of defects identified by user acceptance testing should be small. In practice, it should be a final check before issue. A high defect rate would indicate problems earlier in the development process.

Defects need to be logged and the log need not be any different from the one indicated in Table 17.2. Again, the defects need to be categorized into those that must be rectified and those that can be accepted. Perfect systems do not arise, and even the best systems do have defects.

17.8 Beta Testing

Products that have a huge market are often tested by releasing the product to a selected set of users and eliciting feedback. This is a common mechanism for testing software packages and operating systems and is known as beta testing. The beta testers get certain advantages from an early view of the package, either through special discounts or because they gain an advantage from knowing the package in detail before its official release.

Beta testing is less systematic, in that you are giving the product to people who are not under your direction. On the other hand, it is likely to uncover unusual problems that are not uncovered by routine testing, by virtue of the fact that more people are using the product, that they are usually trying to use it for a purpose, and that they are usually many in number.

Feedback from beta testing requires a more organized procedure. Testers are not likely to want to fill in complex forms. Sometimes the problems they uncover may arise from misunderstandings rather than faults with the product. A common way of handling beta test feedback is to set up a help desk that can be contacted directly by testers, either by email or by telephone.

17.9 Debugging and Processing Feedback

The ideal result of any testing process is a product that has no defects and is ready for deployment. At best, what is likely to happen is that the product has few enough defects to consider for deployment. At each stage of the testing process, there needs to be some assessment made of the defects, and a judgement made about whether to take the system forward or to rectify faults before the next stage.

High severity defects will block progress to deployment. No one would want a car with an engine that did not start, and no one will want a call centre system that cannot check the validity of customers. A judgement may be made that it is worth deploying a subset of the system that has no high severity defects, but most likely there will need to be some repair planned. Project managers need to incorporate time for repairs in their planning. Repairs also need to be tested, and therefore there needs to be consideration of this in the planning.

Moderate severity defects will not automatically block progress, but if there is a high number of these defects then the judgment may be that the system needs some repair work before being acceptable. A car with an indicator switch that does not cancel may be acceptable, but if there are too many niggles like that it will not be acceptable to most customers, and likewise if a system has too many small irritants for its users it will usually create more problems than it solves.

Low severity defects rarely block progress, and they will normally be fed into the development cycle for rectification in future releases. It would take a considerable number of low severity defects before a system was blocked on those alone.

The defects then need to be traced back so that the faults can be uncovered. Development faults will usually result in erroneous data being stored or not being stored at all, validation errors or crashes of the system. Though these are often the most dramatic, they are usually the easiest to fix. Usually the functionality of the system has been provided well enough, and it is a straightforward technical problem.

Systems that are too slow or too difficult to use pose a much greater problem. There is usually then something wrong with the design. This can lead to dramatic revision of the design or architecture to solve the problems.

Systems that are missing functionality result in a trace back to the requirements phase, and it can be a lengthy process to cover up gaps in the requirements and push them through to implementation. However, that missing functionality can often be tolerated, and it may not block release of a version of the product.

17.10 ICANDO Bulk Chemical Ordering

The chemical system has a huge impact on the operation of the business, and a thorough testing strategy will be crucial, in line with a careful deployment strategy that allows for recovery from any undetected problems. The project team decide to engage the various stakeholders in the development process throughout.

17.10.1 TESTING REQUIREMENTS

A series of requirements review workshops are devised to coincide with the scheduled completion of the requirements phase of the planned development iterations. Depending on the aim of the iteration, a suitable set of representative stakeholders are invited to participate in the workshop. We shall consider one workshop for the definition of the requirements for the order-taking iteration, with the requirements as devised in Chapter 8.

The stakeholders involved in the order processing will include call centre staff, sales staff and customers themselves. The workshop is organized with team leaders from two call centres in different countries, who have operational experience of both handling orders and managing day-to-day operations, and two unit managers from different countries who have a broader view of operations. Two key customer representatives are included from companies that take a substantial quantity of supplies from ICANDO, and who have agreed to participate in the beta testing of the electronic ordering over the Internet. Two sales representatives are invited from different countries.

Given the importance of the order-taking element, a two-day workshop is planned. The first morning begins with a general welcome and introduction of the participants, with a statement of the objectives of the day and how the feedback will be captured. The workshop is led by the analysis team, and minutes are taken. After the introduction, there is a presentation on the business process map, the business scenarios and the business workflows. Questions are permitted, but changes to the process flows are not considered at this stage. After the

Table 17.3 Feedback from the order-taking requirements review workshop for the ICANDO Chemicals system

Comment	Importance
There needs to be a way of taking standing orders for customers in some markets, that have a duration of up to a year. The standing order may be adjusted during the year.	Essential
For electronic ordering, customers would like to be able to view the details of their current orders and make changes to them if they have not been despatched without making a call to the call centre.	Desirable
Some customers make repeated amendments to orders, which cause a great deal of disruption. It would help to be able to flag those customers so that sales can use this in the negotiations on prices and contracts.	Useful
Some customers buy fuel from ICANDO, and would like to merge their fuel and chemicals contracts and make orders through the same call centre. Very few customers do want this, and it is considered uneconomic.	Reject

presentation, the workshop is split into two groups who are given the detailed business analysis to review. These groups are facilitated by an analyst who keeps the discussions working, and a second analyst takes a record.

The first group make a number of recommendations, a sample of which is shown in Table 17.3. The recommendations are categorized as essential, desirable, useful or rejected; these categorizations are decided by the workshop. The essential ones must be considered before the requirements move on to the detailed analysis and design stages.

The two groups come back together, consolidate their comments and review the importance. They then move on to the use case models. This begins with a description of what use cases are, and how they fit into the business processes. Then a list of use cases, mapped to business processes, is presented, with the use case diagrams given as an overview. Again, the detailed documents are reviewed by two groups. Comments are gathered, and a sample set of comments is given, a sample of which is in Table 17.4.

Table 17.4 Comments on the review of the use cases for the ICANDO Chemicals system

Comment	Importance
The sales people need to be able to create an order, by calling the centre, for a new client before the contract is fully established. Thus there needs to be a special type of ordering for new customers.	Essential
It is common for customers to ask for a repeat order that is the same as the last one. To save re-keying, it would be useful to be able to have a repeat order use case.	Desirable
Sales staff would like to be able to review the order status of customers and a list of recent orders before making a visit to a customer.	Useful
Customers would like to email sales staff from the Internet ordering facility. However, there are problems with security on this.	Reject

Table 17.5 Comments on the details of the use cases for the ICANDO Chemicals system

Comment	Importance
In the telephone order use case, the system must immediately flag when an order has exceeded the customer's available credit.	Essential
Customers would like to see their available credit on the Internet ordering use case.	Desirable
In the call centre, on the customer validation use case, immediately after validation, the call centre representative should have an immediate view of the last three calls made by that customer, showing the date, time and what type of call (e.g. order, complaint).	Useful

The review then moves on to the details of the use cases. This is a lengthy process, as there are a number of use cases to consider. They are broken up into sections and reviewed in groups, as before. The type of comments gathered are indicated in Table 17.5.

The results of the workshop will involve some revisions to the requirements analysis. Essential items must be addressed, and desirable and useful items will be considered according to the time and resources available.

17.10.2 TESTING ANALYSIS AND DESIGN

Systems analysis and design will be checked using workshops in a similar manner to the requirements documents. However, the stakeholders will be different. The requirements team will be the primary stakeholders in the review of systems analysis, and the requirements team and analysis team will be the primary stakeholders in the review of the design. As with the review of requirements, it is important to collect comments and prioritize them in terms of importance.

17.10.3 UNIT TESTING OF CODE

The unit of testing is chosen as use cases. Each use case is led by a developer, though the implementation will inevitably involve a number of developers. The developer is required to produce a test plan that exercises the use case along all the paths through it. Sample data is devised and related to the use case.

Going back to the use case definition for use case 34, enter order details, a typical test plan for the unit testing of the use case would be as in Figure 17.2. You can see that a great deal of care and attention goes into testing, especially in a business critical application like this. A further test plan for one of the alternatives is given in Figure 17.3.

17.10.4 SYSTEM TESTING

System testing is set up once an integrated release of the system is ready. It involves taking the test plans for the individual use cases and populating them with fresh data. Where there are dependencies between use cases, such as order-taking and despatch, then data can be traced through the use cases.

System testing is done by a special team, set up independently of the developers. It includes expertise in database administration, as a fair amount of the set

Use case number: 34	Use case name: Enter order details

Test number: 1

Objective: Tests the primary path.

Set up: Customer details for customer number 12345 and product codes 55, 66 and 77 must be set up with product names Alpha, Beta and Gamma respectively. Check product code and assign delivery date use cases must be available and unit tested.

Expected results:
1. The order is recorded in the orders database tables.
2. The delivery date assigned that corresponds to the one entered. Check the deliveries table and the order table.
3. A log entry is made on the customer contact details database table, indicating the order number.

Test:
1. Enter orders for product codes 55, 66 and 77 by typing in the product codes in the product code boxes. Use quantities 2 tonnes, 1.3 tonnes and 800 kg respectively. Make sure that the product name comes up as Alpha, Beta and Gamma respectively.
2. Enter a delivery date that is 7 days from the current date.
3. Hit the confirm button; the system should respond saying that the order has been accepted.

Test record:

Date: 21 Aug 2001	Tester: Ken Lunn

Result: The log entry in the contact table did not have the order number.

Date: 22 Aug 2001	Tester: Ken Lunn

Result: Passed.

Figure 17.2 Unit test plan for the primary path of the order entry use case

up and checking will involve examining the changes to the data. The system test team establishes a test data set that supports the use cases to be tested. That data set is restored to the beginning at the start of each system test.

The integrated release to be tested contains a set of use cases that have been unit tested, and the release is authorized by the development team manager on the understanding that the unit tests are complete and acceptable.

System testers are given a set period in which to test the release. They work methodically through the test plans, checking the results and changes to the database. Each time a defect is found they enter the defect in a database and make an estimate of the seriousness of the defect.

The result of the test will be a list of defects, such as Figure 17.4, and a recommendation on whether to progress to user acceptance testing. Normally progress to the next stage is dependent on no serious defects, though there may be arguments for moving on to user acceptance testing of the system to gain some insight into operational acceptability.

Use case number: 34	**Use case name:** Enter order details
Test number: 2	

Objective: Tests the alternative path, where the product code is unknown and has to be looked up in the products database.
Set up: Customer details for customer number 12345, and product codes 55, 66 and 77 must be set up with product names Alpha, Beta and Gamma. Check product code and assign delivery date use cases must be available and unit tested.
Expected results: 1. The order is recorded in the orders database tables. 2. The delivery date assigned that corresponds to the one entered. Check the deliveries table and the order table. 3. A log entry is made on the customer contact details database table, indicating the order number.
Test: 1. Enter 'Alpha' in the product name box. Click on the 'product lookup' button. The product code 55 should appear. 2. Repeat for products 'Beta' and 'Gamma' respectively. 3. Enter a delivery date that is 7 days from the current date. 4. Hit the confirm button; the system should respond saying that the order has been accepted.
Test record: All parts ran successfully.

Date: 21 Aug 2001	**Tester:** Ken Lunn
Result: The product code was not retrieved, and a blank was displayed.	
Date: 22 Aug 2001	**Tester:** Ken Lunn
Result: Passed.	

Figure 17.3   Unit test plan for one of the alternative paths of the order entry use case.

ICANDO System Test – Phase 1, Test 1	
Defect severity	Count
Severe	3
Moderate	42
Low	112
Total	159
Recommendation: The three severe defects need rectification, and the overall defect rate must be reduced to fewer than 100 before progress to user acceptance testing.	

Figure 17.4   Summary report of the first system test for the first phase of the ICANDO Chemicals system

If the release is not allowed to progress, an estimate of the time to repair the defects is needed, and a re-test scheduled. If the release is allowed to progress, then the defects will be addressed in a future release, and the tests reapplied to the next release.

17.10.5 NON-FUNCTIONAL TESTING

Scalability

The system has a requirement for high performance with a substantial number of concurrent users, both in the call centre and with customers doing Web ordering. A test harness is devised that can run on a PC and simulate a user doing a typical set of transactions. These transactions are picked out randomly in proportion to typical use. Because much of a user's time is thinking or talk time, a PC can simulate up to 50 users.

The test harness is run up on a number of PCs, initially at one location, and then with the simulated users from a number of locations. The PCs log response times, and these are collated. A table is drawn up of response times as in Table 17.6. From this it can be read that performance decays between 100 and 200 simulated users to a level that would be considered unacceptable.

Performance can be improved by a variety of means. The server can be changed to a higher performance one. Sometimes the database can be optimized to include better indexes. In a distributed system, network bottlenecks can be a problem. Occasionally there will be some poor coding of a use case that needs to be rectified.

From the above, it might be concluded that the system could be released into beta testing, but that performance would need to be improved significantly for full release.

Security

Given that the system is mission-critical, and that some aspects will be available over the Internet, there is great concern about the security of the system. ICANDO contracts a company specializing in security auditing of systems to make sure that

Table 17.6 Sample scalability tests for the ICANDO Chemicals system

Use case	Simulated users	Minimum response (seconds)	Maximum response (seconds)	Average response (seconds)
Validate customer	20	0.25	3.2	0.7
Validate customer	100	0.25	6.2	0.9
Validate customer	200	0.4	9.5	2.3
Validate customer	1000	1.2	44	8.7
Enter order	20	0.25	2.5	0.4
Enter order	100	0.25	5.7	0.8
Enter order	200	0.45	10.3	1.9
Enter order	1000	1.4	52	9.1

there are no loopholes. This company audits the procedures that are proposed for the system, and they are given opportunities to test the system for breaches.

Reliability and recovery
To ensure that recovery options are working, each system test concludes with a reset of the database to the start, and then applying the journal of changes throughout the system test. The resulting database is then compared with the one that was produced at the end of the system test.

17.10.6 USER ACCEPTANCE TESTING

Once a release is ready for deployment and has passed system tests adequately, a user acceptance test is initiated. This is done by a separate testing team that incorporates representatives from the user community or individuals who have worked in the user community. This team will devise their own test plans, based on the workflows from the business process analysis and from the use case descriptions. They will devise their own test data set.

The approach is similar to system testing, but it focuses on end-to-end execution of business processes. Considerations of usability will be incorporated. Again, a list of defects, categorized by severity, will be produced, as in Figure 17.5. If the system testing has been comprehensive, the number of severe defects should be zero, but there is often in the early stages of system development some severe defect that is detected at this stage.

If there are no severe defects, a judgement can be made about whether to release the system. If the number of moderate defects is high and the urgency of the release is low, then it might be considered wise to repair the defects and retest before release.

Occasionally it is necessary to release a product with severe defects. In this case, the elements with severe defects need to be disabled, or some action taken to make sure that the user community are able to work around the defects.

17.10.7 BETA TESTING

The system is deployed in one country initially. This is selected as the one that will have least impact if there is a failure. Users are given special training, and the staff

Figure 17.5 Summary of the User Acceptance Test report for the first release of the ICANDO chemicals system.

ICANDO User Acceptance Test – Release 1, Test 1	
Defect severity	Count
Severe	1
Moderate	22
Low	34
Total	47
Recommendation: The severe defect relates to the scheduling of deliveries. This can be handled by a work-around in the call centre. The defect rate is high, but acceptable for release into beta testing.	

level is increased through overtime to cope with the familiarization process. The old order-taking system is kept live and available in case the new system has to be switched off.

In the first week, the system is down for two periods of an hour, in which calls are recorded on paper and customers called back when the system resumes. The down times are traced to simple faults in the database configuration.

Over the first month, there are ten down times, one of half a day. Each one is diagnosed. A number of defects are identified, one of them severe. However, the overall beta test is considered satisfactory. It is decided that the system will continue to operate in the call centre, and that a release will be produced that addresses some of the defects identified prior to a careful rollout throughout the company.

17.11 ICANDO Site Safety

The system is primarily a technical feasibility investigation. It is also a standalone system, and though the operation of it is complex, the deployment and multi user aspects are simple. Thus the testing requirements are more limited.

Unit and system testing are carried out by the developers. Two developers are working on this, and they test each other's work. They produce a simple checklist as indicated in Figure 17.6 to ensure that before they release a system they have checked the operation. This checklist is based on the use case definitions.

Acceptance testing is undertaken by a consultant in central services, who produces a list of defects back to the developers. The acceptance test is carried out by running a sample construction and audit based on a real example. Beta testing is undertaken by a site engineer who similarly produces a list of defects. Finally, once the system is considered functionally usable, it is issued to a wider number of consultants and site engineers for evaluation.

```
Add facility
– LPG sphere
– LPG cylinder store
– Office
– Perimeter
– Road
Set facility details
– LPG sphere
– LPG cylinder store
– Office
– Perimeter
– Road
– etc. –
```

Figure 17.6   Checklist for system testing the ICANDO Site Safety system

17.12 ICANDO Retail Petrol Promotions

The complexity and criticality of the retail petrol promotions system is considerably less than for the chemicals system. Therefore less rigour can be accepted. However, it is not deemed acceptable to put a system into the market place that has substantial defects.

The software house contracted to undertake the development work has its own in-house system test team. They test each release of the product internally. The IT manager at ICANDO sets up an acceptance testing team consisting of people who work in the call centre. To facilitate this she calls in a freelance IT consultant who works with the software house and the ICANDO staff to devise test plans. The test plans follow the same pattern for testing use cases and business processes as used in the ICANDO Chemicals system.

To ensure that the system is working to expectations, the IT manager arranges for each internal release of the system to be put through user acceptance testing. This increases her confidence that the system is being developed on schedule and to the quality required.

Beta testing is done by selecting a small number of customers to trial the system. They are given extra reward points to compensate them for their trouble. Towards the end of the beta test phase, a telephone review is undertaken of those customers who have used the system.

REVIEW QUESTIONS

1. **How might you go about testing requirements?**
2. **How might you go about testing systems analysis?**
3. **What is unit testing, and who normally does it?**
4. **How might a unit test for a use case be structured?**
5. **What is a system test and who normally does it?**
6. **How might a system test be devised?**
7. **How are test results recorded?**
8. **Must a system be fault-free before it is considered to have passed the test?**
9. **What is a user acceptance test, and who normally does it?**
10. **How are user acceptance tests devised?**
11. **What is a beta test?**
12. **How might you address non-functional requirements?**

EXERCISES

1. Using the use case and business process definitions you developed for the ICANDO trading system, produce a system and user acceptance test plan.
2. Using the use case and business process definitions you developed for the ICANDO/NeverShut retail system, produce a system and user acceptance test plan.

Deployment, Support and Enhancement

The development team has produced the product and the testing team has provided approval; now it is time to release the product on the unwitting users. There is still much to be done. A fair proportion of this will be carried out in parallel with the earlier stages. The product is not just an item of software. It comes with documentation, training and, in many cases, revision of business practices. There will have to be regular backups and a support organization to handle the product while it is live.

At this point, the weary adventurer will be greeted with plaudits or with jeers. Either the process that has led up to this point has produced something that will be loved and cherished, or there will be nothing but moans and complaints. All fresh deployments have teething troubles, but the pain that has to be endured and the success of the delivery depends on the quality of the software development process and the individuals that produced it.

As with implementation, technical deployment is as diverse as the technologies that might be used. There is little we can discuss here in specific terms, though there are some aspects of deployment strategies that can be considered. Needless to say there is a lot of physical work involved in deployment, including installing computers and networks, installation of operating systems and other support software, and the installation of the application itself.

Deployment of the software is, however, only one small part of the deployment process. In fact, most of the cost and effort of deployment can go into related tasks, such as training, production of documentation and the setting up of a support facility. For new software there may well be a complete reorganization of business alongside the software installation.

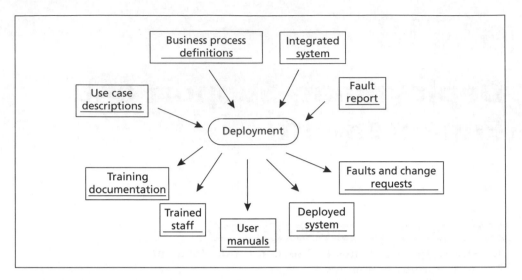

Figure 18.1   Principal inputs and outputs of the deployment stage

In this chapter, a flavour of the aspects of deployment is given. We will look at aspects of documentation, training, migration of data, deployment strategies, risk management, support and enhancement. These are all non-trivial aspects of any project, and can be critical to the success of the project. Figure 18.1 shows the primary inputs and outputs of the deployment stage. The early requirements capture, in terms of business processes and use case descriptions, form the basis for training and user manuals. The integrated system is deployed. Once deployed, faults and change requests will come back through the help desk.

18.1 Documentation

A number of stakeholders require documentation for the support of a product, namely the operations team that keep the system going, the support team that deal with problems, the development teams that will enhance the system in the future, and last but not least the users of the application. For a product that is to be sold, there will also need to be marketing documentation.

Operations documentation needs to explain where to find software for deployment, how to deploy the software, how to start and stop the software, what backups of the data need to be taken, how to restore data, and what precautions and recovery operations are needed to cope with disasters such as a fire. This documentation need not be excessive, but it will take time to produce. Usually the development team will do this, as they have closest knowledge of the application structure. Operations on the whole need not know much about the functionality of the software: just how to get it up and running, and to keep it that way.

Support documentation needs to explain to the support team the actions needed if a user presents a problem. Simple problems can usually be handled by the support team directly, but anything that involves problems with the software will usually require assistance from other parties, usually the developers. Support documentation is usually lightweight, and just needs to identify sources of assistance and provide emergency routines if there are problems that need to be handled urgently.

Development teams need to keep the outputs of analysis and design so that future enhancements to a system can be made. In an incremental delivery, the application will continue to be developed as parts of it are deployed. Keeping good records and maintaining them in a current form is a non-trivial task, and large teams often allocate someone to take prime responsibility for this. It can take up a substantial amount of time to maintain good analysis and design documentation.

User documentation is a description of how the application is to be used. You will be familiar with this type of documentation from software that you have bought for your PC. Following the development process described in this book, the basis for user documentation has been provided in the form of use case descriptions. Screenshots from the application can be used to supplement this. For a substantial application, it is common to utilize technical writers who can take the analysis and design documentation and construct a more accessible description of the system for the users. Developers are notoriously bad at producing this type of documentation, as they tend to have a focus on how it works rather than how it is used.

18.2 Training

Before deploying a system, various stakeholders need training. Training of the operations and support teams is usually done informally through a brief workshop. Training of users, however, can take up a considerable amount of time. They are the ones that need to know all about how to use the system.

Training material can be developed from the user manual or from the use case descriptions. For anything other than a simple system or a system with few users, a trainer is used rather than a member of the development team. The process of training will begin with briefing the trainer. Trainers provide a nice bridge between the technology experts and the end users.

Training will require a version of the system set up for training purposes. It is not sensible to train on the live system, as there may be inadvertent damage to the data. The system will need to be set up with dummy data, and usually there will need to be some process of restoring the system to a common starting point.

For very large applications, such as in call centres, a separate training facility is usually set up. There is usually enough turnover in the workforce for there to be regular training needed for new staff. Users need to be given plenty of time to explore and use a system in a training environment before they use it operationally.

Training is costly. There is the cost of the trainer and the training facility, but most of the expenditure is in terms of the time spent by users in learning the new system. To get some idea of the cost, suppose a call centre with 1000 staff takes on a new system that requires two days training, and that each member of staff costs €100 a day to employ; the total cost of training in terms of lost time and training facilities is likely to be of the order of €250,000!

The cost of not training can be higher than the cost of training. Though there is not the obvious impact of people being taken off productive work, a 20% reduction in productivity caused by introducing a new system without training could, over a month, cost twice as much as training the staff in the first place.

The logistics of training are problematic. Training needs to be as near to the initial use of a system as possible. If large numbers of people need to be trained, then it will need careful scheduling, and inevitably some people may have to be trained well before they can actually use the system live. Much depends on the deployment strategies.

18.3 Data Migration

Replacement applications will usually need to acquire the data from the applications that they replace. For example, a new customer service system would need the customer records from the previous customer service system. This will usually involve some form of conversion of the data.

If the applications both use databases of similar types, the conversion may not be too difficult. However, it would be surprising if the new application did not record some information that the old system did not, and it is highly likely that the structure of the data is different. Encoding of some of the data may differ too.

There will be a need to write special routines to transfer data. Knowledge of the data content for both applications is necessary, and it is usually the database administration team that undertakes this task. The transfer needs to be tested in just the same way that the application is tested, and there will need to be trial runs before the actual transfer of live information into the new system.

18.4 Beta Releases

For products sold in a market place or widely distributed in a large and dispersed organization, a process called beta testing is commonly used. This acknowledges the fact that live use of an application inevitably uncovers problems. After acceptance testing has given the go-ahead, the application is deployed to a limited set of users who use it for real work, accepting a higher risk of failure.

Beta testing will be supported as a live release, with suitable support. Defects will be identified and rectified ready for the full release of the application. In return, beta testing groups will usually be rewarded in some way, perhaps in terms of reduced licensing costs or closer involvement in package specification.

18.5 Deployment Strategies

There are really only two deployment strategies. Either the system is deployed to all the users in one go (known as 'big bang'), or there is an incremental rollout. Wherever possible, incremental rollout should be used. This minimizes risk and allows for rollback if the deployment is unsuccessful or the application has serious problems.

Big bang, however, is sometimes the only possible solution. This is the case when an old system is being replaced, and the new and old systems cannot coexist. Big bang can involve a massive transfer of data to facilitate the change over. If you are contemplating a big bang installation of a substantial system, then all of the quality assurance procedures, such as testing, need to be as rigorous and thorough as possible.

A failed big bang installation can have dramatic consequences. A famous example of a failed installation was for the London Ambulance Service Computer-Aided Despatch System in 1992. The system was designed to facilitate the speedy allocation of ambulances to emergency calls. For a variety of reasons the system rapidly ran into problems and had to be switched off, but only after ambulances had been despatched wrongly and emergency calls not responded to, with obvious dire consequences. Another example of big bang installation was the switch of the London Stock Exchange in 1986 to screen-driven trading, and although this had problems it did succeed.

Incremental installation makes more sense wherever possible. This allows for a small number of users to adopt a system initially, and for that number to grow over time. This way, any problems with the application can be ironed out before it has a massive impact on the operation of the business. It also allows for training of the users in line with the installation.

18.6 Risk Management

Deployment is the riskiest point in any system development. Even a minor fault in the application or the deployment process can cause the system to fail, with dramatic consequences. Thus care needs to be taken that a failure causes the minimal amount of damage. No matter how carefully the application has been tested, the deployment will uncover cracks. If the ship is soundly constructed, a few minor leaks can be tolerated and repaired while still afloat, but if a gaping hole appears then the ship needs to be quickly returned to dry dock before it sinks.

The most important thing to consider is what to do if the deployment fails, or the application fails shortly after deployment. The usual answer is to resort to the previous system. Ideally the old system should be on hot standby, waiting to be called up.

A deployment failure needs diagnosis, repair and then (hopefully) redeployment. Too many failed deployments, however, will ultimately destroy confidence and may result in the cancellation of the application.

18.7 Support and Enhancement

The application is live and the users are happy; now comes the long process of keeping them happy. This is the point at which software developers, and most books on software development, like to leave off. In fact, the vast majority of development work is not on new systems but on continual minor adjustments to existing systems. Applications can last twenty years or more, though in that time they may go through many transformations. At the very least they will be migrated from one hardware and operating system platform to another. Additionally they will go through endless changes, in response to the changing and growing needs of their users. Ninety per cent or more of the development effort may go into the so-called maintenance phase.

I prefer to use the term enhancement, as maintenance has some implication of 'wearing out', as with the maintenance of a motor vehicle. Software does not wear out, but the needs that it is intended to meet do change, and the expectations of the stakeholders change.

Change comes about in many ways. Minor changes come from day-to-day operational problems. A user may ask for a small amount of additional information to be displayed on a screen, or for the layout of a screen to be changed to improve a task. Major changes come about when there are changes in the business, such as adding a new product line that the sales system cannot support.

An organization needs to capture these changes, consolidate them, select the worthwhile changes, prioritize them and implement them. Briefly we will look at the way organizations do this.

18.7.1 SUPPORT

The first point of call for changes is usually the support or help desk. The sort of changes initiated there are basically of two types. Either the system is not doing something properly or well, or there are repeated requests from users asking how to do something that the system does not do.

Typically, a user will ring the help desk and the operator will take details of the problem or issue. The next stage is to prioritize the problem. Three levels of priority are usually assigned. Critical issues will involve the help desk in seeking immediate action. Urgent issues will require examination quickly. Normal issues can be considered in the due course of time.

User support will deal with an issue by firstly checking that a simple problem has not arisen, such as the computer not being powered on or having been unplugged from the network. They will also usually deal with routine matters, such as forgotten passwords. If the problem cannot be solved quickly and easily, they will then determine who best to call to rectify the problem. They will usually have a list of contacts that they will call to seek a resolution to the problem.

Once someone has been identified to check out the problem, the support operator will record the details of the issue and who is acting on it. They will then monitor at regular intervals the progress towards resolving the problem. When a problem is resolved, they will then advise the person who raised the problem and close the issue.

Support logs need to be reviewed regularly for possible enhancements to a system. Frequently recurring problems need action, as they are likely to be causing operational problems for the business and they waste support time and energy.

18.7.2 CHANGE CONTROL

A live application will result in requests for change from many sources. Users and their supervisors will request minor changes to make their day-to-day tasks simpler. Business managers will usually request more substantial changes in anticipation of major changes in the way a business operates. Senior management may be the ones to propose very radical changes in the light of changes in business strategy.

Change proposals need to be recorded and reviewed. The common method is to have a change request form (paper or electronic), that specifies the change, the reasons for change, and the benefits that the change will provide. Change proposals will come from a number of sources within the business.

The change proposals need to be reviewed regularly. Firstly the development team need to group them, looking for related changes. They then need to provide provisional estimates of the cost of making the changes. Once the changes have been checked for viability and costed, a review panel will consider all the changes.

The review panel will consist of various stakeholders in the system, including business managers from areas where the system is used. Inevitably the number of changes will exceed the ability of available resources. The panel must prioritize the changes and choose those that need to be implemented. The review panel will take into consideration all the issues we covered in project inception, focusing on cost and benefits.

Implementation of changes basically means either revising existing use cases or adding new ones. The processes that we have discussed for development of use cases are entirely appropriate for managing the changes. Revised or new use case specifications need to be produced. Any necessary systems analysis for substantial changes is carried out. Design or redesign is undertaken. Then follows construction, testing and deployment. Changes to documentation and necessary training will be incorporated in the deployment.

18.8 Conclusion

Getting the completed system onto users' desks, making sure they are happy, and keeping them that way, is the most important step. It can be quite messy for a new system, as lots of people will be doing things for the first time. It requires careful planning from the project manager and other managers involved in the deployment.

As with implementation, this is very dependent on organization. Therefore the case studies and exercises have been omitted. You may like to consider the issues around the deployment of the trading and retail outlet systems.

REVIEW QUESTIONS

1. **What is the source material for training and user manuals?**
2. **What problems do replacement systems introduce?**
3. **Why are big bang deployments risky?**
4. **How are support and enhancement organized?**
5. **Once a system is deployed, how are changes to the system organized?**

CONCLUSION

Reader's Guide

The main content of the book is complete. This section picks up on a few related items, such as contemporary methods. There are brief answers to review questions abd a UML notation summary. Finally, there is a complete worked example.

Chapter 19: Journey's End

This is the concluding chapter, which covers a few issues not introduced in the main body of the text, such as CASE tools and the Object Constraint Language, which the reader may wish to investigate further.

Chapter 20: Answers to Review Questions

Suggested answers to the review questions supplied at the end of each chapter.

Chapter 21: UML Notation Summary

A summary of the UML notation used throughout this text.

Chapter 22: Worked Example – The Odd Shoe Company

This is a complete worked example using the methods and notations introduced in this book.

CHAPTER **19**

Journey's End

Before we ride off into the sunset, smug in having traversed a difficult terrain, and filled with tales to raise the hairs on our listeners' heads, there are a few discursions that we really did not explore in any depth. I began by saying that this book describes just one route through the jungle. There will be many that will tell you that there are better ways, and the way I have just described is fraught with danger. Well, before we conclude, there are a few things that ought to be mentioned.

The first thing to consider are CASE tools, which help with the development of models at each stage in the development process. These have been developing rapidly over the years, spurred on lately by the development of the UML. Many projects now could not progress without them. However, when you go out and buy your first CASE tool, remember that it is the shovel sellers and whiskey vendors that make the killing in any gold rush, and the majority of miners go home broke.

Software development is a document-intensive activity, from the word processing that goes on in the early stages, through to the source code that makes up the system. Communication is often by documents, sometimes on paper, but most often in electronic form. Managing this flow is a non-trivial activity, and there are document management tools available.

Then there is the methodology war that goes on. Every explorer has a favourite path through the jungle which they claim is the best. There are, however, many types of jungle and many ways through them. Before we close, we ought to discuss some of the major paths around, and we will have a closer look at the Unified Software Development Process, Extreme Programming and Rapid Application Development, which are typical of quite different approaches to software development.

Finally, for those who wish a more formal approach to development, with clearer specification, UML offers the Object Constraint Language. This allows for the precise specification of behaviours and constraints using a mathematical language.

These subjects need more consideration than can be given here. This is nothing more than your initial guide to subjects, such as design, architecture and UML, that deserve whole treatises to themselves. From here your true exploration begins. You've had the Cook's package tour; now you should venture out on your own a little.

19.1 CASE Tools

Computer-Assisted Software Engineering (CASE) is the use of computer systems to aid in the development of computer systems. CASE tools allow you to develop and manage models and code. The dream has been, for a long time, a set of CASE tools to assist in each phase of the development of a system, with integration between the tools so that there is minimal translation in moving between phases.

Figure 19.1 shows a screenshot of the ArgoUML CASE tool.[1] It is a tool for the creation and management of UML models. It is an open source tool that can be downloaded and used for free. The details of the tool are beyond this book. The interface is typical of such tools. In the top left quadrant is a repository that shows the organization of the models, and the items in the models. In the top right

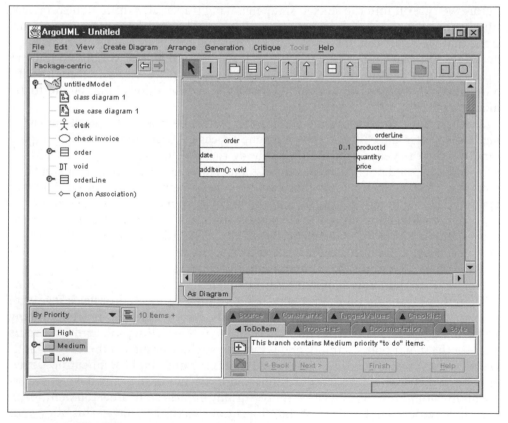

Figure 19.1 A typical UML CASE tool

1 http://argouml.tigris.org/

quadrant is a drawing of a model. Below these are various screens to manipulate the models.

The reality today is that there is a good range of tools available for supporting the individual stages. In particular, there are many tools available now to support the development of UML models, and they often provide integration of features to support development in some programming languages.

It is fair to argue that without CASE tool support, modelling languages such as UML would not be feasible for many applications. Producing models is a time-consuming task. Sharing models and making sure that they are consistent is even more difficult.

19.1.1 EXCHANGE BETWEEN TOOLS

The real barrier to seamless end-to-end CASE tool support is the transfer of information between tools. UML has one feature that is aimed at smoothing this path. XMI (XML Metadata Interchange) is a textual language for describing UML models. CASE tools that support UML should be able to produce XMI versions of the models they produce and import XMI versions.

XMI is a key enabler for supporting integration of tools that support different parts of the software development process. It is, however, only a partial solution, as UML modelling is only part of the software development process.

Individual UML modelling tools have means of integrating with various development languages. This integration is on the whole *ad hoc*, and depends very much on the tool. The best level of integration has the UML modelling tool focused on a particular delivery environment, such as Java. With tight integration like this, it is possible to merge coding and model development.

Looser forms of integration involve embedding documents in models. Some case tools allow the linking of word processor documents with UML models, say to provide a textual description of use cases.

Complete integration is really only possible in a very confined environment with a rigorously defined method. The less well defined the process and tools, the harder it is to integrate. The continual change of languages and approaches has worked counter to full integration, though the convergence of methods and tools as represented by UML and USDP offers some hope on this front.

19.1.2 CODE GENERATION AND ROUND-TRIP ENGINEERING

One of the favourite buzz-phrases in the CASE vendor market is 'round-trip' engineering. This means being able to generate program code from UML models, modify the code and then reimport the code to cause changes to the UML models. This allows models and code to be kept in step. The generation of classes from UML CASE tools is common. The reimporting of classes is less common.

From a project perspective, one of the greatest hurdles to be overcome in managing a model-centric development approach is keeping the analysis, design and implementation models in step. Once they become out of step, the value of the analysis and design models diminishes, and ultimately they fall into disuse. However, without the analysis and design models the application can become much more difficult to maintain.

At present, the only means of enforcing this through technology is through a single development platform that incorporates all aspects of the analysis and design process. For many practical purposes, however, this is impossible. To maintain consistency between models requires management, and appropriate resource to support that.

19.2 Document Management

A software development project produces vast quantities of documents, from minutes of meetings, through requirements reports, to the actual code files for implementation and user/training manuals for operation. Managing these documents is a major undertaking. There are many requirements for the management of documents.

Documents often go through several versions. One version of (say) a design document will relate to one version of an analysis document. There needs to be clear linkage between documents. Therefore some convention is needed for labelling and cross-referencing documents.

Documents go through repeated changes. Sometimes it is important to be able to revert to an earlier document. For example, a developer may be working on a source code file and find that he has made several mistakes and needs to start again.

Software releases are a set of documents that represent a snapshot of the development process. These need to be packaged up and stored. This is particularly important for software vendors, who will frequently have a number of versions of their product in operation with various customers.

A variety of tools exist to aid teams in the management of documents. These allow for the protection of documents from inadvertent or incorrect update, and for the keeping of versions. To use a document, a developer needs to check the document out, update it and replace it according to carefully defined rules. Some of the tools focus on source code, and are known as source code control systems.

19.3 Methodology

Methodology is one of the most abused terms in IT. It is commonly used in place of the word 'method'. A method is a way of doing things, and methodology is the study of ways of doing things. Many people talk about methodology when they mean method.

Methods are extremely important. They are prescriptive routes through the jungle. Follow a method that someone else has defined successfully, and you are less likely to be eaten by a tiger or to get lost in the undergrowth. A method tells you what to do next, and gives you a limited framework for choices. There may be many alternatives within a method, depending on circumstances, but methods are by their nature constraining.

Methodology, on the other hand, is the study of methods. Out of methodology comes new methods. Experienced explorers can share notes, and if they are clever they can build a deeper understanding of the jungle and the paths through it. An experienced methodologist will choose the right method for the task, just as an experienced explorer will choose the right route through a jungle to a particular destination and the right things to put in the kit bag.

There are many phoney wars in the IT world over methods. These show a lack of understanding of methodology. Quite simply, there is no perfect method. Even if you were to drive tarmac roads through a jungle, there would be new jungles to explore with different landscapes and vegetation, and different bits of the jungle that the road never ventured near. Anyone who tells you that 'this is the way to develop software', is expressing his latest love affair rather than capturing beauty in a single phrase. I have had many love affairs with different technologies and methods, and it is only with developing experience I can see beyond those to a bigger picture.

Methods are where much of the research in IT development goes. Methodology is lacking at times, particularly in the understanding of how to match method with organization and task. Even the Unified Process, which defines a framework from which software development processes can be assembled, is more method than methodology.

It is not the aim of this book to elaborate on methodology. I have introduced a method, not a methodology. Below we will consider in very general details some of the established methods. They are not as different in reality as some of their advocates would have you believe.

There are probably three key methods approaches that have emerged in recent years. They have their history in earlier methods. At one end of the spectrum is the Unified Software Development Process, which views software development as a highly staged process, with a considerable amount of construction of intermediate models mostly expressed in UML. At the other end of the spectrum is Extreme Programming, which minimizes the use of intermediate models. In the middle is Rapid Application Development. We shall now look at all three.

19.3.1 THE UNIFIED SOFTWARE DEVELOPMENT PROCESS

The Unified Software Development Process (USDP) (Jacobson *et al.*, 1999) emerged as the unification of a number of methods dating back in some cases over thirty years. It is the product of Jacobson, Booch and Rumbaugh, who were the major instigators of the development of UML. They recognize that UML is not sufficient for the production of good software. A sensible process organization is required.

The USDP is a framework of development workers, development activities, products and workflows. No project is likely to follow the USDP to the letter. Rather, the aim is to select out the parts of the process that are relevant to the current project and organization.

The USDP is 'use case driven'. Use cases are, as defined in this book, pieces of functionality that supply meaningful standalone value. The total use case model defines the functionality of the system. In USDP, use cases are identified by systems analysts, detailed by use case specifiers, prioritized by the architects, prototyped by user interface designers, structured by systems analysts, mapped onto the architecture by designers, and implemented by use case engineers and component engineers. As you can see, the process is fully elaborated with lots of different types of worker. In practice, the workers in the USDP are roles, and one person may take on many roles.

The USDP is 'architecture-centric'. Use cases have both function and form. Function comes from the use case model. Form is dictated by the architecture.

Architecture is the broad overall structure of the application, and the implementation of use cases must fit into that structure. Architecture and use case models must develop alongside each other.

The USDP is 'iterative and incremental'. The overall project is broken down into mini-projects, which need to be delivered internally even if they are not deployed. Iteration is used to control and minimize the risk of a project, and to keep it on track with frequent quality control checks.

The USDP breaks a project down into four phases, as indicated in Table 19.1. The project progresses from inception through elaboration and construction to transition, whereby the software product is delivered. There are five core workflows as illustrated in Table 19.2. These are made up of activities, some of which are illustrated in Table 19.3. The workflows are carried out by people who adopt the various worker roles, some of which are illustrated in Table 19.4. The activities in the workflows produce artefacts, as illustrated in Table 19.5.

Table 19.1   Phases of the Unified Software Development Process

Phase	Description
Inception	This phase determines what the system goals are, what it does in general terms for its major users, what its outline architecture is, and what the costs and time-scales are.
Elaboration	Elaboration covers the detailing of the use cases, the design of the system architecture and the fine planning of the construction.
Construction	Here the product is built. The architecture is filled in with working code.
Transition	The product is tested, the spadework is done for release and finally the product is released.

Table 19.2   Major workflows of the Unified Software Development Process

Core workflow	Description
Requirements	Captures the functionality of the system and obtains agreement of the functionality with the users. These are expressed in a use case model. This is the main workflow of the inception phase and one of the two main workflows of the elaboration phase.
Analysis	Analyses the requirements and structures them, providing a basis on which the architecture can be defined. It moves from a use case definition in terms of external functionality to an understanding of how the use cases operate expressed as use case realizations. This is the key workflow of the elaboration phase, along with requirements.
Design	Design decides the form of the application, and defines the architecture. Use cases are realized through collaborating objects. This workflow mainly straddles the elaboration and construction phases.
Implementation	This phase produces the end product, as components that can be deployed. It is the main workflow of the construction phase.
Test	This workflow verifies the outputs of the implementation in terms of the functional and non-functional requirements. It is a major workflow in the transition phase.

Table 19.3 Typical activities in the Unified Software Development Process

Activity	Description
Find actors and use cases	Identifies the actors and use cases, determines how they interact, and delimits the system from its environment. Part of the requirements workflow.
Prioritize use cases	Determines the order of use case development.
Detail a use case	Describes the flow of events in a use case in detail and how the use case interacts with actors.
Prototype user interface	Produces a prototype of the user interface.
Architectural analysis	Outlines the analysis model and architecture.
Analyse a use case	Determines analysis classes to support the use case behaviour and how they interact.
Analyse a class	Determines the main responsibilities and relationships of a class.
Design a use case	Identifies design classes for a use case, and distributes behaviour of the use case among subsystems.
Design a class	Identify design classes to support the analysis class functionality. Fully elaborate design classes ready for implementation.
Perform system test	Executes a system test on the application.
Evaluate test	Determines the actions to be taken following a test.

Table 19.4 Some of the worker roles in the Unified Software Development Process

Worker	Role
Systems analyst	Responsible for the definition of use case-specific requirements and for delimiting the boundary of the system.
Use case specifier	Provides detailed descriptions of use case behaviour.
User interface designer	Defines the visual and behavioural shape of the user interface.
Architect	Responsible for the integrity of the analysis and design models, and architecturally significant aspects of the system.
Use case engineer	Responsible for use case realizations, making sure that they deliver the functionality specified.
Component engineer	Responsible for the class structure and component structure of the application.
Test designer	Produces the test model and test cases.
System tester	Performs the system tests on the application.

    If you look carefully at the Unified Software Development Process, you will see that the steps are analogous to the ones in this book. Though process has been emphasized, we have worked through the process implicitly. The USDP tries to provide a comprehensive framework for organizations to select and adapt to their own needs.

Table 19.5 Typical artefacts in the Unified Software Development Process

Artefact	Description
Use case model	A set of use cases and actors that define the external behaviour of the system.
User interface prototype	A mock up of the user interface used as an analysis and design tool.
Analysis model	Collection of use case definitions and supporting classes that define the behaviour of the system.
Analysis architecture description	The architecturally significant use cases, with the supporting realizations and key analysis classes such as the entity classes that support the behaviour.
Use case realization (design)	The set of classes and interactions that provide the form and behaviour of a use case.
Integration build plan	The plan of incremental builds for a system.

It would be naive of any organization to adopt the USDP as a standard, without careful pruning and realigning it to the organization's needs. The USDP appears to be for the construction of new software, but as we have argued earlier, a good method can be applied to the major adaptation of many applications originally designed using other methods. You are encouraged to get a good understanding of this method framework as you progress as a software developer.

19.3.2 EXTREME PROGRAMMING

There is a large body of programmers who do not see the value of modelling notations like the UML, who think of documentation as a needless chore, and who see software development processes like the USDP as dinosaurs and brakes on progress. This has prompted the popularity of a method known as Extreme Programming (Beck, 1999), shortened to XP. This is the most prominent of a range of methods sometimes known as light methods because they aim at the minimum amount of formality, documentation and modelling.

The radicalism of the Extreme Programming community is somewhat false, as many organizations adopt light methods of a similar kind by default. Small software houses, for example, focus mainly on coding and do little by way of diagrammatic design. The pressure of time and lack of resources often minimize the amount of intermediate modelling and design that is undertaken.

XP is not, however, an undisciplined method. In fact, it is highly formalized, though it concentrates on certain phases of the fuller, heavyweight methods such as USDP, and omits some of their intermediate products.

XP begins with the collection of 'stories', in what is called the 'Planning Game'. A story is a description of the way a system will be used. In fact, stories are the same concept as use cases. They define the system functionality. Stories are collected in workshops with the potential users of the system, then grouped, refined and prioritized.

Once the stories are agreed, the developers who are implementing the stories are required to develop a test plan for each of the stories. These test plans are agreed with customers. These are analogous to the use case scenarios and primary/alternative path descriptions we considered earlier.

The developers then produce the code to implement the functionality that satisfies the test plans. This is where XP and the USDP differ. USDP produces a large number of intermediate models, such as class diagrams, sequence diagrams, and so on. XP just produces code.

The methods converge again when the code is produced. USDP will produce test plans based on the use case model. XP already has the test plans defined, essentially, as part of the requirements definition.

XP has an additional step after implementation, called refactoring. Code is developed to meet functionality in the first instance. This can compromise the architecture of the system, and is not always the most optimum code. Refactoring aims at improving the quality of the overall system, using various rules for restructuring the code. The restructuring maintains the functionality as defined in the test plans, and aims at improving the performance and maintainability of the application. This is equivalent to the architecture phase that USDP emphasizes, only the positioning of the step is different.

XP has a number of other conventions that are not so much methods as means of improving quality of the product. One of the conventions is that programmers work in pairs, one coding and the other observing. Another is a fixed working pattern, keeping hours to a fixed number, say 40 hours a week. These are mostly to do with project quality assurance and working practices.

XP formalizes common practice in a number of organizations. It is usually only large, well-established development organizations that adopt methods as comprehensive as the USDP. The majority of organizations sit somewhere in the middle, and a fair number are far less structured and organized than XP would dictate. As with USDP, the use of XP needs to be adapted to local needs.

19.3.3 RAD METHODS AND DSDM

Rapid Application Development is a term that encompasses a number of approaches. The core theme is one of frequent, incremental delivery of software, using tools that can quickly construct that software. In truth, they are agnostic on the need for intermediate models. RAD methods fit into the USDP and the XP models perfectly well.

RAD comes with a project management approach designed to minimize risk and maximize the likelihood of successful delivery. The most widely known approach is the Dynamic System Development Method (DSDM).[2] This was developed by a consortium that first met in 1994 with the intention of developing a public domain method for organizing RAD projects.

DSDM is a means of delivering variable functionality within fixed time and resources, rather than the more traditional view of aiming to deliver fixed functionality in a variable time and resource framework. This acknowledges a number of important features.

Firstly, fixing all three parameters, namely functionality, time and resource, is usually doomed to failure. Most projects that try to do this usually overrun,

---

2 http://www.dsdm.org/

consume too much resource, or fail to meet functionality. There are many reasons for this. Projects are notoriously difficult to estimate, and functional requirements are often incomplete, vague or changeable. Pressure is always on to budget for the minimum cost, and unforeseen problems almost always arise.

Secondly, in business environments the requirements for a system can change dramatically in the course of a project. These do not invalidate the project, but if the project cannot adjust then it will be less than optimum on delivery.

Thirdly, the delivery of a product is always some way short of expectations. The realization is often very different from the concept in people's minds. As soon as a product is delivered, people start suggesting better ways to do things.

DSDM has a feasibility study, a business study, a functional model iteration, a design and build iteration, and implementation. The feasibility study is a short phase to determine the suitability of the project and the DSDM method. The business study is another short phase that outlines the main functional and non-functional requirements of the system and determines a baseline architecture.

The functional iteration and design/build phases take the functional requirements through the stages of determining what to build, scheduling the construction, construction and testing. This is really a sequence of phases, each iteration adding to the functionality of the system.

Implementation transfers the tested product into the working environment. This can be done after each iteration of design and build, or after a number of iterations. The scheduling of implementations depends on a number of factors, such as the cost of deployment and the value of a particular stage of the development.

DSDM embodies a number of principles. Users are expected to be actively involved in the development, participating in all stages. Development teams are empowered to take decisions without frequent consultation with senior management. Products should be delivered frequently, through iterative delivery, and testing should be an integral part of the process. Collaboration and cooperation between all stakeholders is essential.

The basic tools of DSDM include the notions of time boxing and Moscow prioritization that we have discussed at length. It is non-prescriptive in terms of models, notations and architectures. It is much more a generic project management method than a pure software development method.

As you can see, much of the concepts of DSDM have been embodied in the USDP and XP. These methods are really a culmination of experiences in projects over a number of years, and it is not surprising that they overlap considerably. Most successful development organizations have adopted the fundamental philosophies of these approaches, though they may not have formally or explicitly adopted the methods.

19.4 Object Constraint Language

A branch of software engineering, known as 'formal methods', aims at a more rigorous specification of systems than we have been discussing in this book. These methods are based on mathematical notations, and are intended for development of systems where the failure of the system can be catastrophic. Examples would be in the control systems for nuclear power stations, or missile guidance systems.

Table 19.6 Typical OCL statements

OCL Statement	Explanation
context Account **inv:** balance >= 0	Objects that are instances of the class Account must always have balances that are greater than or equal to zero
context Account::debit(v:Integer): **pre:** balance >= v **post:** balance = (balance-v)	For the debit operation on an instance of account, that debits an amount 'v', the balance must be at least the value of v for the operation to fire legally, and after the operation the balance must have the value of v deducted.

Once a system has been specified in a formal manner, it is possible to check that the code developed meets the specification. This is like a mathematical proof. Using formal methods, provided the specification is accurate there is a much lower chance of the code having faults.

UML is not a mathematical specification language. However, it is possible to place constraints on a system. One of the means of specifying operation behaviour is through the definition of preconditions and postconditions. These can be expressed in English or a more formal language known as the object constraint language (OCL).

The OCL is an expression language, which means that it has statements that do not change things, but have true or false values. It is more rigorous than English statements, because it allows reference to properties of objects. A full exploration of OCL is beyond this book, but a flavour of the language is given with the expressions and their meanings in Table 19.6. A full description of the language is given in Warmer and Kleppe (1999) and a good summary is provided in Bennett *et al.* (2001).

You can see that OCL is more precise and more concise than English. It is considerably richer in expression than the above examples imply. However, it is at present little used. Greater integration of OCL with CASE tools will encourage its use, and if the CASE tools can generate code from OCL then there is a strong chance that it will gain in popularity.

The use of formal methods is not commonplace. Though it is taught on most computer science courses, it has only caught on in very limited areas of practical software development. In part, this is because it is difficult. Also, where the result of faults is not tragic, it is more cost-effective to iron them out through testing.

19.5 Conclusion

By now you should have some sense of the magnitude of the task of software development. If you are embarking on a career in IT, it will either frighten you or excite you. I have tried to give you some sense of the full sweep of development, from the first seeds of an idea through to the many aspects of implementation and deployment. Along the way you have met notations and methods, and hopefully you have some sense of the stages that any software development must go through.

Every development environment is different in terms of organization, technology and the mix of people that come together to construct software systems. I do not want to preach any particular approach. At times I would lean towards the XP camp, and at others towards the USDP camp. More and more, I see them as differences in emphasis rather than competing methods.

As you progress, you will build your own understanding. The IT industry has one of the most remarkable records of change and rapid evolution in the history of human development. In fifty years we have come from crude laboratory systems that were little more than elaborate calculators to the immense and powerful networks that have seeped into our everyday lives and even into our homes. The next fifty years promise to be just as changeable and dynamic.

The thing that should guide you is enthusiasm, and a sense that underneath all the fads and fashions of software development, and among all the changes in tools and methods, there is an underlying process that software development must follow, just as a butterfly must work through its stages from egg to caterpillar to chrysalis before launching into the summer sun, be it a Cabbage White or a Red Admiral.

Whatever path you take, it will be an adventure.

Enjoy.

REVIEW QUESTIONS

1. What is a CASE tool?
2. Does Extreme Programming generate a lot of models?
3. What does RAD stand for?
4. Is the Unified Software Development Process a ready-made, off-the-shelf methodology that can be applied directly?
5. What is OCL, and why might you use it?

CHAPTER 20

Answers to Review Questions

Chapter 1: Introduction

1. The four major concepts introduced by this book are: organization, process, architecture and notation.
2. UML stands for Unified Modeling Language.
3. The stages of developing software are: conception, business case, business context, system requirements, analysis, design, construction, testing, deployment, support and enhancement.

Chapter 2: Modelling and Notation – The Unified Modeling Language

1. Models allow you to visualize a system before committing a lot of effort in constructing them. They help everyone in a project to communicate and to sort out problems before building the software.
2. The development of computer systems using the notion of object, which are made up of data (known as attributes) and things that can be done to the data (operations).
3. No, object-oriented methods can be used where the implementation language is not object-oriented.
4. UML is a notation, not a method. A notation allows you to write things down; a method prescribes how you go about solving a problem.
5. The key UML models are: business use case diagrams, system use case diagrams, activity diagrams, class diagrams, sequence diagrams, collaboration diagrams, statechart diagrams, component diagrams and deployment diagrams.

Chapter 4: Project Conception and Initiation

1. A stakeholder is anyone or any organization that has some involvement or interest in a project, or who is affected by the project in some way.
2. Stakeholders other than users can have views on the way a system should be developed, or they benefit from the system in some way, or they may find the system threatening and put blocks in the way.

3. Examples of stakeholders would be: users, sponsors, suppliers, various departments impacted by the system, developers.
4. All projects are there to meet some set of goals. It is important to find these out at the beginning.
5. Few projects are totally new, and it is important to know what existing infrastructure is there before planning a new system.
6. A risk is anything that can delay, stop, increase the cost of, or in any other way damage a project.
7. The analysis tools introduced are: stakeholder overview, SWOT analysis, force field analysis, risk register.

Chapter 5: Software Development Life Cycle

1. The stages of the software development life cycle are: requirements analysis, systems analysis, design, implementation, testing, maintenance.
2. Requirements analysis determines the needs of the various stakeholders from a system, and their expectations, producing a description of what the system should do in language that can be understood by all stakeholders, and upon which agreement can be reached.
3. Functional requirements state what a system should do, whereas non-functional requirements state things about how well it should do it (e.g. how reliable it should be).
4. In requirements analysis, the focus is on needs. In systems analysis, a definition of a computer system to meet those needs is produced.
5. Design focuses on the way a system is constructed, whereas systems analysis focuses mainly on the external behaviour of the system and how it interacts with the outside world.
6. Testing is there to ensure that the work of the development team meets the needs of various stakeholders and provides feedback to the development team on any problems.
7. In a waterfall approach, each stage of the software development life cycle is completed in turn. In an iterative approach, there are smaller mini-projects to develop parts of the whole system; that way, analysis, design, implementation, testing and even deployment can take place before all the requirements are defined.
8. A use case is a small, meaningful chunk of functionality.
9. In iterative development, a small number of use cases are developed in a phase (or iteration).
10. DSDM stands for Dynamic System Development Method.
11. Moscow prioritization divides work into things that Must be done, Should be done, Could be done and Won't be done.
12. A charter is a plan to achieve a certain amount of functionality in a phase, based on a Moscow prioritization.
13. The 80/20 rule is a rule of thumb that states that 80% of the benefit comes from 20% of the effort. (Or conversely, 20% of the benefit costs 80% of the effort.)
14. A time box is a fixed period of time in which to achieve a plan. In a time box, there is a prioritized list of things to do, and the developers aim to achieve as

much as possible from that list. At the end, the completed work is delivered, and uncompleted work passed on to later phases.

Chapter 6: Managing the Process

1. The organization types described are: role-based, club, task and existential.
2. Different organization types will approach software development in different ways. Understanding the organization helps to understand what is the best approach.
3. Role-based cultures like to structure their organization very tightly and assign people to slots.
4. Club cultures will not generally force a formal approach to development, unless the key players insist.
5. Task cultures tend to be most focused on results.
6. The steering group for a project sets the goals, monitors overall progress and key risks, keeps track of funding and approves release of funds.
7. Design and definition failures can be prevented by being clear about goals, revisiting and reviewing goals, and making frequent reality checks on progress and what is expected.
8. Risks are easier to address the earlier you find them out. Hidden risks often result in failures or disappointment.
9. Planning depends on good estimation, and this can be difficult in the early stages of a project. An iterative approach allows the team to calibrate their estimation in the first phases of development, so that later estimates are more accurate. Iterative development also allows for refinement of the plan as the project progresses.
10. If a use case is not completed in an iteration, it is carried forward to a later iteration and prioritized with other use cases.

Chapter 7: The Cost–Benefit Model

1. Return on capital employed is the difference between income and expenditure in a business divided by the amount of capital in a business; the capital is the value of all the things in the business.
2. Large projects must have a positive effect on return on capital employed or they cause the business to lose money. You might increase profit by reducing expenditure or increasing income, but if that involves a large increase in capital it might not be worthwhile.
3. Many of the costs of an IT project are not directly related to the IT itself, but cover things like reorganization of a business. The non-IT costs of a project are often much bigger than the IT costs.
4. Cost reduction is most often through improved efficiency of people, which means that fewer people can do a job. Other areas for cost reduction are in reduction of wastage.
5. Revenue impact is difficult to assess, as the effect of any change on a business in terms of how much more it might sell is usually unpredictable.

6. Reducing the amount of capital in a business can free up money for other activities. Increasing capital means that an increase in income or reduction in expenditure is necessary to maintain the return on capital.

7. A cash flow model shows how soon it is before a project actually starts to make a profit. It also shows the likely maximum outlay and the likely maximum profit over a period.

8. If a project looks too risky, it might not be authorized. When people are proposing a project, they tend to hide the risks.

Chapter 8: Business Modelling

1. Understanding the business environment is hugely important. If you do not, you are very likely to deliver a system that no one wants.

2. A business process map is a hierarchical grouping of processes in a business or business area.

3. A scenario is a single execution of a business process.

4. The primary path for a process is the path that is followed most commonly to achieve the goal of the process.

5. The primary path is the one that is easiest to execute, and requires minimal effort. It usually is the one that most people are happy to follow. Hence it is sometimes called the happy path.

6. The best way of dealing with an alternative path is to return it to the happy path as soon as possible.

7. In an exception path, something drastic has usually gone wrong, and the goal of the process is not likely to be achieved. Alternatives are more common and expected, and usually they do achieve the goal of the process. However, the difference between the two is sometimes difficult to see. They are treated the same way though.

8. The basic analysis process is: map out the key processes; identify the primary paths; using the primary paths, look for alternatives; devise alternative paths, returning them to the primary path where possible; determine exceptions and devise exception paths, returning them to the primary path where possible.

9. UML activity diagrams allow you to describe the flows of work in a process.

10. An activity in a UML activity diagram is a point where work gets done. It corresponds to a step in a business process.

11. A transition in a UML activity diagram indicates the movement between activities (and states).

12. A transition is triggered when either an activity completes or some event occurs to cause the activity to terminate.

13. An activity involves some sort of action. A state implies waiting for some event to happen.

14. A swimlane is a column on an activity diagram. It allows you to show where an activity is carried out, say in a particular part of an organization.

15. A decision point is shown by a small diamond. A transition can split into two or more different directions depending on a set of conditions. The conditions are written in square brackets next to the exit lines.

Chapter 9: Requirements Analysis

1. The primary inputs for requirements analysis are a stakeholder analysis, a process map and detailed business processes. The primary outputs are use case descriptions, use case diagrams and GUI prototypes.
2. A use case is a meaningful piece of functionality that can reasonably stand on its own.
3. A non-functional requirement is some statement about how the system should perform that is not directly related to functionality, say a statement on availability or reliability.
4. Some typical non-functional requirements are: scalability, criticality, reliability, security, frequency of use, response and usability.
5. A use case diagram summarizes the functionality of a system and the interaction between actors and use cases. The details of use cases are in use case descriptions.
6. Use case descriptions are not part of UML, but UML diagrams such as activity diagrams may be used as part of the description.
7. In the use case description it is useful to record any non-functional requirements related to that use case, such as security. Some non-functional requirements relate to the whole system and need to be recorded separately.
8. Use cases are there to support steps in business processes. Therefore you map the business processes, identify the process steps using scenario analysis, and then determine use cases to support the process steps.
9. An actor is any person or thing that interfaces with the computer system.
10. A relationship between an actor and a use case means that the actor can exchange information with the use case.
11. In a use case diagram, an arrowed relationship shows who initiated the communication; the communication can be two-way after the initiation.
12. An extends relationship between use cases shows that one use case sometimes invokes the use case that extends it. An includes relationship between use cases shows that a use case always invokes the use case that is included. For an extends relationship the arrow points to the use case that invokes the extension, and for an includes relationship the arrow points to the use case that is invoked.
13. Actors correspond to roles, not people or systems. As a person might well adopt a number of roles in using a system, that person might well appear as a number of actors.
14. Prototypes help various stakeholders to visualize the proposed system. They improve communication, and in particular help to gather the type of information that needs to be exchanged with the system, and how users like to interact with a system.

Chapter 10: Buy, Build or Adapt?

1. Buying software means that you can get the software quicker, and that the quality is likely to be more assured. Building software means that you tend to get software that more closely matches your needs.

2. It can be cheaper to buy software rather than build it, but much of the cost of a project is not related to the purchase or construction of software, so that this is not always the deciding factor.

3. The same approach to determining needs can be used for both the purchase and the specification of software. As with specifying software, it is very important to understand the business environment before entering into a purchase.

4. An RFI is a request for information from a supplier. It states what the business needs are, and asks the supplier to state how its package meets those needs.

5. An RFI should contain a description of the business area that needs the package, such as a process map and process definitions. It will ask the supplier how the package maps onto those needs.

6. An RFT is a request for tender, which invites a supplier to propose a solution to a particular problem. It is more detailed than an RFI, and will ask how a package supports selected business scenarios in fine detail.

7. A demonstrator project is a project to prove that a solution works. It is constrained so that it does not create too much risk if it fails. It should be quick but realistic, and should actually be used.

Chapter 11: Object Concepts

1. The three compartments in a UML class are the name of the class (at the top), the attributes of the class (in the middle) and the operations on the class (at the bottom).

2. In an object-oriented system, data is stored in the attributes of objects.

3. In an object-oriented system, processing is done in the operations on objects.

4. Encapsulation means that the data and operations on data are grouped together, and that access to the data is controlled through operations.

5. Polymorphism means that you can use the same name for an attribute or operation in two or more classes.

6. An object is a particular thing created in the system. A class is the set of all objects with the same name, attributes and operations.

7. An association is a link between two classes that implies that objects in one class can communicate with objects in the other class.

8. A one-to-many association between two classes means that one object in the class at the one end of the association can talk to many objects in the class at the many end; objects at the many end may only talk to one object at the one end.

9. A one-to-one association means that objects in one class can only communicate with exactly one object in the other class, and vice versa.

10. In a many-to-many association, one object in one class can communicate with many in the other class, and vice versa.

11. In an inheritance relationship, objects in a child class have the operations and attributes defined in the parent class.

12. In an aggregation relationship, operations and attributes are not shared between the classes; however, the aggregate object may use the operations on the part objects to implement its own operations.

13. A class diagram consists of classes, with their attributes and operations, and the relationships between classes.

14. Systems can have lots of classes, and it makes sense to produce a number of class diagrams to show different aspects of the system.

Chapter 12: Systems Analysis

1. A domain object is an object that represents a real world entity, such as a customer.
2. An entity object is something that needs to persist over time. Domain objects are usually represented by entity objects.
3. A boundary object manages an interaction with the outside world. A screen would be a boundary object.
4. A control object manages the interaction between a number of other objects. Use cases usually have a control object, or a number of control objects, to manage the interactions.
5. A sequence diagram is made up of a set of objects and interactions between objects. The objects are drawn along the top with lines drawn below them, and interactions between objects are shown as arrows between the vertical lines, in time order.
6. Sequence diagrams are used to work out how objects collaborate to provide the functionality needed by a use case.
7. Use cases are related to sequence diagrams by taking a representative set of scenarios that cover the different routes through a use case, and for each scenario putting together a sequence diagram to determine the interaction between objects to provide the functionality.
8. A collaboration diagram is an alternative to sequence diagrams, showing object interaction in a different way, in two dimensions. Collaboration diagrams look similar to class diagrams.
9. Statecharts are used to show the way a class moves between states.
10. In brownfield analysis, a number of the objects have already been defined. In greenfield analysis, the objects have to be invented.
11. The primary input to systems analysis is the set of use case descriptions, together with any prototypes.
12. The primary outputs of systems analysis are a set of sequence diagrams and/or collaboration diagrams, class diagrams, and possibly statechart diagrams.

Chapter 13: Design

1. UML does not provide a format for the type expression of an attribute. The target implementation language is used.
2. Private visibility means that the attribute or operation cannot be accessed outside the class and *cannot* be inherited. Protected visibility means that the attribute or operation cannot be accessed outside the class and *can* be inherited. Public visibility means that the attribute or operation can be accessed outside the class and can be inherited.
3. If you omit the multiplicity on an attribute definition, it is assumed to be multiplicity of one.

4. The **in** parameter kind on a parameter to an operation means that it is supplied to the operation but cannot be changed by the operation. The **out** parameter kind on a parameter to an operation means that the operation does not use any supplied value, but can set the parameter on return. The **inout** parameter kind on a parameter to an operation means that it is supplied to the operation and can be changed by the operation.

5. A constructor is a special operation that is called automatically when an object is created. It is used to initialize the object. A destructor is a special operation that is called automatically when an object is destroyed, and it is used to tidy up.

6. The objects at either end of an association have a role in that association. The role name is written on the association near the class. It is not necessary to specify the roles in all associations; usually the role is obvious and does not need stating.

7. There is no limit to the number of associations between a pair of classes. However, it is unusual to have more than one or two.

8. A class can have an association with itself.

9. A lifeline on a sequence diagram is a line drawn below an object.

10. Focus of control on a sequence diagram is shown by a rectangle drawn over the lifeline of an object, indicating when that object is active.

11. Repetition on a sequence diagram is shown by drawing a rectangle around the interactions that are repeated and putting a test condition below the bottom right of the rectangle.

12. Branching on a sequence diagram is shown by two or more interactions starting from the same point. Conditions are written against the different paths in square brackets.

13. A design pattern is a commonly used structure that can be copied and adapted in a design.

14. A precondition on an operation is a statement that must be true for the operation to legally fire.

15. A postcondition on an operation is a statement that must be true after the operation has legally fired.

16. Pseudo-code is a way of writing programs in a loose English-like syntax to specify the behaviour of an operation.

17. You can show the structure of a user interface by using a class diagram to show the relationship between the boundary classes that represent the screens in the application. Directional associations can be used to indicate navigation between screens.

18. A UML component is a grouping of objects for implementation.

19. Cohesion is how well objects in a component fit together in terms of related functionality. Cohesive objects tend to communicate a great deal, and are best kept together.

20. Coupling between components indicates how much communication needs to go on between components. In general, it is better to keep coupling low.

21. Reuse can be approached using component-based development, application frameworks and design patterns.

Chapter 14: Database Design

1. Entities in an entity–relationship model only have attributes, not operations. The relationships are data relationships, not paths of communication. Entity–relationship models are used to model entity objects for storage in a database.
2. A relational database stores information in tables with fixed numbers of columns, each column containing a simple type. Tables are linked together using keys.
3. A key in a relational database table is a value or set of values that uniquely identify the record in the table.
4. A foreign key in a relational database table is a key that is used to refer to a record in another table.
5. Normalization is used to improve the structure of a relational database. It prevents duplication of data and unwanted loss of data when records are deleted.
6. A transaction on a database is a set of operations that need to be considered as a whole. They must succeed or fail – partially completed transactions can leave the database in a damaged state.
7. The serializability constraint on a database means that any two transactions must operate as if they happened one after the other, even if they overlap. This prevents them interfering with each other's operations.
8. Atomicity of a database transaction means that it either completely succeeds or has no effect at all.
9. Serializability is enforced in a database by locking records that are used by a transaction.
10. Locking records can result in deadlock where two or more transactions are unable to proceed because they are waiting for each other to release locks on records.

Chapter 15: Architecture

1. Technical architecture concerns itself with the hardware for a system and the software tools, such as CASE tools, databases, programming languages, operating systems, and so forth.
2. Real-time links between parts of a system make sense when the actions in one part of a system have to be acted upon quickly in a remote part of the system.
3. Message queuing makes sense for linking parts of a system when there is no urgency for the information to be passed. This has the advantage that the receiver can work at a different pace and even be offline when the sender issues the information.
4. For component-based development, there needs to be a well-defined and properly managed component repository.
5. In framework-based development, common elements are synthesized into a framework shared by a number of applications.
6. The top tier of a three-tier architecture is the presentation layer, which handles all the interaction. The middle tier is the logic layer, which deals with

the bulk of the application logic. The base layer is the persistence or data layer, which deals with the long-term data in the system.

7. A Web server takes the responsibility of centralizing much of the presentation layer. Thus the presentation layer in a Web application is split between the Web server and the browser.

Chapter 16: Construction

1. For a single-language development with a database, it is sensible to allocate use cases to individual developers.
2. If the presentation language and logic language are different, then it makes sense to allocate the interface to one developer or a small team of developers, and give use cases to individual developers in the logic language.
3. HTML is limited in its functionality, but it is quick to develop and easy to distribute. It needs supplementing with a scripting language such as JavaScript to enable validation at the desktop.
4. Object-oriented languages are not essential for the implementation of the logic layer, though they are increasingly the language of choice.
5. Poor exception handling leads to difficulties in tracing problems. Considerable time and effort can be wasted tracking down problems during development, integration and testing.
6. Integration makes sure that the parts of the system fit together. If integration is too infrequent, then the process of integration becomes costly and difficult.

Chapter 17: Testing

1. A good way of testing requirements is to set up a workshop with representative stakeholders, present the requirements back to them, and gather feedback.
2. A good way of testing analysis is to run a workshop with designers, presenting the analysis and gathering feedback.
3. Unit testing makes sure that a particular part of the system (e.g. a use case) functions according to specification. The developer who creates the unit usually does the unit testing.
4. A unit test for a use case would involve executing a representative set of scenarios from the use case description, with appropriate sample data, to exercise all the paths through the use case.
5. A system test is carried out on a fully integrated system, and this is normally carried out by a testing team within the development environment, but not by the developers who produced the code.
6. Like a unit test, a system test is derived from the use case descriptions.
7. Test results are recorded in some document, sometimes a database. The individual results are fault descriptions with an assessment of the severity of the fault.
8. Systems are rarely fault-free. Normally a system will not be allowed to progress if there are high-severity faults or too many moderate to low-severity faults.
9. A user acceptance test is the final stage of testing before release. It is normally carried out by a special team outside the development environment, but may be made up for particular tests using people from the user environment.

10. User acceptance tests are devised from the business process descriptions and the use case descriptions. The tests focus on usability, and that the use cases support the business processes properly.

11. A beta test is a release to a specially selected set of real users, who use the system. They will report any problems, and normally have extra support and other compensations for using an early version of the system.

12. *Ad hoc* tests may have to be devised to deal with non-functional requirements. For example, if there is a requirement for high scalability, it will be necessary to construct a framework to simulate a high number of concurrent users.

Chapter 18: Deployment, Support and Enhancement

1. The source material for training and user manuals is the business process descriptions and use case descriptions, plus screenshots from the finished application.

2. Replacement systems introduce two main problems. Firstly, data from the old system will have to be migrated to the new system. Secondly, it may not be possible to run the two systems concurrently, and it may be necessary to have a one-off switch, which is a high risk.

3. Big bang deployments that fail can leave users without a system for a long period. That can be very damaging for business and for the reputation of the development team.

4. There is usually a support desk, once a system is deployed, to respond to problems that users have with a system. Users contact the support desk, who deal with minor problems themselves, and refer more serious problems to the relevant parts of the development team.

5. For a deployed system, small changes are gathered through suggestions from users and the support desk. Large changes are usually proposed by management in response to changing business requirements. A change management process is set up to estimate and prioritize changes.

Chapter 19: Journey's End

1. CASE stands for Computer-Assisted Software Engineering. A CASE tool is a computer program that helps with the different parts of software development, such as the drawing of UML diagrams.

2. Extreme Programming tries to minimize the number of intermediate models. Its main emphasis is on the creation of stories and test plans, which correspond to use case descriptions.

3. RAD stands for Rapid Application Development.

4. The Unified Software Development Process is a framework from which you can devise a method; it is too complex and comprehensive to use off the shelf.

5. OCL is the Object Constraint Language, a standard that is part of UML and permits more rigorous statement of constraints such as preconditions and postconditions on operations. It would be used to obtain more accuracy in specification.

CHAPTER 21

UML Notation Summary

UML is an extensive notation. This summary is intended to provide you with a workable set of UML, that covers the majority of day-to-day uses. For a more comprehensive description of UML see Bennett *et al.* (2001).

21.1 Activity Diagrams

21.1.1 PURPOSE

Activity diagrams are flow diagrams. They allow you to describe flows in a variety of situations. They can be used with varying levels of detail and rigour.

21.1.2 USES

Business modelling
Activity diagrams are a powerful way of describing the flow of work in a business. The activities model steps in a business process, and the transitions model the flow from one process step to another. The swimlanes are useful for indicating which area of a business is responsible for a particular activity.

Requirements modelling
Activity diagrams can be used to model the flows within a use case. The activities correspond to steps in the use case. This is a way of consolidating the primary, alternative and exception paths into a single view.

Systems analysis
As for requirements modelling, plus it is sometimes useful to describe the flow that implements a step in a use case if that particular step is complicated.

Design
Activity diagrams can model complex operations. The activities then correspond to small fragments of code that need to be implemented; it is legitimate to embed program statements in an activity.

21.1.3 NOTATION

Start state

This is the entry point in an activity diagram. It may have a label indicating the state, but usually it has no label. There should be a single transition from the start state to an activity or state. There should be only one start state on a diagram.

End state

 This represents an exit point on an activity diagram. It may have a label indicating the state, but usually it has no label. There may be a number of end states on an activity diagram.

Activity

 This represents a step in an activity diagram where work is being undertaken. The activity name should be a brief phrase indicating the work carried out by the activity; for an operation specification, the activity name may be a programming language statement or set of statements. An activity may be entered by a number of transitions. An activity will normally have one exit transition that represents completion of the work of the activity, and this transition will be unlabelled. An activity may have other exit transitions to respond to events that cause termination of the work of the activity, and these transitions must be labelled by the event.

Entry action

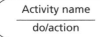 Indicates any action that must take place on entry to an activity. The action can be an English statement or it may send an event, or for detailed design could be a programming language statement.

Do action

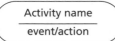 Indicates any action(s) that must take place during the activity. The action can be an English statement, or it may send an event, or for detailed design could be a programming language statement. There may be many do actions.

Event action

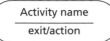 Indicates any action(s) that must take place during the activity to respond to an event. The action can be an English statement, or it may send an event, or for detailed design could be a programming language statement. There may be many event actions.

Exit action

Indicates any action that must take place on exit from an activity. The action can be an English statement, or it may send an event, or for detailed design could be a programming language statement.

State

A state is similar to an activity, except that no work is being done. It is used to indicate waiting for an event. It may have entry, exit and event actions.

Event send

^target.event(arguments)   Sends an event to the object named by target. The event is the name of the event. The arguments are a set of comma-separated values passed with the event.

Transition

transition label →   This shows the transition between activities (or states). The transition label is an optional label, with the format:

event(arguments) [condition]/action

where event is an event that triggers the transition, arguments is a comma-separated list of values supplied with the event, condition is a condition that must be true when the transition fires, and action is an action that must take place when the event fires (action may be an event send, as indicated above).

Fork and join

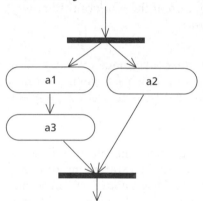

Two or more parallel workflows can be shown by introducing a fork (a thick bar) with one input transition and two or more output transitions. Each of the separate workflows must meet again at a join (a thick bar) with two or more input transitions and one output transition.

Object

An object may be drawn on an activity diagram, to indicate how activities influence objects. The object name or the class name from which the object is drawn (or both) needs to be provided. The object may pass through a number of states, affected by activities, and the state is drawn below the object name in rectangular brackets.

Object flow

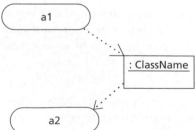

The effect of an activity on an object is shown by a dotted arrow from the activity to the object. An object use by an activity is shown by a dotted arrow from the object to an activity.

Decision point

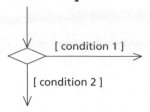

A transition may branch into one of a number of alternative directions by introducing a decision point. A decision point can have a number of input transitions and a number of output transitions. The output transitions have labels that are guard conditions. The guard conditions must determine unique paths. The conditions are written in square brackets, and may be in English or a more formal language such as OCL.

Swimlanes

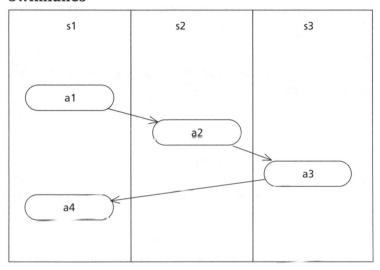

A swimlane indicates an area of responsibility. Swimlanes are vertical (or horizontal) columns with labels at the top (or start) indicating where the work of activities in the swimlane take place (e.g. what department in an organization).

Nested workflows

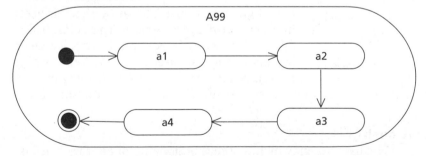

An activity may have a workflow embedded within it. The sub-workflow has a start and one or more end states. If the sub-workflows are complicated, it is better to produce a separate activity diagram for them.

21.2 Use Case Diagrams

21.2.1 PURPOSE

Use case diagrams are used to show the presentation of functionality of a system and its interaction with the outside world. The diagram does not specify functionality.

21.2.2 USES

Business modelling

UML has an extension notation that treats business processes as use cases on a business. This book has not used that notation.

Requirements modelling

Use cases diagrams are one of the principal outputs of requirements definition, together with use case descriptions.

21.2.3 NOTATION

Actor

Actor Name

An actor is any person or thing that interacts with a system. The actor name is a phrase to define the role of the actor. (A real person or thing may adopt many roles, and so may actually appear under a number of actors on use case diagrams.)

Use case

Use Case Name

A use case is a meaningful piece of functionality supplied by the system. The name is a brief phrase to indicate the functionality of the use case; this can be written under or inside the use case ellipse. The use case description is supplied separately, usually as a textual description with possibly some other UML diagrams such as an activity diagram.

Relationship

Actor Name   Use Case Name

A straight line is used to show that an actor interacts with the use case. The relationship allows for two-way communication between the actor and the use case. The relationship may have an arrowhead to indicate who initiates the interaction (sometimes a use case may initiate the interaction, sometimes the actor).

Includes relationship

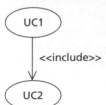

One use case may include the functionality of another use case as part of its execution. The implication is that the functionality of the use case pointed at by the arrow is always included in the use case at the non-arrow end of the relationship.

Extends relationship

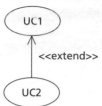

<<extend>>

One use case may extend the functionality of another use case. The implication is that the functionality of the use case pointed at by the arrow sometimes uses the functionality of the use case at the non-arrow end of the relationship.

21.3 Class Diagrams

21.3.1 PURPOSE

Class diagrams show the static structure of a system, with classes and relationships between classes. The diagram is a synthesis of all the possible interactions between objects.

21.3.2 USES

Business modelling
Where entities in the real world have complex behaviour and relationships, it is useful to produce a domain model using a class diagram showing the real-world entities and their relationships.

Requirements modelling
As with business modelling, it is sometimes useful to describe complex behaviour and relationships of real-world entities with a class diagram.

Systems analysis
Systems analysis is beginning to consider the behaviour of the system, and it will model real-world entities together with boundary classes to control interaction with the world, and control classes to manage complex interaction between entity objects.

Design
Design transforms the class diagram provided by systems analysis into a set of classes and relationships that may be implemented in a computer system. Part of the transformation will produce an entity–relationship diagram that is a special case of a class diagram showing entity objects and their attributes that can be stored in a database.

21.3.3 NOTATION

Class

Class Name
Attributes
Operations

A class is a collection of objects with identical structure (ie the same attributes and operations). The class name is a word or phrase to describe the objects in the class, written in the top compartment. The attributes are a list of data items that represent the state and the object in the class, and these are listed in the middle compartment. The operations are a list of things that can be done to objects in the class, and these are listed in the bottom compartment.

Entity class

Entity Class Name

A special type of class used to represent objects that need to persist, and that are usually recorded in a database.

Boundary class

Boundary Class Name

A special type of class used to represent objects, such as computer screens, that control the interaction between the system and the outside world.

Control class

Control Class Name

A special type of class used to represent objects that control the interaction between boundary objects and a number of entity objects.

Stereotype labelled class

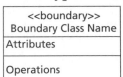

<<boundary>> Boundary Class Name
Attributes
Operations

Instead of using separate icons to show different types of class, it is possible to write a stereotype label at the top of a standard class drawing, with the name of the type of class (e.g. boundary, entity, control) between << and >>.

Inheritance relationship

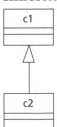

A class may inherit the attributes and operations of another class. The inheritance is controlled by the visibility of the attributes and operations. The inheritance is from the class pointed at in the relationship to the class at the non-arrow end of the relationship.

Aggregation relationship

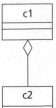

An object in a class may be made up of a number objects from other classes. The class at the diamond end of the relationship consists of objects that are made up of parts, and the class at the other end contains the objects that are parts. An object may be made up of parts from a number of classes.

Relationship

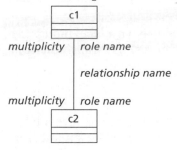

A relationship defines a communication path between objects. An object in one class may communicate with one or more objects in another class. If communication is only allowed one way, then the relationship may be arrowed, indicating the direction of communication. An optional relationship name is allowed. At each end of the relationship there is an optional role name for the role of the objects in the relationship. At each end, there is a multiplicity indicator, which is assumed to be a multiplicity of 1 if omitted.

Many multiplicity

*   If a * appears as the multiplicity of the relationship, then zero or more objects may be related to an object at the other end of the relationship.

Fixed multiplicity

n   If an integer n appears as the multiplicity of the relationship, then exactly that number of objects may be related to an object at the other end of the relationship

Range multiplicity

n..m   If a range is specified, where n and m are either numbers or *, then the number of objects indicated by the range at this end of the relationship can be related to one object at the other end of the relationship.

21.4 Statechart Diagrams

21.4.1 PURPOSE

Statechart diagrams are for modelling the internal state changes of an object. They are a variant of activity diagrams with largely the same notation.

21.4.2 USES

Business modelling
If an entity, such as a contract, has a complex set of states that it can pass through, a statechart model may be useful for modelling the states.

Requirements modelling
As for business modelling.

Systems analysis
As for business modelling. Also, there may be behaviours of boundary and control classes that need to be explained.

Design
As for systems analysis.

21.4.3 NOTATION

Start state

This is the entry point in a statechart diagram. It may have a label indicating the state, but usually it has no label. There should be a single transition from the start state to an activity or state. There should be only one start state on a diagram.

End state

This represents an exit point on a statechart diagram. It may have a label indicating the state, but usually it has no label. There may be a number of end states on an activity diagram.

State

A state is a condition that an object is in, represented by values in its attributes. An object may pass through a number of states during its life.

Entry action

Indicates any action that must take place on entry to a state. The *action* can be an English statement or it may send an event.

Event action

Indicates any action(s) that must take place during the state to respond to an event. The *action* can be an English statement or it may send an *event*. There may be many event actions.

Exit action

```
    State
    Name
  ───────
  exit/Action
```
Indicates any action that must take place on exit from a state. The *action* can be an English statement or it may send an event.

Event send

`^target.event(arguments)`
Sends an event to the object named by *target*. The event is the name of the event. The `arguments` are a set of comma-separated values passed with the event.

Transition

`transition label` →
This shows the transition between states. The transition label is an optional label, with the format:

`event(arguments) [ condition ]/action`

where `event` is an event that triggers the transition, `arguments` is a comma-separated list of values supplied with the event, `condition` is a condition that must be true when the event fires, and `action` is an action that must take place when the event fires (action may be an event send, as indicated above).

Decision point

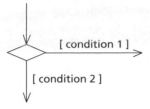

A transition may branch into one of a number of alternative directions by introducing a decision point. A decision point can have a number of input transitions and a number of output transitions. The output transitions have labels that are guard conditions. The guard conditions must determine unique paths. The conditions are written in square brackets, and may be in English or a more formal language such as OCL.

Nested states

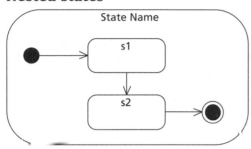

A state may have substates embedded. The substates begin with a start and end with one or more end states. If the substates are complicated, it is better to produce a separate statechart diagram for them.

21.5 Sequence Diagrams

21.5.1 PURPOSE

Sequence diagrams provide a time-ordered mapping of steps in the execution of a scenario into interactions between objects. They are one of the primary tools for elaborating use cases in analysis and design. They are analogous to collaboration diagrams, which present the same information in a different manner.

21.5.2 USES

Systems analysis

Sequence diagrams are the main tool for elaborating a use case and linking the scenarios in a use case to objects in the system that can support them.

Design

Sequence diagrams from systems analysis are transformed at the design stage into interactions between objects that can be directly implemented in the target environment. The diagrams have more detail, and the objects determined at the systems analysis stage may be transformed to fit into the architecture of the system.

21.5.3 NOTATION

Object lifeline

Objects are drawn with a lifeline running down the page. Time runs vertically from top to bottom. The object at the top may be shown by a rectangle, or with an icon to show the type of the object (boundary, entity, control).

Actor lifeline

: Actor

Actors appear on sequence diagrams in the same way as objects. For interactive scenarios, they are usually the source of events that trigger a sequence of interactions between objects.

Focus of control

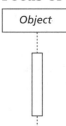

When control enters an object, this can be shown by drawing a rectangle over the lifeline showing the period during which control is within the object. Control is considered to remain in the object if it is waiting for another object to return from a call on an operation.

Object interaction

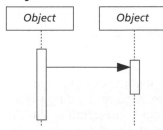

An arrow is drawn between two object lifelines to indicate interaction. The line is usually labelled with either a description of the interaction or the name of an operation that is being called on the receiving object. The calling object may wait for the called object to finish the request, or it may proceed – different arrow shapes are used to show this; see below.

Creating an object

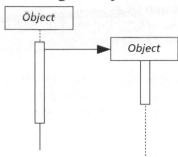

One object can create an object. This is shown by an interaction going into the head of the created object rather than into the lifeline.

Destroying an object

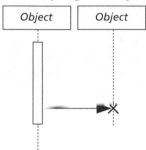

An object may destroy another object. This is shown by an interaction ending at a cross on the lifeline of the destroyed object. The lifeline of the destroyed object then terminates.

Object calling itself

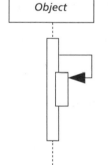

An object may call itself. This is shown by an interaction looping back onto the object. A nested focus of control is shown.

Iteration

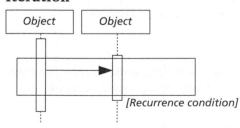

[Recurrence condition]

A set of interactions that repeat can be surrounded by a rectangle, with a recurrence condition drawn to the bottom right of the rectangle. The iteration will continue while the recurrence condition is true.

Procedural or synchronous interaction

When the first object calls the second object, it suspends activity until the second object completes the request. When the second object loses the locus of control, the first one resumes.

Flat interaction

This triggers the second object to start execution. Normally this is asynchronous, meaning that the first object does not wait for a return. However, it can be used if it is unknown whether or not the message is asynchronous.

Asynchronous interaction

This triggers execution of the second object, and the first object continues without waiting for the second object to complete its task.

Branching interaction

Splitting the arrow into two or more branches means that more than one object might be called, depending on some conditions. The conditions are written in square brackets. If the conditions are mutually exclusive, this represents a branch; otherwise it shows potential concurrent execution of the called objects.

21.6 Collaboration Diagrams

21.6.1 PURPOSE

Collaboration diagrams provide a mapping of steps in the execution of a scenario into interactions between objects, drawn in two dimensions in a similar way to class diagrams. They are analogous to sequence diagrams, which present the same information in a different manner.

21.6.2 USES

They are used for similar purposes to sequence diagrams, but present the information in a different way.

21.6.3 NOTATION

Object

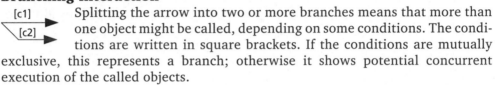

An object in a collaboration. It is common to simply refer to the object as an instance of a class, using the syntax **:classname**.

Actor

Actors usually appear on collaboration diagrams, where they are commonly the source of events that trigger actions in a scenario.

Actor Name

Association

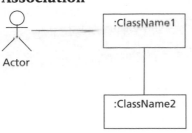

Actor

An association is a line between objects or an object and an actor, showing that communication takes place.

Message

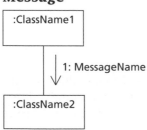

1: MessageName

A message is drawn alongside the association, with an arrow indicating the direction of the message. The messages are numbered, to show the time order of messages. If multiple messages follow the same route, they are listed together with only one arrow.

21.7 Component Diagrams

21.7.1 PURPOSE

Components are groupings of objects for implementation. Component diagrams show the implementation structure of the application.

21.7.2 USES

Design

Component diagrams are used by the designer to indicate where the objects are implemented and how the components interact.

21.7.3 NOTATION

Component

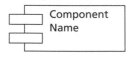

A component is a group of objects for implementation. The objects within a component are usually listed separately.

Dependency

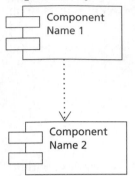

Objects in one component my call on objects in another component. This is shown by a dependency arrow.

Interface class

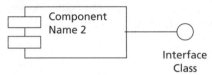

A component may have one or more interfaces. This is shown by drawing an interface class icon attached to the component. There may be a number of interface classes attached.

Dependency on an interface

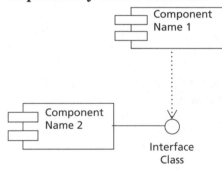

The dependency between components may be shown by indicating which interface is called.

CHAPTER 22

Worked Example – The Odd Shoe Company

The purpose of this chapter is to give you a picture of the stages and models used in a complete project. However, this can only be a sample, as a project of even this modest size would produce hundreds of pages of models and supporting documentation. There is benefit, though, in seeing all the stages together in a concise way, rather than interspersed with the chapters.

22.1 The Odd Shoe Company

Some people have odd sized feet, and some people have only one leg. If you have odd sized feet, either you have to pack up a large shoe for your small foot, or buy two pairs and discard the spare ones, or have pairs made. If you have only one leg, unless you have a false limb, you only need one shoe.

John Peddar, a shoe shop owner, has had enough enquiries to realize that throughout the UK there is a sizeable market for odd-sized shoes and individual shoes. He has contacted suppliers, and he can convince some suppliers to provide stocks of only one shoe, at a small premium, but provided he orders at least 1000 shoes at a time. Then John has a bright idea. If he can sell to all the people in the UK that have odd sized feet, he could buy a large stock of pairs from his normal suppliers and split them. He figures that the number of people with larger left feet will be balanced by the number of people with larger right feet. Similarly, one-leggedness is likely to be evenly distributed.

The only way he can think of reaching such a broadly distributed market cheaply is to use the Internet. He decides to set up a Web site so that customers can browse his stocks, enter orders and receive goods by mail. You are the analyst and designer for the software company he commissions to build his system.

The technical architect has recommended a full database system with the application written in Java and HTML. This is based on John Peddar's estimate that there will be 2000 orders a week, and his requirement to keep substantial records of orders and customers for marketing and analysis.

After your first interview with John Peddar, you come away with the following notes:

1. Customers will need to register with the Odd Shoe Company to make orders. On registration, they need to provide name and address, payment details (credit card etc.), shoe sizes, gender, and any special details.

2. To order, customers will select from the shoe range. The system will tell them if the shoes are in stock or need to be ordered from a supplier. If the shoes are in stock, then the system will tell them how quickly the shoes can be delivered.

3. Customers will want to track their orders online. An order can be waiting for delivery to the Odd Shoe Company, waiting for despatch, waiting for credit clearance or despatched. Before despatch, the customer should have an option for cancelling the order.

4. John would like a weekly report, detailing numbers of customers, statistics on shoe sizes by left and right foot, orders, stocks and cancelled orders.

5. Every month customers will be sent a statement by email, together with a list of special offers. Offers will only be for shoe pairs that are available in suitable sizes for that customer.

6. John wants to keep pictures, prices, stock levels and sizes of all his shoes in a database. When supplies arrive the database will need updating. When goods are ordered, the stock levels should be deducted. If an order is cancelled, the stock levels should be updated accordingly.

You go back to the office, full of enthusiasm, ready to write code. However, your manager is an experienced developer and he sends you back to John Peddar, with clear instructions on the stages you must take the project through.

22.2 Project Initiation

In your next interview, you explain to John about the stages your company requires all projects to go through. You explain about the software development life cycle, and that it is important to address all stakeholders in the project. You talk him through the key stages of the project, and where he will have input.

John Peddar has been doing a considerable amount of research and has gathered a lot of knowledge. Your first task is to compile a list of stakeholders. As a start-up company there is less complexity here, but also more vagueness and uncertainty. Your first attempt at a summary is provided in Table 22.1. You think that there may be some scope for extending this list to cover employees, but as the company has no employees yet, other than John himself, it is hard to get a clear statement about their role. You note that you will need to come back to this analysis from time to time.

22.2.1 GOALS

It is not hard to specify the goal of the project. The goal of the project is to establish a new business, serving a previously untapped market, and to achieve profitability within two years. The service must be launched within six months. John is happy with this.

22.2.2 INFRASTRUCTURE

This project is unusual in that it is a greenfield application. Therefore the project team is able to propose the most appropriate software and hardware infrastructure.

Table 22.1 Stakeholder summary for the Odd Shoe Company

Stakeholder category	Role in project	Project implications	Actions needed
John Peddar	Provide funding	Will be seeking value for money	Agree budgets. Monitor expenditure.
	Monitor and review	Regular reviews of progress, expenditure and risks	Establish regular project progress meetings. Present project plan and costings, progress and risks
	Provide market research and ideas	Will need to be involved in a considerable amount of the analysis.	Establish separate meetings for analysis, as needed.
Suppliers	Provide stock	The cost and reliability of stock delivery will be critical to the business success.	Provisional supplier analysis needed before business plan executed. Contracts need to be in place, with some supplies provided, on company launch.
Customers	Purchase shoes	Need to be sure of size of market, and price sensitivity of market.	Market analysis needs to be undertaken before product launch.
		Need to make sure that the presentation is usable and attractive to the market.	Establish a focus group. Enrol some customers in a trial launch/beta testing.
Software house	Develop software	Ensure software meets business needs.	Conduct thorough business and systems analysis before design and construction.
		Deliver to time, cost and quality.	Adopt iterative development, based on DSDM. Ensure comprehensive stakeholder involvement.

22.2.3 SWOT ANALYSIS OF THE PROPOSAL

You then go through with John the strengths, weaknesses, opportunities and threats relating to the project. John is familiar with this idea, and quickly fills you in. You add one or two ideas of your own.

Strengths
- The concept is new, and likely to be appealing.
- Mail order will be a benefit to people who have mobility problems.
- No one has approached this market in this way before.
- The initial market size suggests a turnover of 100,000 sales is viable in the first year, growing to 200,000 by the third year.

Weaknesses
● Access to the Internet for the market is unknown.
● The market is untested.

Opportunities
● The growth of the Internet creates a unique marketing opportunity.
● The unusual nature of the business will lead to lots of press publicity.

Threats
● Once suppliers get wind of the idea, they may set up in competition.

22.2.4 RISKS

Finally, you discuss the risks with John. You explain that you will be keeping a risk register, and that you will track the risks and review status of actions to address risks at each project meeting. John is most impressed by this.

This is clearly a risky project, but the rewards are considered substantial. John has started a number of successful businesses, and one or two that have failed, so he knows something about risks. Some of the initial risks are shown in the risk register in Table 22.2.

Table 22.2   Risk register for the Odd Shoe Company

Risk	Severity	Likelihood	Owner	Action
Poor quality site would deter rather than attract custom	High	Low	Software House	Good quality and experienced Web designers and developers will be used
Too slow to market, and the competition will gain ground	High	Low	Software House	This will be a priority project, with resource guaranteed
Customers may not be aware or wish to use the Web site	High	Medium	John Peddar	Develop launch promotion
Competition may get wind and beat the Odd Shoe Company to market.	High	Medium	John Peddar, Software house	High confidentiality must be implemented

22.3 Managing the Process

You quickly realize that the business will operate as a club culture. Therefore, heavyweight management structures are not likely to be acceptable. John Peddar will take an active interest in all aspects of the project, and he will act informally as steering group and overall project manager. He likes your software house's approach, and has been particularly impressed with the initial analysis and the approach taken. He therefore is willing to take your advice on managing the development, and delegates control of the software development to you.

You choose an iterative approach, based on DSDM. Regular project meetings with John Peddar are set up. A buy before build policy will be adopted, and the core financial and stock control systems will be purchased. However, from your well-informed knowledge of the e-commerce market place you know that there is no package to support the Web interface that is flexible enough to meet John's needs.

John is satisfied with this. He likes the idea of using standard software wherever possible, but having something unique to go on the Internet.

22.4 Business Modelling

You begin by looking at the business processes in the company and devise a business process map. This is a 'living' document, that allows you to have a good overview of the business. It is a 'helicopter view' of how the business is to operate. There is no one right answer. The aim is to capture as much of the activity of the business and present it as a simple hierarchy. You set aside half a day with John to produce the business process map.

Considering the Odd Shoe Company, its main aim is to buy, market, sell and distribute shoes of different sizes. You then break the top level of the business down into:

- BUYING: the process of buying shoes. The aim is to match buying with market needs. John Peddar tells you that he does not want too much surplus of odd shoes. There will be a lot of negotiation with suppliers in this process to minimize costs. A lot of the information will come from market trends that will be better understood when the business is up and running. Buying will cover ordering, receipt and payment for stock.
- MARKETING: the process of marketing the products and services of the company. John Peddar thinks that there is a unique opportunity brought about by the Internet to reach a large number of people that have significant problems in finding footwear, though this number is geographically widely spread. The thought of an international market is also in John's mind, but he wants to learn the issues in the local market. The Internet will be the key sales channel. However, to get people to know about the company, he believes he will have to market through other means.
- SELLING: the process of selling to the customer. This will primarily be the Internet. John Peddar wants an online shop that presents pictures of shoes and other marketing material. He wants to sell using credit cards in order to remove large issues of credit control.
- DISTRIBUTION: the process of getting the shoes from stock to the customer, dealing with returns and problems with delivery. This will be done by mail and courier services. The aim is to keep the warehouse and stock levels reasonably small, but the nature of the business, where to service one customer two pairs of shoes are split, will mean that stock levels will be higher than businesses trading more traditionally.

After due consideration and discussion with you, John agrees that there will need to be another process to manage the finances.

- FINANCE: the process of managing the flows of money into and out of the company. This involves finding investment money (through loans or share issue), managing bank accounts, setting and controlling budgets.

22.4.1 THE BUYING PROCESS

The market for wholesale shoes is diverse. There are imports, local manufacturers and various ways of acquiring bankrupt stock. John's strategy is to start the business with high-volume, low-cost quality items of a traditional style. That way he feels that he will be able to minimize stock issues. He has many contacts in the trade. His buying process is likely to break down into the following sub-processes:

- IDENTIFYING STOCK CLEARANCES: this is the process of purchasing large volumes of imported goods or stock from companies that have either changed strategy or gone into liquidation. It is a high-risk option, as there is no guarantee on the goods, but the goods can be bought very cheaply. John therefore thinks that, properly managed, this would be a key source of profitable income, and wants to consider this. He will need to attend auctions, determine the value of the goods to his business, determine an appropriate price, and bid and pay for the goods.
- BUYING FROM REGULAR SUPPLIERS: this will be a mainstay approach. John hopes to establish regular purchases. As his business grows, he believes that he will be able to leverage some suppliers into manufacturing individual shoes to specification instead of producing pairs for the mass market. Less risky than stock clearances, there will be less opportunity for high profits. John thinks this will be the mainstay of the business though.
- BUYING SPECIALIST GOODS: this is buying items such as support inserts, shoe stretchers, and so on. John thinks that he will have a market for these goods. However, he wants to defer this until the main product line is available.
- RECEIPT: this is receiving deliveries into stock, checking quality on arrival, logging the stock, and placing in the warehouse. Problem goods will need to be returned to the supplier.
- PAYMENT: this is paying for received goods. On delivery, goods are checked off and logged with the delivery number and supplier on a computer system. Later an invoice will be received that needs to be matched against delivery to ensure that the invoice is accurate. Like any good business, the invoice will be paid within the credit period, but towards the end of that period to improve cash flows.

22.4.2 THE MARKETING PROCESS

Marketing is the key to any business's success. But this has to be done carefully. Bad marketing is worse than no marketing. John's market is geographically widely spread. Once he has a customer, he will expect to keep them. One of the key problems will be getting to his potential customers in the first place. Word of mouth will help, and he has heard that the Internet is good at spreading news informally. There is also the possibility of marketing through chiropodists, who frequently see people with foot problems caused by ill-fitting shoes. Marketing will therefore break down into the following:

- POTENTIAL CUSTOMERS: the process of finding customers. This will involve trade press adverts to chiropodists. John is a shrewd businessman who knows that much free advertising comes from news stories, and he wants to launch his company through local and national press. Having a Web site before this happens is essential. The timing of marketing is important. He knows that he has little control over word of mouth, except by offering an excellent service.

- ESTABLISHED CUSTOMERS: this is the process of building customer loyalty and getting customers to be aware of new products and offerings. He does not expect people to come to the Web site unless they need new shoes. Whenever a special offer comes along, John wants to be able to announce these by email.
- MARKET RESEARCH: this is the process of understanding existing and potential customers needs. It will involve obtaining feedback from existing customers, identifying and interviewing potential customers, and tracking trends in purchases.

22.4.3 THE SELLING PROCESS

Once a customer knows about the company, John wants to do all the selling through the Internet. If the company grows sufficiently, he might consider other channels to market, but he knows that multi-channel selling is expensive. So he wants to focus on one channel, the Internet. This seems to be his best route to a geographically diverse market. It removes the need for publishing and distributing expensive catalogues, and it means he can rapidly exploit opportunities brought about by cheap wholesale purchases. The key sub-processes are:

- PRESENTATION OF GOODS: letting the customer see what goods are on offer. The route chosen is through a Web site that will have pictures of goods, and a list of available sizes.
- SELECTION OF GOODS: this allows customers to select shoes from the Web site. John wants to let people order individual shoes, not just pairs. Thus it must be clear that someone is ordering a left shoe of a particular size and a right shoe of perhaps a different size. John likes the shopping basket idea for customers to acquire goods.
- ORDERING OF GOODS: this is the commitment to purchase. Some goods can be ordered irrespective of current stock levels where John has a regular supply. Some will need to be limited to stock levels only.
- PAYMENT FOR GOODS: John insists that he will take credit card purchases only, and distribute paper invoices with the goods. Immediate validation is not required, but validation and credit clearance will be necessary before goods are despatched.
- TRACKING OF ORDERS: the customer must be able to see at any time where goods are in the process. If they have been ordered from a supplier, rather than from stock, then they will want the option to cancel or adjust the order in some way.

22.4.4 THE DISTRIBUTION PROCESS

John cannot see any way that he can avoid a substantial warehousing process. To deal with cheap volume purchase and the splitting of pairs of shoes, there will need to be a well-managed warehouse. The nature of the goods makes despatch by courier or post most sensible, and John does not want to set up and manage a delivery process. The key distribution processes will break down into:

- RECEIPT OF GOODS: as goods come in, the need to be checked off against orders, checked for quality and that they match the delivery note, and then put into stock.
- RETURN OF GOODS: faulty or wrongly delivered goods will need to be returned.

- ORDER FULFILMENT: from an order, it will be necessary to take goods from the warehouse, pack them and despatch them. Courier details will need to be recorded against the order, and the order marked as despatched. Partial orders can be sent out if there is a wait for some of the order for supply.
- RETURNS: some goods will need to be reintroduced to stock if the customer returns them for any reason. The expectation is that the return rate will be between 10% and 20%, so this needs to be properly managed and resourced.

22.4.5 THE FINANCE PROCESS

This will involve all items to do with money. Some of these are distributed under other processes. Some special areas will be covered by the finance department. These will be:

- BUDGETING: setting and controlling budgets throughout the company.
- SALARIES: all costs related to staffing.
- INSURANCE AND LEGAL: all costs related to insuring the business and making sure it operates legally.
- CREDIT CONTROL: ensuring that payments from credit card companies are timely and accurate.

22.4.6 THE PROCESS MAP

To summarize this, you draw the process map shown in Figure 22.1. John likes this, and asks for a copy that he can use as part of his business planning.

22.5 Technical Architecture

Good business practice in IT is to minimize risk and cost, minimize installation times, and ensure that the IT systems meet the business goals. John Peddar wants to set up his business quickly. Considering the business as a whole, it is clear that the supply aspects of the business are fairly traditional. It is the channel to market that is unusual. The IT market is well supplied with excellent packages for operating a business of this type. Software development is not to be recommended where an appropriate purchase will suffice.

The buying process will be well supported by many packages in the market place. One that is well integrated with stock management looks sensible. Likewise, the distribution process is fairly straightforward, even if the goods being distributed are slightly unusual. Finance is a standard process in any business and there are many finance control packages available. You therefore recommend that the business processes are more fully documented, and that a sub-project is set up to look at the IT market and identify suitable packages. As part of the evaluation, due consideration is needed for the integration of packages with each other and with any bespoke software that is developed.

This leaves the selling process. Though the market for e-commerce products is maturing, there is nothing that quite seems to fit. A quick review of the market and continual monitoring of the market are highly recommended, but it seems that there is a good argument for a bespoke solution in this case. A full analysis and design of the Web site is commissioned.

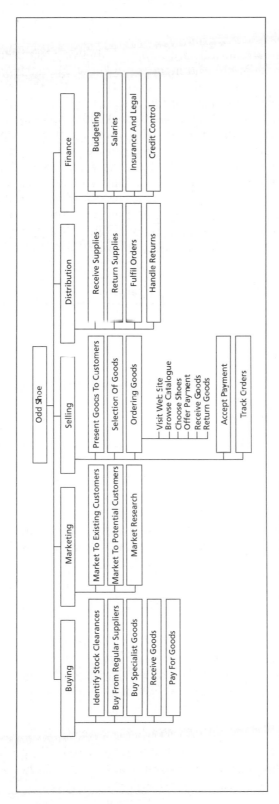

Figure 22.1   The process map for the Odd Shoe Company

22.6 Cost–Benefit

The Odd Shoe Company must be profitable within two years. John Peddar plans to provide the funding himself, and he needs to know the maximum outlay and the point at which the company will break even. He supplies the estimates on trading volumes, warehousing and distribution costs, price and profit margins, and you compile a cash flow as in Table 22.3. John Peddar has based his estimates on selling 20,000 shoes a quarter for the first three quarters of operation, rising to 25,000 shoes a quarter, and that he can buy shoes at €10 a pair and sell them at €25 a pair. He thinks this estimate is conservative, but realistic.

John is surprised by the fact that the company will not have recovered its outlay until the tenth quarter. The high up-front costs of setting up the Internet operation surprise him, but he is satisfied that this is not unreasonable. However, he notes that by the sixth quarter he should be operating at a quarterly operating profit of €200,000. His maximum outlay will be €900,000. He can find the funds

Table 22.3 Cash flow for the Odd Shoe Company

	Q1	Q2	Q3	Q4	Q5	Q6	Q7	Q8	Q9	Q10
Costs										
Development contract	250	250								
Equipment			40	40	40	40	40	40	40	40
Project management	30	30	30	15						
Software licenses										
Hardware/software maintenance			50	50	50	50	50	50	50	50
Testing		30	30							
Contingency	5	5	5	5	5	5	5	5	5	5
Warehousing		100								
Staffing			30	30	45	45	45	45	45	45
Stock		200	200	200	250	250	250	250	250	250
Distribution			20	20	20	25	25	25	25	25
Office costs			10	10	10	10	10	10	10	10
Wastage, damage, bad debt			30	30	30	40	40	40	40	40
Total	285	615	445	400	450	465	465	465	465	465
Benefits										
Revenue			500	500	500	625	625	625	625	625
Total	0	0	500	500	500	625	625	625	625	625
Cumulative costs	285	900	1345	1745	2195	2660	3125	3590	4055	4520
Cumulative benefits	0	0	500	1000	1500	2125	2750	3375	4000	4625
Net worth of project	−285	−900	−845	−745	−695	−535	−375	−215	−55	105

from other business ventures, so he decides to proceed. The cash flow model does show the importance of a successful launch and high sales in the third quarter to ensure business success, but John understands business risk, and he believes in the project sufficiently to take that risk.

22.7 Requirements Analysis

The selling process is the core process that you need to consider for automation. Therefore, you draw up a description of the process and use your company's standard layout for business process descriptions, as in Figure 22.2.

This is then drawn up as an activity diagram, as in Figure 22.3. Drawing up this business process begins to highlight some issues. Presumably the customer may abort the order at any point up to committing the credit card details, so maybe

Business process: 1	**Business process name:** Ordering Shoes

Brief description: The process of the customer ordering shoes over the Internet. Covers the process from the customer's perspective, through to delivery and acceptance of shoes.

Actors: Customer, Web site

Frequency of execution: Expected that the company will take 50 orders per day within 3 months, rising to 500 per day in a year. Expansion to Europe could treble this, and worldwide a tenfold increase.

Primary path:
1. Hear about the Odd Shoe Company.
2. Visit Web site.
3. Identify shoes that suit.
4. Order shoes.
5. Pay for shoes.
6. Shoes delivered.
7. Shoes fit and are acceptable.

Alternatives:
3.1 Shoes not in stock, but can be ordered, so advise customer of likely delay; customer may accept delay or quit purchase.
4.1 Unreasonably large order; advise customer that it cannot be dealt with and suggest they reduce order size
5.1 Problem with credit card, so email customer
6.1 Shoes not delivered, or delivered damaged, so reissue, taking any returns
6.2 Unable to deliver (delivery lost, stock out), so credit customer's card and email apology.
7.1 Shoes do not fit, or are uncomfortable, or customer changes mind, so customer returns them; need to credit customer's card and email them.

Exceptions:
None identified

Change record:
Created: Ken Lunn, 15 Feb 2002

Figure 22.2 Definition of business process for customer purchasing shoes over the Internet

some indication of the cancellation of the order is necessary. It may also be required to reissue returned shoes if it is a quality problem or size problem, rather

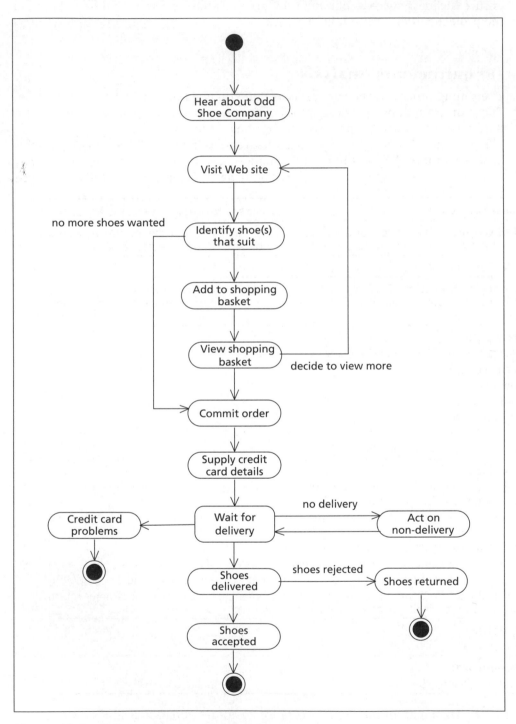

Figure 22.3   Sell to customer process

than a rejection of the shoes outright. Also, aborting the order on a credit card problem may not always be the right thing to do, and some thought needs to go into that. However, from initial interviews, without making too many assumptions, this is deemed to be suitable to review with John Peddar. This is routine procedure: to propose a process and review the proposal with the client. Too much preparation can mean that much time is wasted, but too little and there is little basis for agreement. Once this has been shared with the client, a fuller and more comprehensive analysis will be undertaken, tackling the issues discovered above and any more that come to light.

John is pretty much in agreement with the business process. He finds the activity diagram very readable, and in the process of developing it he made a few minor suggestions to improve the definition of the process.

22.7.1 USE CASE MODEL

The use case model is constructed by examining the business process and determining where an IT function point is needed. You produce a table of process steps against candidate use case, as in Table 22.4.

Figure 22.4 shows the use case diagram you produce that covers a reasonable set of use cases to support the above business process while the customer is online.

Table 22.4   Identification of candidate use cases for the Odd Shoe Company selling process

Process step	Candidate use case(s)
1. Hear about the Odd Shoe Company	None
2. Visit Web site	Visit home page
3. Identify shoes that suit	Browse catalogue; Add to shopping basket; Check stock; Reserve stock
4. Order shoes	View shopping basket; Delete from basket; Amend Quantity; Submit order; Check stock; Reserve stock
5. Pay for shoes	Supply credit card details; Check credit card details
6. Shoes delivered	None
7. Shoes fit and are acceptable	None
3.1 Shoes not in stock, but can be ordered, so advise customer of likely delay; customer may accept delay or quit purchase	Advise customer, no stock
4.1 Unreasonably large order; advise customer that it cannot be dealt with and suggest they reduce order size	Advise customer, oversize order
5.1 Problem with credit card, so email customer	Advise of credit card problem
6.1 Shoes not delivered, or delivered damaged, so reissue, taking any returns	Reissue order
6.2 Unable to deliver (delivery lost, stock out), so credit customer's card and email apology	Credit customer
7.1 Shoes do not fit, or are uncomfortable, or customer changes mind, so customer returns them; need to credit customer's card and email them	Accept returns

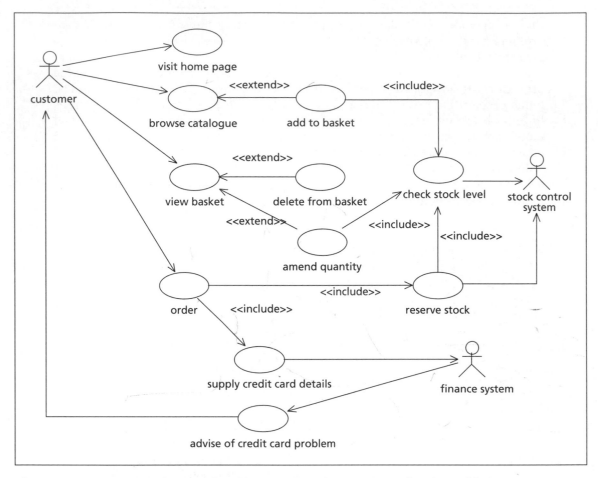

Figure 22.4   Use case diagram for the Internet ordering system for the Odd Shoe Company

In elaborating the use case model, certain questions arise. The IT strategy is to purchase finance and stock control packages. At the time of this preliminary analysis, it is not known what those systems will be, so some assumptions have been made about their functionality. It was assumed that the stock control system could give a real-time answer to questions about the stock levels of particular goods and could adjust stock levels in real time. It was also assumed that the finance system would be able to check credit card details and supply an email response back to the customer. It was decided that, before committing an order, the stock levels would be checked and stock reserved; there is a possibility that, between putting something in the shopping basket and committing the order, the stock may have been sold to another customer.

The use cases for visit home page, browse catalogue and view basket have been described using your company's standard format for use cases below. The first use case, to display the home page, is trivial, and the description is shown in Figure 22.5, and a prototype screen is shown in Figure 22.6. The second use case

Use case number: 1	Use case name: Visit Home Page
Brief description: Displays the home page for the site	
Actors: Customer	
Preconditions: Web site operational	
Postconditions: Home page displayed	
Frequency of execution: Estimated 100 hits per day within 3 months, rising to 1000 within a year.	
Scalability: Up to 100 concurrent users expected	
Criticality: Very. Without the Web site available, the company is not selling.	
Primary path: Customer types URL and Web site displays	
Alternatives: None	
Exceptions: None	
Data requirements: None, other than home page on Web site	
User interfaces: See Figure 22.6.	
Change record: Created Ken Lunn, 15 Feb 2002	

Figure 22.5   Use case description for visiting the home page

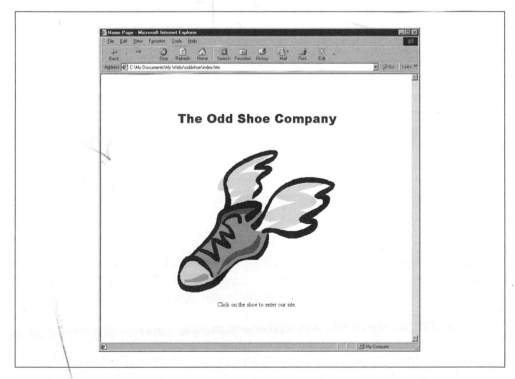

Figure 22.6   Odd Shoe Company home page

Use case number: 2	Use case name: Browse Catalogue
Brief description: The customer will browse through the catalogue of shoes.	
Actors: Customer	
Preconditions: Web site available	
Postconditions: Selected items in shopping basket	
Frequency of execution: Estimated 100 hits per day within 3 months, rising to 1000 within a year.	
Scalability: Up to 100 concurrent users expected	
Criticality: Very. Without the Web site available, the company is not selling.	
Primary path: 1. Customer selects catalogue from home page 2. A list of shoe styles with thumbnail pictures displayed 3. Customer selects a shoe style 4. List of shoes and prices displayed, with thumbnails of shoes 5. Customer selects a shoe 6. Large picture of shoe displayed, with a list of prices, sizes, stock availability and colours 7. Customer fills in quantity, size, foot and colour 8. Customer clicks 'Add to basket'.	
Alternatives: At any time the customer may backtrack to the home page or an earlier page. At any time the customer may abort.	
Exceptions: None identified	
Data requirements: List of shoe styles with thumbnail pictures to indicate shoe style. For each shoe, the sizes available, price, colour, a thumbnail picture and a full picture.	
User interfaces: See Figures 22.8, 22.9 and 22.10.	
Change record: Created by Ken Lunn, 15 Feb 2001	

Figure 22.7 Use case description for the browse catalogue use case

description to browse the catalogue is shown in Figure 22.7, and prototype screens are shown in Figures 22.8, 22.9 and 22.10. The third use case description to view the catalogue is shown in Figure 22.11, with a prototype screen shown in Figure 22.12.

With all the use cases described to this level, you produce a comprehensive requirements document that specifies the functionality of the system. It is readable by the client, so you show this to John Peddar. He makes a few suggestions. He finds the diagrams and screenshots very helpful. The later documents will be less appropriate for the client, and will be used within the development team. You explain to John that the design documents will be available, but that he will not find them too readable. He accepts this, and as he is impressed so far with your approach he is happy to trust you.

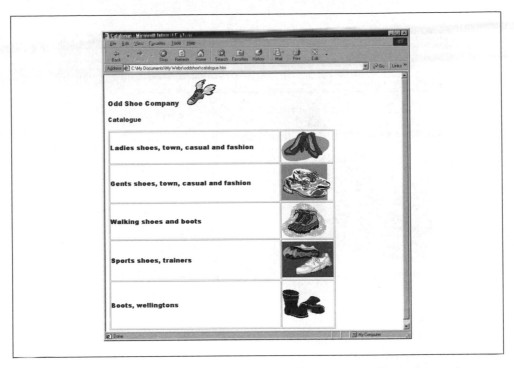

Figure 22.8 The Odd Shoe Company top catalogue page, displaying styles

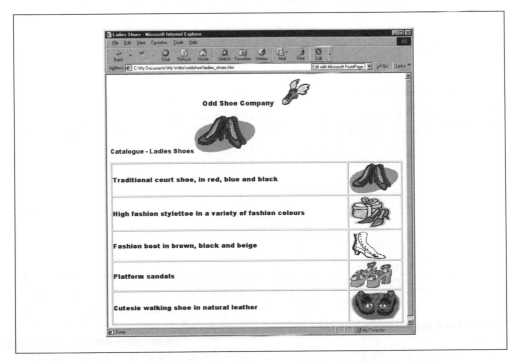

Figure 22.9 The Odd Shoe Company – second level catalogue page, displaying summary for each shoe in style

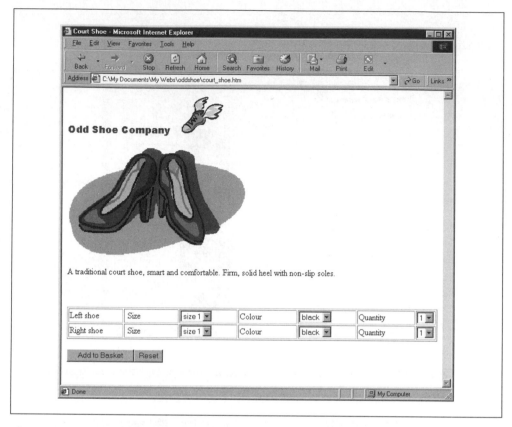

Figure 22.10 the Odd Shoe Company – detailed shoe page

22.8 Systems Analysis

Systems analysis now opens up the requirements to determine in some detail how the system operates. The primary tool you use is a sequence diagram. The process followed is to take scenarios from the use case and provide a sequence diagram that implements the steps in the scenario using interactions between the user, screens and internal objects.

The sequence diagram for the primary path of the browse catalogue use case is shown in Figure 22.13. This is a fairly faithful mapping of the steps of the use case. It would not be possible to implement this directly, as issues such as storage and retrieval of data items in the database have not been considered. Design will have to resolve these issues.

A collaboration diagram shows the same information in a different layout. Figure 22.14 shows a collaboration diagram for the primary path of the add to basket use case. This gives a view of the communication between actors and objects that is not as clear on the sequence diagram. The messages are numbered to show ordering.

You now start looking at some of the classes in the system. You have identified four key entity classes, as indicated in Figure 22.15. Attributes that we can identify from the interactions have been included.

Use case number: 3	Use case name: View Shopping Basket

Brief description: Allows the customer to view the things they want to buy
Actors: Customer
Preconditions: As for browse catalogue, UC002
Postconditions: As for browse catalogue, UC002
Frequency of execution: As for browse catalogue, UC002
Scalability: As for browse catalogue, UC002
Criticality: As for browse catalogue, UC002
Primary path: 1. User clicks on 'Add to catalogue' button on product detail page. 2. System retrieves basket and displays items added 3. Customer clicks on 'Buy' button.
Alternatives: 2.1 Customer wishes to modify the quantity bought, or delete items from shopping basket
Exceptions: None identified
Data requirements: To be determined
User interfaces: See Figure 22.12.
Change record: Created by Ken Lunn, 15 Feb 2002

Figure 22.11   Use case description for View Shopping Basket use case

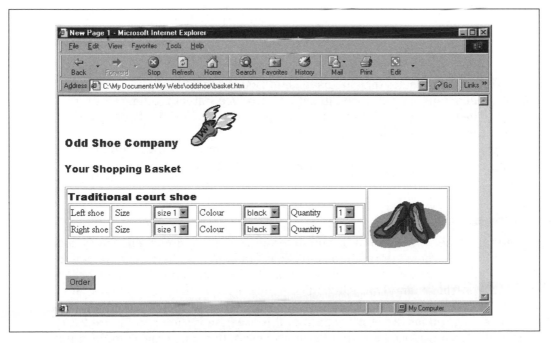

Figure 22.12   Prototype screen for the Odd Shoe Company shopping basket

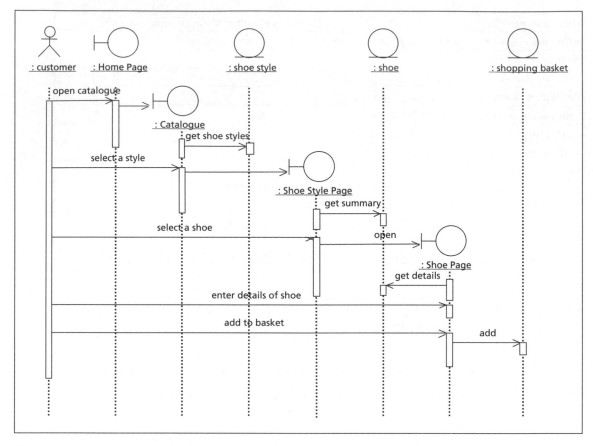

Figure 22.13   Analysis sequence diagram for the browse catalogue use case primary path

Considering the classes that you have identified, none of them have particularly complex behaviour, so it is reasonable not to produce statechart diagrams for any of them. The screen organization is beginning to emerge. Your first cut at a screen organization is provided in Figure 22.16.

Analysis proceeds by elaborating each of the use cases in the manner above, refining the class diagram accordingly and extending the screen organization.

22.9 Design

Design takes the systems analysis and determines how to implement the system. The question of where information is stored is fundamental. In the example of the browse catalogue use case, it is decided that the information will all be stored in the stock control system. Thus when information is required on shoes and styles, a request is made to the stock control system. A first attempt at refining the sequence diagram for the primary path of this use case is shown in Figure 22.17. Here you have introduced a session, a control class, to manage the complex interactions. This is common both to object-oriented design and to Web construction.

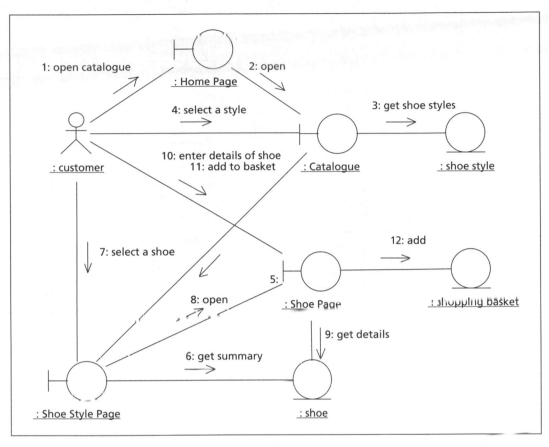

Figure 22.14   Collaboration diagram for the primary path of the browse catalogue use case for the odd shoe company

You redraw this as a collaboration diagram, as in Figure 22.18, where you can see more clearly the role of the session control class. It mediates between the boundary classes, the external stock control system and the entity classes.

You now have operations on the classes to deal with the interactions. These can be added to the class diagrams. The diagram showing the entity objects is shown in Figure 22.19. This class diagram will grow as further scenarios from this use case and other use cases are elaborated. Figure 22.20 shows the revised screen navigation, with operations to indicate the functionality of each screen.

As before, there are no complicated objects, so statechart diagrams are not necessary. The control object is the one that contains most of the behavioural complexity. The sequence diagram has resulted in operations as indicated in Figure 22.21. For the getStyles() operation, you specify it as in Figure 22.22.

Design continues in this way, adding detail and transforming systems analysis, until all the use cases are fully elaborated.

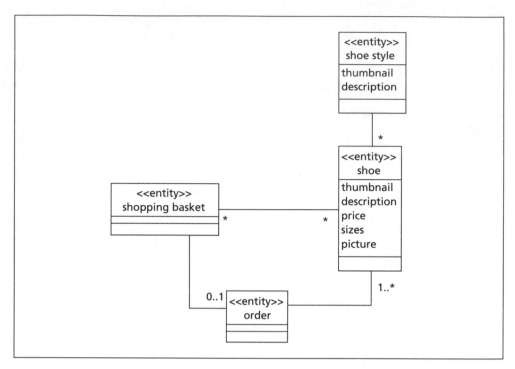

Figure 22.15 Preliminary class diagram, showing the major entity objects and the attributes

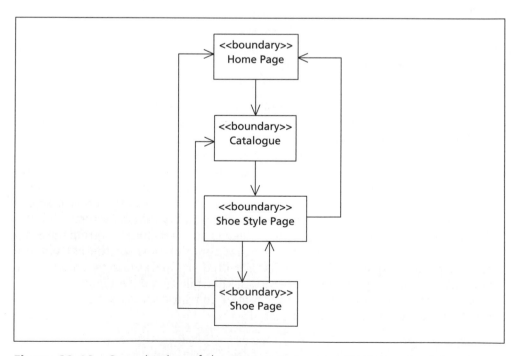

Figure 22.16 Organization of the screens to support the browse catalogue use case, shown as a class diagram

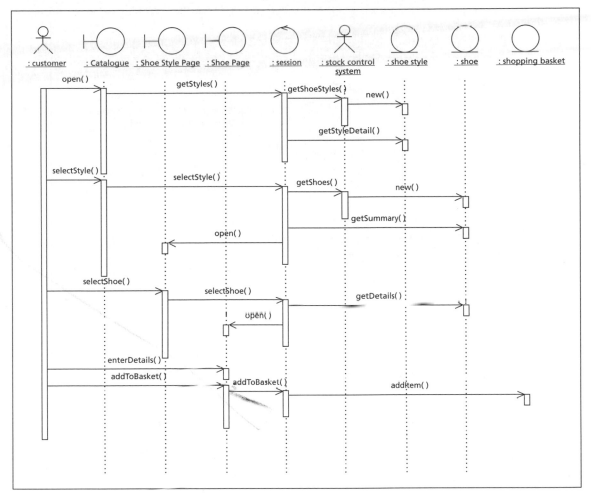

Figure 22.17   Design sequence diagram for the browse catalogue use case

22.10 Implementation

It is really beyond the scope of this book to go into the details of implementation. Java and Java server pages are selected. It is likely, because of the details of the implementation language, that slight revisions to the design will be requested to allow for the limitations and possibilities of the implementation environment.

22.11 Testing

Testing goes back to the requirements and makes sure that the system that is produced meets the requirements, and that it is generally acceptable to the user community. The software house has its own system testing team. Normally the client would supply staff to undertake user acceptance testing, but as John

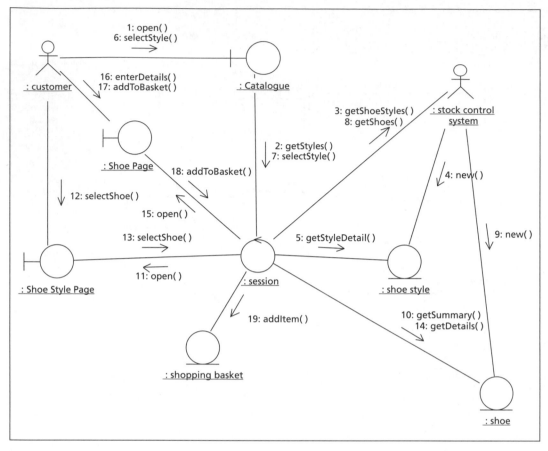

Figure 22.18 Collaboration diagram showing the design for the primary path of the browse catalogue use case

Peddar's business is not operational, a testing consultant is hired to carry out initial user acceptance testing.

System test plans are drawn up from the use case specifications. You produce a plan for testing the browse catalogue use case shown in Figure 22.23.

The testing consultant produces his own acceptance test plans based on the business process descriptions and the use case descriptions. They are similar to the system test plans, but span whole processes, not just individual use cases.

You would like to beta test the system, but there is not really a chance to do this as there is not an established user base. Therefore testing criteria are set high and nothing is issued until it has a very low defect rate. John agrees to have a slow launch, so that market take-up in the first quarter is not dramatic. That way, any failure of the system will not cause too much damage to the reputation of the Odd Shoe Company.

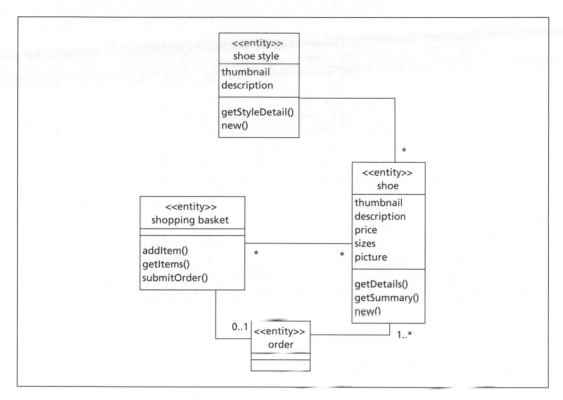

Figure 22.19   Class diagram showing the entity objects with operations and attributes

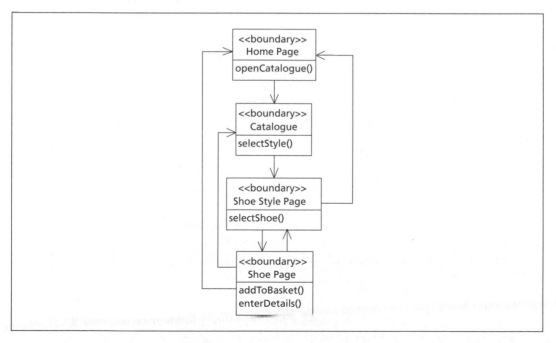

Figure 22.20   Screen navigation extended to show operations indicating what can be done in each screen

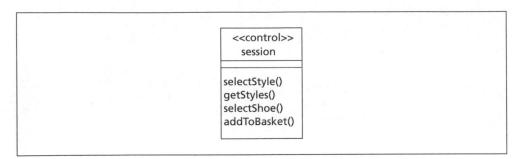

Figure 22.21 The session control object for the Web site

Operation: getStyles()
Class: session
Parameters: None
Preconditions: The stock control system must be online.
Postconditions: A styles page is created and displayed in the browser
Pseudo-code: 1. Call the stock control system for a list of styles. It should return an array of style objects. 2. For each style object, get the detail of the style. 3. Format the styles page, and display.

Figure 22.22 Operation specification for the getStyles operation on the session class

Use case number: 2	**Use case name:** Browse Catalogue
Test plan: 2.1	
Brief description: Exercises the primary path of the use case	
Data: Shoe styles for ladies' shoes, gents' shoes, walking shoes and boots must be set up. For ladies' shoes, court shoes, fashion shoes, walking shoes and sandals should be set up. For gents shoes, ... etc. Prices and stock levels should be set up for each shoe.	
Primary path: 1. Select the catalogue from home page 2. A list of shoe styles with thumbnail pictures should be displayed, with shoe styles for ladies' shoes, gents' shoes, walking shoes and boots. 3. Selects a ladies' shoe style 4. A list of shoes and prices displayed, with thumbnails of shoes, covering court shoes, fashion shoes, walking shoes and sandals. 5. Select a court shoe 6. A large picture of court shoe should be displayed, with a correct list of prices, sizes, stock availability and colours. 7. Fills in quantity, size, foot and colour 8. Clicks 'Add to basket' 9. Now go to the shopping basket page and ensure that the entry is in the shopping basket Repeat the above sequence for each style of shoe and each type of shoe in the style.	

Figure 22.23 Test plan for the primary path of the browse catalogue use case

22.12 Project Development

The project will deliver incrementally a series of use cases, in an iterative fashion. The first use cases will be the browsing of the catalogue and the shopping basket use cases. In the first phase, primary paths and key alternatives only will be implemented. The aim is to show a basic working system within 2 months of project initiation, and for the client to be able to review this. Current estimates suggest that a working system can be delivered into testing within 4 months and that a comprehensive system should be available in 6 months. This should align well with the setting up of the business operations, the purchase and installation of supporting packages, and the preparation and initiation of the marketing plan.

22.13 Conclusion

At the end of the project, a successful system is operational. There have been a few scares on the way, but the staged and well-planned approach that your manager has coached you through has avoided a number of pitfalls that you see you could have suffered if you had followed your instinct and got an implementation team together straight away. John Peddar is very happy with his business, and it is starting to show that it will be profitable inside the time-scale that you had predicted.

Glossary

Activity diagram	A UML diagram used to describe workflows, used in a variety of modelling roles from business process modelling through to the detailed description of operations.
Actor	An external entity (person or system) that interacts with a computer system.
Alternative path	A normally used alternative route through a business process or use case
Application architecture	The large-scale structure of the application software.
Architecture	The large-scale design of the structure of a system.
Association	A logical link between two classes, indicating that instances at either side of the association may communicate with the other.
Atomicity	The property of a database transaction that it must either succeed or fail without side-effects.
Business model	A description of a business operation, using models such as a process map and activity diagrams, with other elements such as a stakeholder analysis.
Class	A collection of objects with identical structure.
Class diagram	A UML diagram that shows classes and their associations, indicating the static structure of a system.
Collaboration diagram	A UML diagram that shows how instances of objects interact to provide functionality, usually in the realization of a use case
Component	A unit of software that implements a logical set of functionality, usually implemented as a set of objects.
Component diagram	A UML diagram that shows the interdependency of components in a system.
CORBA	Common Object Request Broker Architecture – a set of standards defining the interaction of objects in a distributed environment.
Cost–benefit model	A model of cash flows intended to describe how costs and benefits change over time during a project. This is usually handled in a spreadsheet.
Deliverable	A deliverable is a key output of a project. It may be a final deliverable, such as a module of a system to be deployed,

	or an intermediate deliverable, such as a use case definition or a design.
Design	The process of converting the requirements expressed by systems analysis into a set of objects and components that can be implemented in a computer system.
DSDM	The Dynamic Systems Development Method. See http://www.dsdm.org/.
Event	An occurrence (either inside a system or outside) that triggers some activity.
Exception	An unusual circumstance in a business process, use case or operation on a class that requires special action.
Extreme Programming	A method that avoids the use of explicit modelling in the design and construction phase, normally known as a lightweight method.
First normal form	A table is said to be in first normal form if every record has a fixed number of simple fields.
Foreign key	When the key to another table is stored as a value or set of values in another table for the purposes of combining the data in the two tables, this is known as a foreign key.
Functional requirement	A requirement of a system that states what the system should do, usually expressed as a use case (or part of a use case).
Goal	An objective of a stakeholder, or of a business process or use case.
IIOP	Internet Inter-Orb Protocol – a protocol for allowing ORBs to communicate to exchange requests and responses between objects
Iterative development	The development of software in stages, resulting in multiple releases on increasingly functional software.
Join	A way of combining two tables together so that related information can be viewed together.
Key	A value or set of values that uniquely identify a record in a database table.
Methodology	Strictly, the study of methods for the development of software. More commonly used to mean a set of methods and notations used to develop a system.
Milestone	A milestone is a stage of a project where some set of agreed deliverables is provided.
Moscow	This is a prioritization convention that breaks actions or goals into those that Must be achieved for a task to be successful, those that Should be achieved by the task, those that Could be achieved by the task if there is time and resource available, and those that Won't be considered by the task.
Multiplicity	Indicates how many objects at one end of an association may communicate with another object at the other end of the association.

Non-functional requirement	A requirement of a system that states the quality of the system, such as scalability
Normalization	A process of optimizing relational databases to improve the management of data.
Object	The basic building block of object-oriented systems. An object is defined by its attributes, which record the state of the object, and its operations, which define the behaviour of the object.
Object orientation	An approach to the analysis, design and construction of software systems that is based on the notion of objects.
OMG	The Object Management Group, an organization that was formed to create a component-based software market place through the introduction of standardized object software. It has been responsible for the development of various standards such as UML and CORBA. See `http://www.omg.org/`.
ORB	Object Request Broker – a software component that services requests and responses between objects in a distributed environment.
Pattern	A commonly used design that may be adapted to particular circumstances
Polymorphism	The property of objects that two objects of different classes may use the same names for operations and attributes without creating ambiguity.
Postcondition	A statement of the legal results of an operation or use case
Precondition	A statement of the legal conditions under which an operation or use case may fire
Primary path	The most commonly used route through a business process or use case
Process map	A high-level description of a business, grouping together the key processes and sub-processes of a business
Project manager	An individual with overall responsibility for the project, whose role is to plan, resource, monitor deliverables and quality, manage risk and report to the steering group on progress.
Prototype	A quickly produced system used to illustrate a point, generate discussion or test an idea.
RAD	Rapid Application Development, a lightweight method that uses iterative development with frequent releases of versions of software.
Relational database	A database made up of a number of tables, where each table is constructed of records with simple fields, with a fixed number of column headings.
Reliability	A non-functional requirement indicating how well the system performs in terms of availability and prevention of damage to data.
Requirements analysis	The process of providing a definition of requirements of a system, usually expressed as a set of use cases.

Return on Capital Employed	A financial measure to estimate the overall performance of a business defined by the equation

$$\frac{\text{Revenue} - \text{Expenditure}}{\text{Capital Employed}} \times 100$$

RFI	Request For Information. A formal document sent to a supplier asking for information about their product.
RFT	Request For Tender. A formal document sent to a supplier, asking them to tender for business.
Scalability	A non-functional requirement indicating the need for a system to deal with a number of users or transactions in a given period.
Scenario	A single execution of a business or of a system
Second normal form	A table is in second normal form if every non-key attribute is fully dependent on the whole of the primary key, and not on part of the primary key.
Sequence diagram	A UML diagram that shows how the execution of a scenario in a system is implemented in terms of collaborations between objects.
Serializability constraint	The property that two database transactions must operate as if one completed before the other.
Stakeholder	Anyone who has any involvement in the initiation, specification, use, funding or management of a system.
Stakeholder analysis	A component of requirements that describes the stakeholders in the system, their roles and goals.
Steering group	A group responsible for the setting of project goals, control of funding and monitoring of achievement.
SWOT analysis	An analysis of the strengths, weaknesses, opportunities and threats of a situation or proposal.
Systems analysis	The process of providing a comprehensive definition of the external behaviour of a system, in terms of its interaction with the outside world and the types of information it needs to represent.
System test	A suite of tests to determine the acceptability of a system in terms of meeting its defined specification.
Technical architecture	The technical components of a system, such as the servers and networks, and major system software items such as databases.
Third normal form	A database table is in third normal form if it is in second normal form and there are no transitive dependencies.
Time box	A fixed period of time in which to carry out an activity. Usually the activity sets off with a prioritized list of actions or goals, and an agreed resource. Once the time period approaches expiry, the activity is brought to a conclusion.
Transitive dependency	An attribute A is said to be transitively dependent on B if A is dependent on C and C is dependent on B.

UML	The Unified Modeling Language, a graphical notation for the analysis and design of software systems. See `http://www.omg.org/`.
Unit test	A test to determine the correct functioning of a part of a system, such as an individual use case.
USDP	The Unified Software Development Process, a staged process using a series of intermediate models in the production of software.
Use case	A well-defined, meaningful piece of functionality in a system.
Use case description	A detailed description of a use case in terms of its supplied functionality and any particular non-functional requirements it must conform to.
Use case diagram	A UML diagram showing relationships between actors and use cases
Use case realization	A set of objects and their interactions designed to provide the functionality of a system.
User acceptance test	A suite of tests to determine the acceptability of a system in terms of meeting the expectations and needs of the users

References

Allen, P. and Frost, S. (1998) *Component-Based Development for Enterprise Systems: Applying the SELECT Perspective*. Cambridge: Cambridge University Press.

Beck, K. (1999) *Extreme Programming Explained: Embrace Change*. Reading, MA: Addison-Wesley.

Bennett, S., McRobb, S. and Farmer, R. (1999) *Object-Oriented Systems Analysis and Design using UML*. New York: McGraw-Hill.

Bennett, S., Skelton, J. and Lunn, K. (2001) *Schaum's Outline of UML*. New York: McGraw-Hill.

Codd, E. F. (1970) A relational model for large shared databanks. *Communications of the ACM*, 13(6), 377–387.

Connolly, T. and Begg, E. C. (2001) *Database Systems: A Practical Approach to Design, Implementation, and Management*, 3rd edn. Reading, MA: Addison-Wesley.

De Bono, E. (1994) *De Bono's Thinking Course*. London: BBC Consumer Publishing.

Gamma, E., Helm, R., Johnson, R. and Vlissides, J. (1995) *Design Patterns: Elements of Reusable Object-Oriented Software*. Reading, MA: Addison-Wesley.

Handy, C. (1995) *Gods of Management*. London: Arrow.

Jacobson, I. (1995) *The Object Advantage*. Reading, MA: Addison-Wesley.

Jacobson, I., Christerson, M., Jonsson, P. and Overgaard, G. (1992) *Object-Oriented Software Engineering*. Reading, MA: Addison-Wesley.

Jacobson, I., Booch, G. and Rumbaugh, J. (1999) *The Unified Software Development Process*. Reading, MA: Addison-Wesley.

Parikh, G. and Zvegintzov, N. (eds.) (1983) *Tutorial on Software Maintenance*. IEEE Computer Society Press.

Poulson, D., Ashby, M. and Richardson, S. (eds) (1996) *USERfit: A Practical Handbook on User-Centred Design for Assistive Technology*. Loughborough: HUSAT Research Institute.

Pressman, R. S. (2000) *Software Engineering – A Practitioner's Approach*. New York: McGraw-Hill.

Projects in Controlled Environments (2001) Office of Government Commerce: http://www.ogc.gov.uk/prince/.

Senge, P. M. (1990) *The Fifth Discipline*. New York: Doubleday.

UK Office of Government Commerce (2001) *Why IT Projects Fail*. http://www.ogc.gov.uk/sdtoolkit/library/bpbriefings/it_projects.pdf

Warmer, J. and Kleppe, A. (1999) *The Object Constraint Language: Precise Modeling With UML*. Reading, MA: Addison Wesley Longman.

Index